Don't Spend a Dime

The Path to
Low-Cost Computing

James Floyd Kelly

Don't Spend a Dime: The Path to Low-Cost Computing

Copyright © 2009 by James Floyd Kelly

ISBN-13 (pbk): 978-1-4302-1863-0

ISBN-13 (electronic): 1-4302-1864-9

9 8 7 6 5 4 3 2 1

Lead Editors: Joohn Choe, Jonathan Gennick
Technical Reviewer: Steve Nieman
Editorial Board: Clay Andres, Steve Anglin, Mark Beckner, Ewan Buckingham, Tony Campbell, Gary Cornell, Jonathan Gennick, Michelle Lowman, Matthew Moodie, Jeffrey Pepper, Frank Pohlmann, Ben Renow-Clarke, Dominic Shakeshaft, Matt Wade, Tom Welsh
Project Manager: Richard Dal Porto
Copy Editor: Marilyn Smith
Associate Production Director: Kari Brooks-Copony
Production Editor: Ellie Fountain
Compositor: Linda Weidemann, Wolf Creek Publishing Services
Proofreader: Nancy Bell
Indexer: Broccoli Information Management
Artist: Kinetic Publishing Services, LLC
Cover Designer: Kurt Krames
Manufacturing Director: Tom Debolski

Distributed to the book trade worldwide by Springer-Verlag New York, Inc., 233 Spring Street, 6th Floor, New York, NY 10013. Phone 1-800-SPRINGER, fax 201-348-4505, e-mail orders-ny@springer-sbm.com, or visit http://www.springeronline.com.

For information on translations, please contact Apress directly at 2855 Telegraph Avenue, Suite 600, Berkeley, CA 94705. Phone 510-549-5930, fax 510-549-5939, e-mail info@apress.com, or visit http://www.apress.com.

Apress and friends of ED books may be purchased in bulk for academic, corporate, or promotional use. eBook versions and licenses are also available for most titles. For more information, reference our Special Bulk Sales–eBook Licensing web page at http://www.apress.com/info/bulksales.

For Ashley and Decker
and
For Jeff—"Gustav, you're a stinkin' Mac user"

Contents at a Glance

About the Author.. xv

About the Technical Reviewer xvii

Acknowledgments xix

Introduction xxi

CHAPTER 1 The Best Things in Life 1

CHAPTER 2 The PC Element 9

CHAPTER 3 Word Processing 25

CHAPTER 4 Spreadsheets 55

CHAPTER 5 Slide Shows 79

CHAPTER 6 E-Mail and Calendar... 101

CHAPTER 7 Photo Editing 125

CHAPTER 8 Graphics.. 151

CHAPTER 9 Virus Protection 171

CHAPTER 10 Data Backup 191

CHAPTER 11 Personal Finance.. 207

CHAPTER 12 Gaming... 227

CHAPTER 13 Photo Management 243

CHAPTER 14 Internet Phone Calls... 255

CHAPTER 15 Web Logs... 265

CHAPTER 16 Social Networking.. 283

CHAPTER 17 Group Scheduling 301

APPENDIX 311

INDEX 315

Contents

About the Author.. xv

About the Technical Reviewer xvii

Acknowledgments xix

Introduction xxi

■CHAPTER 1   **The Best Things in Life** 1

     Software Wants to Be Free 1

     Software Will Be Free 2

     Open Source.. 2

     Software as a Service 3

     No-Strings-Attached Freebie.................................... 5

     But What About the PC? 6

     Summary.. 7

■CHAPTER 2   **The PC Element** 9

     To Buy or Not to Buy (with Apologies to William).............. 10

         Upgrade or Repurpose an Existing PC 10

         Build a PC 11

         Buy a PC 12

         Great News: Free Software Means More Hardware............. 13

     Five PC User Types 14

     Two Steps to Identifying Your Hardware Needs................. 15

         Step 1: Find a Prebuilt PC............................... 15

         Step 2: Obtain Prices for Individual Components........... 17

     Hardware Focus by User Type.................................. 19

         Type 2, Family Member's PC............................... 19

         Type 3, Gamer's PC....................................... 20

         Type 4, Multimedia Guru's PC............................. 21

         Type 5, Small Business Owner's PC........................ 22

     Summary.. 24

CHAPTER 3 **Word Processing** 25

The Defender 25
The Contenders 28
　　OpenOffice.org Writer 29
　　Google Docs Document 31
Where to Get the Software 34
　　OpenOffice.org Writer 34
　　Google Docs Document 34
Notes on OpenOffice.org Installation 35
Word Processing Features 41
　　OpenOffice.org Writer Features 41
　　Google Docs Document Features 47
Investigate Further 52
Summary 53

CHAPTER 4 **Spreadsheets** 55

The Defender 56
The Contenders 58
　　OpenOffice.org Calc 58
　　Google Docs Spreadsheet 59
Where to Get the Software 62
　　OpenOffice.org Calc 62
　　Google Docs Spreadsheet 63
Notes on OpenOffice.org Calc Installation 63
Spreadsheet Features 64
　　OpenOffice.org Calc Features 64
　　Google Docs Spreadsheet Features 73
Investigate Further 77
Summary 77

CHAPTER 5 **Slide Shows** 79

The Defender 79
The Contenders 81
　　OpenOffice.org Impress 81
　　Google Docs Presentation 83
Where to Get the Software 84
　　OpenOffice.org Impress 84
　　Google Docs Presentation 84

Notes on OpenOffice.org Impress Installation. 85
Slide Show Application Features. 86
    OpenOffice.org Impress Features 86
    Google Docs Presentation Features 94
Investigate Further. 100
Summary. 100

CHAPTER 6   **E-Mail and Calendar** 101

The Defender 101
The Contenders 103
    Gmail 103
    Google Calendar. 105
Where to Get the Software. 105
    Gmail 105
    Google Calendar. 106
Notes on Basic Usage. 106
    Gmail 106
    Google Calendar. 108
E-Mail and Calendar Features. 111
    Gmail Features 111
    Google Calendar Features 119
Investigate Further. 123
Summary. 123

CHAPTER 7   **Photo Editing** 125

The Defender 126
The Contender 127
Where to Get the Software. 128
Notes on GIMP Installation. 128
Basic GIMP Tasks 129
    Add Text to a Photo 132
    Drop Someone into a Photo 141
Investigate Further. 149
Summary. 150

CHAPTER 8   **Graphics** 151

The Defender 151
The Contender 155
Where to Get the Software. 156

Notes on Inkscape Installation 157
Basic Inkscape Tasks 157
    Adjust Your Screen Settings 157
    Add Basic Shapes 159
    Free Drawing 161
    Use Layers 165
    Perform Other Drawing Tasks 168
Investigate Further 169
Summary 169

■CHAPTER 9　**Virus Protection** 171

The Defender 172
The Contender 173
Where to Get the Software 176
Notes on AAP Installation 176
Basic AAP Tasks 180
    Run a Complete System Scan 180
    Schedule Routine Scans 183
Investigate Further 189
Summary 189

■CHAPTER 10　**Data Backup** 191

Your Valuable Data 191
The Defender 193
The Contender 194
Where to Get the Software 196
Notes on Cobian Backup Installation 196
Basic Cobian Backup Tasks 197
    Back Up Files and Folders 197
    Restore Files and Folders 204
Investigate Further 205
Summary 206

■CHAPTER 11　**Personal Finance** 207

The Defender 208
The Contender 209
Where to Get the Software 210
Notes on Money Manager Ex Installation 211

Basic Money Manager Ex Tasks 211
  Create a Database 211
  Import Financial Transactions 216
  Examine Your Personal Finances 223
Investigate Further. 226
Summary. 226

■CHAPTER 12   Gaming 227

The Defender 227
The Contender 230
Where to Get the Software. 231
Notes on Runes of Magic Installation. 232
A Sampling of Runes of Magic Activities 233
  Accept a Quest. 233
  Rent a Mount (Horse). 238
  Change Weapons 240
Investigate Further. 241
Summary. 241

■CHAPTER 13   Photo Management 243

What Is Picasa? 243
Where Can I Find Picasa?. 243
How Do I Use Picasa?. 244
  Use the Photo Tray. 245
  Tag Photos 246
More Great Picasa Features. 248
  Back Up Your Photos. 248
  Eliminate Duplicate Photos. 249
  Create Your Own Screen Saver 251
  Remove Red Eye from a Digital Photo 252
Investigate Further. 253
Summary. 254

■CHAPTER 14   Internet Phone Calls 255

What Is Skype? 255
Where Can I Find Skype?. 256
How Do I Use Skype? 257
  Add Contacts. 258
  Make a Call 260

More Skype Functionality 261
    Send Text Messages to Your Contacts .261
    Set Your Status 261
    Make a Video Phone Call 262
Investigate Further 263
Summary 264

CHAPTER 15   Web Logs 265

What Is Blogger? 266
Where Can I Find Blogger? 266
How Do I Use Blogger? 269
More Blogger Details 275
    Modify the Blog Layout 275
    Turn on AdSense to Make Money 278
Investigate Further 280
Summary 281

CHAPTER 16   Social Networking 283

What Is Facebook? 283
Where Can I Find Facebook? 284
How Do I Use Facebook? 288
    Edit Your Profile 288
    Use the Wall 291
More Facebook Details 292
    Find People You Know 292
    Add an Application 295
Investigate Further 299
Summary 300

CHAPTER 17   Group Scheduling 301

What Is Doodle? 301
Where Can I Find Doodle? 302
How Do I Use Doodle? 302
More Doodle Details 307
Investigate Further 309
Summary 309

APPENDIX. 311
    Get Friendly Reminders 311
    Protect Your E-Mail Address 311
    Brainstorm Online 311
    Find Lost Items. 312
    Selective Web Page Printing 312
    Send Musical Online Postcards. 312
    Design a Room. 312
    Ship and Track Packages. 313
    Create a Web Site 313
    Hard Drive Imaging 313
    Child-Safe Web Browsing. 313

INDEX 315

About the Author

JAMES FLOYD KELLY is a freelance writer who lives in Atlanta, Georgia. He has degrees in both English and Industrial Engineering, because he couldn't decide between majoring in liberal arts or math and science. Fortunately, technical writing uses both sides of the brain, and he has been able to write on a variety of topics, including LEGO robotics, free software, and building a custom computer. James is also the editor in chief of the number one LEGO NXT Robotics blog, The NXT Step (http://www.thenxtstep.com). When not writing, he and his wife enjoy watching their little boy discover all kinds of new and exciting things about the world.

About the Technical Reviewer

STEVE NIEMAN is a systems administrator/teacher's assistant for a private school in Munising, Michigan. He has earned degrees in Accounting and Information Systems, and completed a course in PC repair. Prior to his current job, Steve enjoyed the privilege of being a stay-at-home dad and raising his three kids.

Acknowledgments

Writing a book is not a solitary job, as one might think. The book you're holding in your hands is the result of the hard work of a large collection of people at Apress. The team at Apress did so much more than just fix my misspelled words and tighten up some sentences to make them more readable. During the writing of this book, I actually learned how to be a better writer. And for that, I can thank five outstanding individuals: Dominic Shakeshaft, Joohn Choe, Jonathan Gennick, Steve Nieman, and Marilyn Smith. This group of editors taught me everything from properly using headers to formatting monetary amounts. They suggested new software to cover, new web sites to reference, and, in many instances, new text to add. It was a pleasure working with all of them. (And Jonathan, I will *never again* forget to include introductory text after a new head.)

This is the first book in a new series from Apress, and I'm happy with the final results. I'd also like to thank Ellie Fountain for the layout of the chapters, and Kurt Krames for the nice cover design that is shared by the books in this series.

As for my wife, Ashley, I cannot thank her enough for her support as I changed careers and switched to "this writing thing." She just received 1,000,000 Great Wife points. Spend them recklessly.

And finally, there are three teachers who probably have no idea how influential they were on my education and career choices. Now, only 20+ years late, I must thank Arthur Schang (Physics), Don Louis Lynn, Jr. (Calculus), and Janice Watts (English) for their encouragement and special teaching methodologies that spurred my interest in math, science, writing, and literature. My education and career have both benefited from being a student in their classrooms.

Introduction

Computers are getting cheaper and cheaper. It's not uncommon to find new PCs for sale for under $200 these days. We're not quite at the stage where you can go buy a replacement computer in the same way as you purchase a new toaster, but we're close. In fact, one day computers may be given away with the purchase of a new piece of software.

Ah, software—there's the rub. Software has *not* dropped in price. As a matter of fact, software costs keep going up, and there's no end in sight. It's not uncommon to spend $200 or more for a big-name application to install on your computer. I'm not suggesting that software isn't worth the price. What I'm saying is that it's almost impossible today to spend less on software than you did on the computer to run it!

But there are exceptions. Low-cost software exists. But would you believe that you can get high-quality software that won't cost you a dime? Well, that's what this book is all about: free software.

Free.

No strings attached.

No credit card required.

No 30-day trial period.

Zilch. Nada. Zip.

Don't believe me? That's okay; skepticism is good. I didn't believe that free high-quality software existed either. But now I'm a convert, and that's why I wrote this book.

I'm not anti-Microsoft or anti-Adobe or against any other big software provider, but I don't want to spend a lot of money for software features I won't use. And that's the problem with expensive software these days: feature overload with a matching price overload. Give me some good software that can do what I need it to do, without all the bells and whistles. And if it turns out to be free? Woo hoo! Say it with me: Woo! Hoo!

So, sit down, keep reading, and be prepared for many happy surprises. You may not need every piece of free software I cover in this book, but I'm fairly certain you'll find at least one that you can use (and that will more than cover the cost of the book).

Welcome to the world of free software. And spread the word.

What Type of Software Do You Want?

With the exception of the first two chapters, each chapter in this book is about a different type of software. In many cases, I'll cover the defenders (the popular and usually pricey applications) and the contenders (the free versions), so you can compare their features.

Here's a chapter-by-chapter rundown:

Chapter 1, The Best Things in Life: There are all kinds of free software, but two important categories of free software are open source and Software as a Service (SaaS). This chapter explains how these two types of software differ from just any old free software you find floating around on the Internet.

Chapter 2, The PC Element: Free software will definitely save you money, but you can go one step further by loading it on a computer you already have, or even building your own low-cost PC. This chapter explains how you can save money when it comes to computer hardware.

Chapter 3, Word Processing: One of the most common uses for a computer is composing letters, e-mail, and other types of text files. Most people expect to find some sort of word processing software installed on any computer they use. This chapter covers one of the biggest names in word processing, and then provides two free alternatives for you to consider, along with some sample tasks using each.

Chapter 4, Spreadsheets: Spreadsheets aren't just for accountants. This chapter introduces two free alternatives to the big-name spreadsheet application, along with a collection of sample tasks that demonstrate the usefulness of the 100% free challengers.

Chapter 5, Slide Shows: Presentations are one of the key methods used by businesses and individuals to share information with others. This chapter describes two free alternatives to the most popular slide show application used today. You'll also see some examples of how each application can be used in ways you might not have considered before.

Chapter 6, E-Mail and Calendar: An e-mail address is almost an absolute requirement for living in today's world, and a personal calendar can help you stay organized. One of the biggest names on the Internet today, Google, offers free e-mail and calendar services. This chapter shows you just how handy these two free applications are and why you should use them.

Chapter 7, Photo Editing: A powerful photo editing application that is 100% free to download, install, and use? This chapter introduces you to one of free software's biggest success stories. You will learn where to get it, how to install it, and how to use it.

Chapter 8, Graphics: Applications for creating custom graphics have traditionally been expensive and difficult to use. One up-and-coming application is changing all that. Both professional and nonprofessional users are praising this free software for its features and ease of use. Here, you'll learn about this new application and how to use some of its basic features.

Chapter 9, Virus Protection: All computers are at risk of attack from the malicious software that exists on the Internet and on other users' computers. One of the best antivirus applications available for your computer is also completely free to download and use, as well as extremely easy to set up to protect your computer automatically. This chapter covers this free application, including step-by-step instructions for configuring it so your computer is protected.

Chapter 10, Data Backup: Along with protecting your computer from viruses, you need to consider making backups of all your important files. This chapter introduces you to a free application that will help you make copies of your files, and shows you how to automate the process.

Chapter 11, Personal Finance: You're reading a book about free software because you want to save some money, right? Well, this chapter shows you how a free application can help you track your bank account, including deposits and expenses. Doesn't it make more sense to use a free application for financial tracking than to pay for one?

Chapter 12, Gaming: Online gaming is extremely popular, but unfortunately, it can also be extremely expensive when you're paying a monthly fee to play. This chapter focuses on a free alternative to the biggest name in online gaming. You'll find out how to start playing immediately and have some fun with fellow gamers from around the world.

Chapter 13, Photo Management: If you take digital pictures, you've probably snapped a few bad shots. Bad lighting or red eye can ruin a great picture. And if you have a lot of digital photos on your hard drive, keeping track of them can be a huge time burden. This chapter shows you one of the easiest and most fun applications you can find for solving your digital photo problems, and it's 100% free.

Chapter 14, Internet Phone Calls: This chapter introduces one of the easiest and cheapest ways to talk to your friends and family. If you have an Internet connection and a micro-phone, you can make free local and long-distance calls—even free international calls! And if you have a webcam, you can see the people you're talking with and give them a wave.

Chapter 15, Web Logs: An extremely popular type of media is the web log, or *blog*. This chapter explains how you, too, can start sharing your news, photos, and opinions with the rest of the world by by creating your own blog using an online blogging application that also just happens to be completely free.

Chapter 16, Social Networking: Social networking lets you keep friends, family, and coworkers up-to-date on your vacation news, pictures, videos, and more. This chapter shows you one of the best (and totally free) services for finding friends, old and new, and keeping your list of contacts informed about what's going on in your life.

Chapter 17, Group Scheduling: If you've ever tried to organize any kind of get-together (group movie, birthday party, and so on), then you're going to love the free service this chapter introduces. You will see how to use this online service to narrow down the best time and day for the maximum number of people to attend your next event.

At the back of the book, you'll find an appendix with brief descriptions of some additional free applications and services that I believe are worth mentioning.

Contact the Author

I always like hearing about new software—especially free, good-quality software. If you find something of interest, please let me know. I can be contacted at dsad2009@gmail.com. I'll be post-ing reader submissions, along with my own findings, at http://dontspendadime.blogspot.com.

CHAPTER 1

■■■

The Best Things in Life

As the song says, "The best things in life are free." That statement can apply to numerous things: free coffee, free oil change, free Wi-Fi Internet, and even a free blood pressure check. But how many of us would expect to find computer software on that list? If you're like me, you've discovered that software costs money. You might also be of the opinion that *good* software costs *more* money. And finally, you might have come to the matching conclusion that *free* software must not be that *good*.

Well, I'm here to tell you that I've never been so happy to be wrong. And by the end of this book, I think you, too, will be smiling when you discover that some of the best software in life is free.

Yes, the words *free* and *software* in the same sentence can sometimes still imply computers crashing, flaky installations, and cryptic controls. Unfortunately, the world of free software still has many hurdles to overcome. But rest assured that there are outstanding, five-star, free software applications out there that stand with the best and the brightest. And they're growing in popularity and number every day. This is because they are getting easier to use and install, and are frequently on par in terms of quality (and sometimes 100% better) and features as those from the Big Boys (and you know who I mean). You'll find free software that fills a void that pay-to-use software does not address, and free software written as a labor of love, with no strings attached to its use.

Free software raises many questions. Can this software really offer me the features I need? Can the software be trusted? Who do I contact if I have problems or questions? Are there hidden costs? How do I separate the wheat from the chaff? These are some good questions, and I'm sure you have more. I had my doubts when I started investigating free software, but again, I've never been so pleased to be so wrong.

You're about to discover what I did: the words *free* and *software* do belong together. Let me explain how and why.

Software Wants to Be Free

Without getting too deep into the history of computing, let me summarize the early days of software in one sentence:

In the beginning, there was software, and it was free.

I'm not kidding. One of the biggest shocks to most people is finding out that software originally was free. Students and faculty at colleges and universities would create and share software with one another; no money exchanged hands. Most software at the time was written to fill a void—scheduling software for classes, simple text editing software for term papers, and even rudimentary e-mail software to communicate. Other software (games, for example) was written simply to show off programming skills or provide a nice break between classes and studying. Oftentimes, this software was modified by others to improve it and remove errors (called *software bugs*). But the Iron Age of software (some might even say the Golden Age) didn't last long. For software, as with all things, the *users* turned into *consumers*.

The public today has just come to assume that software is something you buy. Free software has always existed, but any software that is even remotely of interest to ten or more people is typically going to be boxed, priced, and stuck on a shelf.

But many modern-day programmers who create software have looked fondly back on those days and asked, "What would it take to return software to its origins?" What's required to have software shared with everyone, updated and repaired by colleagues, and 100% free to use? The answer is that it wouldn't take much.

Software Will Be Free

Today and any day, you can find all types of free software on the Internet. Just Google "free software," and you'll find hundreds of web sites that collect, summarize, and rate software, in addition to allowing you to download and install it. All right—free software!

But let's be careful here and examine what is meant by *free*. For me, free means I can download it without providing a credit card. But free also means that when I install the program, it shouldn't ask me for a credit card number or an installation key. But again, there are different definitions.

Some "free" software allows you to use it for a specified number of days (30 days, for example), and then requires you to either purchase it or uninstall it. This is often referred to as *trialware* or *shareware*. Other free software can be downloaded for free and installed on your computer, but consists of a slimmed-down version, often with many key features unavailable. The only way you can get the full feature set is to—you guessed it—purchase the full version.

There are many ways to define free, but for the purpose of this book, I want to share three varieties with you: open source, Software as a Service, and what I sometimes call the no-strings-attached freebie.

Open Source

Entire books have been written on the subject of open source software. Here, I'm going to spare you the essay, and simply give you what I feel is a simple, no-frills definition of what open source software is, how it works, and what it means to you.

An open source application is software that has the following characteristics:

- Created using a collaborative effort by individuals who share a common interest in producing an application of the highest quality

- Distributed for free (and kept free)

- Continually refined and improved by reducing bugs and adding features requested by its users

Open source software can include a variety of applications, such as word processors, spreadsheets, games, audio/video editors, and so on.

There are many benefits to using open source software, but the primary one for most people will be its cost: free. But if the software were low-quality, buggy, and not of any real use to people, the fact that it's free wouldn't matter much, because people wouldn't use it. So that's another benefit of open source software: quality.

Open source software is often being developed and tested by a group of knowledgeable programmers. This group might consist of two friends creating a game during their lunch hour. It could just as easily consist of 2,000 individuals scattered around the globe, who may never have met in person, contributing to and debugging one another's work around the clock. But one goal open source developers share is to create something that is of high quality.

And the "free" part of open source doesn't just apply to the application but also to its source code. The *source code* consists of the actual programming code that is used to create the application. If an application is defined as open source, this means that its source code is available for download so other programmers can inspect it and tinker with it. In fact, in some cases, programmers create a completely different version of an open source application by adding features or modifying the look and style. (But the variant source code must also be made available for free download and inspection or it loses the open source label.)

Finally, the group developing an open source application that is popular among users will, inevitably, receive requests for bug fixes and new features. Open source application developers typically are committed to continually improving an application to try to make it the best in class for a particular type of application (such as a word processor or graphics editor).

Open source isn't perfect. I want to make that absolutely clear. A lot of junky open source software is out there. But you can rest assured that the software I identify as open source in this book is some of the best you can find—it meets the high-quality criterion, as well as being free.

Software as a Service

Have you ever used a drive-through (or walk-up) ATM to get some cash? You probably used a computer screen and maybe a keypad to enter things such as your PIN and the amount of cash to withdraw. To get your money, you used software, right? Did you need to install the software on the ATM? Definitely not. You used the software that was already provided by the bank. The bank, on the other hand, had to create the software, test it, debug it, and install it on the ATM for your use. But you don't care how it came to be. Your only concern is that it works properly and lets you get your cash!

For purposes of this book, I'm going to use the term *Software as a Service* (SaaS for short, pronounced "sass") to describe a type of software that is growing in popularity. The primary difference between SaaS and open source software comes down to where the software resides. Is it installed on your computer or elsewhere?

Note Along with where the software resides, there are other differences between open source and SaaS. By the time you finish this book, you'll have a clearer understanding of how to differentiate the two. For now, just keep in mind that SaaS applications can easily be identified by the fact that you don't need to install any software on your computer to use them.

To make this more clear, let's consider online banking for a moment. Most banks allow their customers with Internet access to use a web browser to log in and access their account information. A customer doesn't need to install any special software (other than the web browser, of course), but she uses some very specialized software that's provided by the bank to view her balance, transfer funds, and maybe print out a monthly statement. When she closes the web browser or logs out of the bank web site, the software is no longer running on the customer's computer. That's the basic concept behind SaaS. Use it when you need it, and leave it when you don't. There is no need to install or uninstall the software.

These days, more and more companies are offering various services through their web sites. Some require you to pay a one-time fee (such as paying for two hours of Wi-Fi Internet access at a coffee shop). Others require a monthly subscription (such as an online newspaper subscription for *The New York Times*). These qualify as SaaS, even though they are not free, because the software you use to log in and perform tasks resides elsewhere; you're just accessing it from your web browser.

So what qualifies as free SaaS? Well, one of the biggest names in the industry offers free SaaS, and most people never even think about it. Imagine if you were charged a small fee every time you did an Internet search on Google (see Figure 1-1). You would probably never use it, right? Fortunately, Google makes its search engine completely free to use. It generates revenue from advertisers (yuck!), who place their ads on the right side of your web browser and hope that you'll see something interesting, click their ad, and buy, buy, buy.

Figure 1-1. *Thank goodness that Google doesn't charge every time you click that search button.*

There are plenty more 100% free SaaS web sites. For example, CNN.com offers free news services, and craigslist.org lets you buy and sell items using posted ads. I'm going to introduce you to many free SaaS sites in upcoming chapters. By the time you finish this book, you'll have a collection of SaaS web sites that make your life much easier. You're going to be e-mailing me, asking when *Don't Spend a Dime, Volume 2* is coming out!

No-Strings-Attached Freebie

The last type of free software I'll talk about has been around forever. It's the 100% free application that someone created and put out there for the world to use. This software costs nothing, but also typically comes with nothing—no support, no web site, no phone number, and no updates. Usually, the people who create this type of free software do so because they need a particular functionality and cannot find any existing software that provides it. Typically, these folks share their software with the world, expecting no payment in return (just as in the early days of software!).

Hundreds of web sites offer access to free software. Just do a Google search for "free software" and be prepared to be overwhelmed. One of my favorite places to go when I'm looking for an application to do something very specific is http://www.snapfiles.com. Take a quick look at this web site. In the upper-right corner, you'll see a tab for Shareware and a tab for Freeware. Click the Freeware tab, and you'll see a categorized listing of everything Snap-Files offers that is free, as shown in Figure 1-2. (Be careful—you could spend hours browsing through this site's free software.)

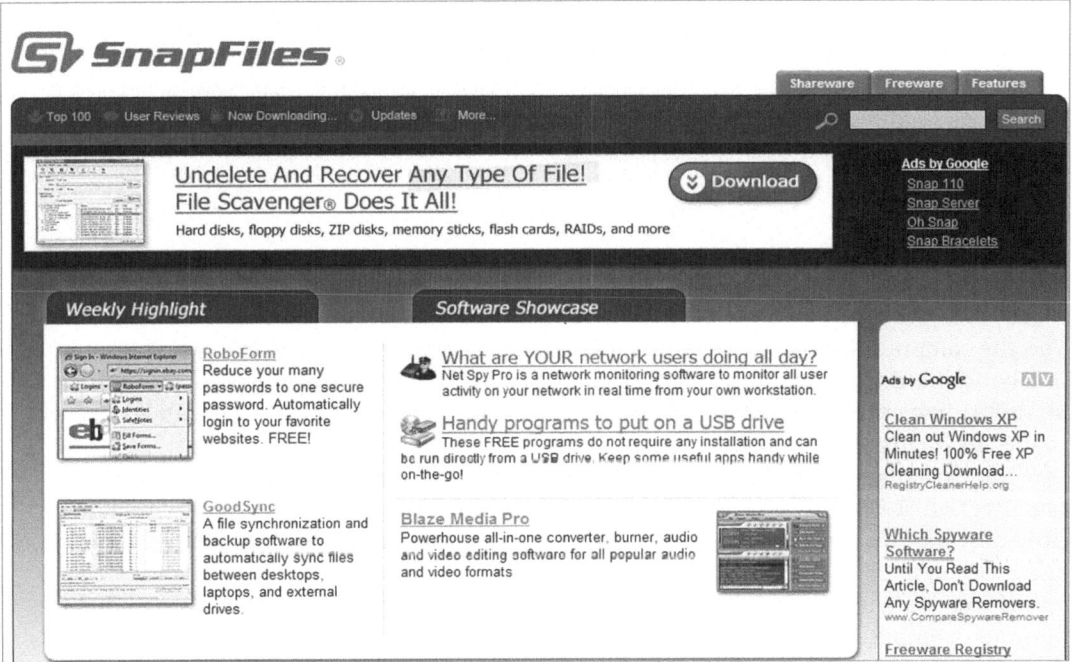

Figure 1-2. *SnapFiles offers thousands of freeware applications for you to use.*

WHAT'S THE CATCH?

You may be thinking that there must be a catch. There's no such thing as free! You're right—sort of. High-quality software that is 100% free with no strings attached does exist. Open source software is the best example. But someone has to pay for those computers that run SaaS, and there are many ways this can occur.

Some companies (Google, for example) cover the costs of their free applications through advertising. Head over to `http://www.google.com` and do a search for "Star Wars." When you see the results page, look along the right edge of the screen. See the small blocks of advertisements? Those companies are paying Google to have their advertisements placed so you (possibly a Star Wars movie fan) can find and buy all kinds of Star Wars memorabilia. But being exposed to ads is not a big sacrifice for access to Google's free applications.

Some companies charge fees for technical support. For example, if you find you have a question about the software, a $25 phone call will get you the answer. Some companies charge fees for multiple users beyond the first user. Others charge a fee if you need customization of the application (such as adding your company name or logo to the application's opening screen).

The methods for generating income vary from company to company, but my best advice to you is to always read the fine print. Spend some time looking around the application's web site, and maybe perform a Google search of the application's name. You're sure to find information that will either verify the software's free cost or give you information about any hidden costs. That said, all of the software I cover in this book is free to download, install, and use. If there are any hidden costs or unusual methods for generating income, I will explain that in the discussion of that application.

But What About the PC?

Yes, the computer (the hardware) costs money. Even if you've been given a free computer as a hand-me-down, that PC required someone to spend money at some point in time. It's an unfortunate truth that there really is no such thing as an open source PC, with all its parts made and distributed for free.

For most of us, obtaining a computer usually requires buying one from a PC company (such as Dell or Acer). This isn't necessarily a bad thing, though. Purchasing a prebuilt PC provides you with a warranty, someone to call when things go wrong, and that new-computer smell (admit it—you like it, too).

If you're buying a new PC, you might want to find a company that allows you to order your new computer without any preinstalled software. Why have them install a $30 antivirus program when you can get some great antivirus software for free? (Chapter 9 tells you where.) Maybe the computer vendor offers to throw in a productivity suite (word processor, spreadsheet, and e-mail application) for only $150 (versus its retail price of $300 at the store). Tell them to forget it! Chapters 3 through 6 show you where to get the same features using reliable, easy-to-use, free software.

The best part of steering clear of pricey off-the-shelf software is that you can take the money you would have spent on that software and use it to get higher-performing hardware. You can put that cash toward a faster processor, more memory, and a larger hard drive. Not only will the free software run more efficiently (and take less hard drive space) on your new computer, but you will also have extended the usefulness of your computer by years.

If you've decided to purchase a new computer or build your own, you'll want to read through Chapter 2 next. There, I'll show you how to determine exactly what hardware you need. Not everyone will need the fastest PC with all the bells and whistles. In the world of computers, people frequently purchase more than they need. If you do this, the computer sellers will love you, but your bank account won't be so happy. Fortunately, open source software and SaaS typically have lower demands for computer hardware, meaning you can save even more money by pairing free software with the lower hardware costs. Now that's a win-win solution!

RECOMMENDED READING

If you have any interest in the history of computers and software, you owe it to yourself to hunt down a few books:

- *Hackers* by Steven Levy (Penguin, 2001) isn't about those troublesome, virus-writing, break-into-computers-and-steal-credit-card-numbers bad guys. Back in the day, the term *hacker* was a positive one (and it's coming full circle and regaining its status). *Hacker* referred to anyone who could take hardware or software and remake it, debug it, tweak it, and do other wondrous things. This book covers from the early days at MIT, when a bunch of model railroad fanatics began experimenting with controlling their trains with simple electronic circuits, to the humble beginnings of Microsoft and Apple. It's some good storytelling.

- *Dreaming in Code* by Scott Rosenberg (Three Rivers Press, 2008) is an entertaining story about a small group of individuals who decided to create an open source application. The book covers the highs and lows, and the successes and failures. It also explains the open source concept in detail.

- *On the Way to the Web* by Michael A. Banks (Apress, 2008) is a history of the Internet, including its origins, its successes, and its mistakes. This is a great read and helps you understand how the Internet got where it is today.

Summary

Many computer users are tired of buying software that is buggy, complicated, and overpriced. And since much of this software is updated every year or two, we can quickly find ourselves in a never-ending cycle of purchasing upgrades.

Enough is enough! With a minimum investment in hardware (possibly even $0), you have a wide selection of free, high-quality software that can save you from this dependency on big-name applications.

My advice is simple. Investigate the options and determine if the free software will meet your needs. If you do find that your needs can be met only by using the features found in an off-the-shelf application, then it's okay to buy that application.

In preparing this book, I made a list of the types of software that would most likely be found on users' PCs. I then picked the most commonly used name brand of each type of software and researched, found, installed, and tested what I believe to be the best, most realistic replacements that are 100% free. Read through the book and discover for yourself how easy it is to never pay for software again.

CHAPTER 2

The PC Element

When it comes to your computer's usable life (well, the amount of time it will be useful to you), the only two things that matter are the hardware and the software. Both hardware and software grow old and become obsolete, but at extremely different rates. There are businesses still running or trying to run Windows 95-generation business software (such as QuickBooks 95) on Windows Vista desktops (a more than 12-year-old operating system's software on the latest version of Microsoft's operating system). And there are many home users who are trying to install and run Word 2007 software on their Windows 98 computer. It's an unfair fact of life, but hardware and software do not grow old gracefully together like that sweet, old couple who lives a few houses down the road.

Note This book is about free software that runs on the Windows operating system. Fortunately, much of the software is also available in Mac and Linux versions. So, when I use the term *PC*, please understand that I'm typically referring to a Windows XP or Windows Vista computer. Feel free to substitute in Mac or Linux if you like, and you can certainly apply much of this discussion to those two types of computers.

It's a hard life cycle to accept: for a few months or maybe a year, there will be large advances in hardware technology, and software might work on a new computer but special features will be disabled for compatibility. And then it flips for a while, and organizations start releasing software that you cannot install on your PC, because that software requires a specific hardware component to be running at a specific speed (a high-end graphic card, for example) or due to some other technological hindrance. Trying to keep your computer up-to-date with the latest and greatest hardware and software is frustrating and expensive. Some suggest it's a conspiracy between hardware and software companies to keep the funds flowing. But there's good news.

The hardware and software update/upgrade dance is quickly becoming an obsolete business method that you're no longer forced to be a participant in, all thanks to free, open source software and Software as a Service (SaaS) web-based applications.

This chapter focuses on hardware, which may seem out of place in a book dedicated to free software. But the information in this chapter is about simply one more way to spend less money—either by refurbishing an existing PC or by buying the minimum hardware you'll need to do the work you require. Either way, I'll offer some guidance on how to get a PC and how that PC should be equipped. The goal here is to save you money, as well get you the proper hardware that's compatible with the software covered in later chapters.

To Buy or Not to Buy (with Apologies to William)

Right now, three (legal) solutions are available when you need the services provided by a computer, such as word processing, gaming, and other types of applications. Here are these solutions, listed in order of cheapest (possibly even free) to most expensive:

- Upgrade or repurpose an existing one

- Build one

- Buy one

By using the free software covered in this book, not only will your computer's useful life span increase, but your overall costs to buy (and then operate) are going to decrease. Need proof? Keep reading.

Upgrade or Repurpose an Existing PC

Saving money, reducing waste in landfills (a huge problem these days), and recycling materials are just a few of the benefits of taking an "obsolete" PC and making it useful again. Most computers aren't actually obsolete—they're simply labeled obsolete because they cannot run the latest and greatest software being sold on store shelves.

For many computer users, having the fastest video card, the largest hard drive, and the highest capacity memory chips on the market just isn't necessary. My parents, for example, do three things with their computer: word processing, e-mail, and Internet browsing. They don't watch DVDs, play graphic-intensive video games, or listen to music/MP3 files. But computer companies spend a fortune on advertising to convince potential customers that they absolutely must have this new computer with a 4GHz processor, 512MB video card, 800GB SATA hard drive, and six USB 2.0 ports in order to be productive and to keep up with the rest of the Internet-connected, high-speed world. But it's all hype! The truth is that extending the life of a PC typically requires only a single upgrade, or two at the most.

Upgrading your PC means buying only hardware that you need and leaving the rest alone. If you have run out of hard drive space and cannot find any files to delete, then buy and install a new hard drive. If your applications are sluggish, buy some more memory sticks and install them. If you're truly trying to keep costs down, upgrading is your best bang for the buck.

Repurposing can mean anything from formatting your hard drive and reinstalling the operating system to simply uninstalling any applications you are not using and freeing up resources for those apps that you do use. Some companies will sell or auction off their surplus computers to employees to use as home PCs. This is also an example of repurposing a PC and giving it a new life. And if you're feeling brave and willing to do a little research on the Web, an old PC can make a great little home server. (A home server is simply a computer dedicated to holding music, pictures, and video and making them available to other computers in your home.)

You are certain to discover that upgrading a hard drive or adding an extra gigabyte of random-access memory (RAM) may be all that's necessary to give a PC an extra year or two of life. It's the dirty, little secret that most computer salespeople will never share with you!

Build a PC

There are many reasons to build your own PC. Being able to choose the exact components you want or learning more about how computers work are two great examples. While it's typically cheaper to do it yourself (DIY), this approach also has plenty of risks, which I'll cover in a moment.

Let's define DIY first, though. When I say DIY, I'm not talking about going to the Dell web site, selecting a base model, and then tweaking it with custom hardware additions. That may feel DIY, but it's not.

What I mean by DIY is performing some research (that includes your computing needs), and then shopping for and purchasing the individual components that will go into your new PC. You might buy the components from a local store or over the Internet. The DIY comes when you take all these components (motherboard, memory chips, hard drive, video card, and power supply, for example), put them together, and install an operating system. *That's* DIY.

Tip There are plenty of books available on building your own PC, but this book isn't one of them. Later in the chapter, I'll show you how to figure out what you need. If you need technical help on putting together a PC (trust me, it's not difficult—I've built dozens!), I suggest three free online tutorials for instructions and discussion on the DIY PC: `http://www.pcmech.com/byopc/`, `http://www.howtogeek.com/howto/the-geek-blog/building-a-new-computer-part-1-choosing-hardware/`, and `http://techreport.com/articles.x/13671`.

If you've done your research and are buying components individually, you're going to save money (web sites such as `pricewatch.com`, `slickdeals.net`, and `newegg.com` are great places to start looking for good deals). You won't be nervous about purchasing "older" hardware, because you know that *older* could mean last month's processor or last year's hard drive capacity.

With many shops (online or not), you'll often find that haggling can lower prices, especially if you can point them to a competitor who is selling the same item at the same price. And you'll also be getting hardware with warranties.

Note While I'm not in favor of purchasing hardware from places such as `craigslist.org`, if you're comfortable doing so and don't mind the buyer-beware risk built into these types of purchases, you can find great deals on hardware. You may be able to make a purchase from one of those PC owners who must have the latest and greatest, and are always ripping components out of their PCs to replace them with the new stuff. Just remember to keep "buyer beware" in your thoughts. Ask questions, and request a photo of the part number or serial number, so you can do a product search and verify that what you're buying is what the seller is advertising.

While you won't save as much money on a DIY PC as you would performing an upgrade on an existing PC, you'll still find the savings substantial when compared to the cost of buying a prebuilt PC.

Buy a PC

I recognize that many people like the idea of a new computer (but there is no such thing as a new-PC smell). One or two big boxes are delivered to your door, and you get to rip into them like it's your birthday. Everything is shiny and under warranty. You turn it on, and maybe take a tour of the operating system, connect the speakers, examine the hard drive, and see all that unused space. Perhaps you'll register a few preinstalled applications online so you can open them and starting typing, playing, or listening. New computers are definitely enjoyable. They're easy to set up and ready to start using.

I'm not going to bash prebuilt computer sellers. They provide a service that's obviously in demand. Not everyone feels comfortable assembling their own PC, and not everyone has an old PC sitting around waiting to be upgraded. PC sellers definitely give you a nice product for the price.

But even when you're buying a new prebuilt PC, there are still ways to save money. You just need to exert some self-control and maybe do a little research to understand what you're buying (or not buying).

First, be aware that most prebuilt PC sellers get you in the door (or on their web site) by offering a low-cost base unit. This unit typically doesn't come with an LCD panel (or monitor) and, in some instances, an operating system isn't even installed. Check the fine print and know what you're buying.

Tip Check the Internet for online coupons, too. PC sellers frequently offer sizable discounts on their computers. Sites such as slickdeals.net are a great place to find online coupons for 20% to 40% off! You simply type in the coupon code at checkout, and the price is adjusted.

Next, most sellers allow you to perform "upgrades" to the base unit by checking boxes next to add-ons or swapping out lower-priced (and lower-performance) components for higher-end hardware. Again, this is where you must show some control and rely on your research on prices and features. Is the 250GB hard drive in the base unit enough, or should you spend the extra $50 to have it replaced with a 500GB hard drive? Here's a hint: obtain prices for the two components individually, and if the "upgrade" costs more than the difference between the two, you'll know it's a bad deal. In this example, the price difference between a 250GB and 500GB hard drive is less than $20 on pricewatch.com—no deal!

What you'll discover is that by the time you're finished reconfiguring the base unit with the hardware that you want, the price will most likely have jumped anywhere from 25% to 100%! And that's just with hardware upgrades. How about the software?

Most base units come with a base operating system, such as Windows Vista Home Basic, not Vista Home Premium—again, check the fine print! You'll then be given the opportunity to upgrade the operating system to a more advanced version of Vista. (Windows XP versions included Home, Pro, and Media Center but, unfortunately, will not be sold after January 2009, and support for the operating system will supposedly stop in October 2009. So, your choice of a Microsoft operating system will be confined to Vista Home Basic, Home Premium, Business, Business Ultimate, or Vista Ultimate.) Make certain to do some research and purchase only the level of operating system that you need.

Note If you want to really show off, consider removing the operating system altogether and installing a free one, such as Ubuntu Linux. Most of the software covered in this book will run on Ubuntu, and if you're repurposing an old PC, you'll truly have a free computer, since the hardware has already been paid for. That means free hardware, free operating system, and free software! One of the best books on installing and using Ubuntu is *Beginning Ubuntu Linux, Third Edition* by Keir Thomas and Jaime Sicam (Apress, 2008). I've read the book, and it is, hands-down, one of the best Ubuntu books on the market.

Finally, while configuring the base unit, you'll be given the chance to add preinstalled applications, such as word processing, spreadsheet, antivirus, and photo/video editing software. You can always purchase this software separately from a local computer store or on the Internet, but PC sellers often give you a slight price break if you buy the software from them. But ask yourself, "Are these applications I really need, or are there free alternatives?" (By the time you finish reading this book, you'll have the answer.)

It's so easy to just check off boxes next to software. When buying a prebuilt PC and configuring its software, buyers can get click-happy and configure the "ultimate PC." Fortunately, at the end of the configuration process, you're presented with the final price of your newly configured computer. Once you're over the sticker shock, you can go back and reconfigure, removing an item here and an application there, until you arrive at a balance of hardware, software, and price that you can handle. Unfortunately, getting to an acceptable price sometimes requires that you remove an application that you feel is important for the work you need to do (or games you wish to play). But remember that any time you save money on software, you have choices. Let me explain.

Great News: Free Software Means More Hardware

Let's not forget the purpose of this book: free software. That will often mean more money to apply to hardware—not just in terms of more components, but also in terms of higher performance. When you *save* $100 by loading a free application versus the off-the-shelf software, that money can be directly applied to the hardware in your computer—whether you're upgrading, building a DIY, or buying a prebuilt new PC. Consider what an extra $100 (or $300 or $400) saved on software can buy when it comes to a processor, hard drive, or other components: faster speeds, more features, higher capacities, and, ultimately, a *longer, more useful life for your PC.*

Throughout the remaining chapters, I'll cover brand-name applications that cost anywhere from $30 to $40, all the way up to $500 or more. Keep these prices in mind as you decide whether you absolutely require the brand-name software, can substitute the free competitor, or don't need that type of application at all. It adds up quickly. By the time you finish this book, you may be surprised that you've substituted $300, $400, or maybe even $500 worth of name-brand software with free software options. Pocket those savings, or splurge on that larger LCD screen that will let you view all your free software in greater color and clarity! You might even consider purchasing another PC. That $500 will buy a nice, portable ASUS Eee PC that you can take with you on the road.

Five PC User Types

Whether you're considering building your own PC or buying a prebuilt one, I highly recommend that you first examine your computer needs. Why? Because if you can identify the type of software you will run on your computer, you can spend the appropriate amounts on the hardware that you need, and spend less on the hardware that you don't need.

There's really no surefire method for doing this, so I'll just offer one possible solution that divides computer users into what I call *user types*. For simplicity, I categorize all computer users into five types:

Type 1, Bare-Bones: The Bare-Bones PC user requires the most basic of computing needs: e-mail, word processing, basic graphics and sound, and antivirus protection. This user may or may not be comfortable with computers, but does live in the twenty-first century and recognizes that Internet connectivity makes life easier, so will want either dial-up or broadband service. This user is likely concerned about cost, so basic hardware, without any bells and whistles, is fine (and because this computer may be upgraded at a later time).

Type 2, Family Member: The PC will be used and shared by all members of a household. High-speed Internet is a necessity, as is e-mail, word processing, spreadsheets, and good speakers and video display capabilities for music, movies, and games. Upgrading is always an option, so this computer doesn't necessarily need the most advanced hardware. Price is important, but so is performance. The Family Member PC user is willing to play a game of give-and-take to get the best balance of price and performance. And because so many people will be using this PC for a variety of reasons, antivirus software is an absolute requirement.

Type 3, Gamer: The Gamer requires the best of all possible hardware, including video, sound, processor, memory, and storage. This user never knows what game he will be running next, so it's safest to have the latest and greatest hardware installed, or at least have a computer that can be readily upgraded to the newest stuff. The Gamer is more concerned with performance than cost, so sticker shock isn't a concern when selecting components. Components should be easy to swap out (as well as a case that allows quick changes), because this user is never happy with last month's hardware.

Type 4, Multimedia Guru: The Multimedia Guru works with video, audio, and photographs and requires the best visual experience possible, as well as fast hard drive access and superb sound quality. Multimedia takes up a huge amount of space, so storage is always a concern. A large LCD is almost always present, and no rinky-dink video card will suffice. The Guru may also dabble in music mixing and editing, so a quality sound card is an absolute must-have. Cost may be a factor, but the Guru knows that you get what you pay for and will settle for trade-offs, as long as they don't affect the applications she runs.

Type 5, Small Business Owner: The Small Business Owner must carefully balance cost with functionality. This user is looking for the best price for the best hardware, and is usually willing to shop around for the best deal. The software installed on a small business computer typically includes productivity applications (word processor, spreadsheet, and so on), as well as antivirus and data backup software. Video can sometimes be important, but sound quality is an easy sacrifice for most Small Business Owner users. The small business PC typically has a mix of good-quality hardware, but not necessarily the most recent or best.

The user types aren't super-specific. You may be having a hard time deciding which type you fall under, but that's okay. These are merely to help demonstrate how pricing can vary depending on your hardware and software needs. Keep these five types in mind as we take a virtual shopping trip to first look at prebuilt PCs, and then at the hardware required to build an identical (or as close to identical as possible) DIY computer. Ultimately, you'll fall into your own unique type—let's call it Type *<Your Name Here>*—because you'll be the one customizing your new computer.

Two Steps to Identifying Your Hardware Needs

Now I'm going to show you a two-step process to identify the type of hardware you need. You should perform these steps no matter what type of PC you plan on purchasing. As an example, I'll demonstrate how to pick a Bare-Bones PC. In the next section, we'll look at PC shopping for the other four types.

Caution Keep in mind that the only software you're receiving with the name-brand computers is the operating system (Windows Vista) and, in a few instances, Outlook Express, Microsoft Works, and 30-day evaluation copies of various applications. Don't be fooled—Microsoft Works is not the same as Microsoft Office, so you're not getting Word, Excel, or Outlook. And 30-day evaluations are just that: trial software that will stop working in 30 days and require you to purchase if you wish to continue using them. As you read through the remaining chapters in this book, you'll find the additional pricing required for various applications. Software can often double or even triple the cost of a computer.

Step 1: Find a Prebuilt PC

Your first step in our virtual shopping trip is to find a prebuilt PC that will fit your needs. For now, I'm searching for a good Type 1, Bare-Bones PC. Remember that the Bare-Bones user is looking to save money and needs only enough hardware to run the most basic of applications, such as an e-mail app and Internet browser. There's no need to buy the largest hard drive or the fastest processor, so I'll keep this in mind as I browse for a PC.

I'm paying a visit to dell.com. For a Type 1, Bare-Bones PC, I've located the Inspiron 530s base unit, which has a starting price of $279 (plus any tax and shipping).

Inspiron 530s

Intel Celeron 440 processor (2.00GHz, 800 FSB)

Windows Vista Home Basic Service Pack 1

No monitor

16X DVD+/-RW drive

1GB dual-channel DDR2 SDRAM at 667MHz, 2 DIMMs

250GB serial ATA hard drive (7200 RPM)

Integrated Intel Graphics Media Accelerator 3100

Integrated 7.1 Channel Audio (sound)

One-year limited hardware warranty (not on-site service, so you'll send it in for repairs)

While I've now identified a very basic computer that could satisfy a Bare-Bones PC user's hardware requirements, I'd like to make a few changes.

First, I want to upgrade that Celeron processor to a dual-core processor. That will be the most expensive hardware upgrade, but the processor is just too important to skimp on. Next, I need a monitor. Dell will let me add a 17-inch widescreen LCD for $180.

Figure 2-1 shows the system summary. Note that the computer comes with a network card (10/100 Ethernet) built in to the motherboard, keyboard, and mouse, and a 30-day evaluation copy of McAfee security software (antivirus, anti-spyware). It does not come with speakers or a floppy drive (which is really old technology anyway, so don't let that bother you). Finally, Dell throws in a copy of Microsoft Works.

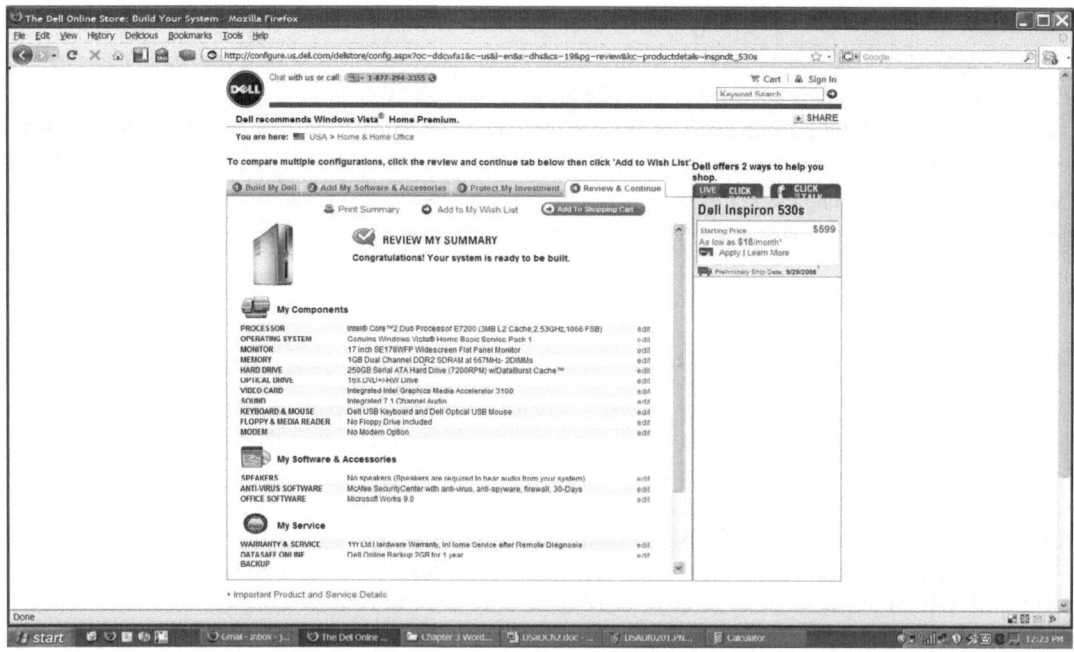

Figure 2-1. *The Dell Bare-Bones system choice (with an upgraded processor and monitor added)*

As shown in Figure 2-2, after upgrading the processor and adding the monitor, shipping ($35.00), and tax ($38.04), my total price is now $672.04. That's not too bad for a basic PC that should give me years of service when I combine it with the free software covered in this book! Now that I've picked the Type 1, Bare-Bones computer I'm considering purchasing, it's time for step 2.

Caution As you move through the checkout process, notice how many other products and accessories Dell asks you to consider purchasing: printer, wireless mouse, mouse pad, flash drive, and even a digital photo frame! Just stay focused, and buy only what you need. That means the computer . . . the computer . . . the computer—stay focused!

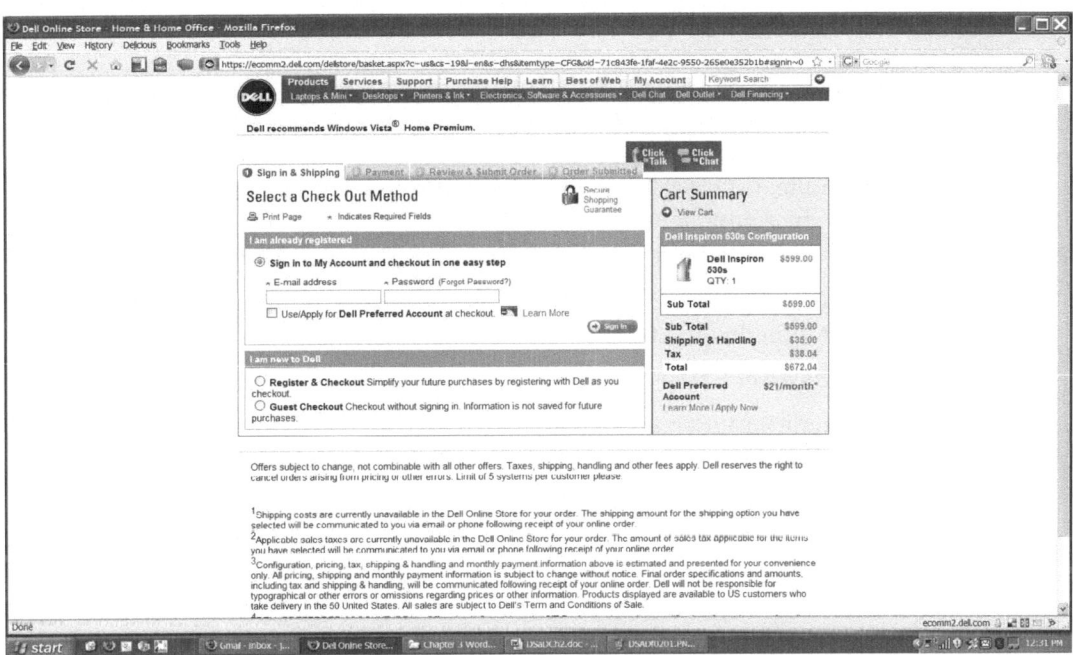

Figure 2-2. *Final Dell Type 1, Bare-Bones computer price with shipping and taxes*

Step 2: Obtain Prices for Individual Components

The second step in the process can be performed using information from a web site such as pricewatch.com, or by simply visiting your local PC store and doing some price checks. The following list shows prices that I obtained from a local PC store in Atlanta, Georgia. In some cases, I couldn't find the exact matching component as the Dell Inspiron 530s. In those situations, I priced a component that would be considered a step or two higher in speed, performance, capacity, or all three.

ASUS All-in-One Motherboard LGA775	$54.99
Intel Core 2 Duo Processor E7200 (2.53GHz, 1066 FSB)	$139.99
Windows Vista Home Basic Service Pack 1	$99.99
17-inch LCD (not widescreen)	$169.99
16X DVD+/-RW drive	$34.99
1GB dual-channel DDR2 SDRAM at 667MHz	$30.00
250GB serial ATA hard drive (7200 RPM)	$59.99
Integrated Intel Graphics Media Accelerator 3100	On motherboard
Integrated 7.1 Channel Audio (sound)	On motherboard
One-year limited hardware warranty	Provided in store
ATX midtower case and power supply	$39.00
Assembly	No charge

The total is $628.94 (plus $38.00 tax), for a savings of around $5, and I get a faster processor. That's probably not enough justification for having a custom PC built, and I would probably prefer to order the name-brand Dell.

But wait just a minute. Let me tell you what else happened during my visit to the local PC shop. I printed out the components for my Dell choice and showed them to the computer technicians. After a few minutes of discussion, they agreed to build me the following computer:

ASUS All-in-One Motherboard LGA775

Intel Dual Core Processor E2180 (2.0GHz, 800 FSB)

Windows Vista Home Basic Service Pack 1

20-inch widescreen LCD

20X DVD+/-RW drive

1GB dual-channel DDR2 SDRAM at 667MHz

250GB serial ATA hard drive (7200 RPM)

Integrated Intel Graphics Media Accelerator 3100 (on motherboard)

Integrated 7.1 Channel Audio (sound) (on motherboard)

One-year limited hardware warranty (provided in store)

ATX Deluxe case and power supply (with front USB)

Assembly (no charge)

Total price: $604.97

For almost $50 less, I get the original Inspiron 530s hardware configuration, but with a faster DVD burner and larger LCD (20-inch), and no shipping costs. The larger LCD will be great on my eyes, and that $50 I saved will buy an additional 2GB DDR2 SDRAM (memory).

I didn't have to haggle (but I'm sure I could have gotten a little better deal if I had pushed). I simply showed them what I was willing to spend on a Dell PC, and they provided me with a better computer at a lower price. Even if I had elected to buy the components myself and put the PC together, I would have saved a few dollars. For a Type 1 computer, however, savings of between $30 and $100 should be your goal. And remember that the money you save can immediately be applied to purchasing better hardware—maybe more memory, a faster processor, or more hard drive capacity.

You can save even more money when you begin investigating purchasing your own Type 2, 3, 4, and 5 PC and components versus buying prebuilt PCs.

Hardware Focus by User Type

In the previous section, I gave you an idea of how to price a computer for a Type 1, Bare-Bones user. Here, I'll note the hardware that you should focus on when pricing a computer of the remaining four user types. I'll provide an example of a PC for each type, and point out where you should spend your money.

Type 2, Family Member's PC

A good PC for a family has a little of everything. Sound, video, and storage are just as important (and not just to the kids' games) as a decent processor and a healthy amount of RAM. A good example of a computer of this type is the HP a6560t (http://www.hp.com).

HP a6560t

Intel Core 2 Duo Processor E8400 (3.0GHz)

Windows Vista Home Premium Service Pack 1

20-inch widescreen LCD

128MB NVIDIA GeForce 9300

16X DVD+/-RW drive

2GB dual-channel DDR2 SDRAM at 800MHz

320GB serial ATA hard drive (7200 RPM)

Sound Blaster X-Fi

Standard HP speakers and keyboard/mouse

One-year limited hardware warranty

Total price: $975.16 (includes free shipping and $55.18 tax)

A 320GB hard drive is more than enough (for now) to satisfy the storage needs of most families, and 2GB of RAM will guarantee that Windows Vista runs properly. While the video card isn't the best on the market, 128MB will satisfy any game players in the house, as well as make Internet browsing easier on the eyes. Add a nice sound card, some speakers, and a DVD burner so users can back up their photos and listen to their music, and this PC is a perfect little solution for the Family Member user.

■ **Tip** When considering the purchase of a Family Member's PC, focus on storage (hard drive), memory (RAM), and the processor. Video and sound are frequently included on the motherboard, and require no additional purchase of special hardware. Try to get the best (longest) warranty you can, too. Having more users means more wear and tear on a computer, and a good warranty can protect your investment.

Type 3, Gamer's PC

The Gamer's PC focuses on performance in four areas: video, sound, memory, and processing speed. Secondary concerns are usually storage, but gamers will frequently buy low-end hard drives to get the higher storage capacity; if a hard drive dies, they just replace it and keep on playing.

A typical Gamer's PC will put the money into the processor, a lot of RAM, a super-fast video card, and a high-quality sound card. If a sacrifice must be made, most gamers will go with a lower-priced sound card first, and then maybe a little less processor speed, before they'll skimp on RAM or the video card. Keeping that in mind, Alienware (http://www.alienware.com) has created what has to be one of the most impressive (at least, for now) PCs for playing games: the Area-51 High-Performance Gaming PC (see Figure 2-3).

Alienware Area-51 High-Performance Gaming PC

Intel Core 2 Quad Q9400 Processor (2.66GHz, 1333MHz FSB)

Windows Vista Home Premium Service Pack 1

22-inch widescreen LCD

512MB ATI Radeon 4870

20X DVD+/-RW drive (SATA)

2GB dual-channel DDR3 SDRAM at 1066MHz

1TB serial ATA hard drive (7200 RPM)

Creative Sound Blaster X-Fi XtremeGamer

Gigabit Ethernet port

Keyboard/mouse

One-year limited hardware warranty

Total price: $2916.53 (includes $124.00 shipping and $165.00 tax)

As you can see, this PC doesn't skimp on the hardware. It includes top-of-the-line sound and video, plenty of RAM, a 1 terabyte (TB) hard drive, and a 22-inch widescreen monitor. Again, when pricing a Gamer's PC, remember the big four: video, sound, memory, and processing speed. Focus your spending there, and you'll find the latest and greatest games run with no problem.

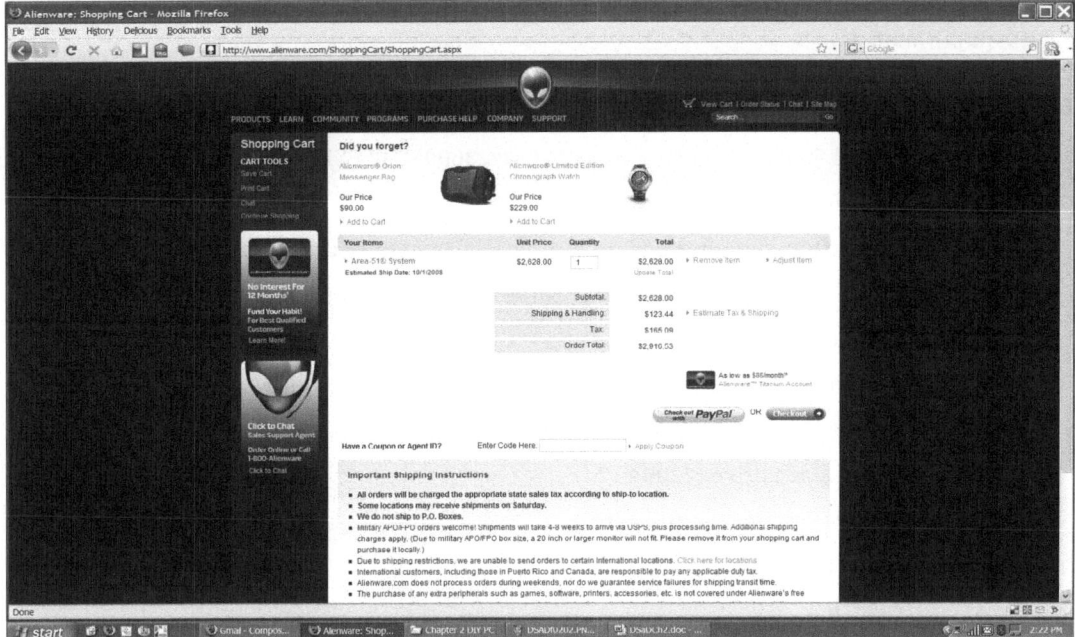

Figure 2-3. *Almost $3,000 for a computer, and a picture to prove it*

Tip Yes, that's $3,000 for a computer. But this is the Gamer's PC, remember? Price is no option. Well, okay, maybe you consider yourself a Gamer but can't imagine paying $3,000 for a computer. In that case, remember the concept of trade-offs. Do you really need the fastest processor, fastest RAM, highest capacity hard drive, and newest video card? Savings can be found by just taking one or two "steps" back in hardware level. You'll still end up with a speed-demon gaming PC. You'll be surprised at how much a video card or sound card drops in price once the latest version is released by a manufacturer, and you can take advantage of this. Research the latest hardware releases, and then just pull back a little (not much) and buy something in the ballpark. A Gamer's PC is always going to be a little higher in cost, but that's the price for wanting to play those high-performance games.

Type 4, Multimedia Guru's PC

The Multimedia Guru is all about videos, photos, and music. This user's PC is focused on providing the best video and sound possible, allowing the viewer to appreciate every color and sound at the best possible quality. This means that hardware usually focuses on the video and sound cards, as well as the hard drives. While viewing and listening are important, the ability to edit (both sound and video) is also paramount, so this PC requires a lot of storage space and fast spinning hard drives to supply the video and sound to the screen. A typical PC for this type of user might include the Gateway LX series (http://www.gateway.com), designed specifically for the multimedia fan.

Gateway LX 6200

AMD Phenom X4 9500 Quad Processor (2.2GHz, 3600MHz FSB)

Windows Vista Home Premium Service Pack 1

Built-in TV tuner (for watching and recording TV from your computer)

15-in-1 media card reader (because the Multimedia Guru uses them all)

256MB ATI Radeon 3200

18X DVD+/-RW drive (SATA)

8GB dual-channel DDR3 SDRAM at 1066MHz

750GB serial ATA hard drive (7200 RPM)

8-channel Dolby surround-sound card

Gigabit Ethernet port

Keyboard/mouse

One-year limited hardware warranty

Total price: $857.99 (includes $29.00 shipping and about $48.00 tax)

It's an impressive PC, but before you get excited about the price, let me point out that this PC does not come with an LCD monitor. This is a good thing—as a Multimedia Guru, I would much prefer to pick the size and quality of my LCD panel myself, and not have that decision made for me. So I need to budget between $200 and $500 for a good-quality, large viewing area LCD screen. But for less than $1,400, a Multimedia Guru will find this PC can easily handle viewing, editing, and storing every photo, song, and video.

Tip The Multimedia Guru's PC could easily double as a Gamer's PC with that large amount of RAM and sizable hard drive and fast processor. The video card ideally should have 512MB, and the sound is built into the motherboard (rather than being a separately installed sound card). A true Gamer might balk a little, but it's more than enough for the Multimedia Guru. So, if this is your type of PC, remember to focus on storage (hard drive size and a lot of space), memory (for handling the sound and video sent to and from the hard drive), and the video card (no less than 256MB). Feel free to skimp a little on the sound card and DVD burner. You don't really need the fastest burner, and the most crystal-clear sound card isn't necessary, unless you're in the music production industry.

Type 5, Small Business Owner's PC

Small business owners have a variety of items to consider when it comes to a PC. It can be difficult to nail down exactly what hardware is important and what isn't. Some small business owners use their PC strictly for writing letters, managing spreadsheets, and e-mail—all tasks that can be handled with standard productivity software. Other business owners run specialized software that is specific to their industry, such as advanced accounting software for CPAs or medical record keeping software for doctors' offices.

The best advice I can offer is to examine the minimum and suggested hardware requirements that come with all of the software you plan on using. Most software will detail the minimum specifications and suggested specifications for how much hard drive space is required, how much memory is needed, and if any special hardware is required (such as a scanner or DVD/CD burner). I recommend purchasing a PC that includes the highest suggested hardware requirements for your software (replace *suggested* with *ideal*, and you'll get a better idea of what the software manufacturer actually means). If your word processing software states it requires a minimum of 512MB of RAM, and your accounting software requires a minimum of 1GB of RAM, you know you must go with the higher value. But if the accounting software "suggests" an amount of 2GB, then you need to determine if the cost of the added hardware (memory) is within your budget.

An example of a typical small business PC that you might find for sale is the Dell Vostro (http://www.dell.com) business series.

Dell Vostro 420

Intel Core 2 Quad Q6600 Processor (2.40GHz, 8M, L2Cache, 1066FSB)

Windows Vista Business with Service Pack 1

20-inch widescreen LCD

256MB ATI Radeon 3450 video card

16X DVD+/-RW drive (SATA)

3GB dual-channel DDR2 SDRAM at 800MHz

500GB serial ATA hard drive (7200 RPM)

Integrated 5.1 sound (on motherboard)

Gigabit Ethernet port

Keyboard/mouse

Three-year on-site, next-business day warranty

Total price: $1437.00 (includes $81.00 tax and free shipping)

This is a great PC for a small business owner. It has plenty of hard drive space, RAM, and a fast processor. And notice that three-year on-site service warranty. Dell sends a technician to your office the next business day. (I've used this feature and can verify that Dell's on-site service is the best in the industry.)

Where does this PC skimp? Well, the DVD burner isn't the fastest available, and although the video card is nice (256MB), it has on-board sound (on the motherboard), rather than a sound card. The 20-inch LCD screen is nice, too, but business owners often have a multitude of applications running at the same time, so a larger screen might be better, but it costs more.

Tip All in all, a small business owner should never go bare bones. A simple computer just isn't going to be able to handle the demands of high-end business software. Likewise, there's no reason for a small business owner to load up a new computer with the highest quality of computer hardware. Leave that to the Gamer. You have a business to run and costs to watch. Stick with a decent-sized hard drive, load up as much RAM as you can afford, select a reasonable processor, and you're (pardon the pun) in business.

Summary

You've absorbed a lot of information in this chapter, so I'm going to keep this summary short and sweet. I'll offer you a list of things to keep in mind as you upgrade/repurpose an older computer, build a custom PC, or buy a prebuilt one:

- Keep your existing PC and upgrade its hardware to save money.

- If you absolutely must get a new PC, identify the software you need to help you determine the hardware to purchase with a new computer.

- Identify the brand-name software that you want to use, and add the prices into your calculations for a new PC.

- Compare prices of prebuilt computers with the cost to build it yourself.

- If you're willing to substitute free software, consider using the money saved to upgrade the hardware.

- Never be afraid to ask for a better price from a local computer shop. Show them exactly what you want to buy from a competitor.

- Accept the fact that hardware technology changes quickly, and do not fall into the trap of believing you must have the best, fastest, and shiniest products under the hood of your PC.

In a nutshell, save money on software when and where you can, and pump that money back into your hardware, business, or hobby.

That's it, really. Computers change so quickly, there's no reason to get upset when you find that your video card is considered "obsolete" at the computer store and no longer sold. Don't get angry when that $200 you spent on a 1TB hard drive three months ago will now buy you 2TB. And don't yell at your computer when its video card sputters and lags a bit when you're playing that new game. Instead, reflect back on the money you saved on the software installed on your computer. And when the time comes, upgrade the hardware and smile, knowing that your computer has many more years of usefulness left in it.

CHAPTER 3

■■■

Word Processing

Your new computer has an operating system installed, and you can play a card game or two and browse the Internet. Now it's time to start loading up your new machine with some great free software. That's what I'm going to show you how to do in this book. We'll start our discussion of free, alternative software solutions with one of the most common activities: word processing.

Grade school children, college students, business professionals, retirees, and everyone in between have most likely used a computer to write a letter, and I'm sure you have, too. You might run into the occasional individual who uses only a typewriter or paper notepad, but common practice in today's world is to use word processing software. In fact, chances are, word processing is most of what you'll do with your computer. According to a 2003 survey of United States workplaces (`http://www.bls.gov/news.release/History/ciuaw.txt`), word processing ranked behind only Internet browsing and e-mail as the most widespread computer activity.

So, it's no surprise that plenty of word processing products are vying for your attention and your dollars. I've used close to a dozen different word processors over the years, and I can't make up my mind which one I like the most (but the two that I recommend in this chapter come close to being at the top of the list). One thing is for certain, however, and that is the biggest name today in word processing is Microsoft Word. It comes installed on many new computers (bundled with other Microsoft products such as Excel and PowerPoint) and is considered by many to be the gold standard for word processing applications (but opinions do vary). It also comes with a gold standard price.

I use Microsoft Word—it's a great product. There's simply no escaping it in my line of work. But I sure don't like having to pay through the nose every few years to get the latest upgrade. So, I keep my eyes open for alternatives, and so should you. In this chapter, I'll cover two of my favorite alternatives to Word. Both of them are 100% free, and their full complement of features may surprise you.

The Defender

Microsoft Word is widely considered to be the standard for word processing applications. With more than ten years of development and version releases, Word continues to beat out many competitors, including Corel WordPerfect and Lotus Symphony Documents. The most current version, Microsoft Word 2007, comes bundled in the Microsoft Office software suite.

Note The previous version, Microsoft Word 2003, is still extremely popular with users. The user interface changed drastically between 2003 and 2007 versions of Word. Microsoft replaced the standard toolbars with a new interface called the Ribbon. Opinions vary on the Ribbon; some like it. I don't. Thus, my search for alternatives began.

MICROSOFT OFFICE SUITE

The Microsoft Office suite is a grouping of productivity applications. Combinations depend on the version of Office you purchase and may include any or all of the following:

- Word, a word processing application

- Excel, a spreadsheet application (covered in Chapter 4)

- PowerPoint, an application that allows you to create slide show presentations (covered in Chapter 5)

- Outlook, an e-mail, calendar, and address book application (covered in Chapter 6)

- Access, an application for creating information databases

When you first open Microsoft Word, the graphical user interface (GUI) provides you with a blank page and a handful of buttons and menus along the top of the screen. It can take some time to learn the locations for different tools and options, but the most common needs of a user—such as underlining or boldfacing text, setting margins, and changing the font or font size—are all easy to locate.

Microsoft does a good job (some might say too good) of hiding many of the power features that most users won't be needing, while providing the most commonly used features in plain sight. For example, Figure 3-1 shows a document with the reviewing options displayed at the top of the screen. Every now and then, I need to go on the hunt: click menu A, click tab B, click button C, click drop-down menu D . . . you get the picture. Unfortunately, it's a fact of life when dealing with powerful applications: software developers are limited to how many buttons and features they can put on the screen and must hide/bury everything else. (Yet another reason for downloading and installing a simpler, more streamlined application.)

One important item you should be aware of regarding Microsoft Word is the file format it uses: .doc. The .doc format is more common today than the original text file type developed decades ago: .txt. You'll come across many documents these days saved using the .doc format, simply because Microsoft Word is found on so many computers (both Macintosh and Windows versions are available). Any word processing application that you consider using should be capable of opening and saving files with the .doc file extension. But there's a new twist.

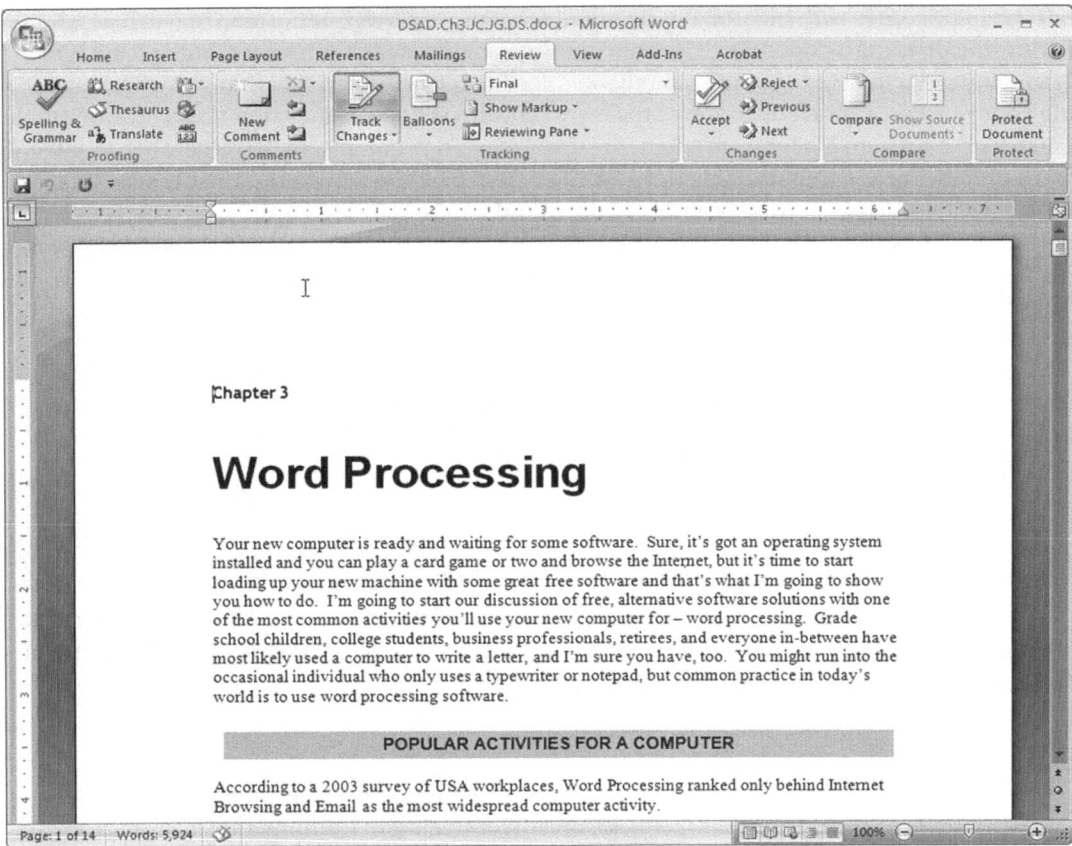

Figure 3-1. *Editing a standard business letter using tools found in Microsoft Word 2007*

■**Note** When you hear the term *file type*, don't cringe. It simply refers to how an application stores a file. Most operating systems (Windows included) allow the user to simply double-click a file to open it. But how does the operating system know which application to use for a specific file? Say you have a mixture of files on your computer, including word processing, spreadsheet, graphics, and music. How does Windows know when you double-click Hey_Jude.mp3 to open your music player instead of your spreadsheet application? Windows simply looks at the file type (mp3 in this example) and opens the appropriate application that you installed (or was preinstalled).

Microsoft Word 2007 uses a new file type: .docx. That additional x thrown in there means that Word saves your file using XML code. I really don't want to get into a discussion of XML here. The bare minimum you should be aware of is that adding in the XML code does give word processing documents more flexibility when making them available on the Internet, but the price comes with bloated file sizes and sometimes slower performance (such as when saving and opening a document). Results vary from computer to computer, but at least Word 2007 allows you to save using the old reliable .doc file format. Keep that in mind when sending your word processing documents to coworkers and friends. If they don't have the ability to open .docx files, you'll hear from them for sure. To avoid problems, try to remember to save word processing documents using the .doc file type. Then you can be reasonably sure that others will be able to open, view, and/or edit your documents.

I think Microsoft Word is a good application, and it definitely delivers on word processing features. I've selected Word in the past simply because of its variety of built-in tools. These include grammar and spell checking, mail merge capabilities, and too many formatting choices to remember—font, font size, bold, italics, bullets, columns, tables, and so on. I hear just as many people complain that Word has too many features as the number of people who complain it needs more. But for many professionals (myself included), the investment in time (learning/training) and money makes Word a difficult application to give up.

Note A complete list of the features in the latest version of Microsoft Word can be found at http://www.microsoft.com/word. Be aware that you could spend hours sifting through the volume of information that Microsoft provides. This information also demonstrates the complexity of Microsoft Word and the number of features that are built in to this powerhouse application.

But that doesn't mean I'm not looking for the day when I can stop spending big bucks every two or three years to get the latest, greatest Word version. Rumor has it that Microsoft is now considering a subscription model for its Office suite. This means you'll pay a yearly or monthly subscription fee, and get any updates and upgrades free during the subscription period. No thank you.

The good news is that many competitors are catching up to Microsoft Word. If you don't necessarily need all the bells and whistles that Word offers, there are many *free* alternatives that are taking a bite out of Microsoft's market share. And even if you do need those power features, competitors are constantly adding and upgrading their own products, ensuring that the day is coming when all the features you do need will be available. (You did catch the *free* part, right?)

Two applications that I find myself using with more frequency include OpenOffice.org Writer and Google Docs Document. Read about them here, and then download and install them on your new low-cost computer. You may find yourself jumping (or is that writing?) on the free software bandwagon.

The Contenders

I'll admit that it's difficult to find an alternative to Microsoft Word that matches it feature-for-feature and provides an identical user interface. But I've found one application that does come close: OpenOffice.org Writer. OpenOffice.org Writer has enough features to satisfy even the most demanding word processing power user.

Another alternative is a member of the Google Docs family called Document. Google Docs Document doesn't come close to offering all of Word's features, but it's extremely easy to use, comes with a clean, uncomplicated user interface, and provides the most common features that typical users are likely to require. I use it frequently for those quick-and-simple writing requirements. Document also has a great sharing feature that makes it really easy to allow others to view and edit your documents (more on that in the "Google Docs Document Features" section later in this chapter).

OpenOffice.org Writer

OpenOffice.org Writer is the word processing application that is part of the OpenOffice.org software suite. Just as certain versions of Microsoft Office contain a word processor, spreadsheet, slide show/presentation, and e-mail application, OpenOffice.org provides a similar collection.

OPENOFFICE.ORG SUITE

OpenOffice.org comes as a single downloadable file that allows you to choose from a list of software applications to install on your computer. The latest version is 3.0. Some of the applications include the following:

- Writer, a word processor application

- Calc, a spreadsheet application similar to Microsoft Excel (covered in Chapter 4)

- Impress, a presentation/slide show application similar to Microsoft PowerPoint (covered in Chapter 5)

As shown in Figure 3-2, OpenOffice.org Writer has a simple user interface. As you can see, the number of toolbar buttons and menus is substantially less than what you'll find in Microsoft Word. But don't let that fool you—Writer is a powerful and feature-rich application.

After installing the software, you might consider selecting the Help ➤ OpenOffice Help menu option. A quick glance through the online help documentation will give you a good idea of the various things you can do with Writer. From the same Help menu, you can also choose the What's This? option. When this feature is active, you can hover your mouse pointer over any button, and a small text box will pop up to let you know what it is and how it works. Click any open area of the screen to turn off the What's This? feature.

Give yourself some time to become familiar with all the features that Writer offers. We'll walk through a few sample tasks in the "OpenOffice.org Writer Features" section later in the chapter, but for now, just experiment a little. Type a short letter to a friend, and then try out some of the options such as boldfacing, changing the font, and modifying the margins.

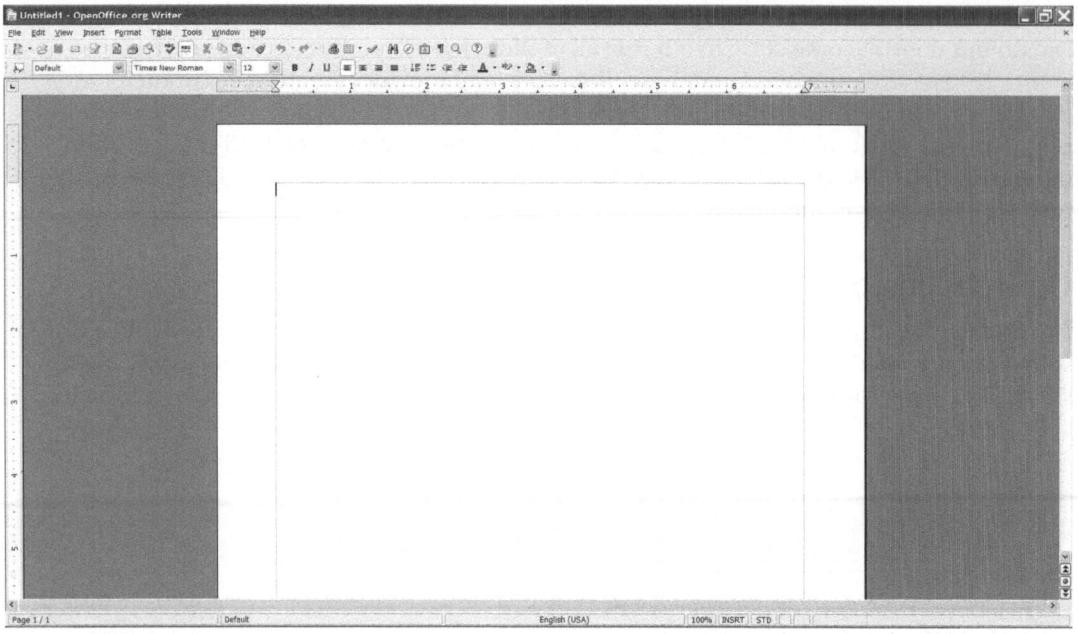

Figure 3-2. *OpenOffice.org Writer has an uncluttered and easy-to-use interface.*

Note Yes, I'm one of those people who play around with software before consulting the manual. With Writer, I found the user interface so similar to Word that it was several weeks before I needed to go to the help documentation—it was that easy and familiar to use.

The basics of Writer are straightforward. You have a "what you see is what you get" (WYSIWYG) view of the document. You have menu options and buttons that can apply to the entire document or to a selection within the document. But if there's a task you simply cannot figure out, start with the Help ➤ OpenOffice Help option. If that doesn't provide a solution, your next step is the OpenOffice.org web site and its help forum, found at http://support. openoffice.org.

Unlike with Microsoft Word, you'll find that the help community for OpenOffice.org, as with most other open source projects, is user-run and very responsive. You can sift through previous questions, post your own queries, and offer help to others who might be looking to do something that you've already figured out. I've posted many questions and received answers the same day, and even some within a few minutes. The number of OpenOffice.org users out there is growing, and those willing to provide support are always quick to help a newcomer.

The OpenOffice.org web site offers much more than a place to ask questions and get answers. The site provides additional downloads such as templates and clipart that can be used in Writer and the other OpenOffice.org applications. Just visit http://www.openoffice.org and click "I want to do more with my OpenOffice.org."

Tip While you're at the OpenOffice.org web site, be sure to do a search for Professional Template Pack I and Professional Template Pack II. These add-ons contain an amazing number of freebies, from resume samples to presentation themes and more.

Google Docs Document

The next word processing application I'm anxious to introduce you to comes from a company you might be familiar with: Google. Google started out as a simple Internet search company in 1998, but has since extended its reach into many other areas, including e-mail, online maps, scheduling/calendar tools, and word processing.

Google now offers its own software suite called Google Docs, which I absolutely *love*. While Google Docs doesn't come close to providing all the features of Microsoft Office, it continues to surprise users by adding new tools and features regularly. And what's the best part besides it being free? There is no software to install or updates to download. The software is maintained by Google, and all that's required to use it is a live Internet connection.

This is our first example of SaaS (Software as a Service, discussed in Chapter 1), where the normal functions of an application installed on your computer's hard drive are instead used within your web browser.

GOOGLE DOCS SUITE

The Google Docs collection of applications is maintained by Google and available using your Internet web browser. The following applications are currently available:

- Document, a word processor application

- Spreadsheet, a spreadsheet application similar to Microsoft Excel (covered in Chapter 4)

- Presentation, a presentation/slide show application similar to Microsoft PowerPoint (covered in Chapter 5)

After you've created a Google account and logged in to Google Docs (see the "Where to Get the Software" section coming up next), you'll find the user interface is similar to that shown in Figure 3-3.

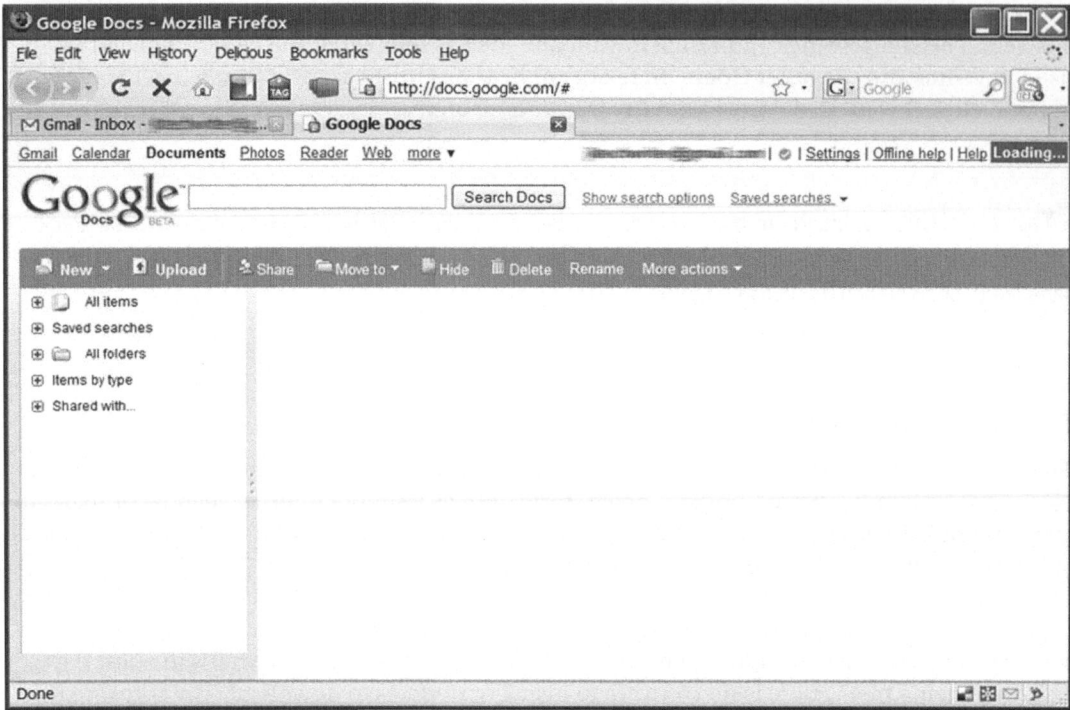

Figure 3-3. *The Google Docs user interface is completely contained within a web browser.*

To begin using Google Docs Document, simply click the New menu on the left side of the screen and choose Document from the drop-down list. Document opens, ready to use, as shown in Figure 3-4. Yes, it's that easy.

As with OpenOffice.org Writer, Google Docs Document has an uncluttered toolbar (Word 2007 Ribbon-haters may appreciate the simplicity) and is intuitive to use. We'll walk through a few sample tasks using Google Docs Document later in the chapter, in the "Google Docs Document Features" section, but in the event that you encounter a problem or are trying to figure out how to perform a specific task, select the Help ➤ Google Docs Help Center menu option. The online help section offers you the ability to search using keywords, as well as a listing of favorite topics to click to learn more. Finally, Google offers its users the ability to suggest new features for inclusion in future updates to Google Docs by clicking the "Let us know" link.

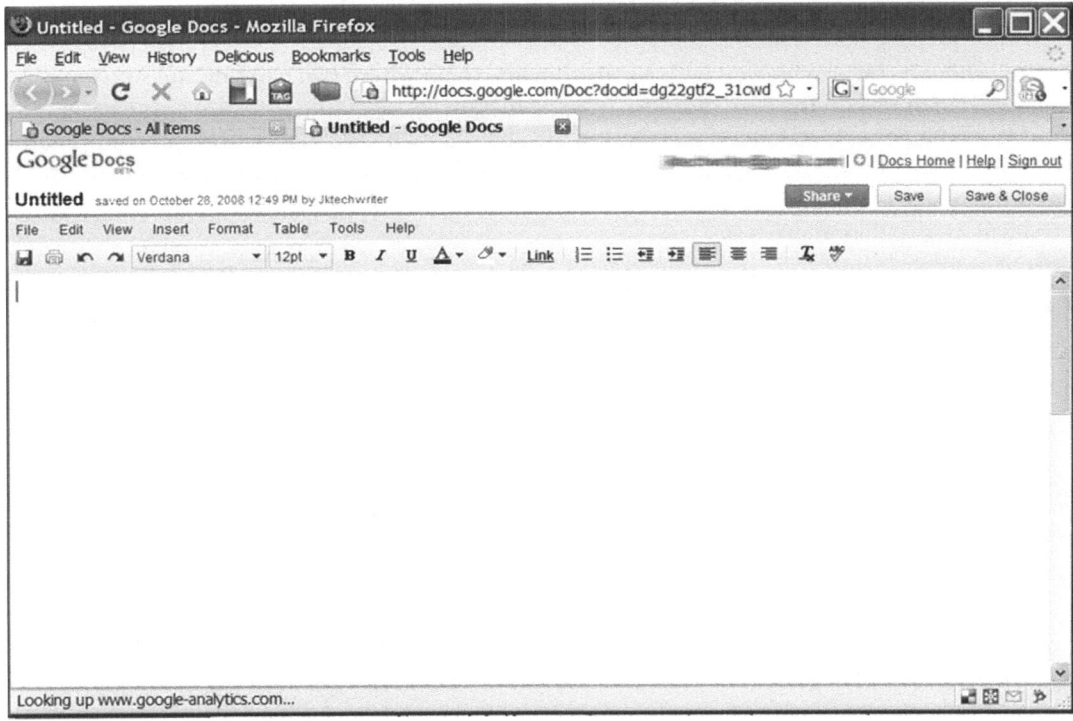

Figure 3-4. *Document opens in its own browser window.*

POTENTIAL USER GROUPS AND BENEFITS

While everyone can potentially benefit from free word processing software, I can think of three user groups that are most likely to gain the largest advantage by using OpenOffice.org Writer or Google Docs Document. These include college/university students, small business owners, and retirees. Here's why:

- *Students*: Instructors who require students to submit digital files (as opposed to paper printouts) typically request that documents be saved in Word format (either .doc or .docx). Both OpenOffice.org Writer and Google Docs Document allow you to save your final versions in .doc format, satisfying this requirement. (OpenOffice.org 3.0 will support the .docx and .odf formats as well, so OpenOffice.org will be able to fully compete with Word 2007 when it comes to saving files in standard formats.)

- *Small business owners*: Business owners intent on keeping expenditures under control will find that the features provided with Writer and Document should satisfy most of their initial needs. From simple business letters (with the ability to embed graphics such as a company logo) to standard invoices, small business owners can use Writer and/or Document, and spend those important dollars in other areas such as advertising or payroll.

- *Retirees*: Whether on fixed income or not, many retirees would rather spend their retirement income on travel, hobbies, and possibly grandchildren. Google Docs Document and OpenOffice.org Writer are not only free, but also simple to use. Not having to spend hours learning all the bells and whistles frees up time that is better spent enjoying retirement. My mom and dad are retired, and I was happy to be able to provide them with OpenOffice.org and save them some serious cash. It's got all the features they need, and it is easy to use to boot.

Where to Get the Software

In each chapter, I'll provide you with a web address (URL) where you can find the software to download or use (in the case of SaaS). In most instances, installing software is as easy as double-clicking the downloaded installation file and following the instructions. In some chapters, I may provide additional installation steps if the installation is tricky or has some unusual steps that you should know about. In this chapter, I'll take you through the OpenOffice.org application installation process.

OpenOffice.org Writer

Here's how to get Writer from the OpenOffice.org site:

1. Visit http://www.openoffice.org/.

2. Click "I want to download OpenOffice.org." Then click the big, green Download Now! button and follow the instructions.

3. During the download, take note of the web page that opens. It contains links that allow you to provide feedback, ask questions, and volunteer to help further develop the product.

Once the OpenOffice.org download is complete, you're ready to install and begin using Writer. Jump ahead to the "Notes on OpenOffice.org Installation" section to get started.

Google Docs Document

Follow these steps to get started with Google Docs Document:

1. Visit http://docs.google.com.

2. If you already have a Google account (for Gmail or another Google service), log in. Otherwise, click the Get Started button and follow the instructions to create your free user account.

Note You can also take a tour of Google Docs or watch a video from the Welcome to Google Docs page (http://docs.google.com). Just click the Take a Tour or New Features link to investigate Google Docs before you sign up.

Once you log in to Google Docs, you might be surprised to find that there's no software to install. As I've noted, Google Docs is this book's first introduction to SaaS. Once you're logged in, you're ready to begin using Document (or any of the other Google Docs family of applications).

WHICH ONE SHOULD I USE?

You can choose to use either OpenOffice.org Writer or Google Docs Document, but if you're wondering if I have a favorite, my answer is "depends." With Document, remember that you're keeping your files stored on Google's hard drives, located somewhere other than on your own computer. The upside here is there's no software to install and your hard drive won't be filled up with application files. With Writer, however, you'll need to install software on your computer, and any files you create are also stored on your hard drive. This may or may not matter to you.

Ultimately, it comes down to taking a test drive. The easiest order would be to use Google Docs Document first, since it doesn't require you to install any software. Use it and figure out if it fulfills your software needs. If it doesn't, move on to OpenOffice.org Writer—download it, install it, and try it out.

This advice works for pretty much all the software you'll be introduced to in this book. Since the software is free, there's very little risk to trying it before you consider spending any money on a commercial product.

Notes on OpenOffice.org Installation

I'm going to walk you through installing the OpenOffice.org software using a set of screenshots. (As noted, Google Docs Document does not require installation on your computer.) Software seems to always be in a state of change, so don't stress if my images don't match exactly what you're seeing. And if you make an incorrect selection, you can always uninstall the application or simply click the Back buttons to start over.

We'll go through the steps to install Writer. You'll also be given the chance to install Calc, the OpenOffice.org spreadsheet application covered in Chapter 4, and Impress, OpenOffice.org's presentation application covered in Chapter 5.

1. After you download the OpenOffice.org 3.0 installation file, double-click the icon. You will be informed that a temporary folder will be created to unpack the installation files, as shown in Figure 3-5. Click the Next button.

2. Click the Unpack button. Once the files are unpacked, OpenOffice.org will begin the Installation Wizard, as shown in Figure 3-6. Click the Next button.

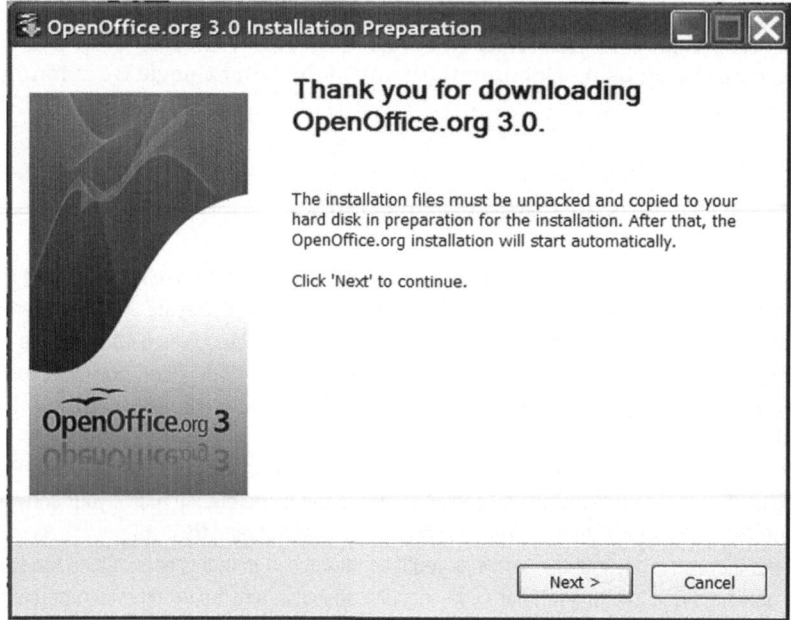

Figure 3-5. *To install Writer, OpenOffice.org will unpack the installation files.*

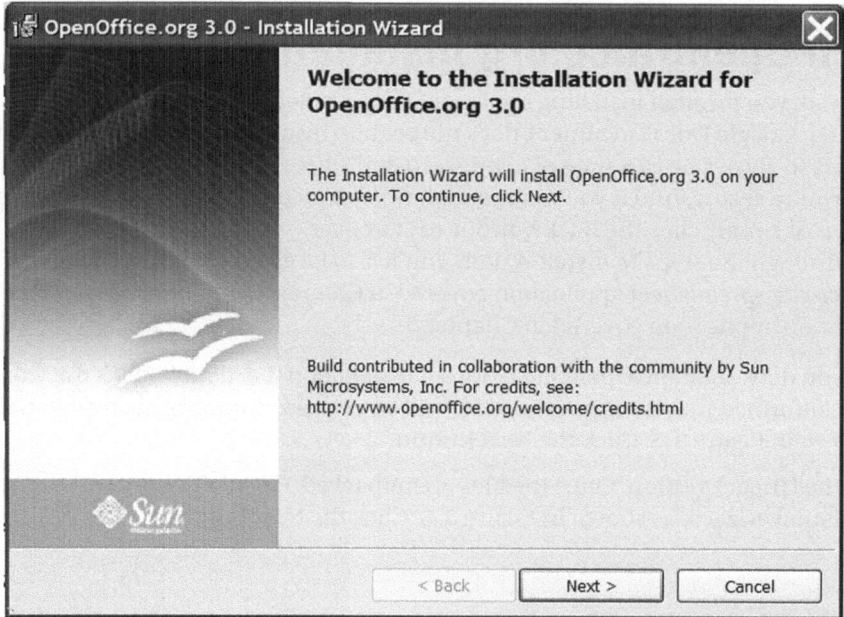

Figure 3-6. *The Installation Wizard will allow you to install OpenOffice applications.*

3. You will be asked to enter your name (filling in the Organization text box is optional), as shown in Figure 3-7. If you wish for others who use your computer (logged in under a different account) to be able to use OpenOffice.org, you can leave the default selection of "Anyone who uses this computer (all users)." If you don't want this option, select the "Only for me" radio button. Click Next.

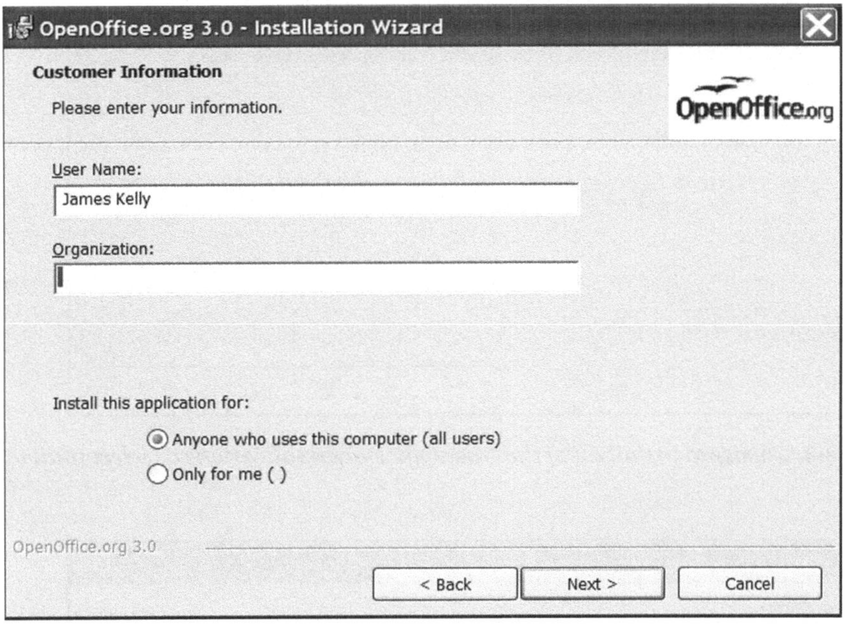

Figure 3-7. *Provide a user name and, optionally, your organization, and select who may use OpenOffice.org.*

4. The next Installation Wizard screen provides you with two options for setup. You may install the full OpenOffice.org software suite (Writer, Calc, Impress, Draw, and Base) by leaving the Complete option selected. Alternatively, choose the Custom option to pick which applications you wish to install. For this example, Custom has been selected to demonstrate how to install the Writer application (and allow you to choose Calc and Impress for Chapters 4 and 5), as shown in Figure 3-8. Click Next to continue.

5. The Custom Setup screen lists the individual applications that can be installed. By default, all applications are configured to be installed. For this example, you want to deselect all the applications except Writer, Calc, and Impress. First, click the icon showing a hard drive and a small arrow pointing downward next to OpenOffice.org Draw. You will be presented with a list of options, as shown in Figure 3-9.

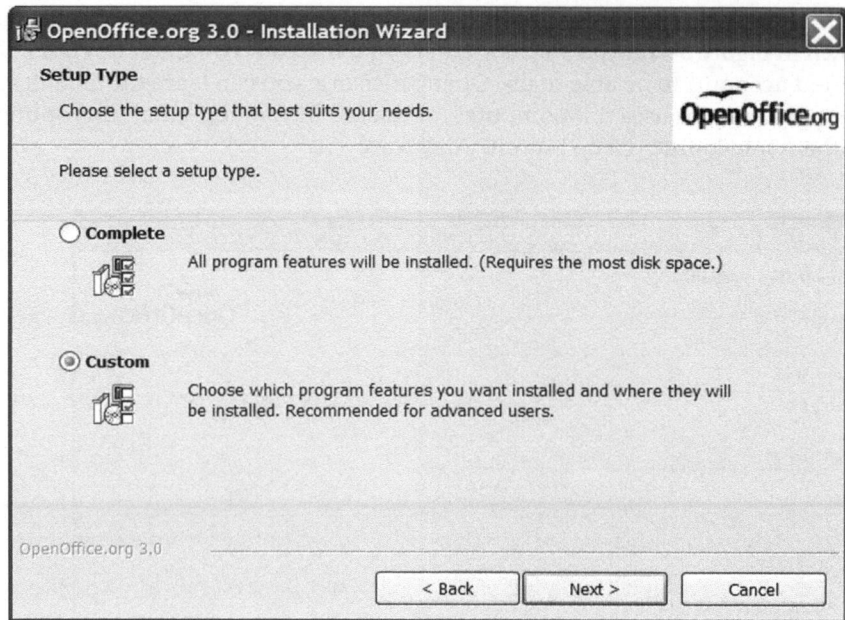

Figure 3-8. *Choose to install all of the OpenOffice.org applications or select individual apps.*

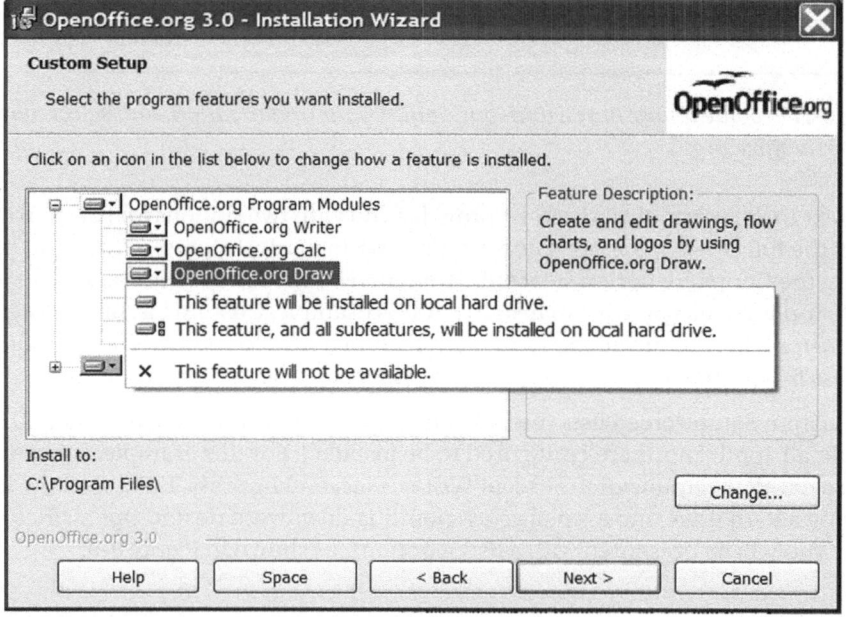

Figure 3-9. *Installation options for each OpenOffice.org application will be listed in a drop-down menu.*

Note Of course, you can choose to install the other OpenOffice.org applications, such as Math, and the Optional Components selection, now or at a later time. For now, I'll assume you have chosen to install Writer, Calc, and Impress.

6. To prevent an application from being installed, select "This feature will not be available" from the menu. A red X will be added to the left of the application's name.

7. Repeat steps 5 and 6 for every application you wish to deselect. Figure 3-10 shows only three applications will be installed at this time (Writer, Calc, and Impress). Click Next to continue.

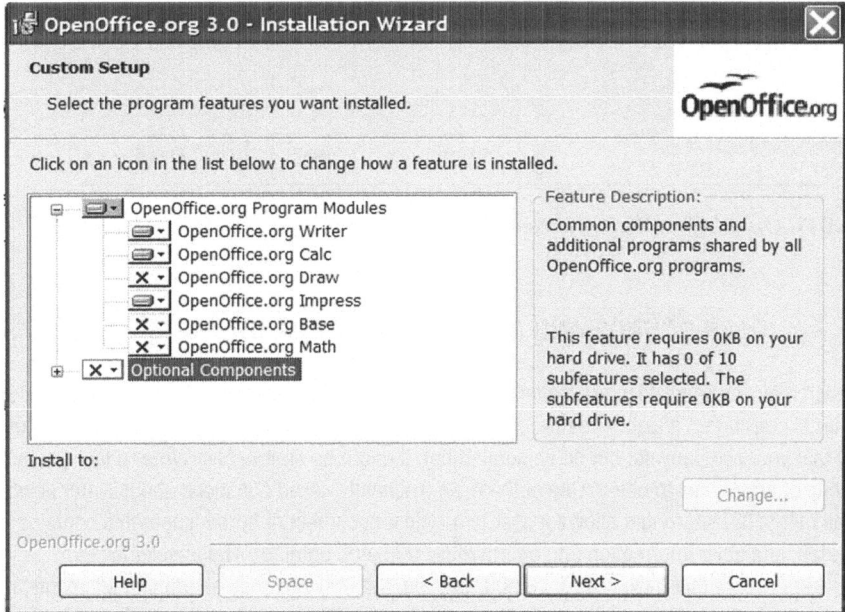

Figure 3-10. *All applications except for Writer, Calc, and Impress have been deselected.*

8. The Ready to Install the Program screen appears, as shown in Figure 3-11. Click the Install button to start the installation.

9. Click the Finish button when the Installation Wizard has completed the installation.

You're finished! Get ready to start using Writer.

Note You may delete the OpenOffice.org installation folder after you've installed all the applications you wish to use.

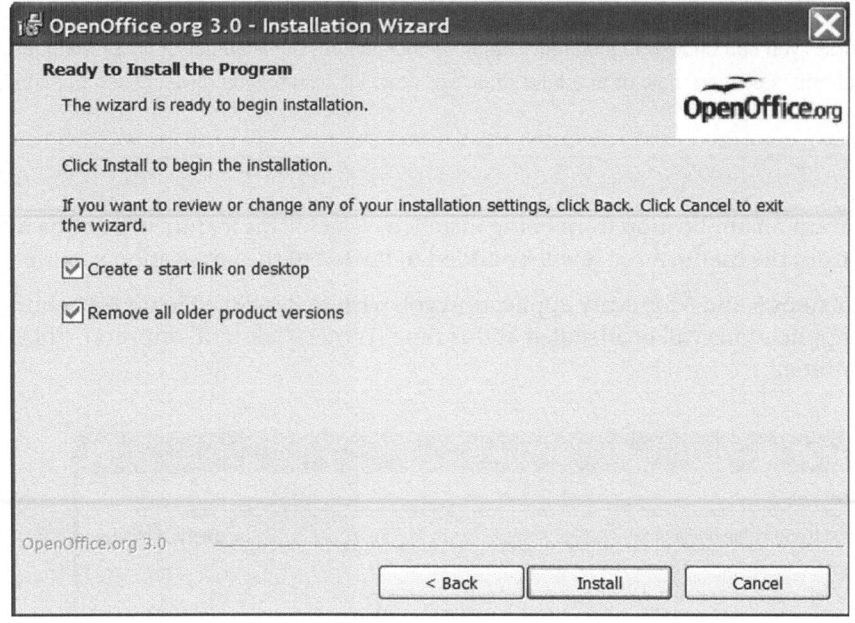

Figure 3-11. *OpenOffice Writer is ready to install.*

OPEN SOURCE AND SAAS FOR BIG CORPORATIONS

Can a corporation move to OpenOffice.org Writer for its word processing requirements? Absolutely. OpenOffice.org Writer is considered a stable, feature-rich word processing application. Are there any functions found in Word that your company cannot do without? If not, it might be time to give Writer a test run by allowing a small group of employees to use it. One of the most frequently asked questions about Writer is whether it supports mail merge (a feature that allows a user to merge a document or spreadsheet that contains names, addresses, and other information into a form letter for batch printing). The answer is yes.

For large corporations that have 1,000, 10,000, or even 100,000 desktops all running Microsoft Word, consider the savings that can be realized by eliminating it from the budget and moving to OpenOffice.org Writer. How much can you save? Consider that a single user license for Microsoft Word 2007, called *per-seat licensing*, can run around $200 and requires a minimum five-license purchase (meaning you can install it on five computers). And that's just for Word. Similar costs exist if your company needs to install Excel, PowerPoint, Outlook, and Access on users' desktops—a fee for each application multiplied by the number of desktops on which to install them. Ouch!

Many companies, plus education and governmental entities, have already eliminated Office products. They have discovered a reliable, easy-to-use option that's 100% free.

Word Processing Features

Now that your word processing software is installed, you're ready to try it out. We'll walk through some common tasks with OpenOffice.org Writer, and then do the same with Google Docs Document.

OpenOffice.org Writer Features

We can't delve into every feature provided by Writer. To do so would require an entire book on just that one bit of software. Instead, the next few sections will highlight several features that are useful, and that might even surprise you. You'll see a good sampling of what Writer can do for you, and you'll get a grasp on how the user interface works.

Add a Logo to a Business Letter

Writer makes it trivial to make your business correspondence look professional by adding your business logo to your letters. Here are the steps to follow:

1. Create a template letterhead with an address and any other information you wish to include. Figure 3-12 shows an example. Then click in the upper-left corner of the document to place the insertion point there.

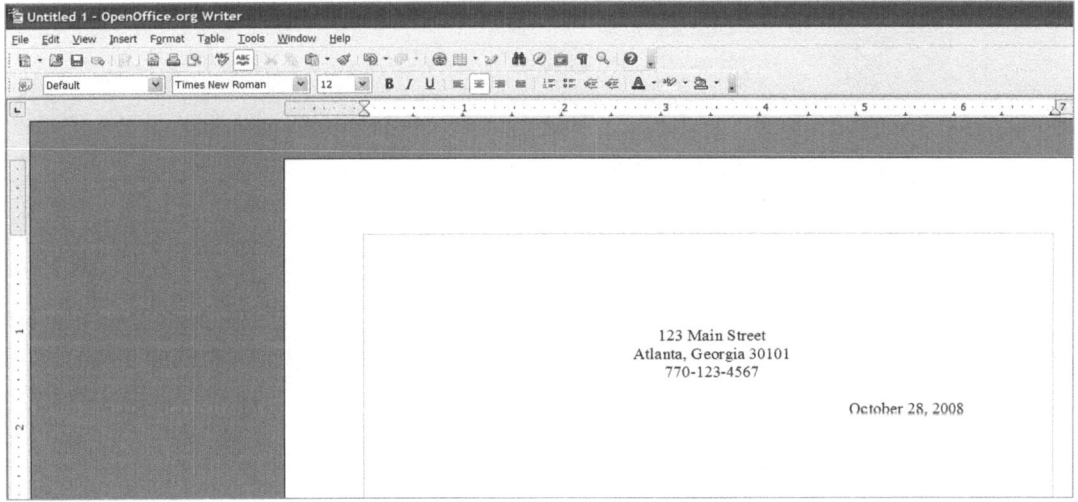

Figure 3-12. *Create a letterhead template in OpenOffice.org Writer.*

2. Select Insert ➤ Picture ➤ From File, as shown in Figure 3-13.

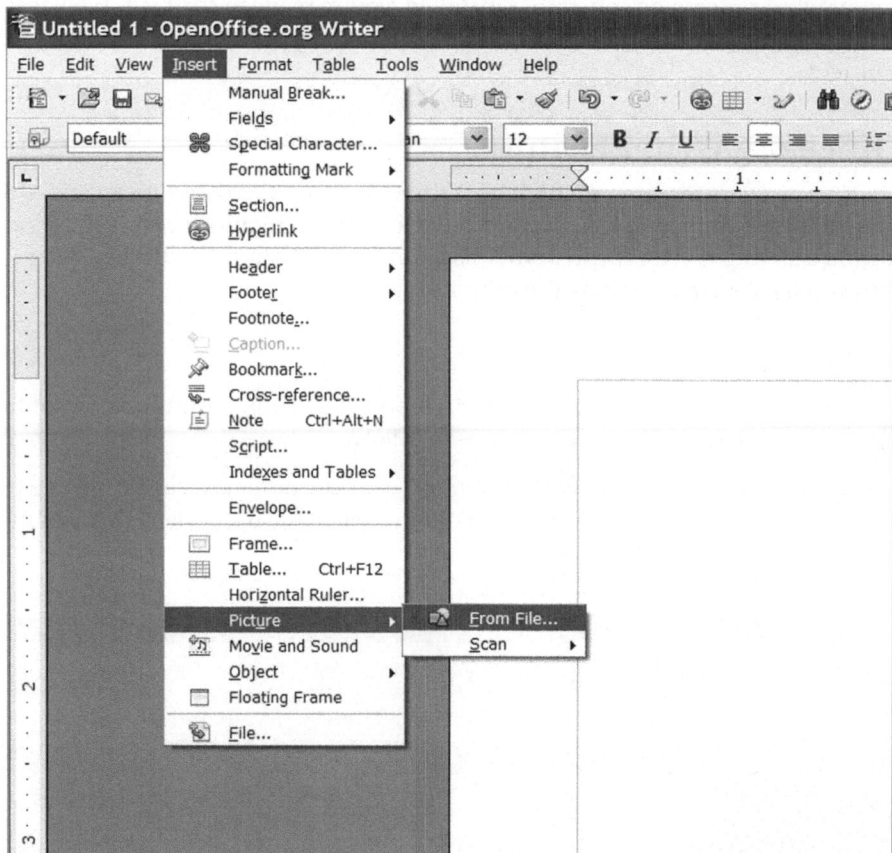

Figure 3-13. *Select to insert a picture (your logo) using the Insert menu.*

3. From the Insert Picture pop-up window, browse to the location of your logo file, select the image, and click the Open button. The logo will be added, as shown in the example in Figure 3-14.

4. Use the left-justify or right-justify buttons on the toolbar to position the logo. You can also resize the image by clicking any of the green squares surrounding the image box and dragging the mouse. Hold down the Shift key to enlarge or shrink the image without changing the height-to-width ratio.

Figure 3-14. *Your logo can be centered and resized as desired.*

Save Your Work As a PDF Document

You can save your OpenOffice.org document in a variety of file formats. One popular choice is as a PDF file. Here are the steps for exporting your document as a PDF:

1. After creating your document and formatting it as desired, select File ➤ Export as PDF, as shown in Figure 3-15.

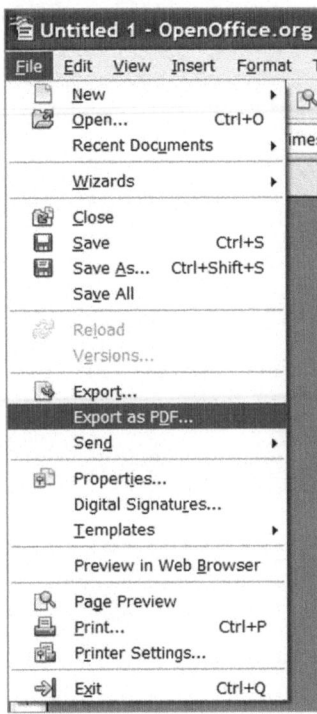

Figure 3-15. *Choose to export your file in PDF format.*

2. In the General tab of the PDF Options dialog box, shown in Figure 3-16, tweak the PDF settings if you know specifically how you wish to save the file, or just accept the default settings.

3. Optionally, click the Security tab in the PDF Options dialog box. As shown in Figure 3-17, you can add a password so the file cannot be altered, as well as set restrictions on who can open and edit the file.

4. Click the Export button to proceed.

5. In the Export dialog box, provide a name for the PDF file and browse to the folder/location to save the file.

6. Click the Save button to complete the task.

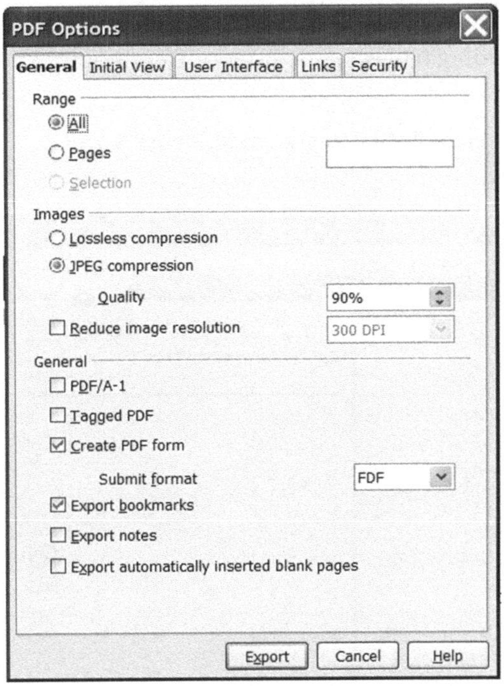

Figure 3-16. *Select PDF settings or accept the defaults.*

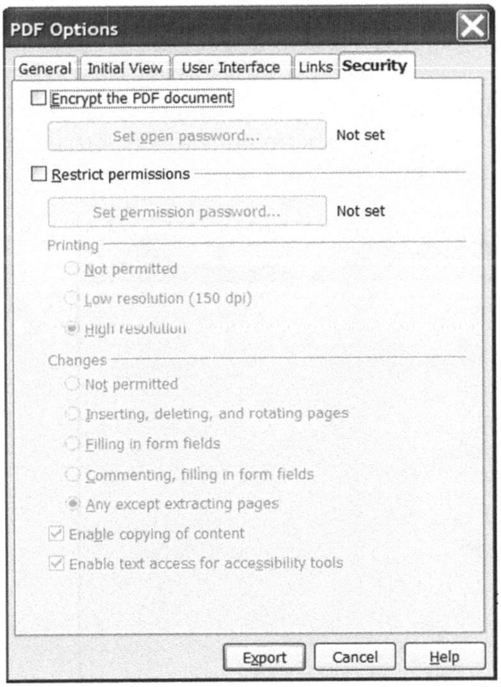

Figure 3-17. *You can set security options for your PDF file.*

Create a Simple Table

Another common word processing task is adding tables to documents. Here's how to do this in OpenOffice.org Writer:

1. In your document, select Table ➤ Insert ➤ Table, as shown in Figure 3-18.

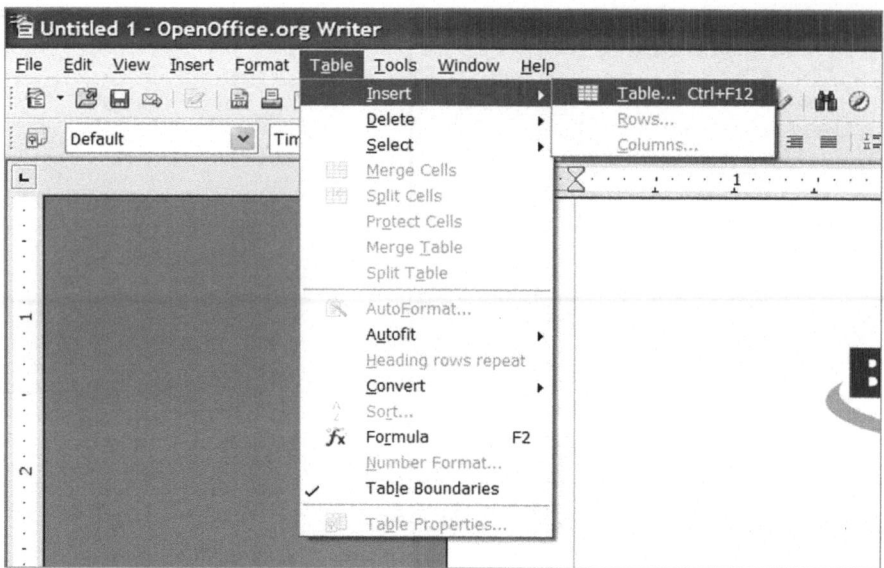

Figure 3-18. *Choose to insert a table into your document.*

2. In the Insert Table dialog box, select the number of columns and rows, as shown in Figure 3-19. You can click the AutoFormat button to experiment with layouts, colors, and title bars. Click the OK button to add the table.

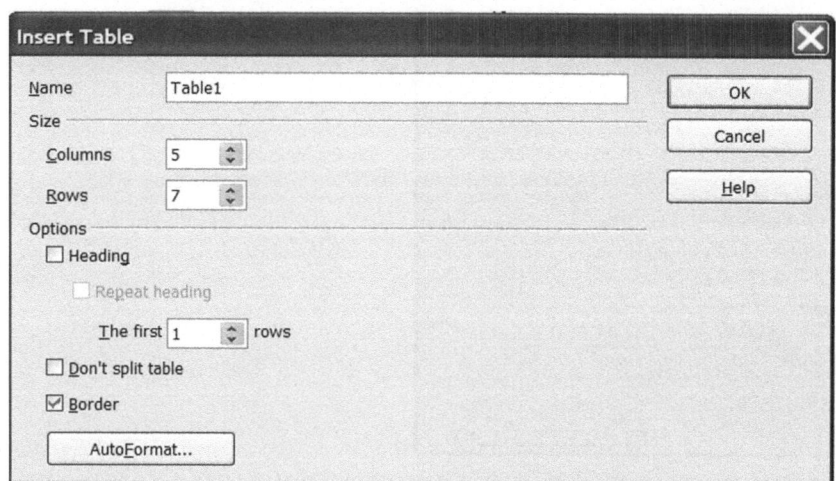

Figure 3-19. *Choose the number of rows and columns for your new table.*

3. Your new table will be inserted into the document, as shown in Figure 3-20. Add labels for each column if desired. To enter data in a cell, simply click inside it and type.

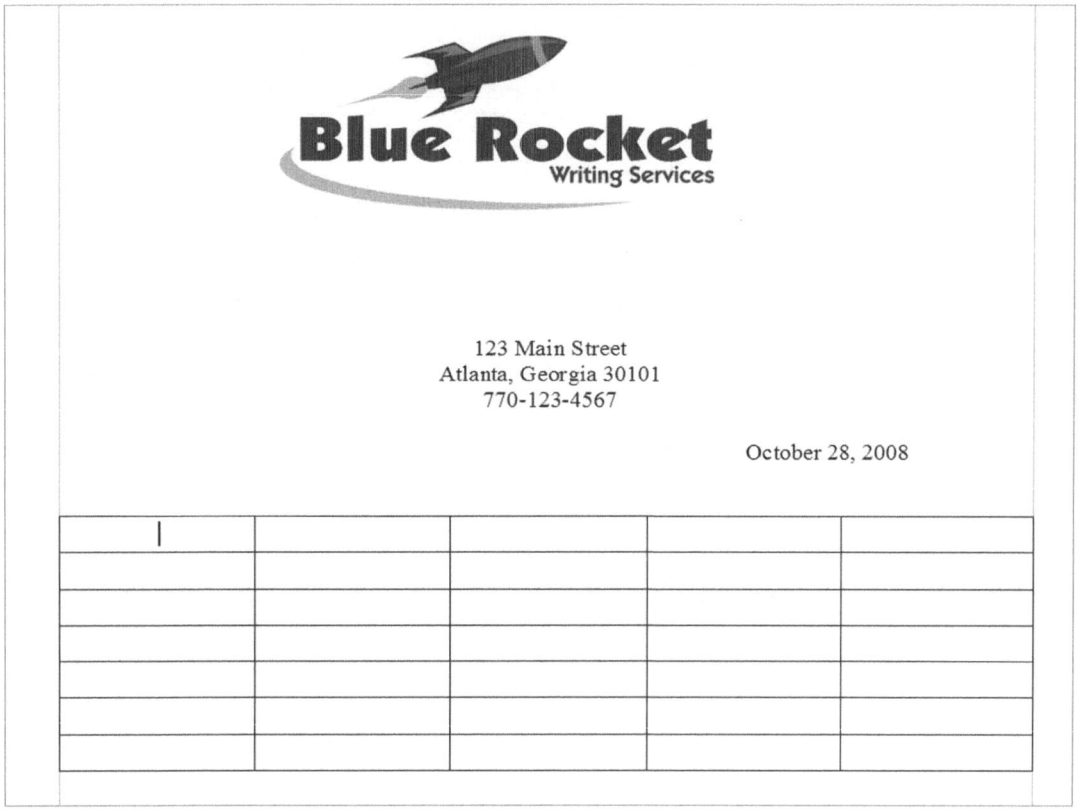

Figure 3-20. *Your new table is ready for you to begin entering information.*

Google Docs Document Features

As a SaaS, Google Docs Documents has a different look and feel than Microsoft Word and other desktop programs, so it may take some practice to become familiar with it. However, it also offers some valuable features not found in typical word processing programs.

Collaborate on a Document with a Friend

Google Docs has an exceptional sharing feature. Even getting close to this type of functionality with Microsoft Word or other Microsoft Office applications would require the purchase and configuration of a very complicated and expensive service called Microsoft SharePoint Server, which comes with Windows Server products (and requires an entire slew of licensing fees, in addition to expensive consultant work and a dedicated server). SharePoint offers plenty of other features besides collaborating on documents, but for sharing applications it isn't even close to the simplicity provided by Google Docs.

Here's how to share a document you've created in Google Docs Document:

1. From the Google Docs home page, place a check in the box next to the document you wish to share, as shown in the example in Figure 3-21. Then click the Share button on the toolbar.

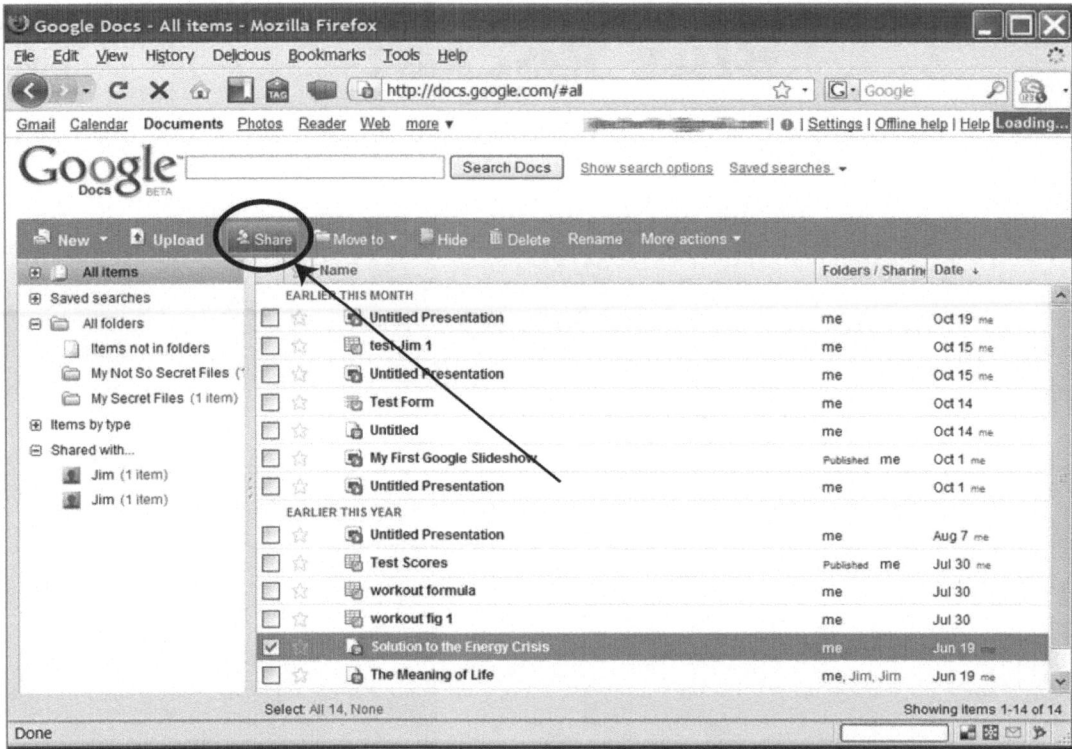

Figure 3-21. *Sharing a document you've written is as easy as clicking the Share button.*

2. When the Share this File window opens, enter your friend's e-mail address in the Invite People text box, as shown in the example in Figure 3-22. Uncheck the boxes labeled "Collaborators may invite others" and "Invitations may be used by anyone." Then click the Invite Collaborators button.

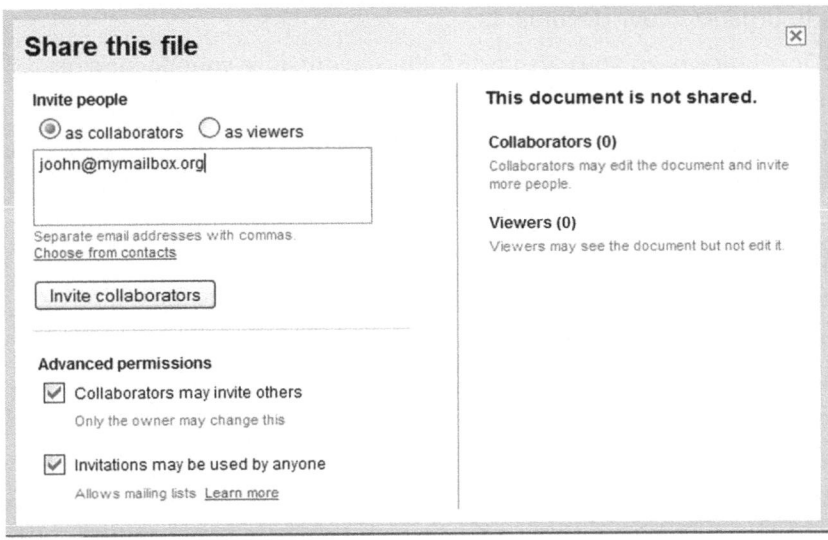

Figure 3-22. *You can give others the ability to modify your document or only view it.*

3. In the "Tell these people about the file?" window, enter a brief message, as shown in the example in Figure 3-23. Then click the Send button.

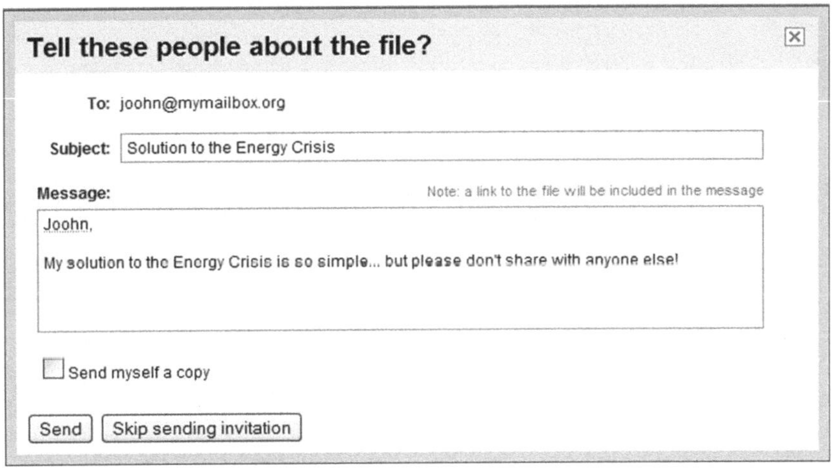

Tell these people about the file? ☒

To: joohn@mymailbox.org

Subject: Solution to the Energy Crisis

Message: Note: a link to the file will be included in the message

Joohn,

My solution to the Energy Crisis is so simple... but please don't share with anyone else!

☐ Send myself a copy

Send   Skip sending invitation

Figure 3-23. *Let those you invite know a little about the document you're sharing.*

Your friend will receive an e-mail that contains a hyperlink he can click to view and edit the selected document.

Create Folders to Organize Your Documents

On the Google Docs home page, you can create folders to organize your documents, as follows:

1. Click the New button to see the drop-down menu shown in Figure 3-24. Select Folder from this menu.

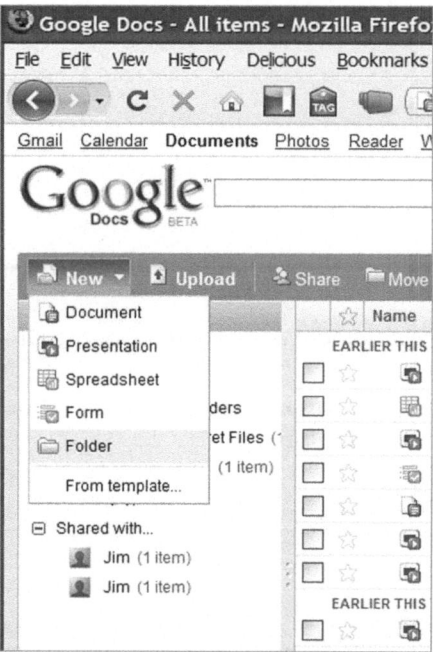

Figure 3-24. *Create folders in Google Docs to help organize your files.*

2. Your new folder appears. Place a check next to the folder and click the Rename button to give it a more memorable name, as shown in the example in Figure 3-25. Press Enter when you're finished.

3. Optionally, create a subfolder (a folder within a folder) by clicking one of your existing folders and choosing to create a new folder (step 1). Your new folder will be placed inside the existing folder you selected.

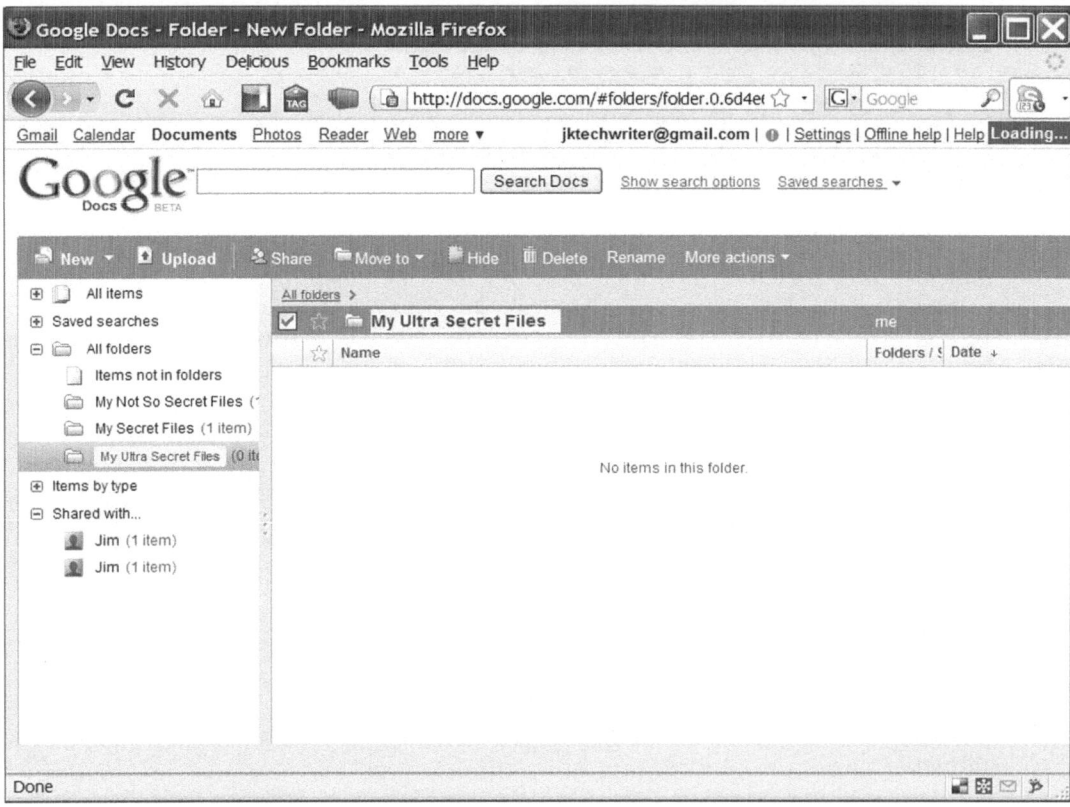

Figure 3-25. *Giving your folders useful names will help you find what you're looking for later.*

Download the File from Google Docs to Your PC

By default, your documents are stored on Google's computers, most likely hundreds (if not thousands) of miles away, and can be accessed only from a computer with an Internet connection. If you wish to save a document to your own computer or for transfer to a flash drive or writable CD/DVD, you can download the file, as follows:

1. Open the Google Docs Document file you wish to download.

2. Select File ➤ Download file as, and on the fly-out menu, pick the format for saving the document. Figure 3-26 shows an example of saving the document as a PDF file.

3. In the browse window that opens, browse to the location on your hard drive where you want to save the file.

Once the file is saved on your computer, you may edit it as desired.

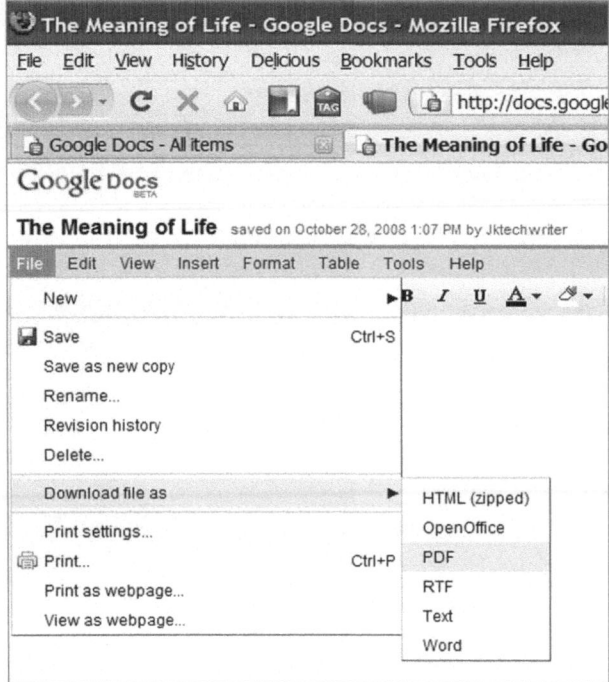

Figure 3-26. *You can save your Google Docs files to your own computer in a variety of formats.*

Investigate Further

There are more free word processing applications available, but be advised that many of these applications come with no user support and little documentation. These freebies are often the work of a single programmer and are made available "as is."

Caution Always scan your downloads for viruses and spyware. With free applications, it's not buyer beware, but downloader beware. I've been bitten by the infected download, and it's no fun to try to clean up the mess it makes. (The free antivirus software we'll cover in Chapter 9 can fix that.)

Here are two additional word processing applications that I submit for your consideration:

- AbiWord, available from http://www.abisource.com/
- KWord, available from http://www.koffice.org/kword/

For more word processing apps to consider, visit the following web site:

```
http://webworkerdaily.com/2007/06/22/10-free-minimalist-word-processors/
```

Here, you'll find a list of free "Minimalist Word Processors." Google Docs and AbiWord are listed, as well as some others that you might find useful.

Summary

There's no arguing that Microsoft Word is an extremely useful and popular application. Most users are familiar with its GUI and the location of popular buttons, tools, and other options. This familiarity is certainly an argument for sticking with the application.

If you are considering purchasing Microsoft Word, you should examine your specific word processing needs and compare those requirements to the features available in Word, OpenOffice.org Writer, and Google Docs Document. Even the most advanced writer might discover that 99% of the features required can be found in Writer or Document. If you find some missing features that are absolutely required for your word processing needs, Microsoft Word is ready and available for purchase and installation.

But if you are like most people, your requirements are fairly basic: change fonts, change font sizes, add some boldfacing here and some italics there, perform a spell check or mail merge, and occasionally highlight some text and track some editing changes in different color. Consider giving OpenOffice.org Writer or Google Docs Document a whirl before making a purchase. You might be pleasantly surprised to find that all of your word processing needs can be met with a simple and free software alternative.

Microsoft Word: $229 ($400 bundled with Microsoft Office 2007 Standard)

OpenOffice Writer: $0

Google Document: $0

CHAPTER 4

■ ■ ■

Spreadsheets

After word processing (covered in Chapter 3), the next most commonly used "office" application is a spreadsheet program. Entire books have been written on the use of spreadsheets. From financial calculations to household budgets to gym workout routines, spreadsheets have a variety of uses.

While spreadsheets take care of some behind-the-scenes operations—such as averaging, summing, and calculating interest rates—if the user (you) wishes to make the spreadsheet useful in any way, you do need some knowledge of formatting and creating formulas (both demonstrated in this chapter). For a quick-and-dirty calculation, most users simply plug numbers in to cells, generate a formula or two to act on those numbers, get the results, and delete the file. But if the spreadsheet is to be used to make dissemination of information easier for others, you'll find that spending some time making your spreadsheets pretty will pay off in both ease of use and accuracy.

If you've never played with a spreadsheet before—perhaps because you think a spreadsheet application costs too much or takes too much time to learn—you'll discover here how easy it can be to get started using spreadsheets. A lot of tasks that people commonly try to accomplish with a word processor—such as a complex table, a list of reminders, or a schedule handout—can be done efficiently and for free with one of the spreadsheet applications recommended in this chapter.

As with word processing, the big name in spreadsheets comes from Microsoft. Microsoft Excel (part of the Microsoft Office suite) is considered by most users to be the standard for spreadsheet applications, but other products are popular. Some other commonly used spreadsheet applications include Lotus Symphony Spreadsheets (part of the Symphony suite), Corel WordPerfect Office suite's Quattro Pro X4, and Apple's own spreadsheet application Numbers, which comes bundled in the iWork suite.

But this book's focus is on alternatives to the commercial packages, and plenty are available, including two free and powerful spreadsheet applications that can go head-to-head with the big names.

TYPICAL USES FOR SPREADSHEETS

While spreadsheets had their start in the business world, users have never felt restricted to using them for only accounting purposes. The following are some examples of real-world uses of spreadsheets to keep in mind as you read through this chapter:

- *Recipes*: List the ingredients in one column and the amounts in a second column.

- *Exercise routines*: Keep track of your exercises, including weight amounts and number of sets and repetitions.

- *Scripts and novels*: Scriptwriters have created custom templates for filling in dialogue, as well as scene descriptions and actor movements. Book writers have long used spreadsheets to help manage complicated plots and chapter content.

- *Car buying*: Many spreadsheet templates allow you to fill in values such as the car's price, the interest rate, and your trade-in value to calculate your monthly payments.

- *Mailing lists*: Combined with a good word processor, spreadsheets can be used to store name, address, city, state, and ZIP code information, and provide these to a text document for printing. The feature is called *mail merge*, and OpenOffice.org Writer and Calc support it.

- *Rosters*: Keep track of your contacts in a single location, and sort through them easily. This method has the benefit of being very easy to load into a custom database. This is great for small businesses, non-profit organizations, or even video game guilds or clans.

The Defender

Like Microsoft Word for word processing, Microsoft Excel is widely considered to be the standard for spreadsheet applications, with more than 90% of the market according to a recent estimate. Competitors such as Corel's Quattro Pro X4 and Lotus Symphony Spreadsheets are also popular, but more books and web sites are dedicated to Excel than to any other spreadsheet application. Microsoft Excel 2007 is the current version, and it comes bundled with the Microsoft Office suite.

Figure 4-1 shows a new spreadsheet open in Excel. As with Microsoft Word, users of Excel will find the typical gamut of buttons—for formatting, printing, saving files, and so on. As in most Microsoft products, hovering the mouse pointer over a button will provide a small tool tip window that gives a brief description of the button's purpose. Excel has plenty of power features, too, hidden deep within pull-down menus. There are plenty of online resources and books that can give you as much detail on Excel as you care to learn.

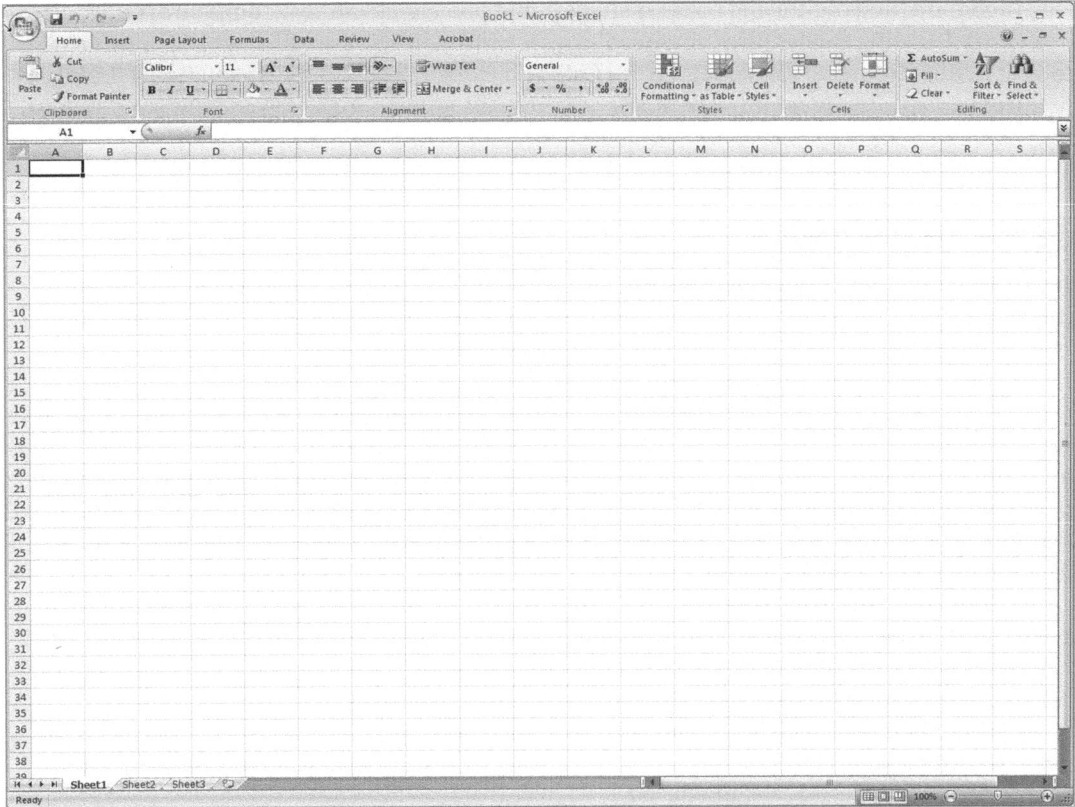

Figure 4-1. *A typical Microsoft Office 2007 spreadsheet consists of rows and columns of cells.*

Most users will find that the list of actual features they tend to use while working in a spreadsheet is quite short. Formulas that perform operations such as averaging and summing are on that list, as well as the ability to format cells with colors and fonts. Because this list is short, the likelihood of you finding these same features and tools available in Excel competitors is very high.

Excel saves files in the .xls format and the new .xlsx format for Excel 2007 (refer back to Chapter 3 for a discussion of file types). The .xls format has become an industry standard, and you'll find most spreadsheet applications will offer the option to save your spreadsheet files in this format.

Excel is popular because it works, and it works well. It's a powerful application, and Microsoft has expanded the product over the years by adding so many new features that it's quite likely no single person knows them all. (A complete list of the features found in the latest version of Microsoft Excel can be found at http://www.microsoft.com/excel.) But many people consider this abundance of features one of Excel's major flaws. Sure, power users may not be able to do without Excel and those hidden features that justify its price. But since Excel isn't sold in price increments based on how you will use the product, you've been forced to buy the same application as Joe the Super-Accountant and pay the same price—until now.

Before shelling out the big bucks, I suggest that you check out two competitors to Excel and see if they offer the features you need in a spreadsheet. The spreadsheet alternatives we'll look at in this chapter are OpenOffice.org Calc and Google Docs Spreadsheet. If you find that features you absolutely require are missing from these applications, you can always purchase Excel later.

The Contenders

It's true that Excel is feature-packed, but you don't need to worry that you'll be sacrificing power for cost if you switch to a competing application. OpenOffice.org Calc is also crammed with powerful functions, and many users who switch to Calc agree that the two products are fairly well matched.

Calc looks and feels similar to Excel, but when you consider how a spreadsheet works, this really shouldn't come as a surprise. Data is entered in rows and columns. Rows are numbered, and columns are given letters. Where a row and column intersect, you have a cell. The cell ID is its column letter and row number, such as cell A1. To select a cell for data entry or modification, you click it with the mouse. And, as with Excel, you can use formulas that perform calculations on the values in cells.

The other alternative covered here is Google Docs Spreadsheet. If you do not need a lot of bells and whistles with your spreadsheet application, I think you'll find this Google Docs application right up your alley. While it doesn't have every feature imaginable, it does have the most reliable and popular features that the majority of users will need.

One of the nicest features of Google Docs Spreadsheet is its simplicity. Most features are available with a single click or within a single menu. There are no hidden power features to spend time searching for—what you see is what you get.

I suggest that you try both Google Docs Spreadsheet and OpenOffice.org Calc, and then decide which one provides the best results for you.

OpenOffice.org Calc

OpenOffice.org Calc is the spreadsheet application that is part of the OpenOffice.org software suite (introduced in Chapter 3). Just like OpenOffice.org Writer, Calc has a user interface that is simple to use and easy to navigate.

Calc contains extensive help documentation. Figure 4-2 shows the general OpenOffice.org Help window that appears when you select the Help ➤ OpenOffice Help menu option from Calc. You can type keywords in the search box at the top of the tab on the left side of the window to find topics of interest. Double-click an item listed in the tab, such as an entry on the Index tab, and the right side of the Help window will provide links to relevant topics and articles. Remember that you can also hover the mouse pointer over any button in the Calc application to see a tool tip showing its function.

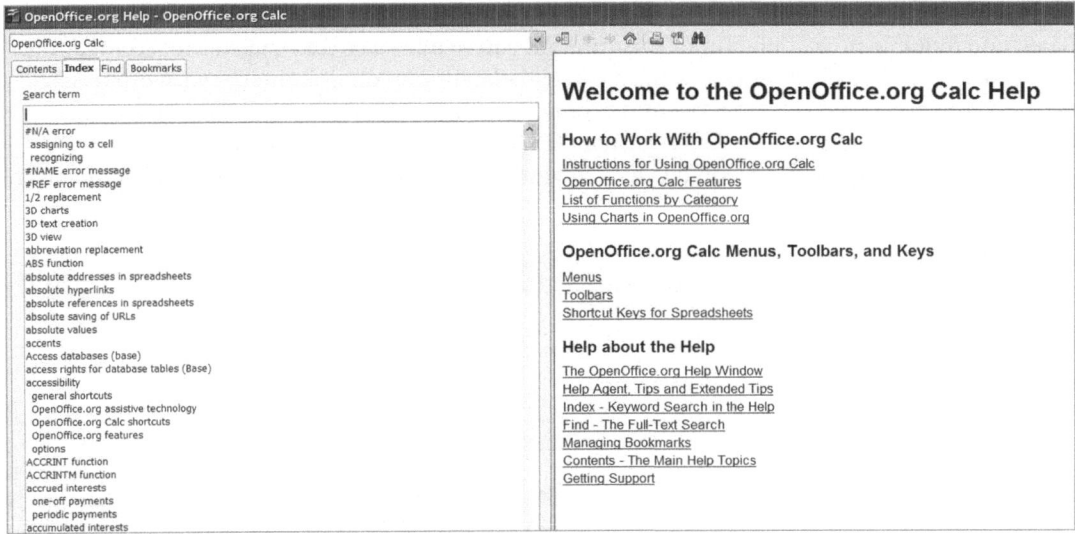

Figure 4-2. *OpenOffice.org Calc has detailed Help documentation built-in.*

As with any application that's new to you, you can learn quite a bit by simply experiment-ing with the buttons, clicking menus, and examining the features offered. I'll show you some sample tasks that you can perform using Calc shortly, but for now, try out the application by entering text and values in various cells. You'll find that features such as copying, pasting, deleting, and moving entries work in Calc just as they do in other spreadsheet and word pro-cessing applications.

The OpenOffice.org web site (`http://www.openoffice.org`) and its help forum (`http://support.openoffice.org`) are great places to start if you have questions that aren't answered by the built-in help documentation. You can post your questions and sift through other topics that might be of interest to you. The site also provides templates and clipart that can be used in Calc and the other OpenOffice.org applications. Just visit `http://www.openoffice.org` and click "I want to do more with my OpenOffice.org."

Google Docs Spreadsheet

Google offers its own spreadsheet application called Google Docs Spreadsheet, which works just like Microsoft Excel (and most other spreadsheets as well). Google Docs Spreadsheet may not have all the features of Excel, but Google continues to develop new tools and features for this application, expanding its usefulness and power.

Tip The Google Docs Spreadsheet window has a New features link in the upper-right corner (see Fig-ure 4-4). Click it to get a rundown on all the updates Google has added.

As with Google Docs Document (covered in Chapter 3), Google Docs Spreadsheet is a SaaS, and requires no installation of software. All you need to use it is an Internet connection. And just as with Google Docs Document, you can collaborate on documents with other users, access your spreadsheets from any computer with an Internet connection, and save your spreadsheets in a variety of standard formats (Excel, PDF, HTML, and so on).

Once you've logged in to Google Docs (if you haven't already done so), you'll find the user interface is similar to that shown in Figure 4-3.

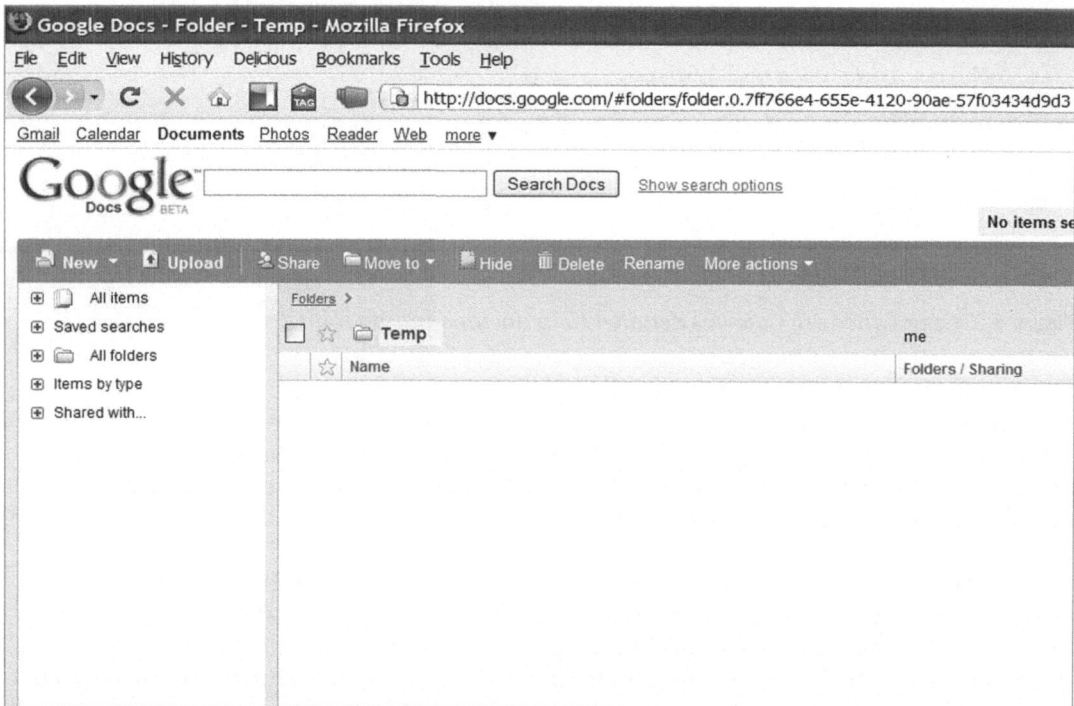

Figure 4-3. *You use Google Docs applications within a web browser.*

To begin using Google Docs Spreadsheet, click the New menu on the top-left side of the screen and choose Spreadsheet from the drop-down list. A new spreadsheet opens, ready to use, as shown in Figure 4-4.

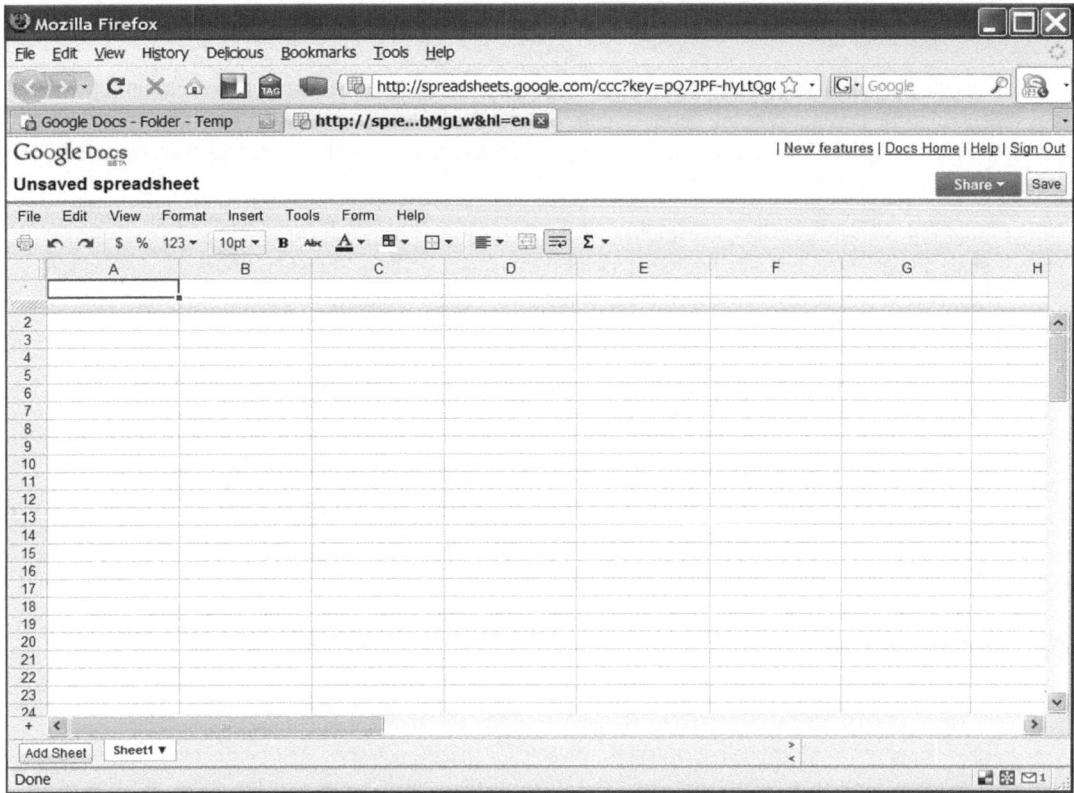

Figure 4-4. *Google Docs opens a new spreadsheet in its own browser window.*

I will take you through a handful of tasks using Google Docs Spreadsheet later in the chapter, but the Help menu is always available if you need assistance. Choose Help ➤ Google Docs Help Center, and use the search feature by entering keywords (or entire phrases and questions) related to the information you need.

■**Note** Remember that Google gives you the ability to suggest features for inclusion for future updates by clicking the "Let us know link" in the online help.

POTENTIAL USER GROUPS AND BENEFITS

Just as some groups of users are likely to gain the largest advantage by using free word processing software, as discussed in the previous chapter, certain groups can potentially reap huge benefits from free spreadsheet software such as OpenOffice.org Calc and Google Docs Spreadsheet: These include college/university students, small business owners, working groups, and retirees. Here's why:

- *Students*: Spreadsheets can be extremely useful for organizing daily schedules—timetables of classes, study groups, work, and let's not forget social events (a.k.a. parties). Students in business classes will, sooner or later, find spreadsheets are a required part of some coursework. Using Google Docs Spreadsheet, students can access their worksheets from any computer on campus that has Internet access.

- *Small business owners*: Not having to spend large amounts of money on software is one way small business owners can give their business a boost. Spreadsheets are a fairly typical application used by most business owners, and what better way to save money and keep your business organized than using a free spreadsheet application? From tracking inventories to maintaining customer mailing lists, OpenOffice.org Calc or Google Docs Spreadsheet can fill an immediate need for software at zero cost.

- *Working groups*: Sharing and collaborating on spreadsheets often introduces errors. If your work involves sharing and collaborating on a single spreadsheet, a Google Docs Spreadsheet project can reduce inefficiency and errors that come from needing to share multiple versions of an important spreadsheet within a working group.

- *Retirees*: Common uses of spreadsheets for retirees include tracking of retirement income and maintaining a budget. Since many retirees are on a fixed income, knowing where the money is being spent is as important as allocating how much is available for specific activities. An OpenOffice.org Calc spreadsheet would be perfect. It doesn't need to be shared, and it is easily customizable, allowing retirees to create spreadsheets that are extremely specific to their financial situation.

Where to Get the Software

If you read about getting the word processing software in the previous chapter, you'll find the material here basically the same. OpenOffice.org Calc is available from the OpenOffice.org site, and Google Docs Spreadsheet just requires a Google account to use.

OpenOffice.org Calc

OpenOffice Calc is part of the OpenOffice.org suite of software and requires an installation file to be downloaded to your computer. Follow these steps to obtain Calc:

1. Visit `http://www.openoffice.org/`.

2. Click "I want to download OpenOffice.org" to obtain the latest version.

3. During the download, take note of the web page that opens. It contains links that allow you to provide feedback, ask questions, and volunteer to help further develop the product.

Once the OpenOffice.org download is complete, you're ready to install and begin using Calc. Jump ahead to the "Notes on OpenOffice.org Calc Installation" section to get started.

Google Docs Spreadsheet

Google Docs Spreadsheet differs from OpenOffice.org Calc in that there is no software to install. Follow these steps to begin using Google Docs Spreadsheet:

1. Visit `http://docs.google.com`.

2. If you already have a Google account (for Google Gmail or another Google service), log in. Otherwise, click the Get Started button and follow the instructions to create your free user account.

Note You can also take a tour of Google Docs or watch a video from the Welcome to Google Docs page (`http://docs.google.com`). Just click the Take a Tour or New Features link to investigate Google Docs before you sign up.

Once you log in to Google Docs, you're ready to get started. Feel free to open a new spreadsheet and experiment, as discussed in the previous section.

Notes on OpenOffice.org Calc Installation

The steps for installing OpenOffice.org applications are covered in Chapter 3. Refer to the "Notes on OpenOffice.org Installation" section in that chapter for instructions.

If you've already run the Installation Wizard to install another OpenOffice.org application, but did not choose to install Calc at that time, choose the Modify option when you run the setup program.

Following the instructions in Chapter 3 takes you to the Custom Setup screen shown in Figure 4-5. Remember that to prevent an application from being installed, click the small triangle next to an application's name and select "This feature will not be available." A red X will be added to the left of the application's name. To select an application for installation, select "This feature will be installed on local hard drive." Figure 4-5 shows that Calc has been selected to be installed at this time, along with Writer and Impress.

After you choose the OpenOffice.org applications to install and click Next, the File Type screen will appear, asking if you wish to make OpenOffice.org Calc the default application when opening Excel spreadsheets (any file name ending with .xls). (For OpenOffice Writer and Impress, you will also be given the option to allow those applications to open .doc and .pps files, or Word and PowerPoint files, respectively.) Accept this offer, and click Next.

After you've completed the installation, you're ready to start using Calc.

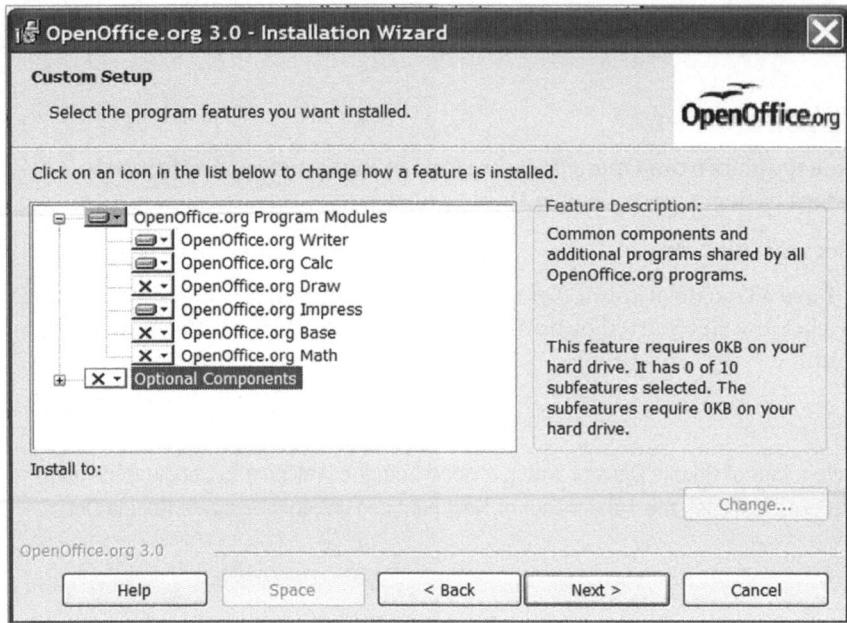

Figure 4-5. *Writer, Calc, and Impress are selected to be installed.*

Spreadsheet Features

Now you're ready to try out your spreadsheet software. We'll walk through some common tasks with OpenOffice.org Calc, and then do the same with Google Docs Spreadsheet.

OpenOffice.org Calc Features

To give you an idea of how the Calc user interface works and the features available, the next few sections walk you through formatting and publishing a spreadsheet, as well as performing calculations within it.

Jazz Up Your Spreadsheet with Colored Column Headers

Creating column headers that can be read quickly makes your spreadsheet more legible (and pretty!). Here's how:

1. After creating your spreadsheet, select a group of cells that you want to be colored. You can use the standard mouse and keyboard techniques to select cells. Clicking the row number selects the entire row, and clicking the column letter selects the whole column. In the example in Figure 4-6, the column headers—Date, Exercise, Set 1, and so on— are selected.

2. Select Format ➤ Cells.

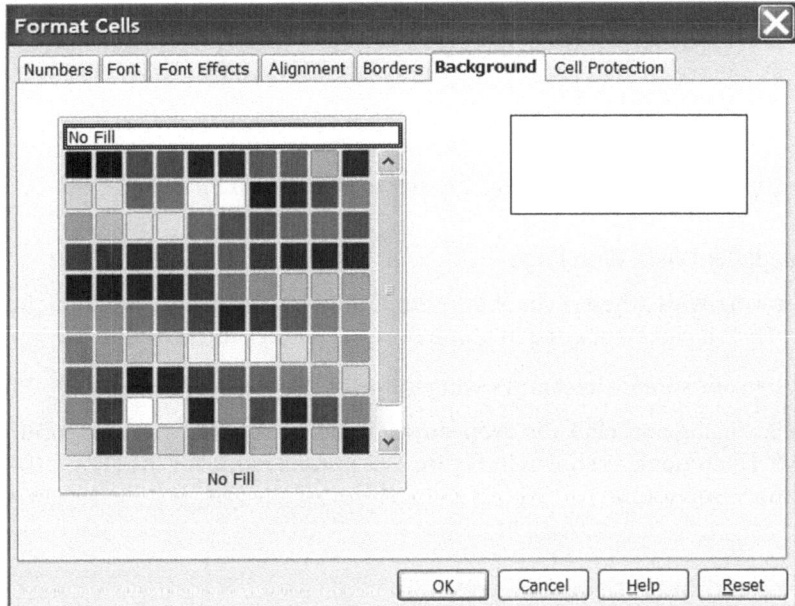

			SET 1	WEIGHT	SET 2	WEIGHT	SET 3	WEIGHT	SET 4	WEIGHT		Subtotal	
1													
2	DATE		EXERCISE	SET 1	WEIGHT	SET 2	WEIGHT	SET 3	WEIGHT	SET 4	WEIGHT	Subtotal	
3	5-Dec		Deadlift	5	135	5	135	5	135	5	135	2700	
4			Dumbell Incline Press	5	60	5	70	5	90	5	100	1600	
5			Cable Row	5	35	5	65	5	95	5	95	1450	
6			Wide Grip Pulldown	5	85	5	120	3	140	5	120	2045	
7			Woodchop - Left	5	35	5	42.5	3	50	5	42.5	750	
8			Woodchop - Right	5	35	5	42.5	3	50	5	42.5	750	
9													
10	7-Dec		Squat	5	85	5	95	5	115	3	125	1850	
11			Dumbell Incline Press	5	40	5	45	5	50	5	50	925	
12			Cable Row	5	100	5	120	5	140	5	140	2500	

Figure 4-6. *Select a grouping of cells that you wish to format with some color.*

3. In the Format Cells dialog box, click the Background tab, as shown in Figure 4-7.

Figure 4-7. *The Background tab lets you apply a color to selected cells.*

4. Click the color you wish to apply to the selected cells, and then click the OK button. The color will be applied, as shown in the example in Figure 4-8.

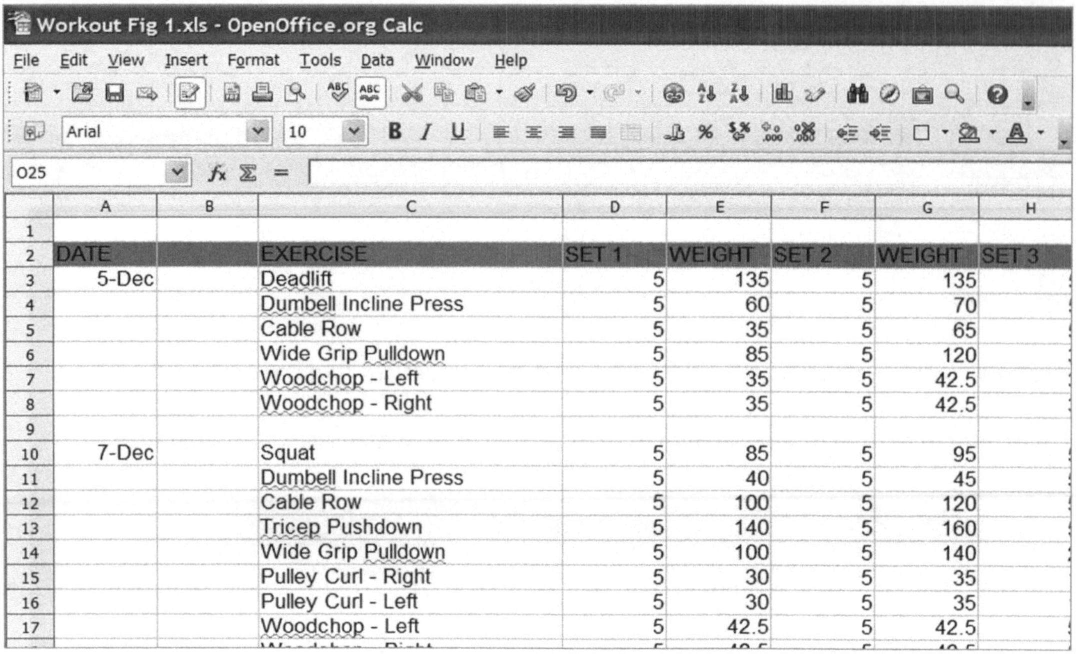

Figure 4-8. *Color is applied to the cells, making it easier to distinguish the column heads.*

Publish Your Spreadsheet As a Web Page

You can share your work with others, even if they don't have a spreadsheet program, by saving it as an HTML file. Then it can be opened in a web browser. Here's the procedure:

1. After creating your spreadsheet and saving it, select File ➤ Save As.

2. In the Save As dialog box, click the drop-down menu for the "Save as type" option and select HTML Document, as shown in Figure 4-9. Enter a name for the HTML file, and then click the Save button.

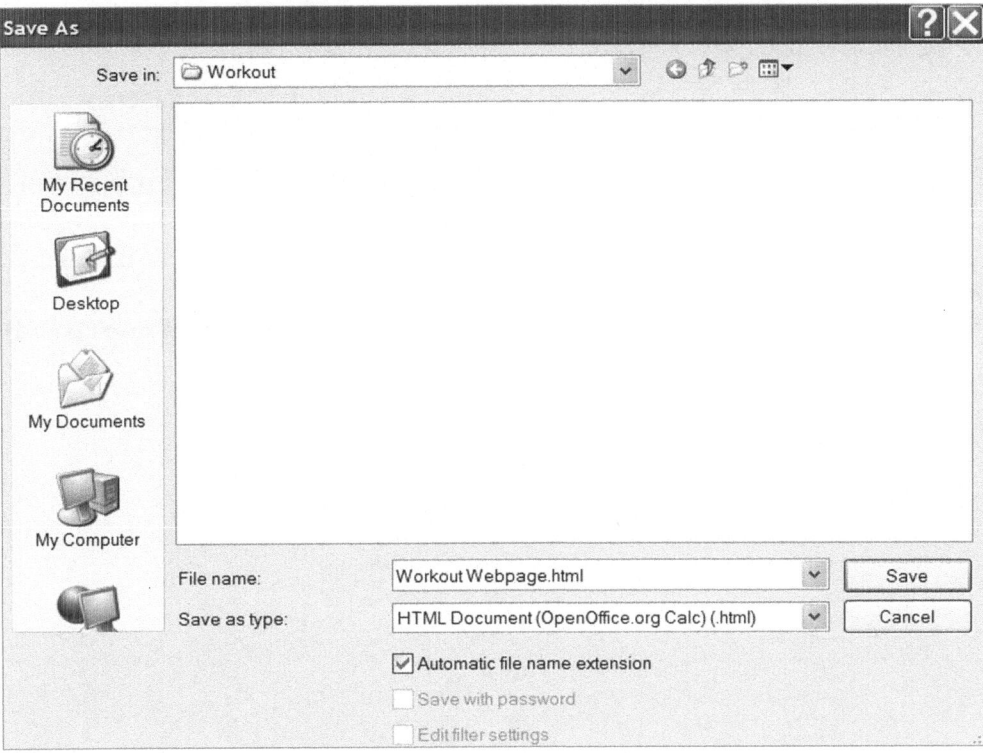

Figure 4-9. *HTML is one of the file type options available for saving a spreadsheet.*

3. You might receive a warning that some formatting options in your spreadsheet may not be able to be retained in an HTML document. Click the "Keep current format" option.

4. Browse to the HTML file you saved and double-click it. Your spreadsheet will now open in your web browser, as shown in Figure 4-10. You may upload this file to a personal web site or e-mail it as an attachment.

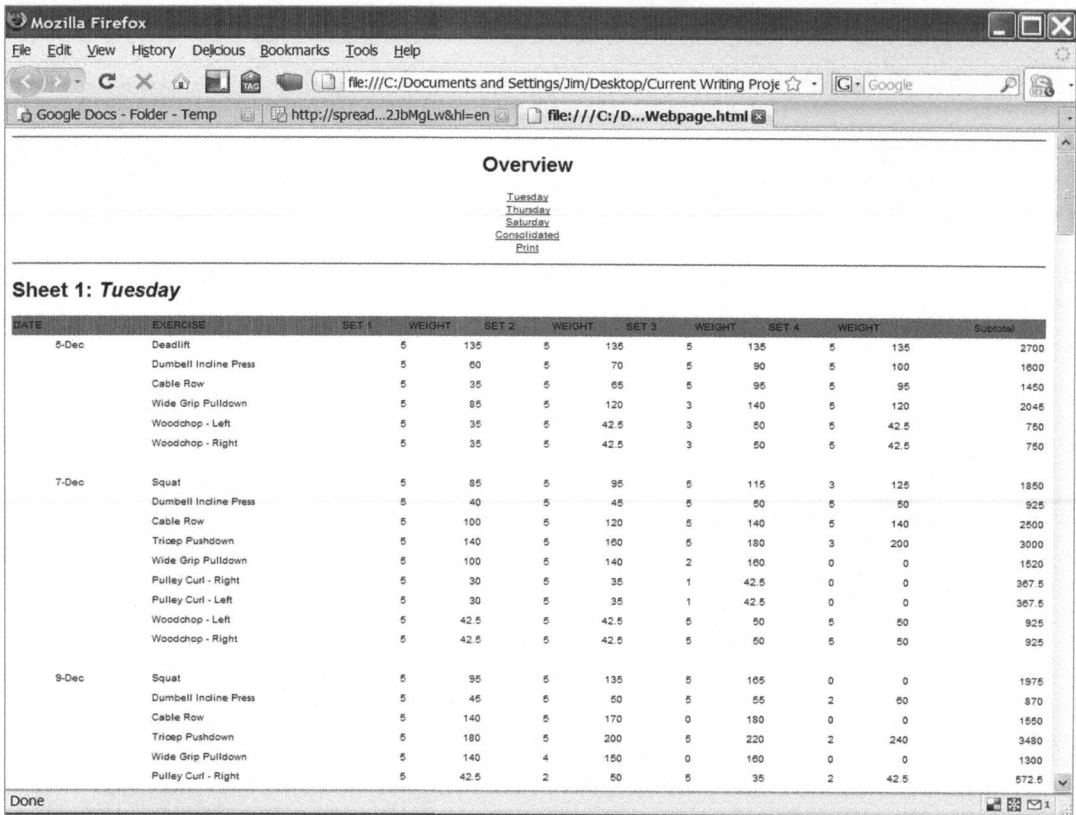

Figure 4-10. *Your spreadsheet can now be viewed in a web browser.*

Find a Formula/Function and Apply It to a Spreadsheet

Formulas are the most powerful and commonly used feature of spreadsheets. In fact, until you start working with formulas, spreadsheets are basically word processor documents that are divided into cells. Learning how to use formulas unlocks the real power of spreadsheets. As you'll see in this example, applying formulas is slightly more complex than formatting or saving your spreadsheet, but the reward is that you'll be a real, honest-to-goodness spreadsheet analyst.

In this example, we want to multiply the number of repetitions in a set of an exercise by the amount of weight used, and record those values in the Subtotal column, as shown in Figure 4-11. Once all the subtotals are calculated, we will then get the grand total.

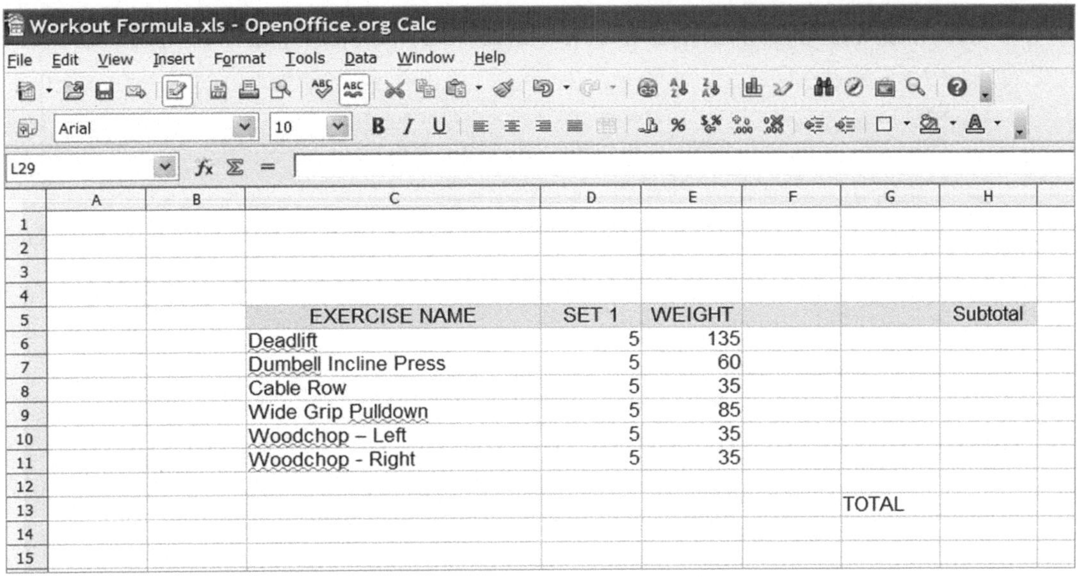

Figure 4-11. *Use formulas to determine the total amount of weight used.*

With the spreadsheet shown in Figure 4-11 created, follow these steps:

1. Click the cell in the Subtotal column that will contain the result of your calculation. In this example, first select the cell corresponding to the row holding the Deadlift data, as shown in Figure 4-12.

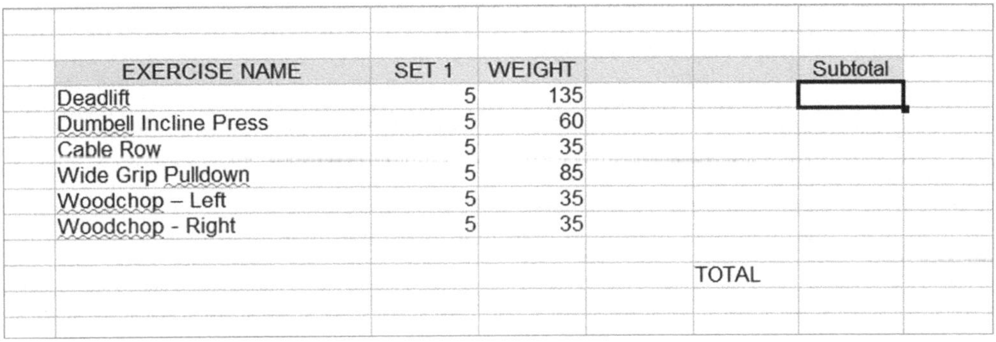

Figure 4-12. *Select a cell that will hold a calculated value.*

2. Select Insert ➤ Function.

3. In the Function Wizard's first page, scroll down the list of functions to find your formula. A description of the calculation performed by the formula will be provided. In this example, choose PRODUCT (because we want to multiply the value in the Set 1 column, the number of repetitions, by the value in the Weight column), as shown in Figure 4-13. Then click the Next button.

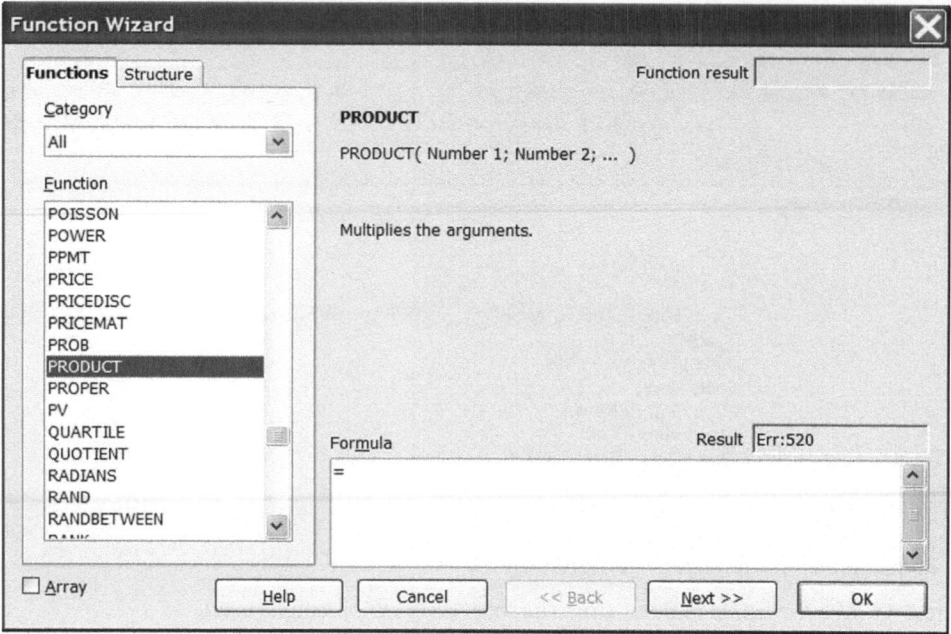

Figure 4-13. *Select the function to be applied to selected cells.*

4. The next page of the Function Wizard is waiting for the values that will be multiplied together. Each value is given a variable name of Number *x*, and you can either click a cell to assign that cell ID or type in the cell ID. Figure 4-14 shows that cell D6 has been selected for Number 1 and cell E6 has been selected for Number 2.

5. Click the OK button. The product of the two selected cells will be calculated for the Subtotal column's cell.

6. Repeat steps for 1 through 5 for the remaining rows. When you've finished, the Subtotal column will contain a group of values, as shown in Figure 4-15.

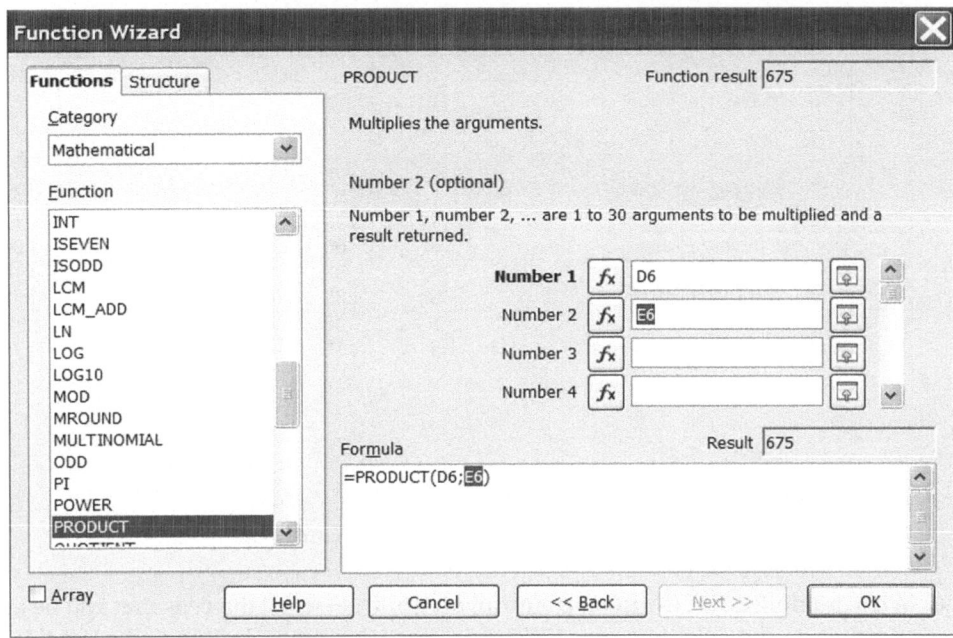

Figure 4-14. *Select the values that will be multiplied together.*

EXERCISE NAME	SET 1	WEIGHT		Subtotal
Deadlift	5	135		675
Dumbell Incline Press	5	60		300
Cable Row	5	35		175
Wide Grip Pulldown	5	85		425
Woodchop – Left	5	35		175
Woodchop - Right	5	35		175
			TOTAL	

Figure 4-15. *All the subtotals have been calculated.*

7. Now we need to sum all the values in the Subtotal column and display that value in the Total cell. Click the cell where the Total value will be displayed, and then click the Sum button. As indicated in Figure 4-16, the Sum button is the one with the uppercase sigma character.

Figure 4-16. *Click the Sum button after selecting the Total cell.*

8. While holding down the mouse button, drag and select all the cells that will be added together, as shown in Figure 4-17. Then release the mouse button and press the Enter key. The total will be displayed, as shown in Figure 4-18.

■**Note** You can also use Ctrl-click and Shift-click to select a collection of cells that you wish to use in a calculation. Hold down the Ctrl key while you click to select cells that are not adjacent to one another. Alternatively, hold down the Shift key, click the first cell and the last cell, and any cells between the start and end cells will be selected.

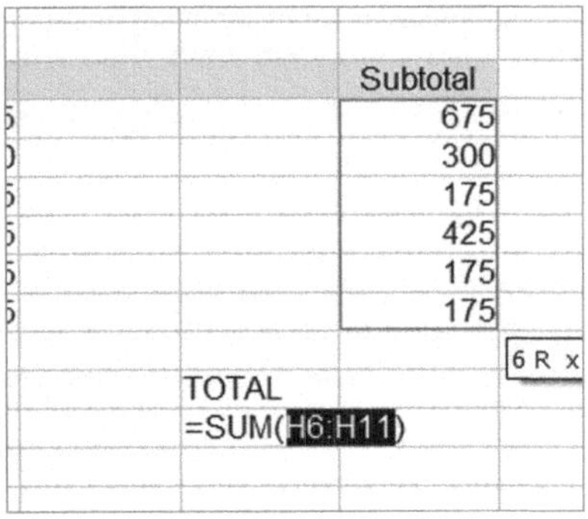

Figure 4-17. *Sum all the subtotal values to calculate the total value.*

EXERCISE NAME	SET 1	WEIGHT			Subtotal
Deadlift	5	135			675
Dumbell Incline Press	5	60			300
Cable Row	5	35			175
Wide Grip Pulldown	5	85			425
Woodchop – Left	5	35			175
Woodchop - Right	5	35			175
				TOTAL	
				1925	

Figure 4-18. *The total value of all the weights used during the workout appears on the spreadsheet.*

Google Docs Spreadsheet Features

Google Docs Spreadsheet is the right tool when you need to share your spreadsheet and make sure it is kept up-to-date, and you are not concerned with customizing it and keeping it private.

Here, I'll show you how to create a chart from your spreadsheet and how to share a spreadsheet with others.

Create a Chart

Google Docs Spreadsheet can create charts as easily as Excel does. And the chart you create is immediately shareable after you publish its spreadsheet; it doesn't need to be e-mailed around. Here are the steps for adding a chart:

1. After you have created a spreadsheet with data, select Insert ➤ Chart.

2. In the Create Chart window, shown in Figure 4-19, select the type of chart you wish to use. For this example, select a Bars chart.

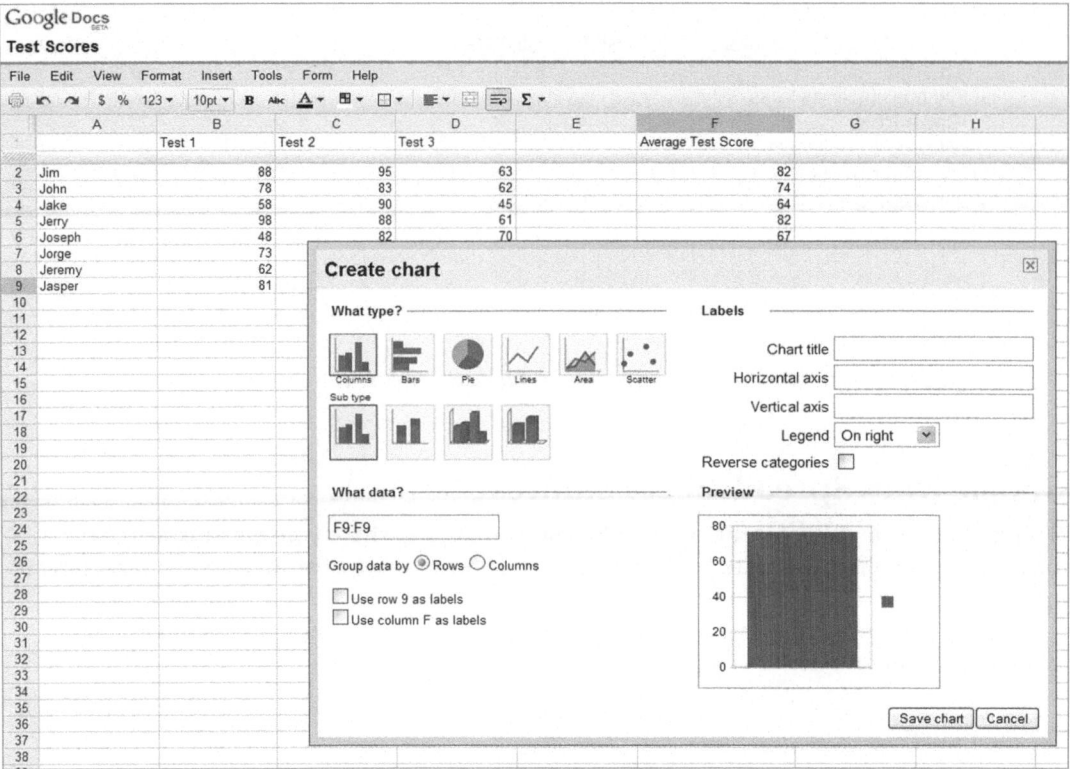

Figure 4-19. *Creating a chart using data from your spreadsheet is extremely simple.*

3. In the Labels section of the window, add labels for the chart title, horizontal axis, and vertical axis, as desired. For this example, title the chart **Test 1 Scores**. Name the horizontal axis, which will provide the test scores, **Scores**. Name the vertical axis, which will list the student names, **Student Names** (see Figure 4-20).

4. Use the mouse to select the data in the spreadsheet you want to include in the chart. For this example, remember to include column A, which contains the student names, and row 1, which contains the test number. The cell range appears in the What data? box, as shown in Figure 4-20.

5. Check the preview of the chart. Make changes if necessary. Then click the Save chart button.

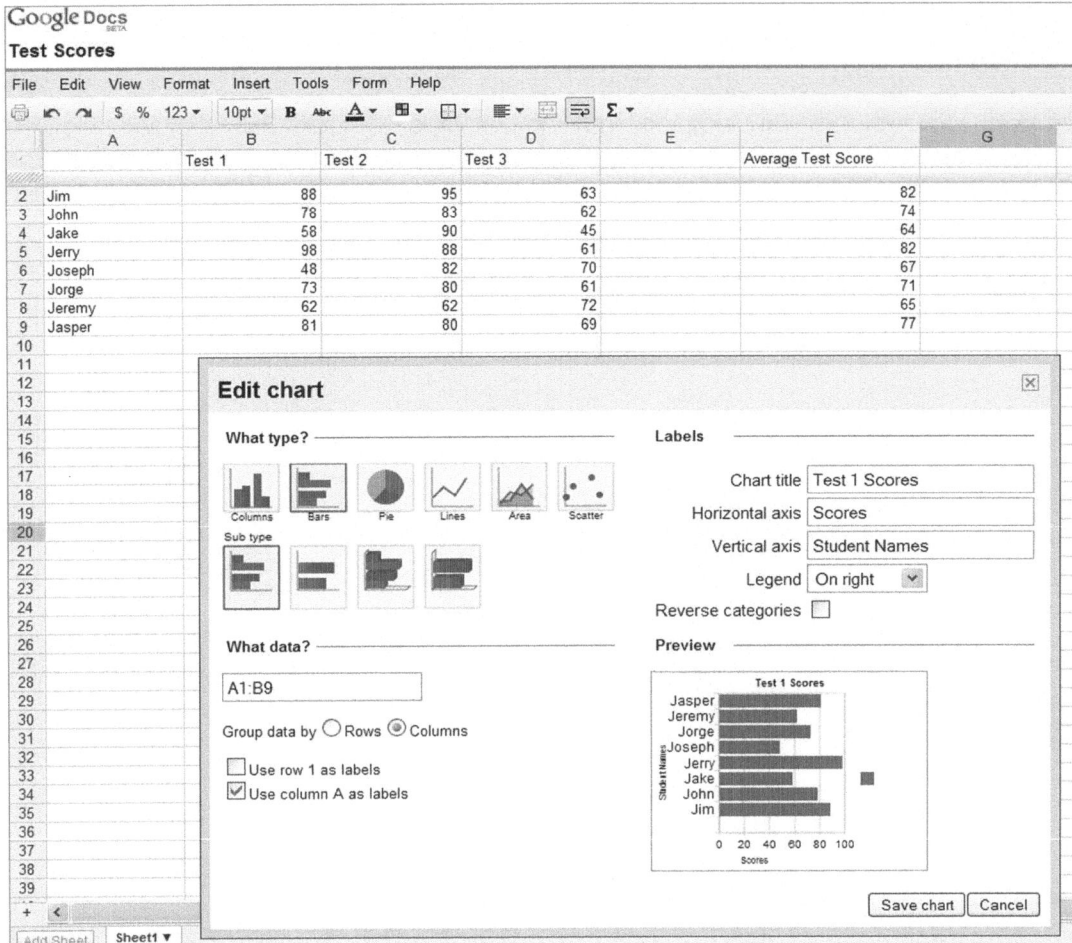

Figure 4-20. *Provide labels and select the data to be included in the chart. This figure shows the settings that appear when you choose to edit a chart, which are the same as those in the Create Chart window.*

The chart is created and inserted into your worksheet, as shown in Figure 4-21. You can click the chart to select it; drag and drop it where desired; or use the drop-down menu to edit, delete, save, or move the chart.

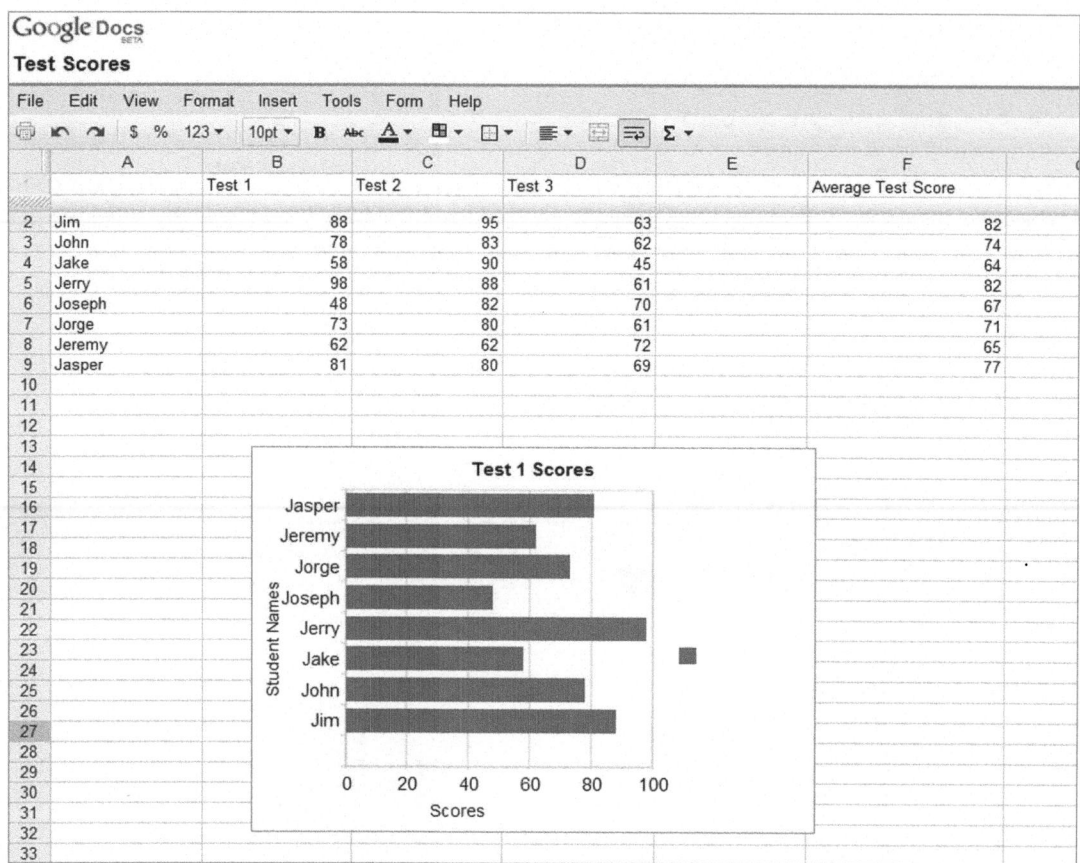

Figure 4-21. *The final chart is saved inside your spreadsheet.*

Publish Your Spreadsheet

After you've set up a spreadsheet, you can share it with your coworkers or family, even if they don't have a spreadsheet program. This is a huge plus to using Google Docs Spreadsheet. OpenOffice.org Calc will put your spreadsheet into HTML web page, but it won't publish it.

However, before you choose to publish your spreadsheet, be aware that no security is provided, so anyone with the URL may view the spreadsheet data. It is also possible that your published data might be found using an Internet search. Additionally, keep in mind that since your data is residing on Google's servers, Google is entitled to verify that the content doesn't violate any of its Terms of Service. Realize that your "private" spreadsheet data might not be so private if Google is allowed to examine it. So, for business purposes, Google Docs Spreadsheet might not be the best solution.

You can choose to publish a spreadsheet and make it available to anyone with Internet access as follows:

1. Open the spreadsheet you wish to publish (such as the one in Figure 4-21).

2. Click the Share button in the upper-right corner of the window to see the drop-down menu shown in Figure 4-22.

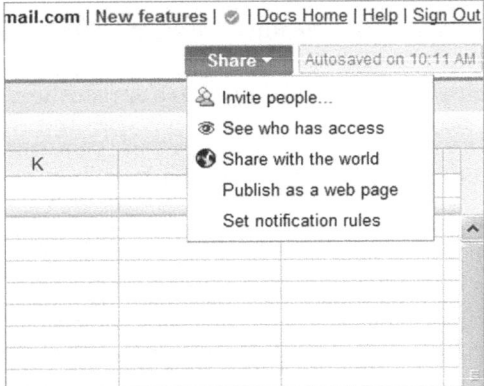

Figure 4-22. *The Share button gives you options for publishing your spreadsheet.*

Note Other options here include the ability to stop publishing and to republish if changes have been made. You can also choose individual sheets (Sheet1, for example) if your spreadsheet contains multiple sheets. Additional features are available, such as subscribing to the published Google Docs file.

---

3. Select the "Publish as a web page" option. You will be given a URL.

4. Provide the URL to any users who wish to view your spreadsheet.

Investigate Further

Google Docs Spreadsheet and OpenOffice.org Calc aren't the only free spreadsheets out there. Here are two additional spreadsheet applications that are enjoying popularity:

- Gnumeric, available from `http://www.gnome.org/projects/gnumeric/`

- Simple Spreadsheet, available from `http://www.simple-groupware.de/cms/Spreadsheet/Home`

Summary

Spreadsheets are useful, no doubt. The question for you is whether your spreadsheets require (or might ever require) advanced calculations and features not found in the free spreadsheet software.

Before making an expensive purchase, it's definitely worth a bit of investigative time on your part. Examine and experiment with OpenOffice.org Calc, Google Docs Spreadsheet, or one of the other free spreadsheet applications. Compare your needs to what is available in these free applications. If you find them lacking, then by all means invest in the product that gives you what you need.

Many spreadsheet users may be surprised to find that the functions and features they require don't make up too long a list. Google Docs Spreadsheet and OpenOffice.org Calc continue to expand their features, so it is likely that everything you'll need in a spreadsheet can be found in one of these free but powerful applications.

- Microsoft Excel: $400 (bundled with Microsoft Office 2007 Standard)

- OpenOffice.org Calc: $0

- Google Docs Spreadsheet: $0

■ ■ ■

Slide Shows

Before slide show applications came along, anyone giving a presentation had to rely on some low-tech solutions: handouts, overhead projection, and sometimes even a chalkboard. These days, if you need to display information, pictures, or other items to a group of any size, a slide show application is your best bet.

Early slide show applications could support only text, text formatting, and the occasional embedded GIF or BMP image. Today, most slide show applications can support video and audio as well.

Modern slide show applications, also called *presentation* software, allow a presenter to use color, animation, and sound to engage viewers, hold their attention, and deliver information in a more memorable way. This isn't to say that all slide shows are enjoyable. Many are bland or crammed with too much information. The key to creating a useful presentation is being aware of the capabilities of your application and not overusing the available features.

The current big name in presentation software is PowerPoint from Microsoft. PowerPoint is part of the Microsoft Office suite. Of course, since I'm mentioning it in this book, you can guess that there are free applications that offer features similar to PowerPoint. In this chapter, we'll focus on two alternatives: OpenOffice.org Impress and Google Docs Presentation.

Note One thing that presentation software is great for is building a family photo album, ready to go in slide show format. Slide shows are also seeing usage outside the boring-your-friends crowd, in settings as diverse as storyboarding for animation or personal organization, index-card style.

The Defender

Microsoft PowerPoint is king in the business world. Would you believe that many large corporations require their employees to take PowerPoint training and to learn how to use a standardized corporate template for all presentations they create?

PowerPoint works like the other Microsoft Office applications. A toolbar of buttons runs across the top of the screen, and drop-down menus offer a substantial number of features. In the main work area, you enter your text, place pictures and other items, and select from background themes or create your own. Figure 5-1 shows a slide show in PowerPoint.

PowerPoint saves files in the default `.ppt` format, and PowerPoint 2007 also offers the new `.pptx` format (similar to the `.docx` and `.xlsx` files that Word and Excel create). Opening a `.ppt` or `.pptx` file requires PowerPoint and gives you the ability to edit the slide show. The `.pps` format is also popular. This format creates an encapsulated file that can be opened and viewed (but not edited), even if PowerPoint is not installed on the computer.

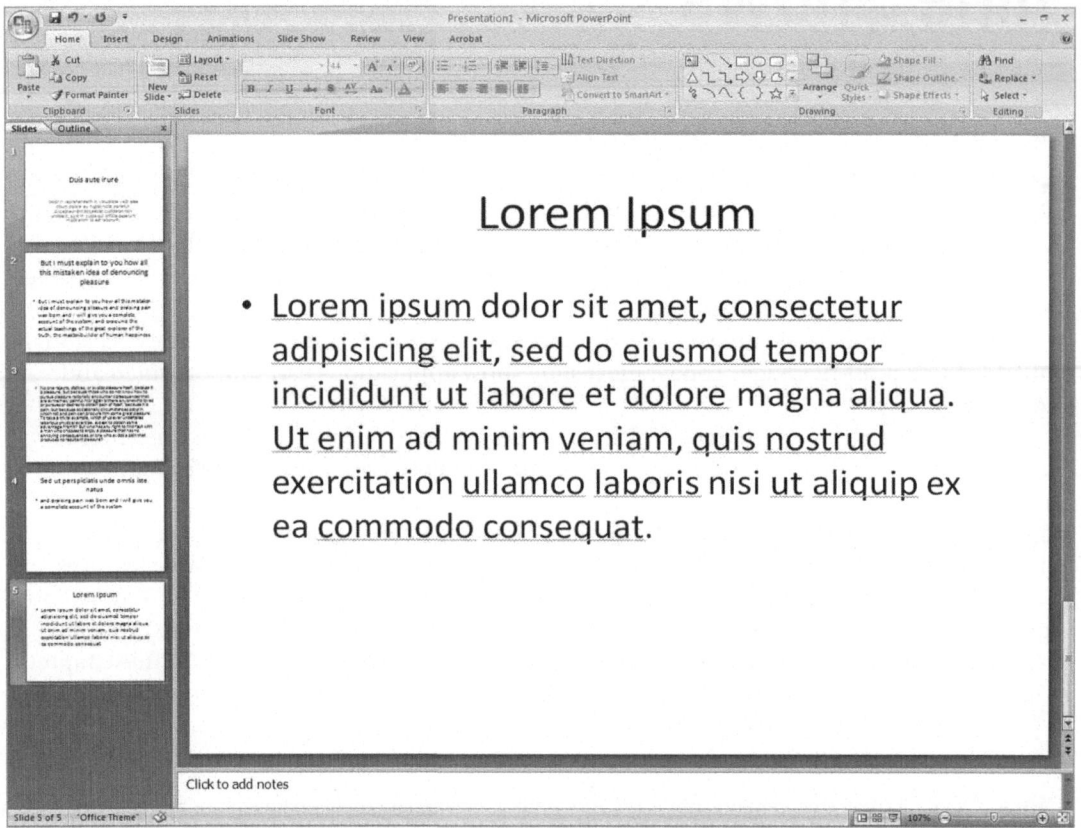

Figure 5-1. *A Microsoft PowerPoint slide show*

With PowerPoint, you can embed images, video, recordings, and more. Text can be entered and font sizes changed. Color can be applied to text, as well as to graphic elements such as arrows (used for drawing the eye to specific points on a slide). You can select a presentation theme that will be applied to every slide you create. The theme controls items such as the background color/image, font sizes and colors, and placement of a company logo.

There is no arguing that PowerPoint has set the bar for slide show applications. With all the built-in templates and clipart, a new user can have an impressive presentation up and running in very little time. Built-in help files and online support are also available.

PowerPoint is feature-filled (a complete list of the features found in the latest version of Microsoft PowerPoint can be found at `http://www.microsoft.com/powerpoint`), but as with most Microsoft products, you may find yourself using only a handful of basic features. And you've probably guessed by now that PowerPoint isn't cheap. As Chapters 3 and 4 demonstrated, many users are paying for features that are readily found in free applications. And again, I recommend that you examine a few of the competing (and free) products and determine if they offer the features you need. Two applications you should consider testing are OpenOffice.org Impress and Google Docs Presentation.

The Contenders

If you need to create slide shows, whether for work or personal reasons, you have options other than Microsoft PowerPoint. If you've read through Chapters 3 and 4, you know that OpenOffice.org has its own slide show/presentation application called Impress. If you've discovered the power of OpenOffice.org Writer and Calc, then it won't come as a surprise that OpenOffice.org Impress offers a full range of features—for free. I use it when I need to make a slide show, and I've found it to be easy to master.

A less feature-packed but still extremely useful slide show creation tool is Google Docs Presentation. It requires no installation, and is extremely simple to use, totally free, and always being improved by its Google programming team.

OpenOffice.org Impress

Impress is the OpenOffice.org slide show application, and, as its name implies, it's definitely impressive. Each time you open the application, you're immediately led through a small set of steps to help you select the basic look and design of your presentation.

Figure 5-2 shows the start of a wizard that will guide you through creating a new presentation. You can cancel the wizard if you like, but if you're new to presentation software, I suggest walking through it the first time to see what decisions and options are available. The wizard gives you the opportunity to quickly set up a presentation template that will be used throughout your entire slide show. Any selections you make while using the wizard can be changed later.

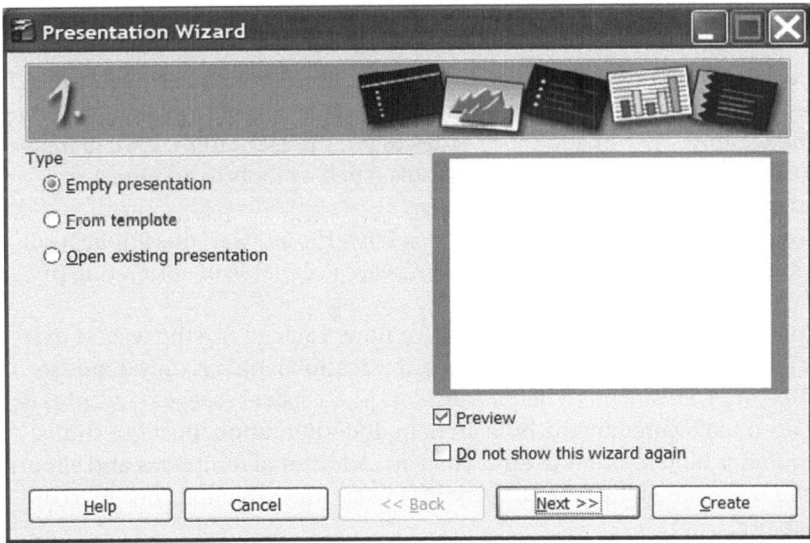

Figure 5-2. *OpenOffice.org Impress has a great wizard to help you get started.*

As you step through the wizard, you'll choose whether to start a new presentation, open an existing one, or select a template (such as a slide show layout with company logo). Additional selections include prebuilt templates and simple effects. Finally, click the Create button, and you'll be presented with your selected template (if you chose one; otherwise you'll see a blank screen), as shown in Figure 5-3. From there, you can start working on your slide show.

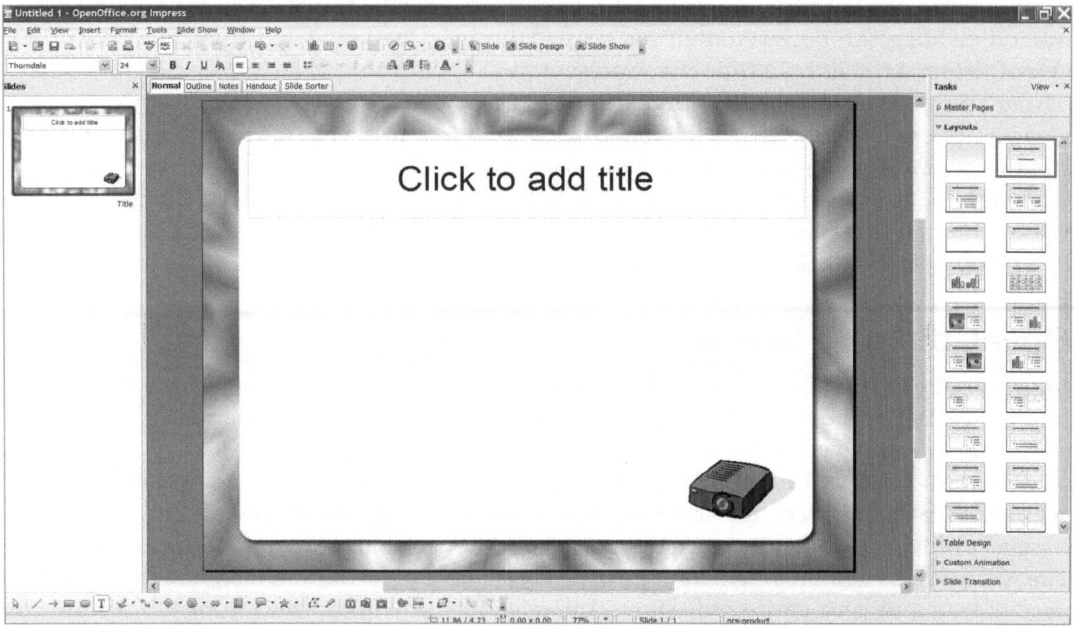

Figure 5-3. *An OpenOffice.org Impress slide show with a preconfigured template, ready for your information*

In Figure 5-3, you can see the main work area in the center of the window. The toolbar along the top offers access to many features, and various layouts that can be applied are visible along the right edge of the window. As you add more slides to your presentation, a small image of each will be visible in the left panel. Custom drawing tools (such as tools to add lines and shapes) are available along the bottom edge of the window.

As I said, Impress doesn't skimp on features. If you're a PowerPoint user, this application is going to prove to you that the OpenOffice.org suite of software is capable of competing in the big leagues.

I'll cover some sample tasks later in the chapter, but for now, you can use the wizard to try out the software. And as with all the other OpenOffice.org applications, help is only a mouse click away. The OpenOffice.org web site has a help forum (http://support.openoffice.org) if you have questions that aren't answered by the built-in help documentation. Post questions, search existing topics, and offer help to other users if you can. Additional templates and clipart are available for download by visiting http://www.openoffice.org and selecting "I want to do more with my OpenOffice.org."

Google Docs Presentation

Google Docs has its own slide show application called Presentation. Like the Google Docs applications I recommended in the previous chapters, Presentation is SaaS, and requires no installation of software. All you need to use it is an Internet connection. Your presentation will be saved online, on Google's servers, and available to you whenever you log in to your Google account from any computer connected to the Internet.

To use Google Docs Presentation, simply log in to Google Docs, click the New menu, and select Presentation. As you can see in Figure 5-4, Presentation looks similar to Impress. You add text, video, and images to the workspace in the center of the screen, the toolbar is available along the top of the browser window, and images of the slides in the presentation are displayed in the panel on the left.

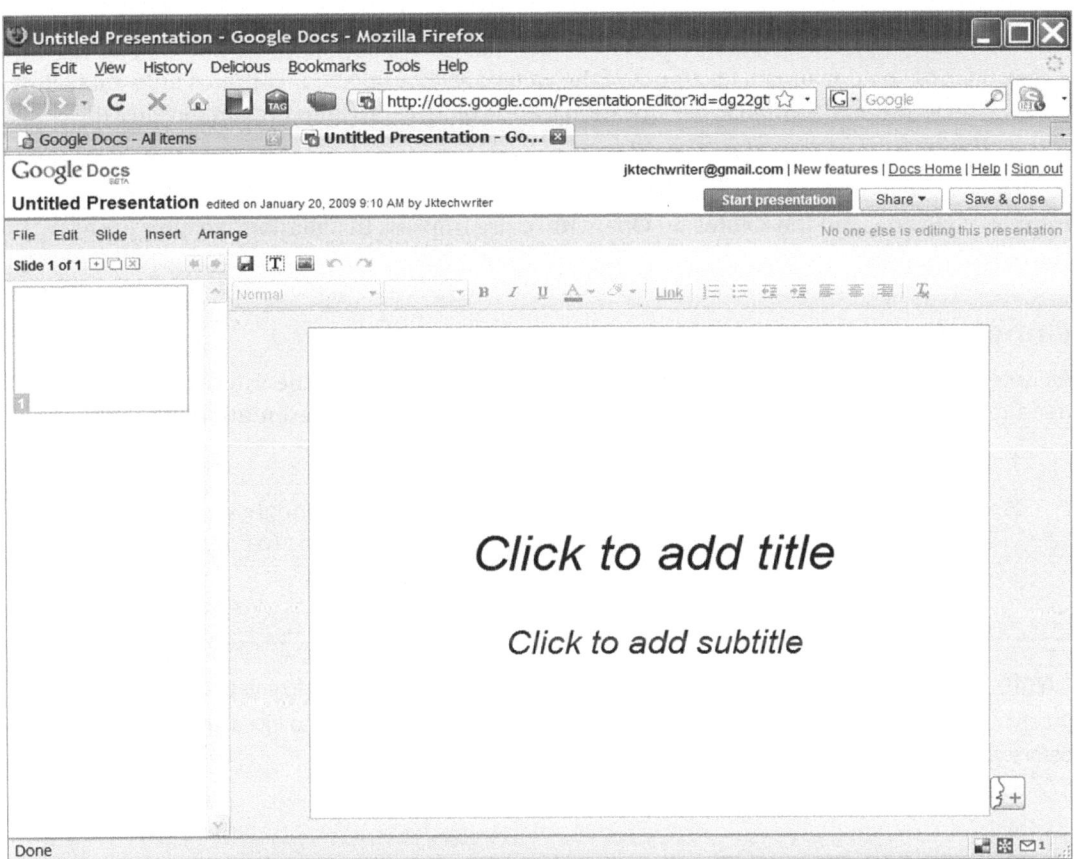

Figure 5-4. *Presentation starts with a blank title slide, ready for your additions.*

I'll walk you through a handful of sample tasks using Google Docs Presentation later in the chapter. For now, you can try creating some slides and see what the toolbar and menus have to offer. The Help menu has options for viewing simple tutorials on performing specific tasks.

Where to Get the Software

You're not going to find OpenOffice.org Impress or Google Docs Presentation at a store. OpenOffice.org Impress, another creation of the OpenOffice.org project, is available for download as part of the full OpenOffice.org package. Google Docs Presentation is available from `docs.google.com`.

OpenOffice.org Impress

OpenOffice.org Impress is part of the OpenOffice.org suite of applications. Here are the general steps to follow to install OpenOffice.org:

1. Visit `http://www.openoffice.org/`.

2. Click on "I want to download OpenOffice.org" to obtain the latest version.

3. During the download, take note of the web page that opens. It contains links that allow you to provide feedback, ask questions, and volunteer to help further develop the product.

Once the OpenOffice.org download is complete, you're ready to install and begin using Impress. Skip ahead to the "Notes on OpenOffice.org Impress Installation" section to get started.

Google Docs Presentation

As noted earlier, Google Docs Presentation is a SaaS, delivered over the Internet. You don't need to install anything. All you need is a Google account. Access Presentation as follows:

1. Visit `http://docs.google.com`.

2. If you already have a Google account (for Gmail or another Google service), log in. Otherwise, click the Get Started button and follow the instructions to create your free user account.

Note You can also take a tour of Google Docs or watch a video from the Welcome to Google Docs page (`http://docs.google.com`). Just click the Take a Tour or New Features link to investigate Google Docs before you sign up.

Once you log in to Google Docs, you're ready to get started. Feel free to open a new presentation and experiment, as discussed in the previous section.

Notes on OpenOffice.org Impress Installation

The steps for installing OpenOffice.org Impress are almost identical to those described for installing OpenOffice.org Writer and Calc, covered in Chapters 3 and 4.

To install OpenOffice.org Impress, follow the instructions in the "Notes on OpenOffice.org Installation" section in Chapter 3. If you've already run the Installation Wizard to install another OpenOffice.org application, and did not install Impress at the time, choose the Modify option when you run the setup program.

Following the instructions in Chapter 3 takes you to the Custom Setup screen shown in Figure 5-5. To choose Impress for installation, click the small triangle next to its name and select "This feature will be installed on local hard drive" from the drop-down menu. To prevent an application from being installed, select "This feature will not be available" from the drop-down menu. Figure 5-5 shows that Impress has been selected to be installed at this time, along with Writer and Calc.

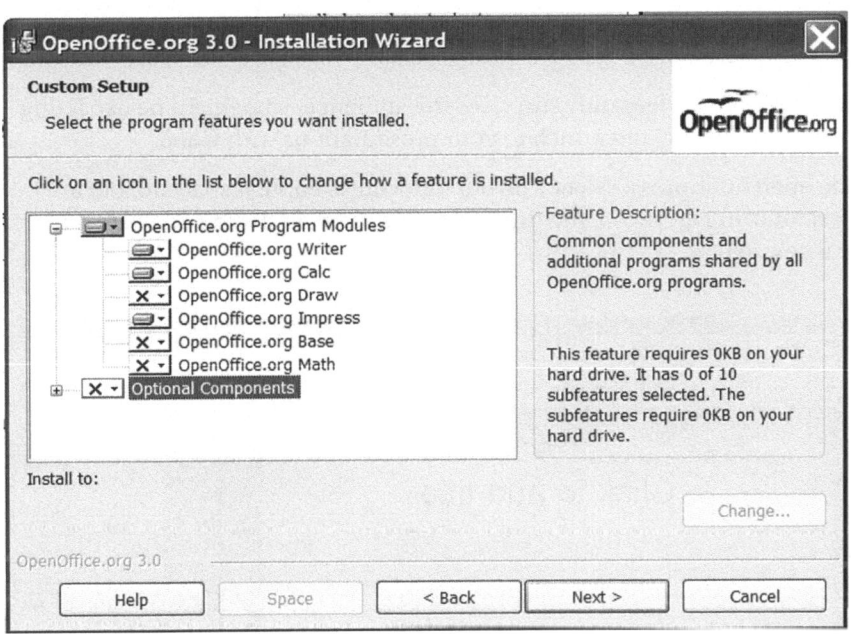

Figure 5-5. *Select OpenOffice.org applications to be installed on your hard drive.*

After you click Next in the Custom Setup screen, you will see the File Type screen, asking if you wish to make OpenOffice.org Impress the default application when opening a PowerPoint presentation (any file name ending with `.ppt`). For now, place a check in the box for Microsoft PowerPoint Presentations and click Next.

The Ready to Install Program screen will appear next. Simply click the Install button to start the installation.

When the Installation Wizard is finished, click the Finish button. You're now ready to start using Impress.

Slide Show Application Features

This section walks you through a handful of sample tasks that can be performed using the free presentation software. I won't cover the basics of creating slides and adding text, because those are such easy tasks. Instead, I'll cover some interesting, not-so-obvious tasks that will prove useful in adding a bit of flash to your presentations.

You'll notice how OpenOffice.org Impress allows you to create rich presentations that are portable and don't require an Internet connection. Google Docs Presentation is well suited for simpler slide shows that will be presented online.

OpenOffice.org Impress Features

OpenOffice.org Impress doesn't disappoint for feature richness. Everything you can do in PowerPoint, you can do in Impress. Here, I'll show you how to add video to a slide and use some of Impress's drawing tools.

Add Video to a Slide

Adding video to a slide show often pleasantly surprises the audience, who might be expecting only text and pictures. Here's how to add punch to your presentations with video:

1. With your slide open in Impress, select a layout that allows enough space to add a video. In the example in Figure 5-6, the third template down in the left column of the Layouts pane is selected.

Figure 5-6. *Select a template for the slide where you will add video.*

2. Enter a title and any other text you would like to appear, and format the text if desired. Figure 5-7 shows a title and some text added to the slide.

Figure 5-7. *Prepare the slide with a title and text, if desired.*

3. Select Insert ➤ Movie and Sound. Browse to the location of your video and select it, as shown in Figure 5-8. Then click the Open button.

4. Drag the inserted video box and place it where you want it to play from the slide, as shown in Figure 5-9.

Figure 5-8. *Find the video to be inserted into your slide.*

Figure 5-9. *Place the video in the desired location.*

5. To test that the movie works, select Slide Show ➤ Slide Show (or press the F5 key). Your movie should begin to play (including any audio), as shown in Figure 5-10.

Figure 5-10. *View the video you inserted into your slide.*

Modify a Slide with Drawing Tools

You can add some interesting effects to your slides using the tools on Impress's Drawing toolbar. Here's how:

1. Add a new slide by clicking the Slide button, as shown in Figure 5-11. The slide will appear in the left pane with the other miniature views of your existing slides.

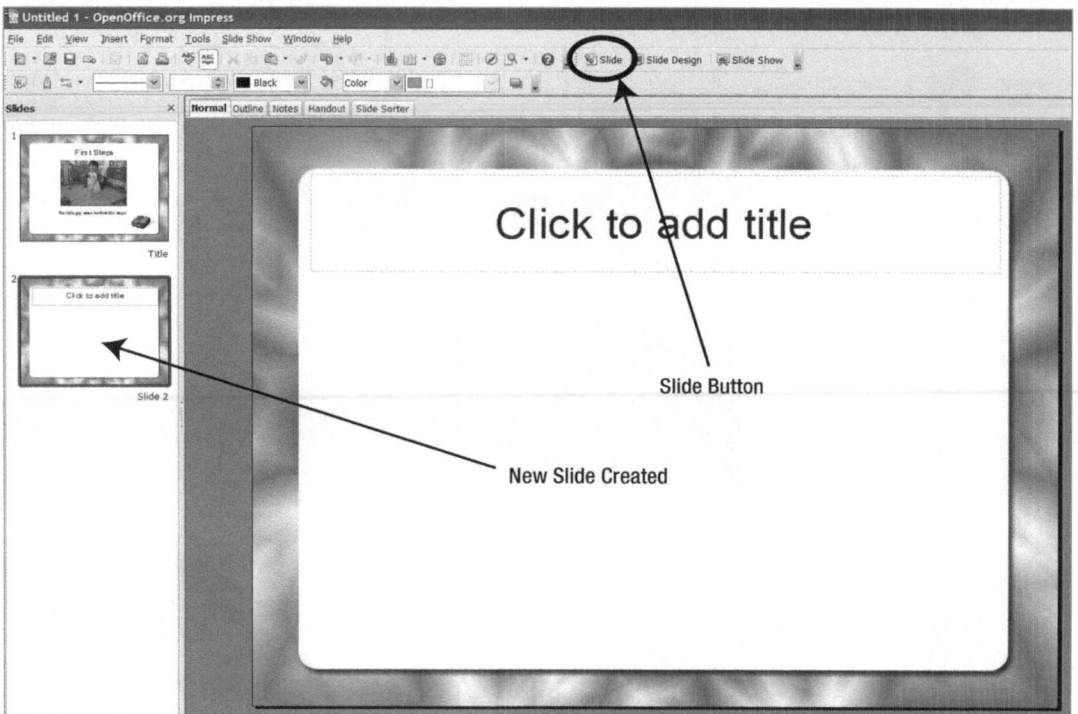

Figure 5-11. *Add a new slide to your presentation by clicking the Slide button.*

2. Add a title and some pictures to the slide. Figure 5-12 shows an example with two photos inserted.

Figure 5-12. *Add a title and pictures to the slide.*

3. Let's add a text balloon to a photo. In the Drawing toolbar along the bottom edge of the Impress window, click the text balloon button. A fly-out menu appears, offering a choice of shapes for the text balloon, as shown in Figure 5-13.

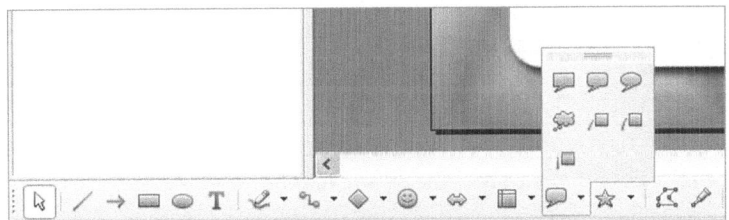

Figure 5-13. *Add an effect such as a text balloon to your images.*

4. Drag your mouse to size and shape the text balloon, as shown in Figure 5-14. After it is placed, you can use the small boxes around the text balloon to resize and move it as desired.

Figure 5-14. *Draw the text balloon on screen, and then resize it as desired.*

5. To add some text to the balloon, click the Text tool on the Drawing toolbar, as shown in Figure 5-15, and then click where you would like to place the text.

Figure 5-15. *Select the Text tool to add text inside the text balloon.*

6. Enter you text in the box, as shown in Figure 5-16. You can use the small boxes surrounding the text to resize and move it.

7. For fun, let's add a small graphic to the second image with some additional text. Select the heart shape from the Symbol shapes tool fly-out and place it where desired. Then add some text to it, as shown in Figure 5-17.

Figure 5-16. *Adding text to the text balloon is as simple as using the Text tool on the toolbar.*

Figure 5-17. *Add some additional effects to finish the slide.*

Google Docs Presentation Features

While not as rich (yet!) as OpenOffice.org Impress, Google Docs Presentation is still a capable presentation tool. Here, I'll show you how to pick a theme, add pictures and video, and publish your slide show.

Change a Slide Show Theme

When you first open Presentation, the slide show template shows a clean (and very dull) page, ready for your additions (refer back to Figure 5-4). Here's how to choose another theme:

1. With your slide open in Presentation, select Edit ➤ Change theme, as shown in Figure 5-18.

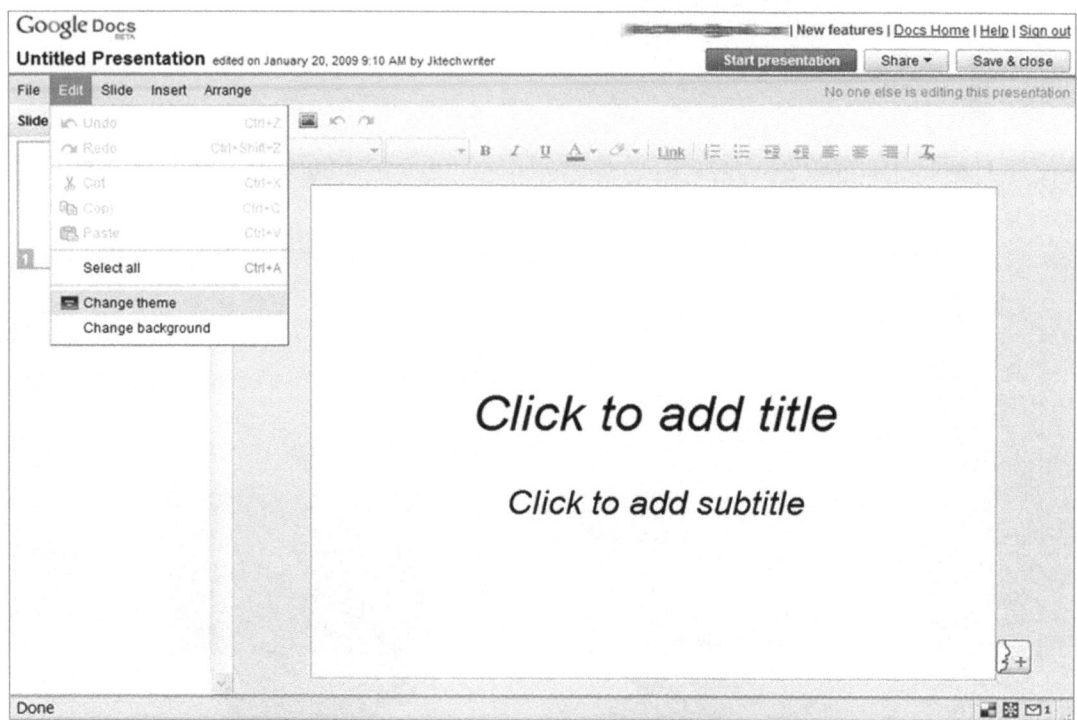

Figure 5-18. *The default slide show template is boring, so change the theme.*

2. You will see a window that offers a variety of templates, as shown in Figure 5-19. Select one, and the background will change instantly, as shown in Figure 5-20. Keep in mind that your selection affects all the slides in your slide show; you cannot choose multiple themes.

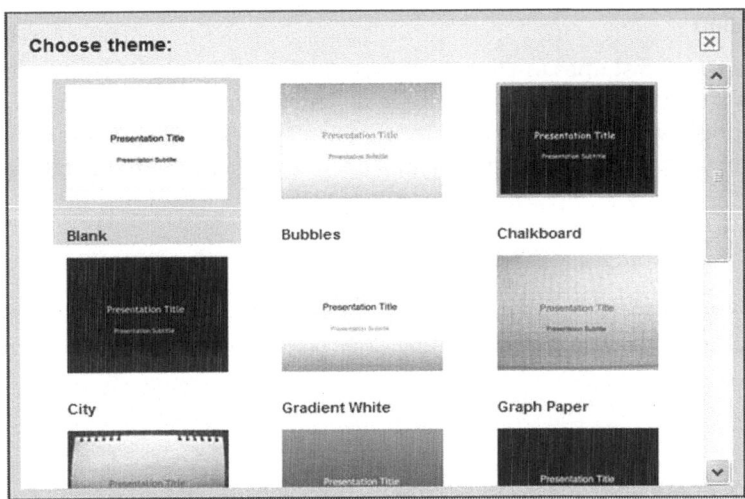

Figure 5-19. *Google Docs offers a variety of theme templates for your slides.*

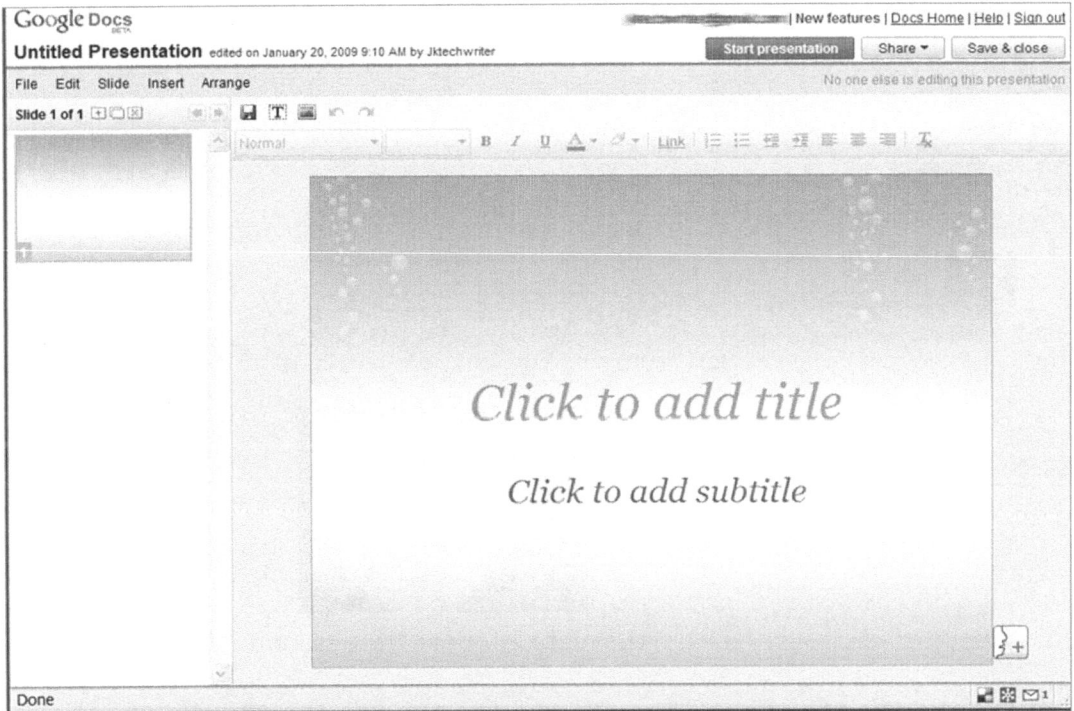

Figure 5-20. *Change the background to something more visually appealing.*

You can change the background template as many times as you like, and the change will be applied to all the slides in your presentation file.

Insert a Picture and Video

You can insert text, images, and shapes in your Presentation slides. Google Docs also allows you to insert video, but it must be hosted on youtube.com. The video in your presentation will be sent from YouTube's web service (another form of SaaS provision!). This means that in order for the videos in your slide show to play, you'll need to present them on an Internet-connected computer.

■**Note** A big difference between Google Docs Presentation and OpenOffice.org Impress is that Impress will let you save your presentations offline. With Presentation, important parts of your presentation will stay on Google's servers.

Here's how to add a photo and video:

1. With your slide open in Presentation, select Insert ➤ Image. Browse to the location of the desired image and click the OK button. Your photo will be inserted into the slide, as shown in Figure 5-21. You can resize and move the photo as desired.

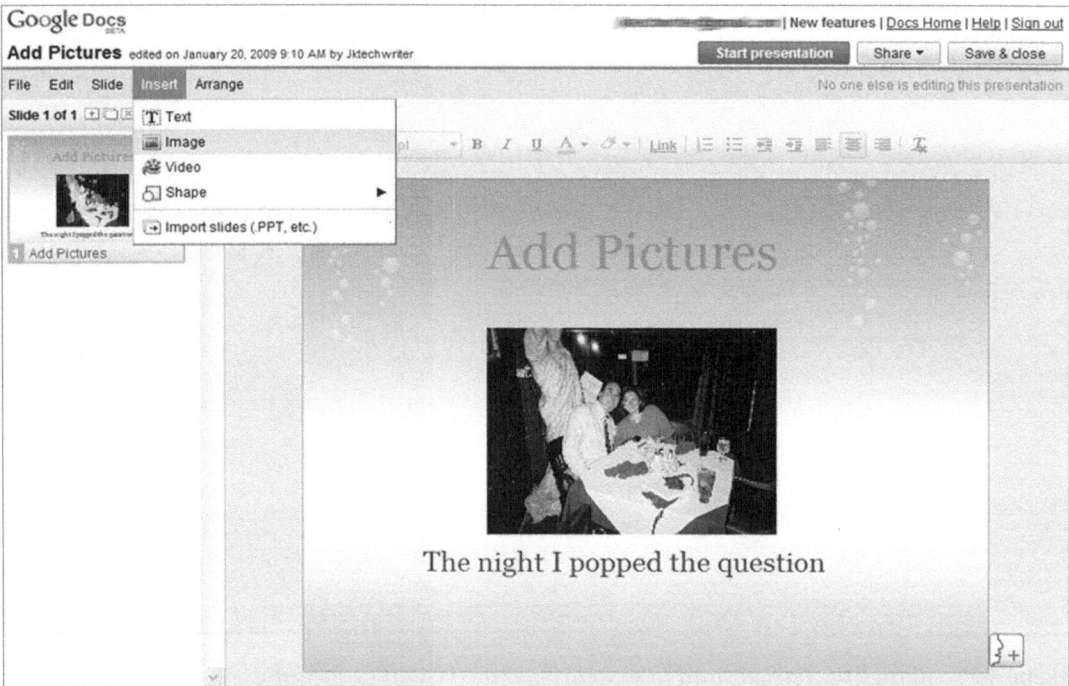

Figure 5-21. *Inserting images is simple using Presentation.*

2. Select Insert ➤ Video. Browse to the YouTube video you wish to insert (use the Search feature to find a specific video), and place a check mark next to it, as shown in Figure 5-22. Click the Insert Video button to insert the video.

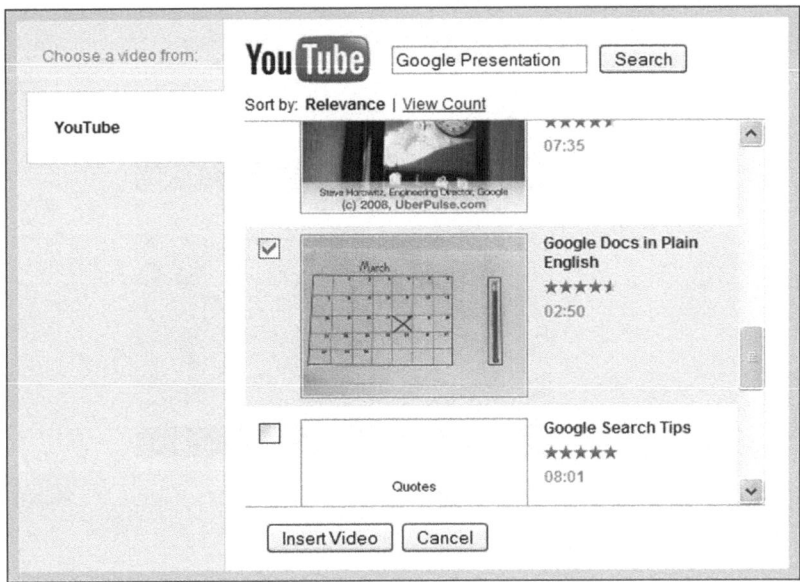

Figure 5-22. *Insert YouTube videos into your Presentation.*

3. Your video will be placed in the slide, as shown in Figure 5-23. You can resize and move it as desired.

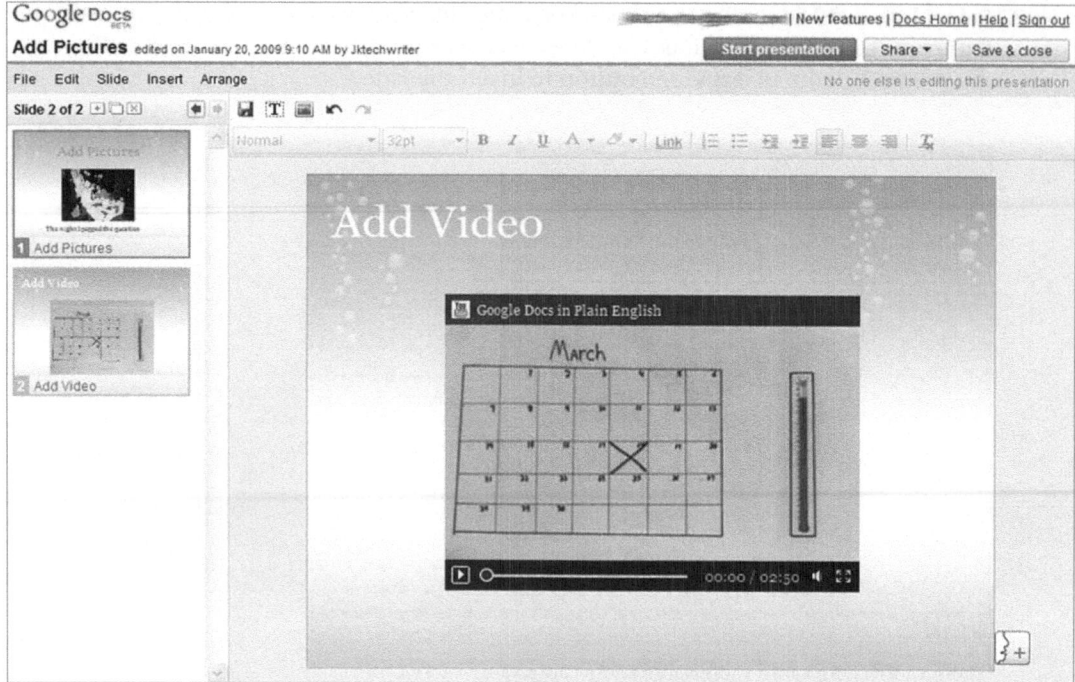

Figure 5-23. *Your video will be embedded into your slide show.*

Publish Your Presentation

You can publish your Presentation slide show and make it available to anyone with Internet access, as follows:

1. Click the Share button in the upper-right corner of the Google Docs screen and select the Publish/embed option, as shown in Figure 5-24.

2. Click the Publish document button. You will be given the URL link to e-mail to those you wish to see your slide show, as shown in Figure 5-25. You also have the opportunity to change the size of the presentation (the choices are small, medium, or large). HTML code is provided so you can embed it (place not only a link, but the full slide show) in a blog or web site. Click the Stop publishing button if you no longer want to share the slide show.

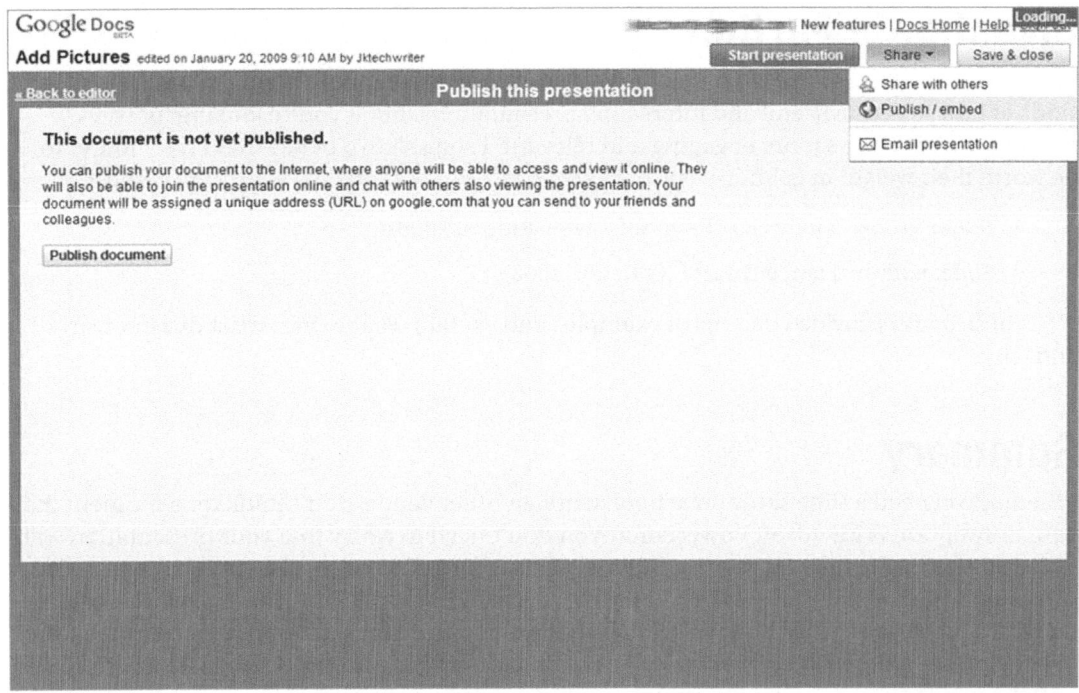

Figure 5-24. *Publish your slide show to share your creation with the world.*

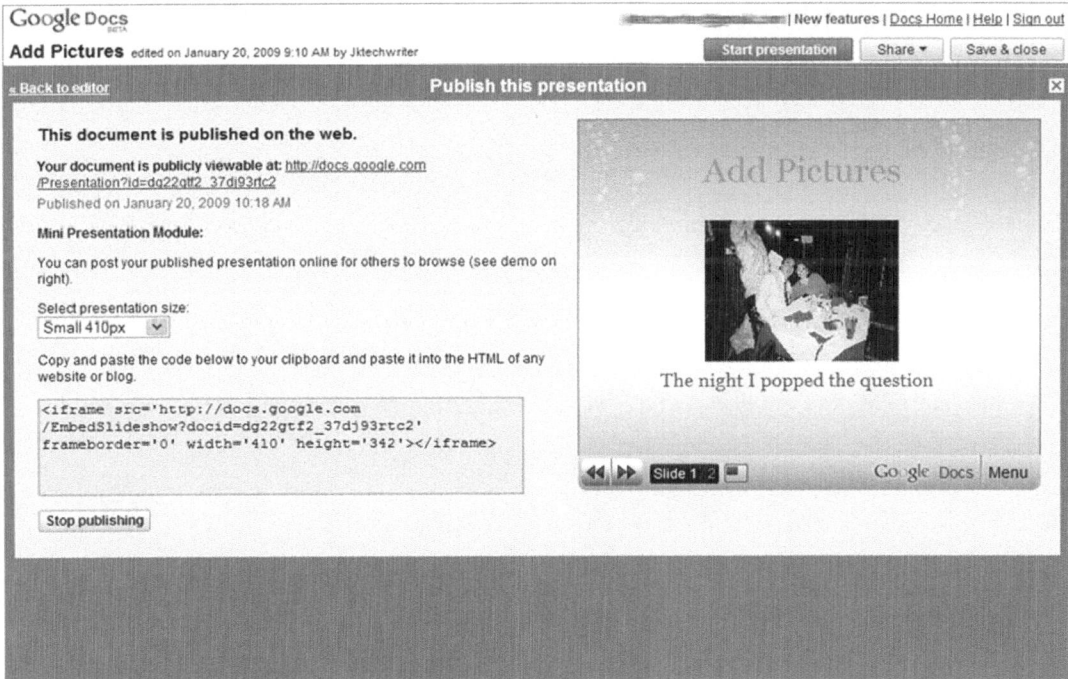

Figure 5-25. *Options are provided for sharing your presentation.*

Investigate Further

Slide shows are an art form all to themselves. Of course, you can find plenty of online discussions of how to create useful and interesting presentations. But if you're looking for ways to make your slide shows more engaging and relevant, I suggest two books that I have found to be worth their weight in gold:

- *Presentation Zen* by Garr Reynolds (New Riders, 2008)
- *Slide:ology* by Nancy Duarte (O'Reilly, 2008)

These books provide you tons of examples and explain what works, what doesn't work, and why.

Summary

Whether you need a slide show for school, work, or other venue, don't think for a moment that your only option is Microsoft PowerPoint. You don't need to worry that your presentation will lack eye-catching features if you use Impress. This OpenOffice.org application has a ton of features that will give your slide shows plenty of punch and polish. If you don't need a lot of glitz and glamour in your slide show, you'll find that Google Docs Presentation has enough features to get your slide show up and running in a minimum of time. And the ability to share your Presentation slide show over the Internet immediately is a huge bonus!

- Microsoft PowerPoint: $229 (or $400 bundled with Microsoft Office 2007 Standard)
- OpenOffice.org Impress: $0
- Google Docs Presentation: $0

■ ■ ■

CHAPTER 6

E-Mail and Calendar

I love e-mail. And I love my calendar application. E-mail helps me to keep in touch with my family and friends (and my editor, a member of both groups). My calendar reminds me where I'm supposed to be or what's due and at what time (the Chapter 6 draft is due tomorrow!). My calendar will even send an e-mail message to me as a reminder (or a text message to my mobile phone, if I prefer)—how cool is that?

One day it hit me how dependent I had become on both of these applications. Like my mobile phone and my vehicle, my e-mail and calendar tools had become indispensable to both my personal life and my work. And just like losing my mobile phone or having the car in the shop for repairs, if my e-mail and calendar were to become unavailable, I would quickly become stressed and unproductive.

I never gave much thought to having reliable access to my e-mail and calendar. I was using Microsoft Outlook, one of the most widely used personal information management applications (PIM, for short). My e-mail was stored on my laptop's hard drive, as was my address book and my calendar. Everything was going smoothly. And then my Outlook application crashed.

I was able to recover most of my e-mail and all of my contacts, but not my calendar information. It took hours of work, and my stress levels were off the chart. A few weeks later, a friend at my favorite coffee shop (with free Wi-Fi Internet access) listened as I told him this horror story. He pulled out his laptop and proceeded to introduce me to Google's e-mail application, Gmail, and Google Calendar. An hour later, I was a convert. And you may be, too, by the end of this chapter.

The Defender

I never thought I would walk away from Microsoft Outlook. It's a popular application and comes bundled with Microsoft Office. "Light" versions—Outlook Express or Microsoft Mail—come installed as the default e-mail client on most Windows computers. Since I was paying big bucks for Microsoft Word, Excel, and PowerPoint, it would be a waste of money not to load and use Outlook, right?

Outlook is definitely the king when it comes to e-mail, address book, and calendar features. After you install Outlook, it can be configured to receive your e-mail, and you can begin adding contact information to your address book. You can create filters (special rules that can help you eliminate junk e-mail or send special e-mail messages to specific locations). You can create a signature (with your name, phone number, and web site address, for example) to appear automatically at the bottom of all your sent messages. You can add appointments to your calendar. (A complete list of the features found in the latest version of Microsoft Outlook can be found at http://www.microsoft.com/outlook.)

Outlook's user interface uses a familiar folder storage design (which some users find cluttered—this author included), as shown in Figure 6-1. E-mail messages are placed inside folders with names such as Deleted Items, Sent Items, and Inbox. Clicking a folder on the left side of the screen displays that folder's messages in the middle of the screen. Clicking a message allows you to view its contents on the right side of the screen, or you can double-click to open the message in full-screen view.

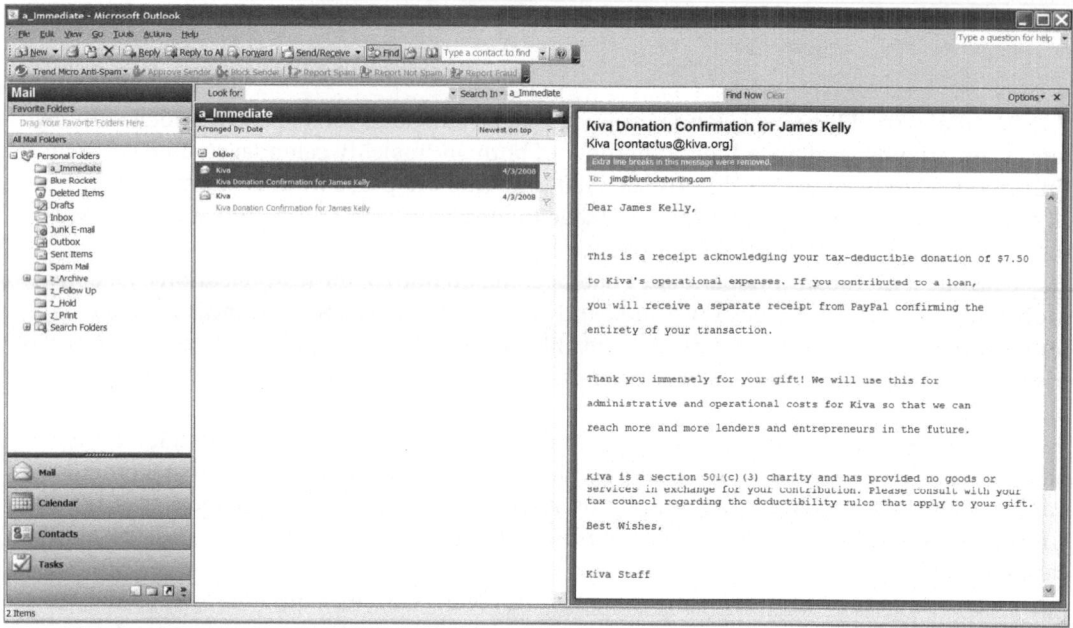

Figure 6-1. *Outlook uses a folder hierarchy to store e-mail.*

But here's the main problem with Outlook (besides the fact that it is expensive): your data—every bit of it—is stored on your hard drive. This means that if you want to send an e-mail message, check your calendar, or find a contact's phone number, you need to be sitting at your computer. Basically, if you're sitting at a friend's computer or using an Internet kiosk, access to your Outlook e-mail and calendar just isn't possible.

Yes, there are options for accessing Outlook, but for most users, they aren't practical. For example, you could use remote access to your computer (medium difficulty and involves configuring your computer to allow another computer to access your hard drive) or use Microsoft Exchange Server to hold your data (high difficulty and expensive to purchase as well as maintain).

Outlook has several other drawbacks:

- A lot of experienced users don't like the way that Outlook is coded. By modern standards, it's a real resource hog. To see for yourself (if you're running Outlook), press Ctrl+Alt+Del, click Task Manager, and click the Processes tab. Typically, you'll find that OUTLOOK.EXE is taking up 40MB to 50MB of system RAM.

- By default, Outlook plays a "mail-received" sound and pops up an e-mail alert in the lower-right corner of your screen. Besides being irritating, these messages are very high priority, so they may pop up in the middle of a movie or while you're playing a game.

- Searching for a specific e-mail message can be time-consuming if you have a lot of messages. Outlook does provide a search tool that allows you to search all folders at once, but it isn't as powerful or fast as the one provided by Google for its Gmail application.

As for Microsoft Outlook's calendar, I can say that while it is a powerful tool with plenty of features, I would still prefer to be able to access it from any computer or my mobile phone. And I'm not willing to spend the money to rent a server and install my own copy of Microsoft Exchange Server on it ($699 for the standard version) or purchase the server hardware and Windows Server 2007 operating system software ($2,000 or more) to run Exchange and have those options!

Because Outlook comes with Microsoft Office, most people get their first experience with e-mail and a calendar by using this PIM at work. That familiarity with Outlook typically makes it the first consideration for a home computer. But Outlook isn't the only game in town.

If you read about Google Docs in the previous chapters, you probably will not be surprised to learn that Google has an e-mail application and calendar application that are both free, easy to use, and unbelievably powerful.

The Contenders

Google's e-mail application, Gmail, and Google Calendar are both completely free, and they might change the way you deal with e-mail and scheduling. Both applications are SaaS and available from any web browser, including mobile phone browsers, with Internet access.

Here, I'll give you a brief overview of each application. Later in the chapter, I'll show you some more sample tasks that are sure to convince you to give Gmail and Google Calendar a try.

Gmail

Gmail is an online e-mail application that is offered as a free service by Google. You can access Gmail from any computer (or mobile phone) with Internet connectivity. It offers more storage space than most people will ever need: currently 7GB per user (and Google is always increasing that number). Consider that most corporate e-mail administrators will cap employee inbox size at 2GB or 3GB. If you exceed your quota, you need to either erase messages or archive your old mail. In contrast, Gmail's storage space is so big you can use it as file storage!

Gmail stores all of your active e-mail in the Inbox container, as shown in Figure 6-2. There are no folders. This can take some getting used to initially, but once you understand a bit more about Gmail's capabilities, you won't give it another thought.

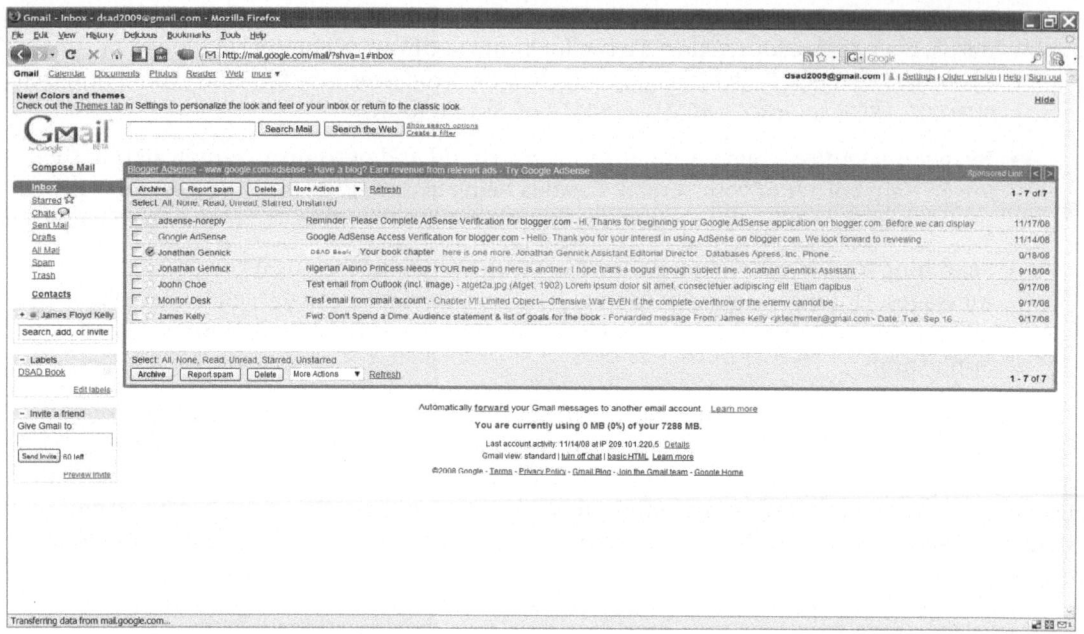

Figure 6-2. *Gmail displays your e-mail and shows how much storage space is available.*

Gmail offers all the standard features you would expect in an e-mail application, such as the ability to send attachments, add a signature, and so on. You'll also find a basic contacts tool that lets you store a contact's e-mail address, phone number, and physical address information, as well as a built-in instant messaging/chat application.

Google is constantly updating Gmail, adding a new feature or two just about monthly. You can enable or disable features to suit your preferences. In the "Gmail Features" section later in this chapter, I'll show you how to view the optional features and enable those that you find interesting.

Tip Google's programmers added a new feature just recently that feels like it was made just for me. I frequently forget to include an attachment with my messages. Gmail's new Forgotten Attachment Detector now pops up an alert when it detects words such as *attach*, *attachment*, or *attached* in the text of a message. Outlook doesn't do that! The Forgotten Attachment Detector can be enabled from the Labs tab of the Gmail Settings screen (click the Settings link in the upper-right corner of the Gmail screen to display the Settings screen).

Using Gmail is easy, and most of its features are fairly intuitive. If you need assistance, just click the Help link in the upper-right corner of the screen (see Figure 6-2). Google provides help files as well as access to a special Gmail forum, where you can post questions and get answers from other Gmail users and sometimes even Google programmers.

Google Calendar

I'm secretly addicted to Google Calendar. This amazing and free tool keeps this scatterbrained writer organized, informed, and on time for my daily appointments and deadlines. I can access my calendar from any computer whenever I like. I can access it from my mobile phone. It e-mails me reminders. Calendar lets me schedule new events by sending it text messages. It updates automatically with my favorite TV shows and sporting events. And it plays a mean game of Snake (available from Labs tab of the Settings screen, accessed by clicking the Settings link in the upper-right corner of the Gmail screen)!

Google Calendar is one of many Google applications that are available to you once you're logged in to your Google account. Look along the top left-edge of the screen, and you'll notice Gmail, Calendar, Documents, Photos, and more available as links, as shown in Figure 6-3. Clicking a link will open that Google tool in its own window or tab.

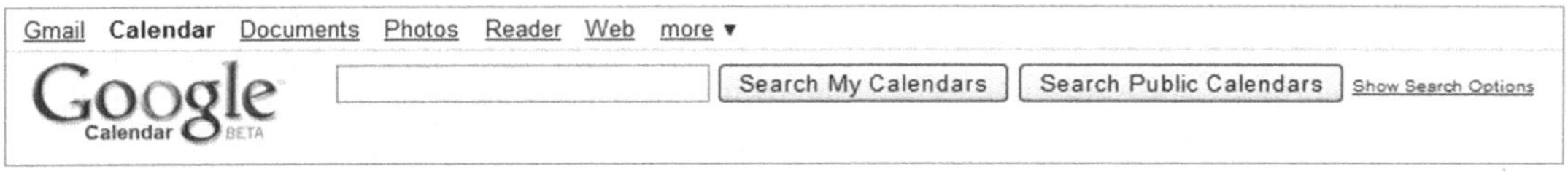

Figure 6-3. *Google Calendar is one of many free Google applications.*

Google Calendar allows you to view your calendar in various forms, including daily, weekly, and monthly views. You can create multiple calendars (such as a work calendar and a family calendar) and even make a calendar available for viewing by other Google users (such as a sports calendar for keeping up with your kids' games and practices). There's a lot of cool stuff you can do with a publicly shareable calendar that you might not have ever considered. For instance, I like to keep track of when *MythBusters* is on, so I can TiVo it or watch it with my son.

Google Calendar allows you to use multiple methods for entering new events in your calendar. You can enter them using the keyboard, send them via a text message from your mobile phone, and even add them from within an e-mail. And Google Calendar has the same level of online help available as Gmail, if you should need it.

Where to Get the Software

Gmail and Google Calendar do not require you to install any software. Both applications are tied together, however, so you cannot use Calendar without a Gmail account.

Gmail

Gmail is a SaaS, so there's no software to install. Follow these simple instructions to get started using it:

1. Visit `http://mail.google.com`.

2. Click the Sign up for Gmail button.

3. Follow the instructions to create your Google account.

4. Once your account is created, log in to Gmail.

Google Calendar

There's no software to install to use Google Calendar either. Follow these steps to access and use it:

1. Once you log in to Gmail, you can access Google Calendar by clicking the Calendar link along the top-left edge of the screen (see Figure 6-3). Calendar will open in its own window or tab.

2. If you've never used Google Calendar before, provide the additional information requested, and then click the Continue button to open the application.

Notes on Basic Usage

Gmail and Google Calendar are incredibly intuitive to use, but a lot of the neatest features are hidden away behind a clean "only-what-you-need-to-see" web interface. Here, we'll take a look at some of the basics of using these applications. In the upcoming "E-mail and Calendar Features" section, we'll explore some of the other interesting features available.

Gmail

If you're familiar with Outlook or another e-mail application, using Gmail may feel a little strange at first, but its unique interface will quickly become easy for you to navigate and use.

Figure 6-4 shows the basic Gmail interface. On the top-left side of the screen is a Compose Mail link. I'll give you two guesses as to what that link does for you.

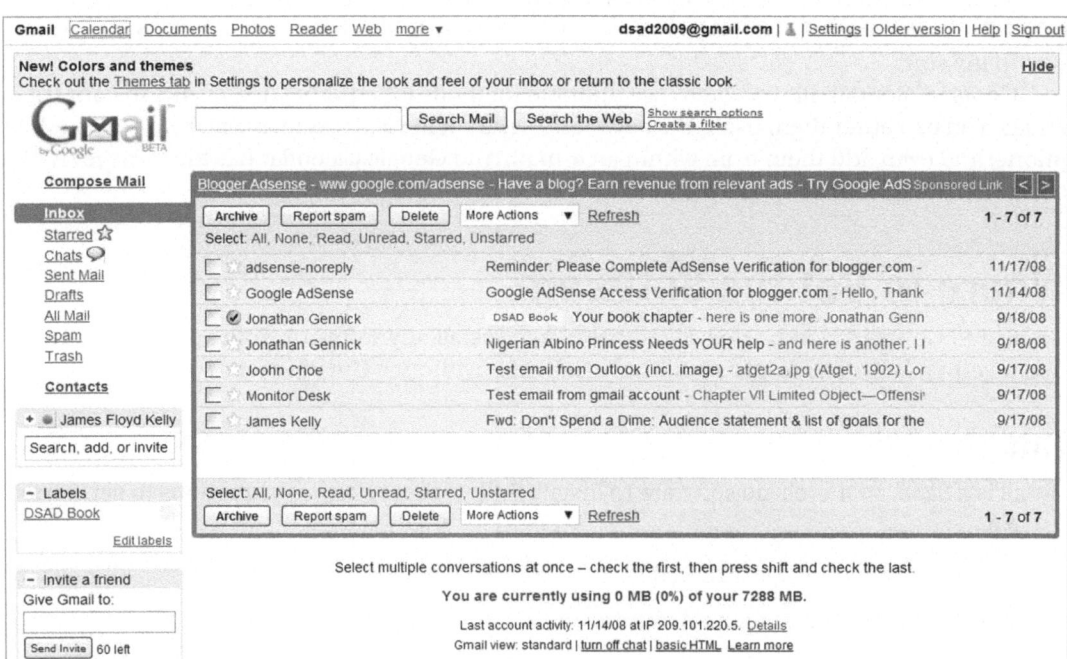

Figure 6-4. *Google Mail has a unique user interface but it's extremely easy to use.*

Below the Compose Mail link is a list that includes Inbox, Starred, Chats, Sent Mail, Drafts, All Mail, Spam, and Trash links. For now, just think of these as folders that you can click to see what's inside. Most of the labels are self-explanatory. Chats will keep an archive of any chat discussions you have. Starred will allow you to filter all your mail and display only those messages you have starred.

When you first open Gmail, your Inbox is selected, and any e-mail you have in the Inbox will be displayed. Notice that each e-mail message has a check box, a small star icon, the name of the sender, subject line (with a short preview of the first few words in each message), and the date or time of the e-mail.

The check box allows you to select a single message or multiple messages before performing an action (such as deleting messages or marking messages as unread). The check boxes are also handy when applying a label to multiple messages, as you'll see in the "Gmail Features" section later in this chapter.

The star provides a nice visual reminder of important messages, for example. Click the star icon for e-mail that you want to mark (perhaps to follow up on later), and the star becomes a solid color, as shown in Figure 6-5. When you select the Starred link in the column on the left, only starred messages are displayed.

Tip If you really enjoy the star feature, you can extend it. Gmail lets you add new shapes and colors. Click the Settings link in the upper-right corner of the Gmail screen, and then click the Labs tab. Look for the Superstars add-on.

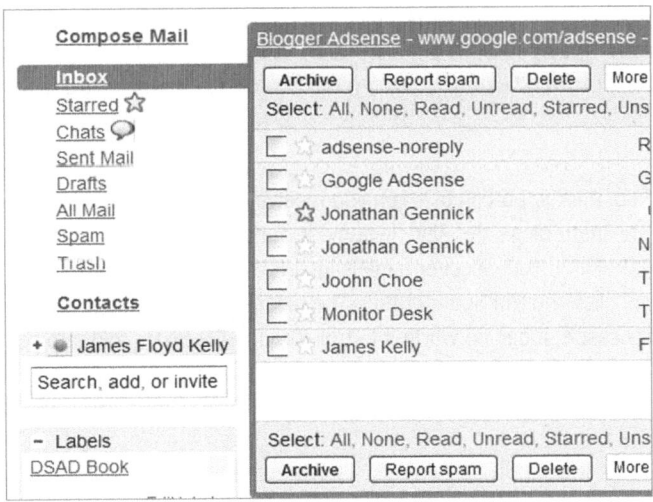

Figure 6-5. *Stars are useful for marking important messages that you don't want to forget.*

To open a message, simply click it, and it will appear in full-window view, as shown in Figure 6-6. You can print the message, reply to it, delete it, and so on, as typically offered by e-mail applications. Also notice the Archive button at the top of the message window.

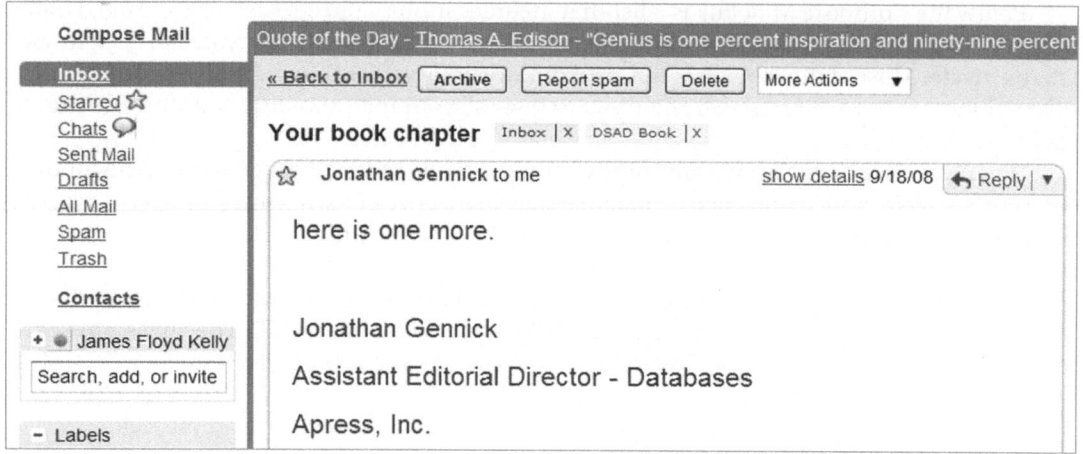

Figure 6-6. *You have many options available to you after reading an e-mail message.*

One of the containers that Gmail provides is All Mail. When you select Archive for an e-mail message, it goes into the All Mail list. Because Google gives you more than 7GB of e-mail storage space, this shouldn't be a problem for most users. How many times have you deleted a message and then months (or years) later wished you could have it back? Well, with the Archive ability and the All Mail section, you can push that e-mail out of your Inbox but not worry about it being deleted. That said, the Delete button doesn't really delete a message, but instead moves it to the Trash container. If you absolutely want to delete the e-mail in the Trash, click the Empty Trash now link (but use it with caution, because an e-mail deleted from the Trash is gone—period).

Also notice the Report Spam button. If you receive a piece of e-mail that is spam, click this button. The message will be moved to the Spam container, and that sender will be blocked from sending you any more e-mail. Additionally, Gmail's own spam filter will be updated.

Note While Gmail's spam filter will get rid of a large portion of spam you receive (it goes directly in the Spam container), it doesn't always catch every spam message. Also, in some instances, a legitimate message might be tagged as spam (by you or by Gmail). If you discover a message in the Spam container that isn't spam, simply place a check next to it and click the Not Spam button. The message will be put in your Inbox. If you think you've missed an e-mail message, it can be worth it to troll through the Spam folder to see if Gmail kicked it there by accident.

Google Calendar

My best suggestion for using Google Calendar is to learn a few shortcut keys. What I mean is that navigating Google Calendar and adding events/appointments is as easy as pressing a single key on your keyboard.

First, learn how to change the view of your calendar (daily, weekly, or monthly are the most popular). Google Calendar couldn't make this any easier. Just press the M key to change to monthly, W for weekly, and D for daily. If you don't want to use your keyboard, you can change views by using the tabs along the upper-right edge of the window, as shown in Figure 6-7.

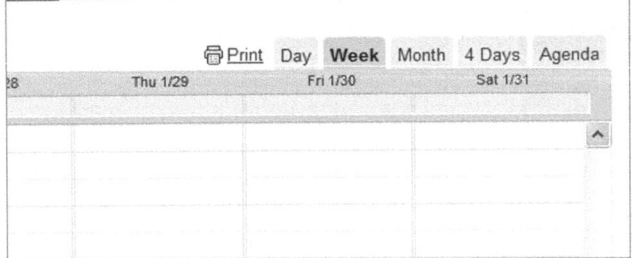

Figure 6-7. *Change your Calendar view to daily, weekly, monthly, or other layout.*

I prefer the monthly view and will use this view for the remainder of this chapter's Calendar discussions. So, for now, press the M key or select the Month tab before continuing.

One of the most important things you'll do with your calendar is add events. Google gives you two simple ways to add a new event to your calendar:

- Click the day or time to add an event. In Figure 6-8, I've clicked January 27 and added a new event called Truck Oil Change. Press the Enter key or click the Create Event button, and the event is created.

- Click the Quick Add link or press the Q key or your keyboard. The Quick Add box appears, as shown in Figure 6-9, where you can enter a description, time, and even a date. Press the Enter key, and the event will be added to your Calendar.

Figure 6-8. *Adding a new event is as simple as clicking a date in your Calendar.*

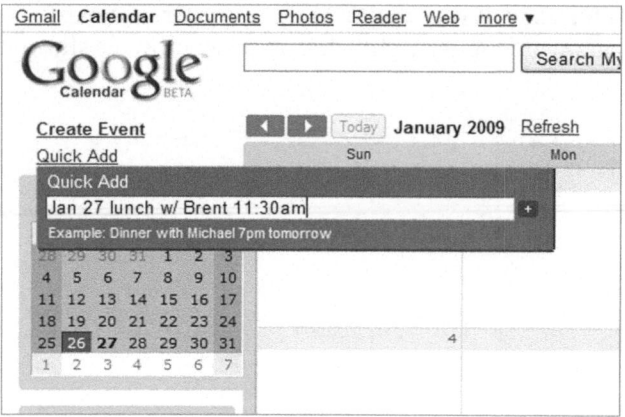

Figure 6-9. *The Quick Add feature allows you to specify exact details.*

You can change the description of an event or add more details by clicking the event and selecting the "edit event details" link, as shown in Figure 6-10. This will open a new window that will allow you to make changes and configure reminders and other settings (I'll cover the reminder and sharing options in the next section). When you're finished, click the Save button.

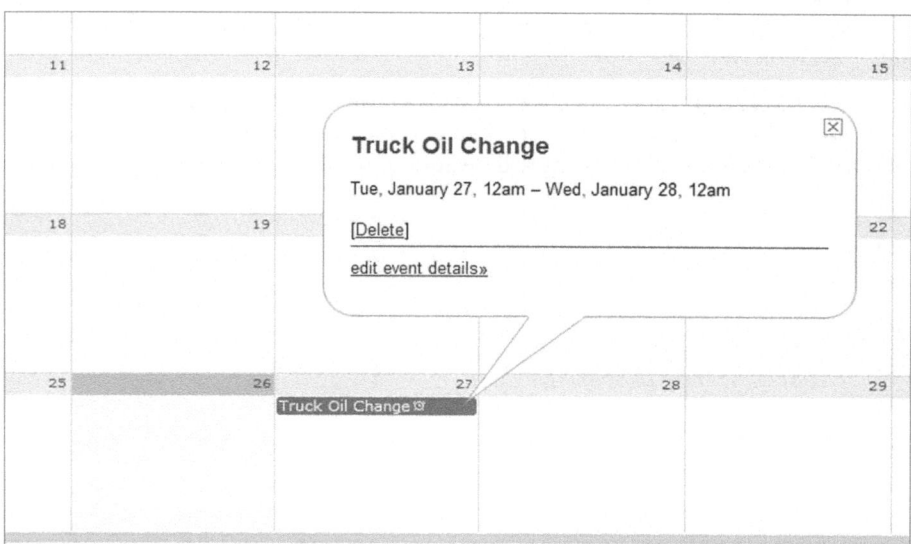

Figure 6-10. *Edit an event to provide more details such as time or location.*

To delete an event, click the event and select the Delete link. Confirm that you wish to delete the event, and it will be removed from your Calendar. You can also drag and drop an event from one date to another (click the event description, hold down your mouse button, and drag it to another day).

Like Gmail, Google Calendar is easy to use, and most of the features are fairly intuitive. It's hard to make a mistake in either tool, and assistance is just a click away using the Help link in the upper-right corner of both applications.

E-Mail and Calendar Features

There are many things you can do using Gmail and Google Calendar. I'll describe some of my favorites here. As you use these applications, you'll find that there are dozens of other hidden gems. Gmail and Google Calendar are certainly worth getting to know!

Gmail Features

Gmail offers some powerful features that can help you handle your e-mail. Here, we'll look at how to use Gmail labels, enable and disable options, and add a contact.

Set Up and Use Labels

As you've seen, Gmail doesn't use folders, as are used in Outlook and many other e-mail applications, but don't let this dissuade you from trying it out. Gmail provides a feature called *labels* that, in my opinion, works even better. Here's how to create and use labels with your Gmail messages:

1. From the Gmail screen, click the Edit labels link, as shown in Figure 6-11.

Figure 6-11. *Click the Edit labels link to add a label.*

2. Enter a description of the label, as shown in Figure 6-12, and then click the Create button. Create as many labels as you like.

3. Return to your Inbox. Notice that your new label appears under the Labels section on the left.

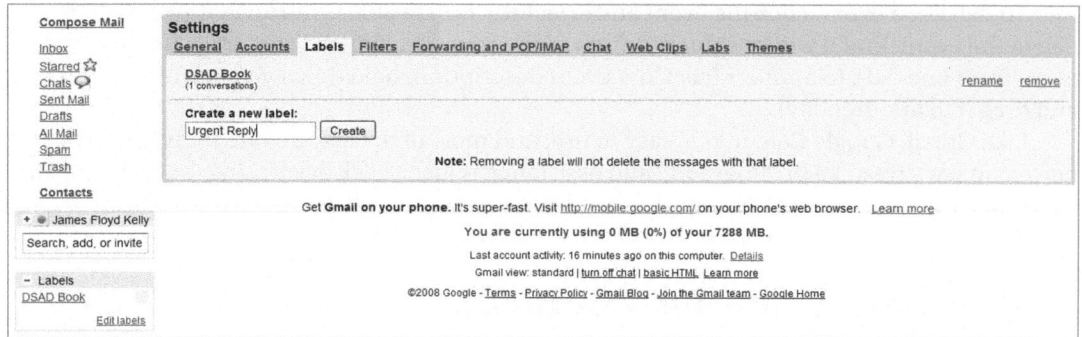

Figure 6-12. *Enter a description for your label.*

4. Place a check in the box next to a message you wish to label.

5. From the More Actions drop-down menu, select your new label, as shown in Figure 6-13. The message you checked will now contain the color-coded label, as shown in Figure 6-14.

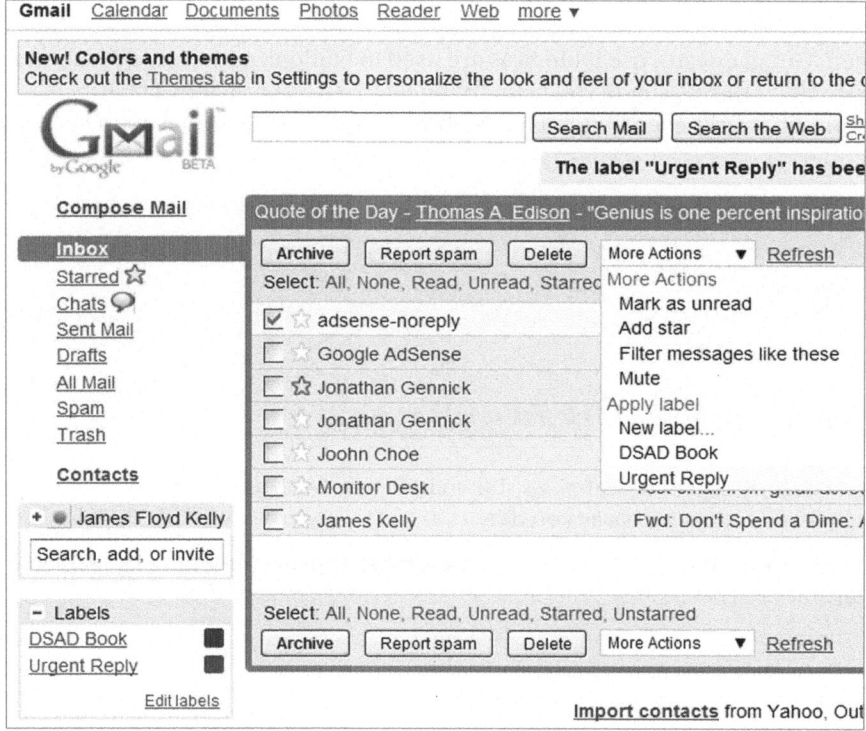

Figure 6-13. *Add a label to an e-mail message to make it more visible and searchable.*

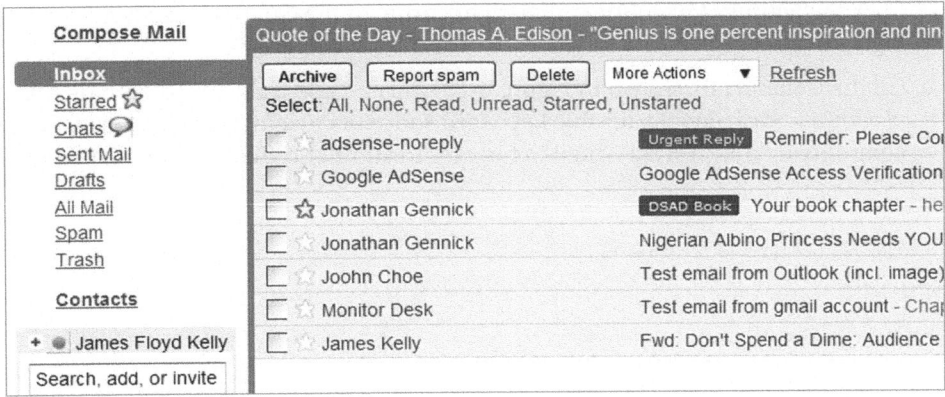

Figure 6-14. *Your label is added to the e-mail message, preceding the subject.*

Create multiple labels and assign them to your messages. They make e-mail messages easier to pick out of your Inbox. Additionally, you can use each label as a filter (to view only those messages that contain that label) by clicking the label's name, as shown in Figure 6-15.

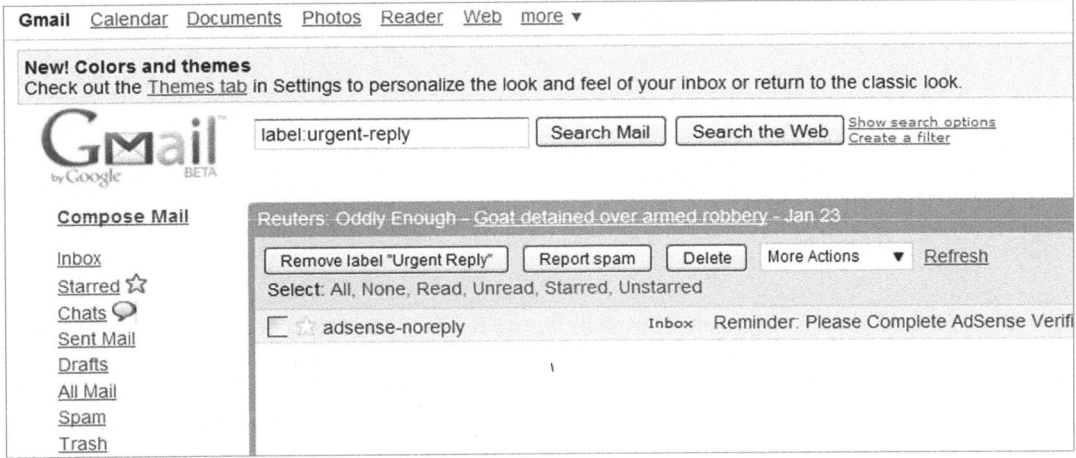

Figure 6-15. *Use labels to filter your messages.*

You can edit your labels and change the name assigned to them by clicking the Edit labels link (see Figure 6-12).

View and Enable/Disable Special Options

Gmail offers many special options that you can turn on and off to suit your preferences. Follow these steps to view these options and turn enable or disable them:

1. Click the Settings link in the upper-right corner of the Gmail screen (refer back to Figure 6-4).

2. On the General tab, shown in Figure 6-16, you can add a signature, turn on and off a vacation notice, enable/disable keyboard shortcuts (useful for assigning special keys to common actions), set up Gmail to forward to another e-mail address, and more.

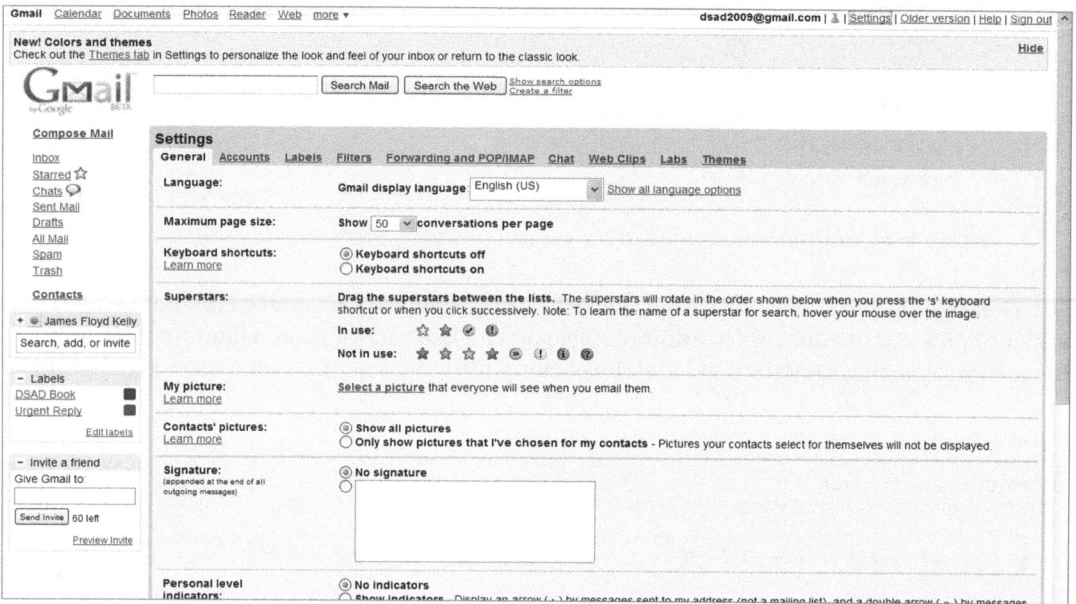

Figure 6-16. *The General tab of Gmail's Settings screen has many special features you can use or ignore.*

3. Click the Labs tab. This tab, shown in Figure 6-17, contains experimental features that Google allows you to enable or disable. Click the Learn more about Gmail Labs link if you need help or more information about a specific feature. Click the Enable or Disable radio button to turn on or off a feature. In the example in Figure 6-17, the Superstars feature is enabled. This gives you additional stars and colors to mark your messages.

4. Click the Save Changes button at the bottom of the Settings screen after making your selections.

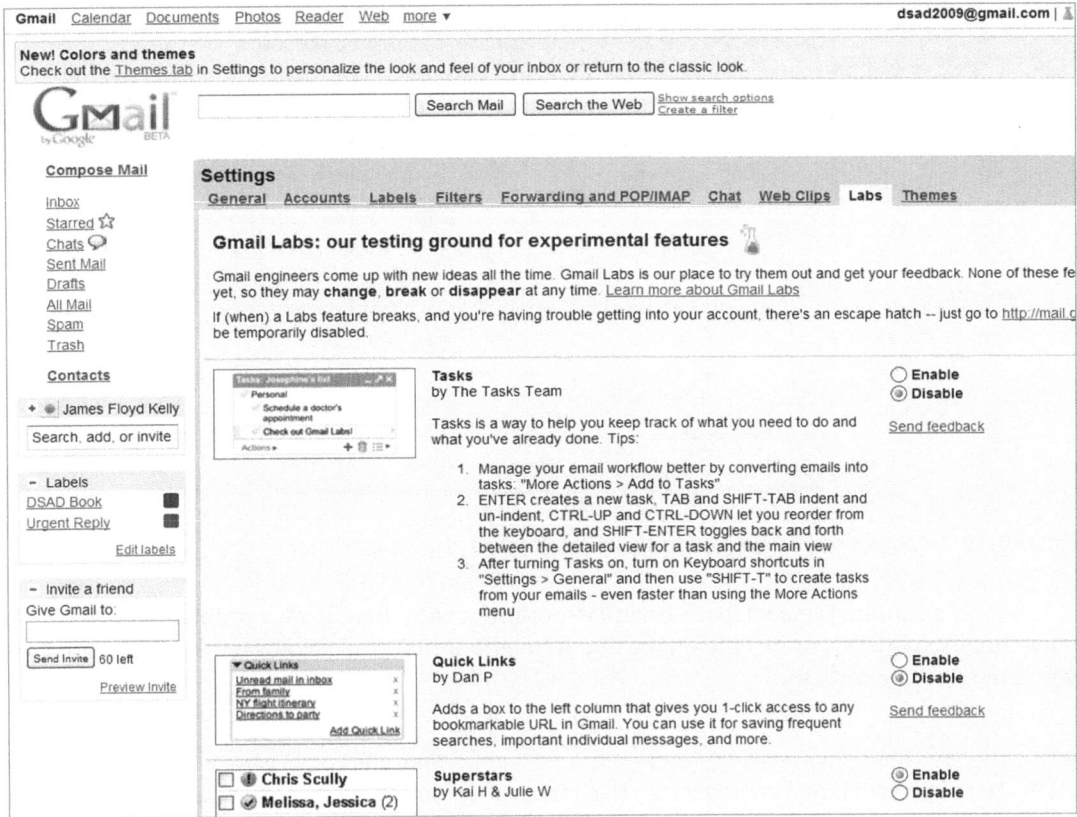

Figure 6-17. *Select the Enable or Disable button for specific Gmail Lab features.*

After enabling the Superstars feature, for example, you can select additional icons (clear star, yellow star, blue star, green check mark, red exclamation, and clear) by clicking the mouse and cycling through the options to the left of the sender's name back in the Inbox. Figure 6-18 shows the result of selecting the green check mark for a message from Google AdSense.

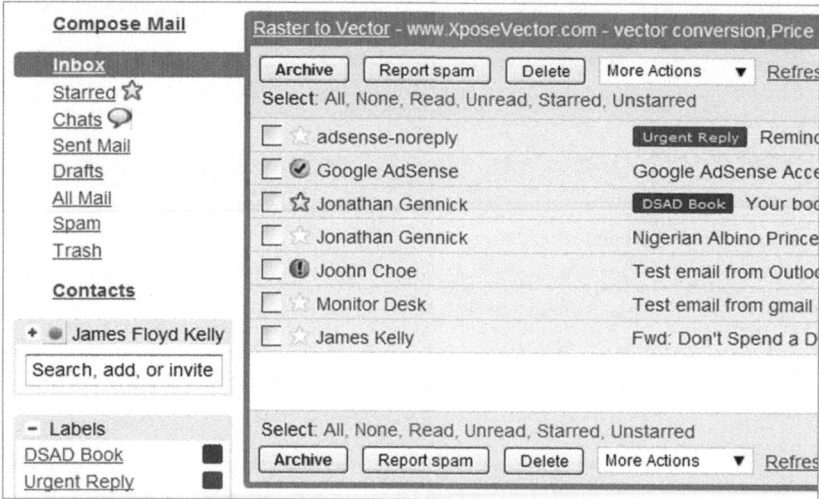

Figure 6-18. *Messages can be flagged with starts, colored circles, and more.*

Enable additional special features and experiment with them to determine if they make your Gmail experience more efficient or fun. Remember that you can always disable them if you don't find them useful.

■**Tip** You might want to also investigate the Themes tab of the Gmail Settings screen, which can give your Gmail user interface an interesting new look.

Add a Contact

Gmail isn't going to be useful to you without some friends, family members, and work colleagues to receive e-mail. Follow these steps to start building your contact list:

1. Click the Contacts link in the Gmail screen (refer back to Figure 6-4). The contacts management screen will appear, as shown in Figure 6-19.

Note Gmail will automatically add anyone you e-mail to your Suggested Contacts list, so your list may or may not be empty at this point. However, only those people in your My Contacts list will show up on the contact list in the screen shown in Figure 6-19.

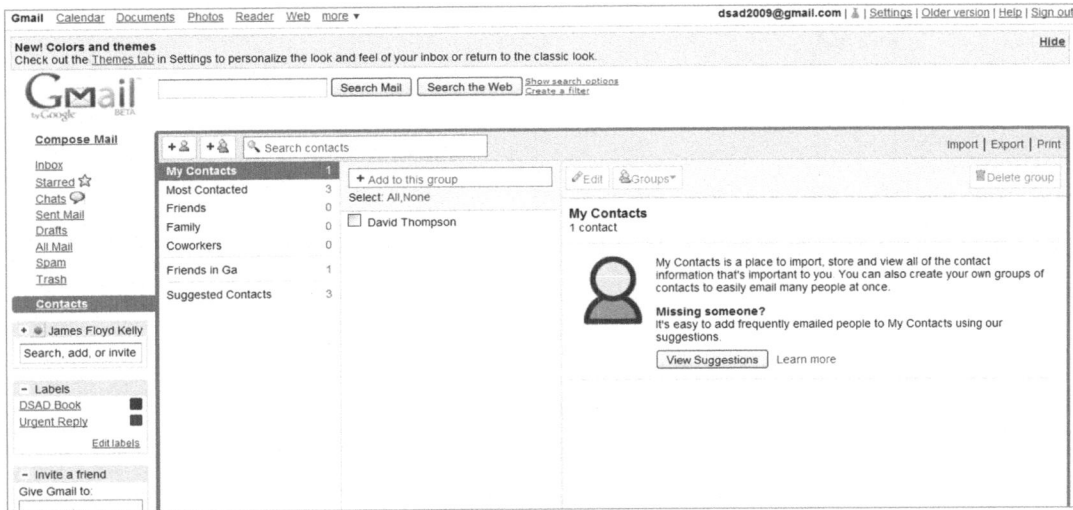

Figure 6-19. *The contacts management screen*

2. To add a new contact, click the New Contact button, as shown in Figure 6-20. Enter information for that contact, and then click the Save button.

3. Your new contact will be added to the My Contacts list, as shown in Figure 6-21. Click the Add a picture link to browse and assign a photo of the contact. You can also click the Groups button to assign the contact to any special groups (or click New group to create a group and add this contact). If you later want to remove this contact, click the Delete contact button.

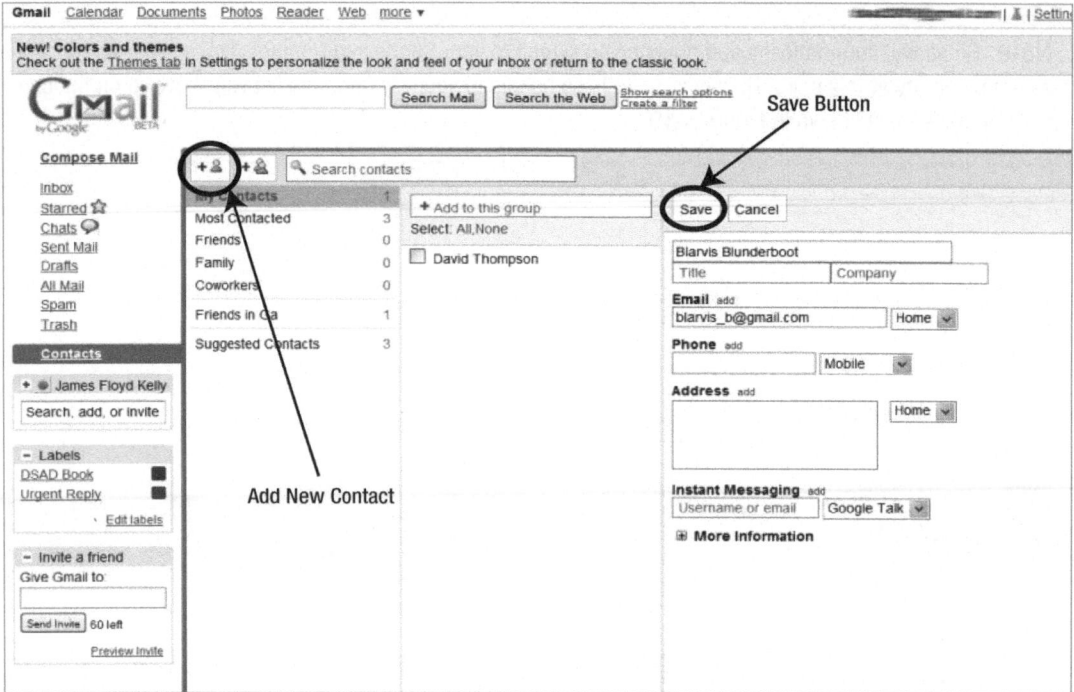

Figure 6-20. *Click the New Contact button to add a new contact, enter contact information, and then click the Save button.*

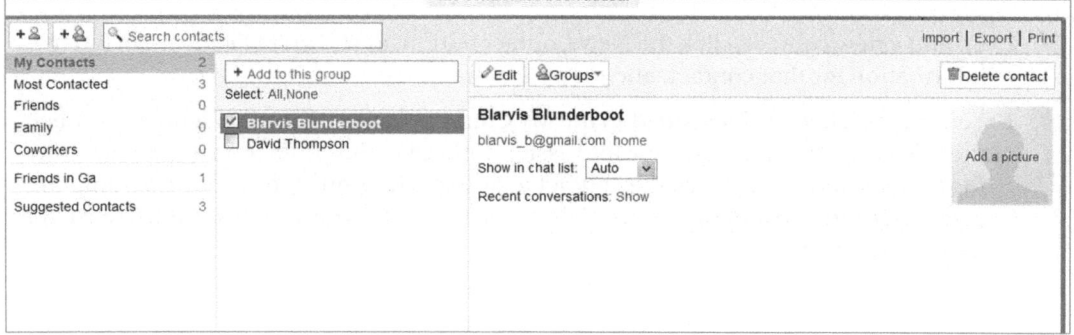

Figure 6-21. *A new contact added to the Contacts management screen*

Your contacts will also be available from the main Gmail screen. Simply hover your mouse over the contact to see the options available. More features to investigate with your contacts include viewing Google Map directions to a contact, adding the contact to your Chat list, and viewing recent chat conversations. You can easily start a chat session from the main screen this way. (Some people leave the Gmail chat window open all day, as a type of mini-mailbox.)

Google Calendar Features

The real strength of Google Calendar lies in how easy it can make your life—maybe in ways you might never have considered! At its best, Google Calendar is like having a personal assistant to keep your schedule.

Create an Appointment with Text Messaging

One of my favorite features of Google Calendar is the ability to add appointments even when I'm not sitting in front of a computer.

If your mobile phone supports sending and receiving text messages, you can create a new Calendar event by texting a description, time, and date to GVENT (48368), as shown in Figure 6-22. Google Calendar will send you a reply text message indicating the event was successfully added. The next time you view Calendar, you will see the new event, as shown in Figure 6-23.

Figure 6-22. *Send a text message to GVENT (48368) to add an event to Google Calendar.*

Figure 6-23. *Your text message event will be added to your Google Calendar.*

Receive Text Message Reminders on Your Mobile Phone

To receive reminders on your mobile phone, you must first enable Google to communicate with your mobile phone. Here's how to set up the communication and choose to get reminders:

1. Click the Settings link in the upper-right corner of the Google Calendar screen.

2. In the Settings screen, click the Mobile Setup tab.

3. Select your country, enter your phone number, and select your Carrier from the drop-down list. Then click the Send Verification Code button.

4. The code will be sent to your mobile phone. Enter that code in the Mobile Setup tab. You will see a "Phone number successfully validated" message, as shown in Figure 6-24. Click the Save button.

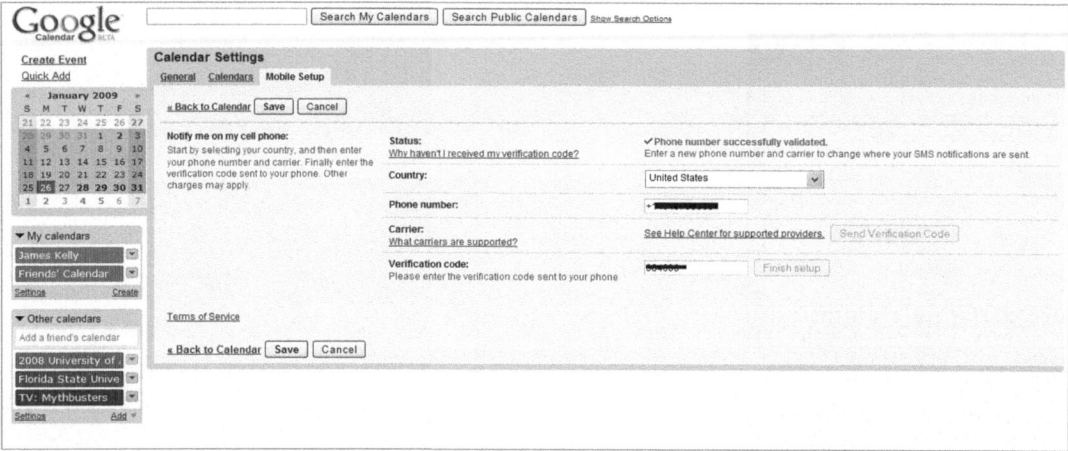

Figure 6-24. *The Mobile Setup tab allows you to set up your mobile phone to receive text message reminders.*

5. Click an event on your calendar and select the "edit event details" link.

6. The event's details screen will open. In the Options section, select SMS from one of the reminder drop-down menus, as shown in Figure 6-25. (Alternatively, you can click the Add a reminder link to add Email as another option for notification, in addition to Pop-Up and SMS). Next, select minutes, hours, or days from the drop-down menu, and enter a specific numeric value. Click the Save button to enable the reminder.

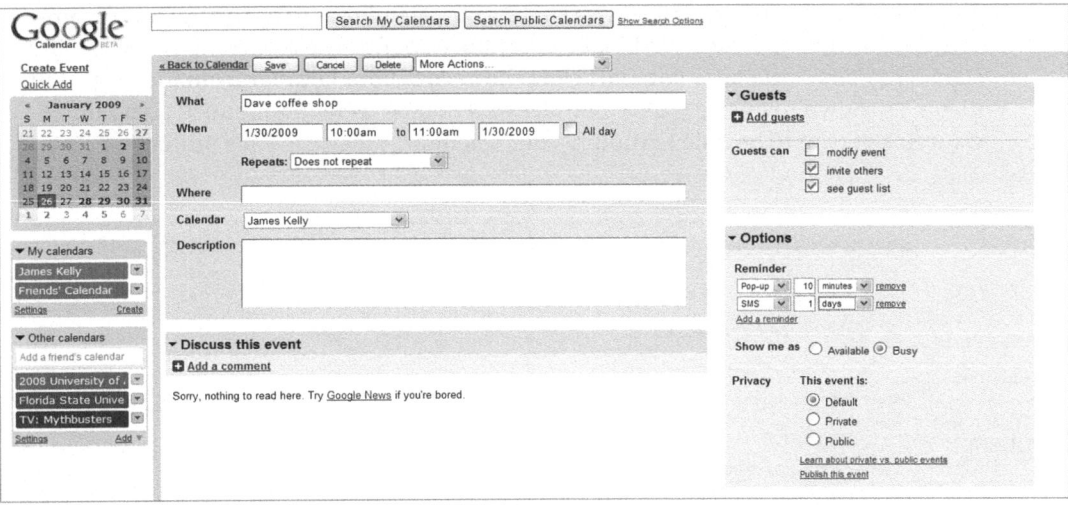

Figure 6-25. *Use SMS and a time (in minutes, hours, or days) to notify you in advance.*

Share Your Calendar

What's great about Google Calendar is that you can make your calendar viewable by others using an HTML web page. Here's how:

1. Click the Settings link in the upper-right corner of the Google Calendar screen.

2. Click the Calendars tab, as shown in Figure 6-26.

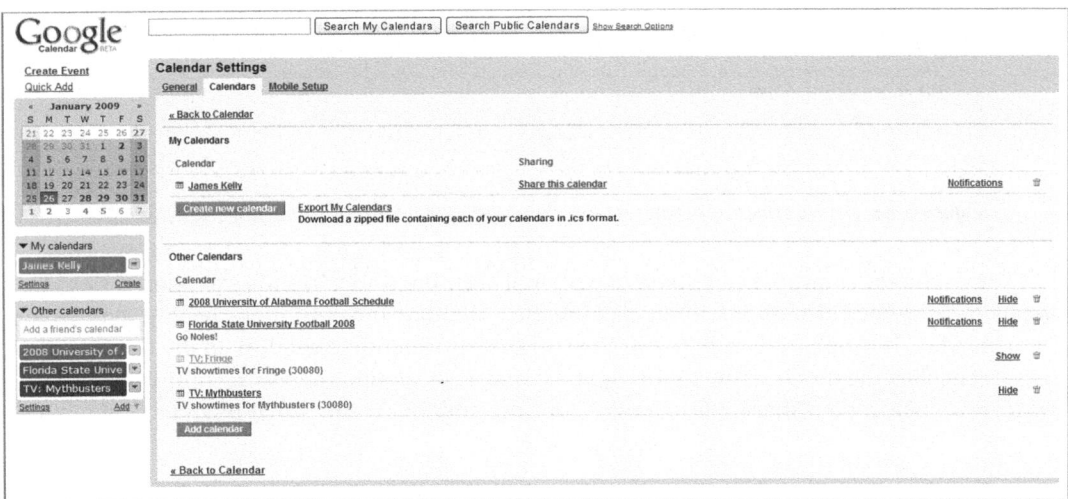

Figure 6-26. *The Calendars tab offers the option to share your calendar.*

3. Click the Share this calendar link.

4. You will see a screen that will let you share your calendar with everyone (not recommended) or with specific individuals. Enter the e-mail address of someone who will be allowed to view your calendar and select the permissions settings from the drop-down menu, as shown in Figure 6-27. ("See all event details" is recommended if you don't want this person to be able to modify your calendar.) Click the Save button.

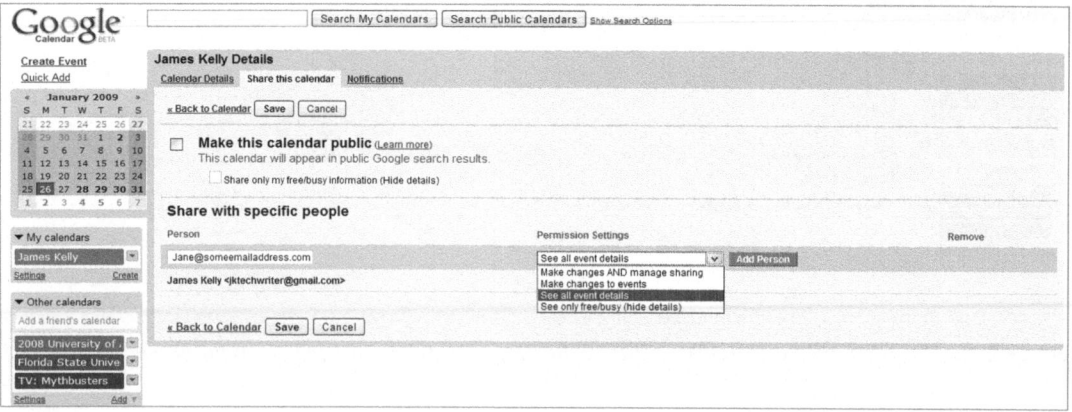

Figure 6-27. *Select permissions for sharing your calendar.*

5. If the person you are giving access to your calendar does not have a Google Calendar account, you will receive an alert like the one shown in Figure 6-28. Click the Invite button to send that person an e-mail message that will allow her to create an account and view your calendar.

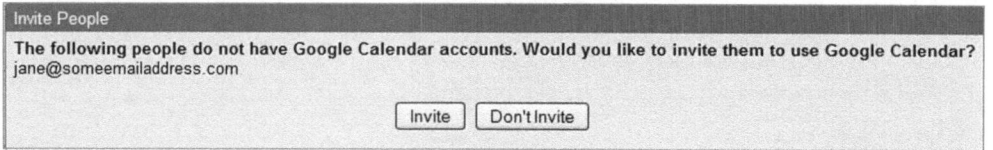

Figure 6-28. *Invite those without a Google Calendar account to view your calendar.*

You can create multiple calendars (a personal calendar and a friends calendar, for example) by clicking the Settings link, then clicking the Calendars tab, and then clicking the "Create new calendar" button (see Figure 6-26). Next, in the My Calendars section on the left side of the screen, click the down arrow to the right of your new calendar to see the options shown in Figure 6-29. Select the "Share this calendar" option, and follow the previous steps to share it.

Figure 6-29. *Create a new calendar and share it instead of your personal calendar items.*

Investigate Further

Although dozens of free e-mail and calendar applications are available, I simply cannot imagine using anything other than Gmail and Google Calendar. These two applications go hand-in-hand, and I highly encourage you to create a Google account and try them out.

The following are some useful web sites that provide more details on using Gmail and Google Calendar:

- Mirror Outlook in Gmail: `http://www.cnxn.ca/GmailMirror.html`

- 50 Google Calendar Tips : `http://blogoscoped.com/archive/2008-01-21.html`

- How to Organize and Categorize Messages with Labels in Gmail:
  `http://email.about.com/od/gmailtips/qt/et032006.htm`

Summary

Gmail and Google Calendar work great separately, but together they are a powerhouse combination that can help you stay organized and in touch with friends, family, coworkers, and everyone else on the planet.

E-mail is here to stay—there's no avoiding it if you wish to live and work and play in this modern world. And if you're as busy as the next person, it's nice to have a calendar application to help you remember important dates like birthdays and anniversaries, super-important dates like that job interview, and not-so-important dates such as the original TV episode airing of *Fringe*.

Gmail and Google Calendar are two of my most valued computer applications. The fact that they're both totally free to use makes me smile when I think about the money I'm saving and laugh when someone asks why I don't use Outlook.

- Microsoft Outlook: $109.95 (or $400 bundled with Microsoft Office 2007 Standard)

- Gmail: $0

- Google Calendar: $0

CHAPTER 7

■ ■ ■

Photo Editing

It's hard for me to imagine a time when I took pictures using rolls of film, but in reality, it was only about eight years ago that I purchased my first digital camera. I was able to take pictures and have them stored on a small memory card that fit inside my camera. At the time, my memory card limited me to about 90 pictures, but that was still more than the standard 24 exposures I could take using a single roll of film. Digital photography was definitely the way to go.

Today, buying a camera typically implies a digital camera. Sure, some professional photographers still use film, but for ease of use, you just can't beat digital. Getting your pictures printed on paper is as easy as inserting the memory card into a store's kiosk and selecting the photos you wish to purchase. Kiosks also offer options such as the ability to crop, add text, and remove red eye (the effect that sometimes results from a camera flash).

Along with the photo kiosks, plenty of online digital photo printers (such as snapfish.com) are available. They will not only print your images and mail them to you, but they also offer custom services that let you add pictures to mouse pads, coffee mugs, calendars, and more items than you can imagine.

Owning a digital camera lets you capture all those special moments: your child's first steps, that great vacation, and your first house. But a digital camera also helps with some more mundane tasks, such as providing an insurance company with photos of damage done to your vehicle by a negligent driver or taking pictures of the serial numbers on all your home electronics.

If you're at all like me, you've been known to take a bad picture. Maybe the lighting was poor, with the sun behind your subject instead of in front. Wouldn't it be great to be able to clean up some of those bad photos, saving them from deletion?

Well, the good news is that there are numerous applications out there that allow you to modify and edit your digital photos. Some of these applications are extremely powerful and come with features that professional photographers have been known to charge huge amounts of money to provide. Other applications provide only a single feature (red-eye removal, for example) but do it well.

In this chapter, I'll introduce you to the two biggest names in digital photo editing. One is the industry standard and comes with the industry-standard price (hint: it's high). The other is an open source hit that remains completely free.

The Defender

When it comes to digital photo editing, the leader of the pack belongs to Adobe. Adobe Photoshop is the product most professional photographers and graphic artists turn to for any kind of digital photo manipulation.

Photoshop has an interface similar to many popular applications, as shown in Figure 7-1. A toolbar along the left edge gives you access to tools to edit a photograph in the large workspace in the center of the application. Menus along the top provide additional options, including the ability to turn on and off additional windows and toolbars.

Figure 7-1. *Adobe Photoshop is a popular digital photo editing application.*

You won't hear too many people who use Photoshop say that the application doesn't have enough features. In fact, "Photoshop is just too complicated" is a frequent complaint. (A complete list of the features found in the latest version of Adobe Photoshop can be found at http://www.adobe.com/photoshop.)

Photoshop is certainly popular and powerful. There's even a professional organization dedicated to the application. Check out the National Association of Photoshop Professionals (NAPP) web site at http://www.photoshopuser.com and learn about its annual Photoshop conference held to discuss the application and provide training. For me, that's a sure sign that this application goes a little beyond my basic needs.

Professional photographers and graphic artists are sure to appreciate the power of Photoshop, but the cost of Photoshop is just a bit too steep for the features that most of us will use.

Wouldn't it be nice to have a lower-priced application that gives you the features of Photoshop if and when you want them, but also keeps the user interface simple and non-intimidating? (And by lower priced, I mean free, of course.) Well, you're in luck. A group of like-minded computer programmers decided to create an application that can compete, head-on, with Photoshop. And, because it's open source, they're giving it away.

The Contender

Whether you need to perform some simple edits to a digital photograph or do more complex cropping and cleanup work, you're going to love GIMP. GIMP is an open source digital image editing application that is totally free to use.

One of the first things you'll notice about GIMP is its slightly different user interface. When you open the application, you'll see two separate windows, as shown in Figure 7-2. This may seem a little odd at first, but you'll quickly adjust and understand why GIMP works as it does.

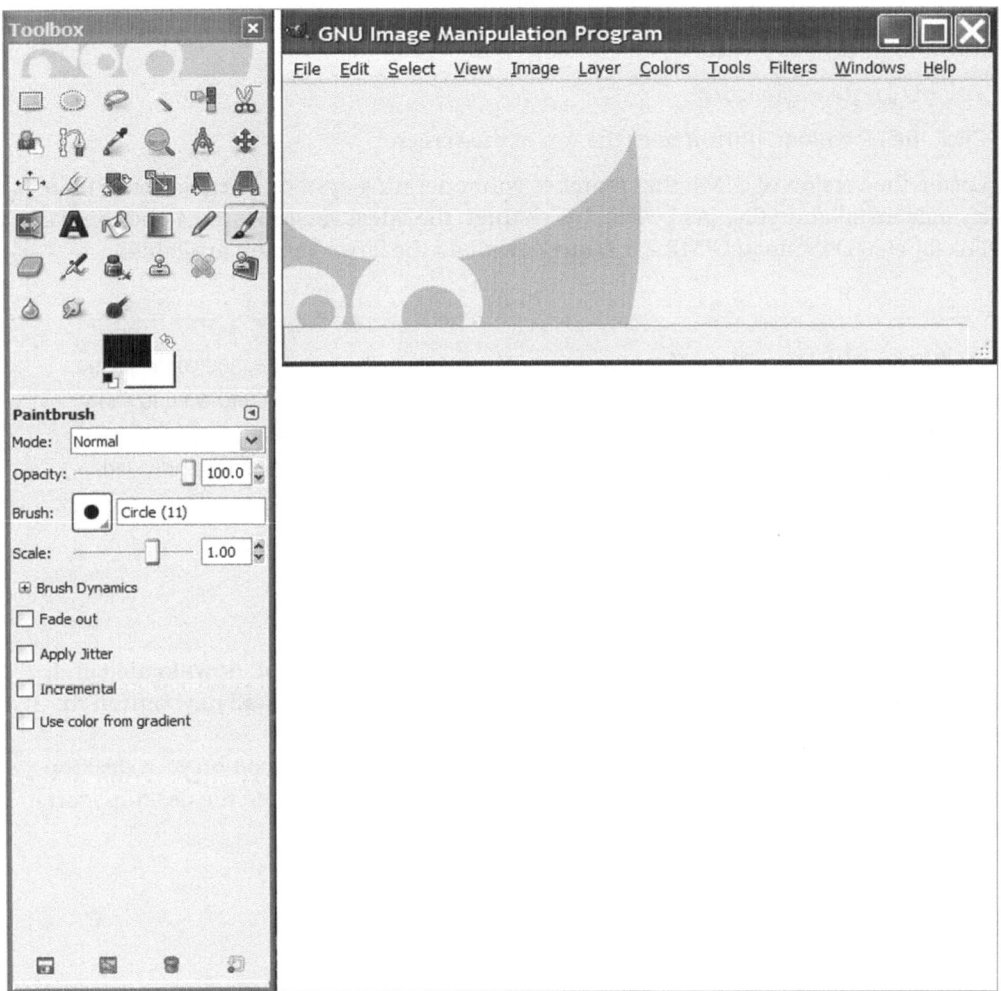

Figure 7-2. *GIMP opens two simple windows when you first run the application.*

Like Photoshop, GIMP is a powerful application in the hands of someone who knows how to properly use all its features. Entire books have been written on GIMP, and an abundance of web sites provide tutorials and examples of what can be done using this application.

So, let's get started. Up next, I'll tell you where to get GIMP, explain how to install it, and then show you some simple tasks you can perform with this great application. Once you start using GIMP, you'll begin to discover all sorts of useful (and sometimes strange) tweaks you can perform on your photos. See the "Investigate Further" section of this chapter for my recommendations for online help and resources when you're ready to dig deeper into GIMP's collection of amazing abilities.

Where to Get the Software

You'll need to download a software installation file that will be used to install GIMP on your computer. To get the software, perform the following steps:

1. Visit `http://www.gimp.org`.

2. Click the Download button near the top of the screen.

3. Locate the version of GIMP that matches your operating system. For Windows, there is a single installation file. (As I write this chapter, the latest version is 2.6.4 and there is a link labeled Download GIMP 2.6.4, but download the latest version available.)

■**Note** Is GIMP completely free? Yes. There are no advertisements in the software, and you'll see no pop-ups asking you to upgrade or buy a premium edition. If you like the application and want to show your support of the project, you can make a tax-deductible donation by visiting `http://www.gimp.org/donating/` and clicking the Make a Donation button or by sending a check to the address provided.

Notes on GIMP Installation

Installing GIMP is extremely simple. Double-click the installation file you downloaded and, after reading through and accepting the license agreement, click the Install now button to begin the installation process.

When the installation wizard finishes, you'll find a GIMP shortcut icon on your desktop. Double-click the icon to open and begin using GIMP. (You can also delete the desktop icon and open GIMP by selecting it from the Start menu.)

Basic GIMP Tasks

To really take advantage of GIMP, you need to have a basic understanding of something called a *layer*. Once you understand layers and how they work, you'll be able to do some amazing things using GIMP.

Layers are not actually that complicated. Just imagine a stack of magazines on the floor, as shown in Figure 7-3.

Figure 7-3. *A stack of magazines is a perfect example of how layers work.*

Notice that the magazine on top of the stack is completely visible—none of the words or images are hidden. The magazines below it, however, are partially obscured. You can make out the name of one of the magazines and see a glimpse of the cover on another one, but that top magazine (or top layer) is the only one in the stack that is totally viewable.

I don't want to take up all my floor space, but I would like to be able to glance down and see the titles of my magazines, so I'll reorder the stack (layers), as shown in Figure 7-4.

Figure 7-4. *I can rearrange the layers to see more (or less) of each magazine.*

Now that I can see my magazine titles, I'm going to throw some more items on top of the stack: a couple of business cards and some sticky notes, as shown in Figure 7-5.

But now I realize that the most current issue of one of my magazines is at the very bottom of the stack. It's a simple matter to move that magazine up to the top of the stack (but below the business cards and sticky notes). Now that all the layers on the floor of my office are organized the way I like them, I move the business cards and sticky notes around a bit so I can see more of the magazine layer beneath them. Figure 7-6 shows how I finally organized all the layers in my stack.

If you're wondering what all this has to do with GIMP, let me explain by walking you through a typical activity using GIMP: adding some text to a digital photo.

Figure 7-5. *My layers are a mixture of magazines, cards, and notes.*

Figure 7-6. *All the layers in my stack are ordered and positioned as I prefer them.*

Add Text to a Photo

In this example, I'll show you how to create a customized digital photo that you can e-mail to various friends and family. We'll add some text that will not change from photo to photo, as well as some other text that will be a personal message to the recipient.

To begin, open GIMP by double-clicking the desktop shortcut or selecting it from your Start menu. When GIMP opens, you'll see a couple of windows (see Figure 7-2).

Now, follow along with the procedure, and the concept of layers will begin to make sense.

1. Drag and expand the windows to give yourself some more working room. Figure 7-7 shows how I've expanded the workspace window on the right.

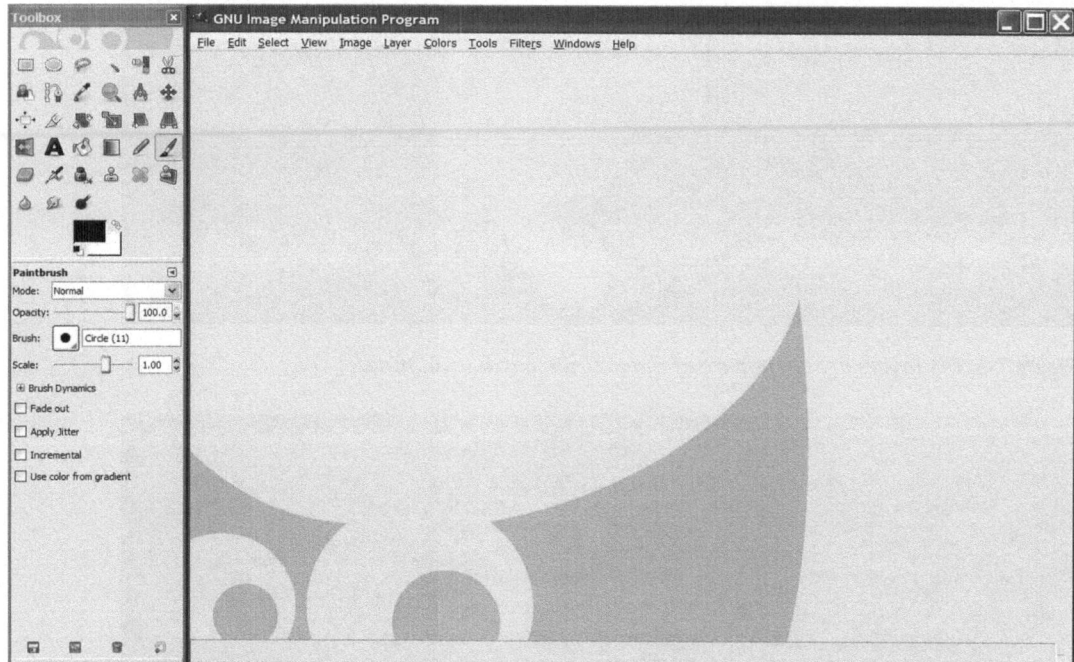

Figure 7-7. *Expand the GIMP windows to give yourself more working room.*

2. To open the digital photo you wish to edit, select File ➤ Open, as shown in Figure 7-8. In the dialog box that appears, browse to the location of the photo you wish to edit, select it, and click the Open button.

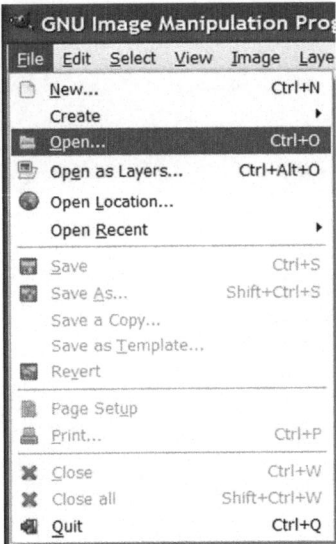

Figure 7-8. *Open a digital photo that you wish to edit.*

Your photo will open and appear on the workspace, as shown in Figure 7-9. Just as in my stack of magazines, this photo is the first item in my stack, and currently the only item. Because we want to add some text to this photo, the text will need to be placed on top of the photo, correct? To do this, we need to add a layer; that is, the text must be added to the top of the stack.

Note Think of everything you wish to add to a digital photo as an item. That item will go above or below your photo. If it's above it, it can obscure the entire photo or just part of it. If the item is below the photo, the photo will most likely obscure the entire item.

Figure 7-9. *Your digital photo will open in the workspace, where you will perform your edits.*

3. Select Windows ➤ Dockable Dialogs, and then select Layers, as shown in Figure 7-10.

    The Layers window will appear, as shown in Figure 7-11. The layer at the top of the list in this window is equivalent to the item at the top of a stack. It will sit on top of any layers below it. In this example, there is currently only one layer, named Background. The Background layer will typically be the photo you are opening to edit.

Figure 7-10. *Open the Layers window to view all the layers you've added to the stack.*

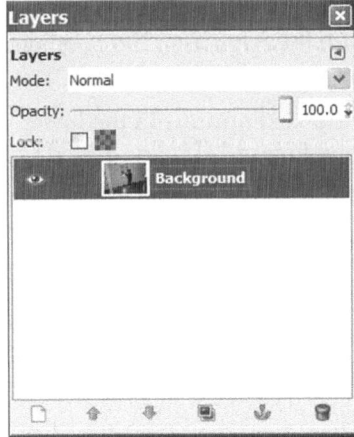

Figure 7-11. *The Layers window shows all the layers in your stack and their order.*

4. To work with a layer, click it in the Layers window. In the list, the layer will turn blue, indicating it is the layer you are currently working on. (In Figure 7-11, the Background layer is selected.)

5. Drag the Layer window to the right of your workspace and expand it a little, as shown in Figure 7-12. Now you can view the tools in the left window, your workspace in the center window, and your layers in the right window.

Figure 7-12. *I organize GIMP with the Toolbox window on the left, workspace in the middle, and Layers window on the right.*

6. To add text, select the Text tool (the tool button with the large *A*) in the Toolbox window and click in the photo where you wish to place the text.

7. Type the text you wish to add. Then you can use the Text options in the lower part of the Toolbox window to format the text. As shown in Figure 7-13, I've added my greeting in the upper-left corner of the photo and changed the color, font, and font size of the text.

Notice that after you've added the text, a new layer is added in the Layer window, as shown in Figure 7-14. The layer has the name of the text you added and appears at the top of the layer stack. So, when you add an element (such as a shape or text) to your photo, GIMP automatically creates a layer for you.

Figure 7-13. *Use the Text tool to add your text and modify the font, font size, and color as desired.*

Figure 7-14. *The text that you added exists in its own layer.*

8. Layers can be moved up and down the stack easily. Try it. Click your text layer and, while holding down the mouse button, drag it down the stack. Release the button when the layer is where you wish to place it in the stack. Figure 7-15 shows that the new text layer is now below the Background layer. It looks like the text disappeared! Because the photo takes up the entire screen, it is essentially covering the text, making it invisible. Now, drag the text layer back to the top,

Figure 7-15. *Moving layers up and down will change what is visible in the workspace.*

9. Next, let's add a personal message. Once again, select the Text tool and add the text for that message where you want it to appear. In Figure 7-16, I've added a message to my parents. Notice that a new layer appears at the very top in the Layers window. I've placed this new message so that it slightly covers the other text layer.

10. Because the new message is the topmost layer, it appears on top of the original greeting text. Drag this top layer down one level in the stack and drop it under the greeting layer. You'll see that the text changes places, as shown in Figure 7-17. The greeting is now sitting on top of the personal message.

Figure 7-16. *Adding another item (more text, in this case), adds another layer.*

Figure 7-17. *Swapping the top two layers doesn't improve the readability.*

11. Drag the personal message text to the lower-right corner. As shown in Figure 7-18, now both messages can be read. In this arrangement, it doesn't really matter which text layer is on top.

Figure 7-18. *Move text items around in their respective layers until the image is acceptable.*

So, why not just put all the text on the same layer? Well, you could do that, but separating the text into two different layers allows you to make changes to one layer without altering any work done in another layer. Let's see how that works.

12. To save this first image and text, select File ➤ Save As and give the file a name.

13. Click the personal message layer and change it, as shown in Figure 7-19. The greeting stays in place, as does the original photo. Now you can continue to change the personal message, so you have a personalized image to e-mail to each person.

Layers are powerful. You can move them up and down the stack, delete them, copy them, and more. Now that you understand how layers work, let's look at another fun thing to do with GIMP.

■**Tip** If you're interested in learning more about the use of layers, I highly recommend *Beginning GIMP, Second Edition*, by Akkana Peck (Apress, 2009). This book goes into great detail and provides many examples of the power of layers.

Figure 7-19. *Changes made in one layer will not affect elements in other layers.*

Drop Someone into a Photo

With GIMP, it's easy to clip items out of one photo and put them into another. This is a useful for placing an absent family member into a family photo, or for inserting a friend into a humorous photo (just don't use it to place anyone at the scene of a crime or in a compromising situation!).

Here's how you do it:

1. Open a photo containing the person you wish to clip out, as shown in Figure 7-20. In this example, I want to clip the little sleeping fellow on the couch and place him somewhere more interesting.

2. Click the Scissors tool in the Toolbox window, as shown in Figure 7-21.

Figure 7-20. *The first step is to open the photo that contains the item you want to clip out.*

Figure 7-21. *The Scissors tool will let you cut out a person or object in a digital photo.*

3. Click anywhere on the edge of the person (or object) you wish to clip out. Figure 7-22 shows that I've clicked the edge of the subject's ear, indicated by a small colored dot.

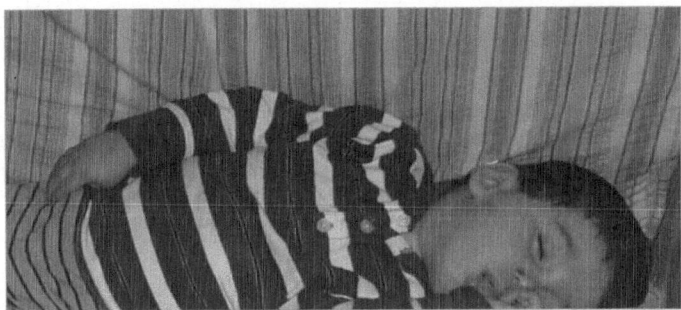

Figure 7-22. *Start by clicking a spot along the edge of the person or object using the Scissors tool.*

4. Using your mouse, click points around the edge of the person or item. GIMP does a good job of examining the surrounding image and connecting the dots around the subject. Figure 7-23 shows my progress as I click around the sleeping figure.

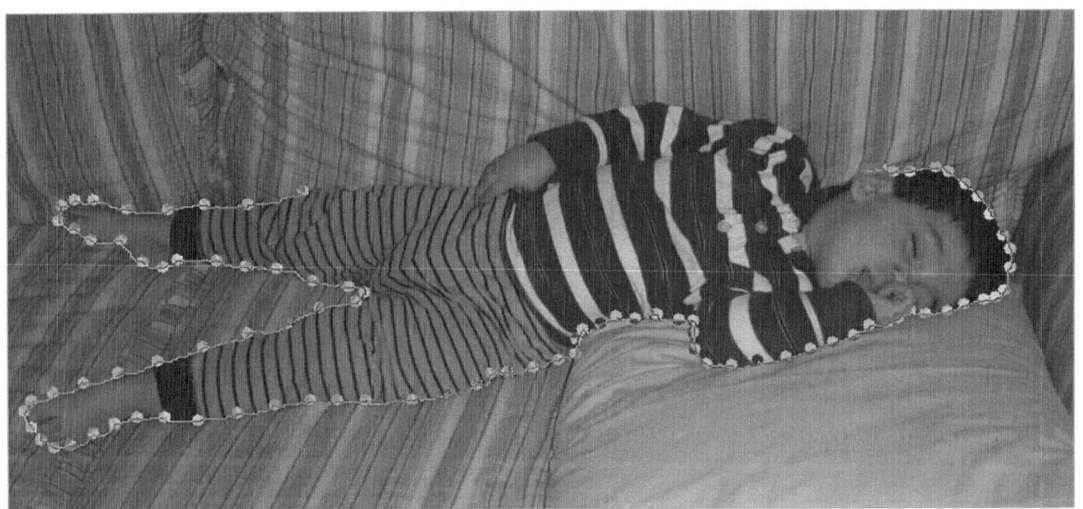

Figure 7-23. *You must select points along the edge of the person or object using the Scissors tool.*

5. As you near the completion of surrounding the subject using the Scissors tool, click the original starting point (see Figure 7-22), and then click inside the area you've defined. The dots and connecting lines will change to an animated line (called *marching ants*) to indicate the item that has been selected to be clipped, as shown in Figure 7-24.

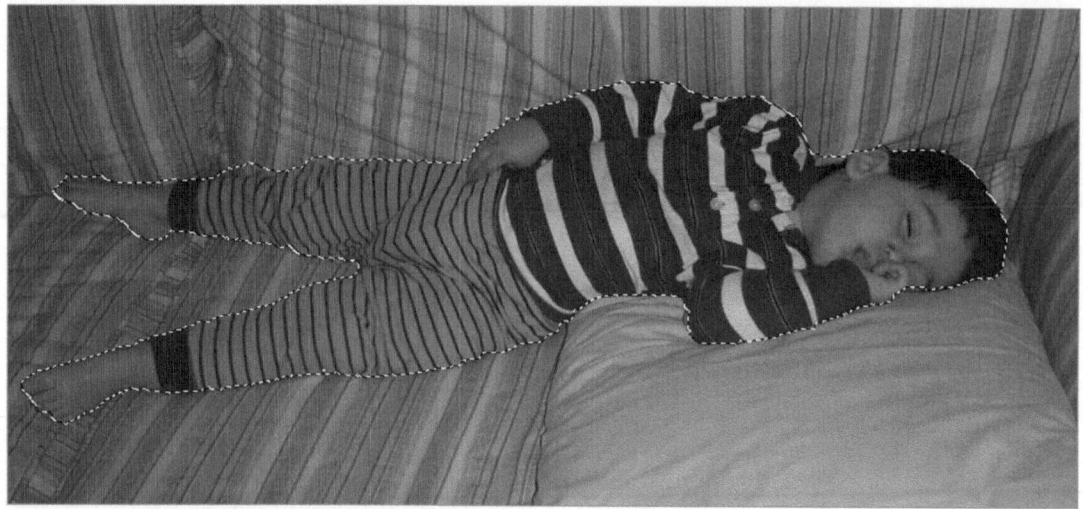

Figure 7-24. *Your subject will be selected when you've completed clipping with the Scissors.*

6. Select Edit ➤ Cut. Figure 7-25 shows that the subject has been successfully removed from the original photo.

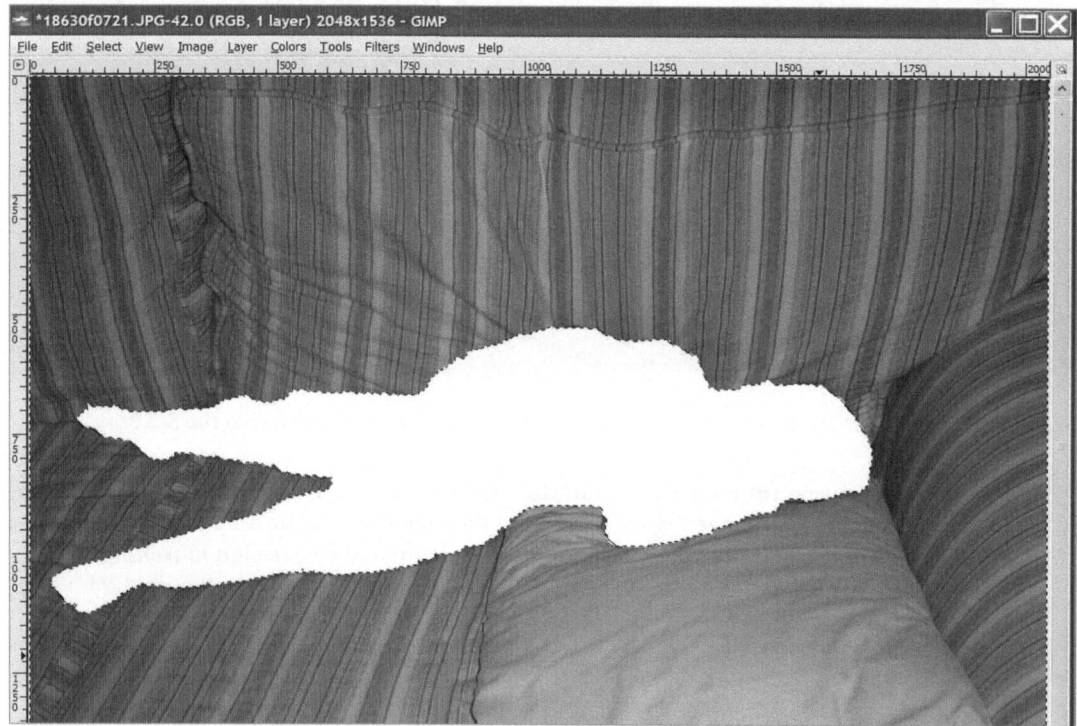

Figure 7-25. *Cutting the subject from the original photo leaves a blank white space.*

7. Select File ➤ Open as Layers, as shown in Figure 7-26. From the dialog box, choose the photo in which you wish to place the clipped person or object.

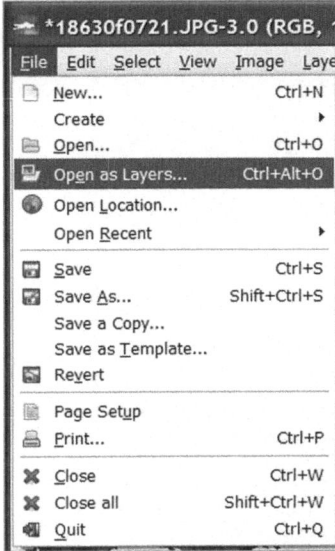

Figure 7-26. *Open a new digital photo as a layer.*

8. The digital photo you selected will be added as a layer above the Background layer, as shown in Figure 7-27. Also, notice that the marching ants line appears superimposed over this layer, showing where the image will appear when you paste it. But there's one more step to perform before putting the clipped subject back into the photo.

9. Adding a new layer will allow you to paste in the clipped subject, resize it, and move it around without affecting the layers below it. To do this, select Layer ➤ New Layer. Figure 7-28 shows the new layer, which I named Subject.

Figure 7-27. *The border of the clipped subject appears over the new layer.*

Figure 7-28. *The new layer will be used to modify the clipped subject.*

10. Click the newly added layer to select it.

11. Select Edit ➤ Paste. The outline of the clipped subject will appear, as shown in Figure 7-29.

Figure 7-29. *The clipped subject is back but needs to be resized and placed in a better location.*

12. Right-click inside the clipped image, click Layer, and then select Scale Layer, as shown in Figure 7-30.

13. In the Scale Layer dialog box, make sure that percent is selected from the top drop-down list, and then type in a number (such as 80 for 80%) in the Width and Height fields, as shown in Figure 7-31. Then click the Scale button. You may need to experiment with the percentage value until you're satisfied with the final size.

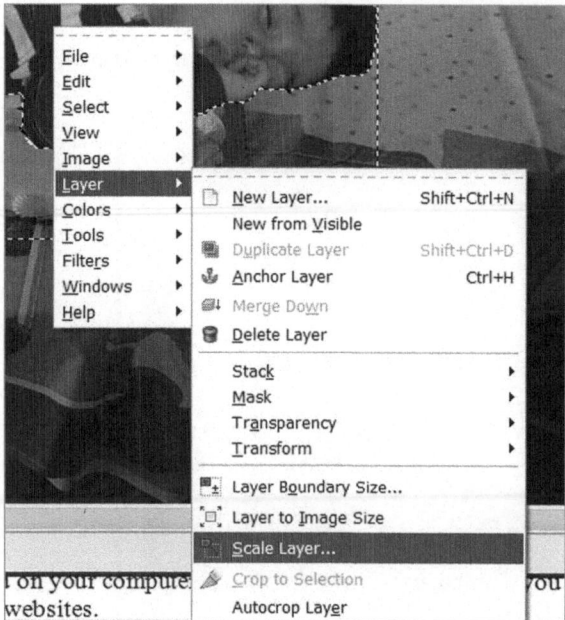

Figure 7-30. *The clipped image needs to be scaled down in size.*

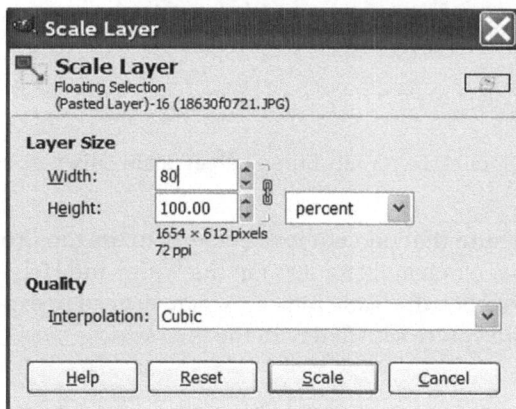

Figure 7-31. *Scale down the clipped image to a size that fits well with the new background.*

14. Click the clipped subject, hold down the mouse button, and drag it to a different location. Figure 7-32 shows the final image with the sleeping boy reduced slightly in size and placed behind his birthday cake.

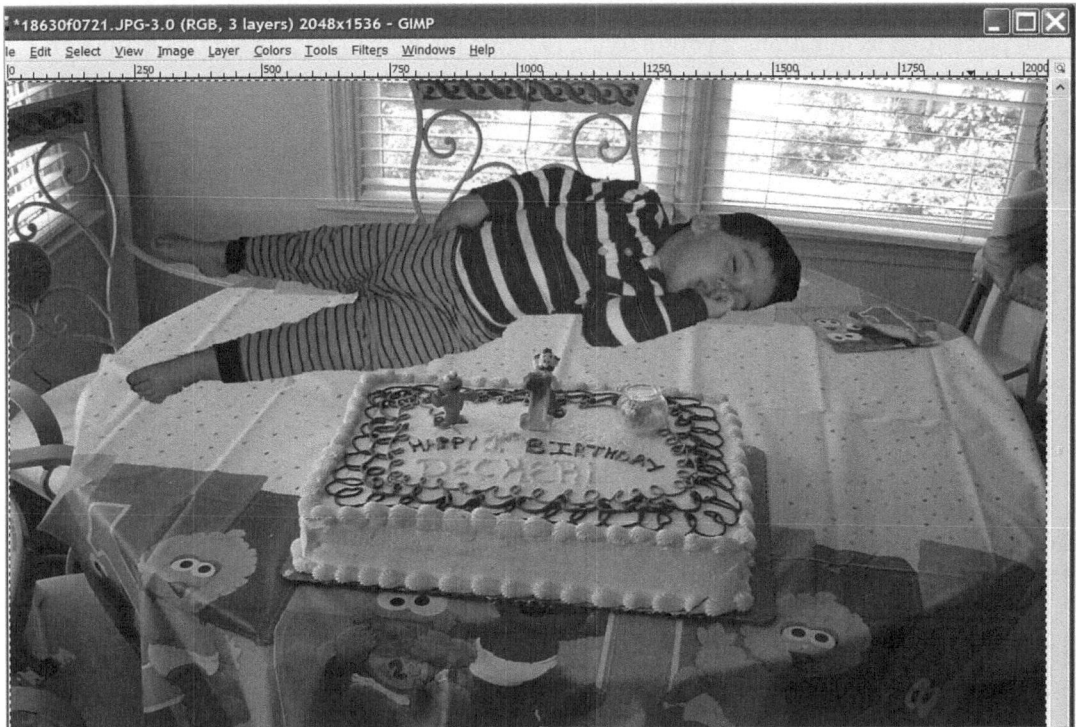

Figure 7-32. *The new image shows a little boy too tired for cake.*

This is just one of the many fun effects you can add to digital photos with GIMP. An abundance of possibilities exist for editing your photos with this extremely powerful application.

Note GIMP can also do things such as remove red eye or improve images that are overexposed. However, such fixes are much easier to perform with Picasa, as you'll learn in Chapter 13.

Investigate Further

Entire books and web sites are dedicated to GIMP. For starters, I highly recommend the same book I read, cover to cover, when I was learning this application: *Beginning GIMP* by Akkana Peck (Apress, 2006), which has been recently updated in a second edition (Apress, 2009).

The following are some excellent online resources for GIMP:

- GIMP User Manual: http://docs.gimp.org/en/

- GIMP wiki: http://wiki.gimp.org/gimp/

- GIMP Tutorials (including red-eye removal): http://www.gimp.org/tutorials/

- GimpTalk discussion forums: http://www.gimptalk.com/forum/

You'll find a ton of tutorials at the Tutorials site. And the online discussion forums are great places to post questions if you're trying to figure out how to do something unusual or possibly complicated.

Summary

A few months ago, I participated in a group photo that had more than 100 people in it. One of the group members (Frank) was late and disappointed that he didn't make it into the photo. But we didn't need to leave him out. I asked him to stand approximately where the group was standing when the photo was taken and snapped a photo with only Frank in the image. I was able to use GIMP to clip him from the second photo and place him (well, just his shoulders and head) in the original photo. After the group photo was printed, no one could tell the difference.

GIMP is a fun tool. You may find it as addictive as I do for adding special effects and text to photos.

The developers of GIMP never stop working to improve the product; they are always adding new features and effects. GIMP is one of the rare open source applications that may have exceeded the big name, pay-to-use applications in terms of ease of use and functionality. Give it a spin. Visit some of the online resources I suggested in this chapter. I think you'll agree that this 100% free photo editing application is one outstanding tool.

- Adobe Photoshop: $699

- GIMP: $0

■ ■ ■

Graphics

I am not embarrassed to admit that I cannot draw. My stick figures are horrible, with mis-matched arm lengths, feet pointing in the wrong directions, and oversized heads that no neck could possibly support. I may be the only person in the world who cannot draw a symmetrical five-pointed star.

But all that changed when I began to use my computer to assist me with creating simple geometric shapes and ensuring that symmetry exists where it's needed. Suddenly, I could draw perfect squares, circles, and stars. My hand drawings typically still look like the crayon masterpieces of a two-year-old, but the graphics I create using my computer are starting to show promise.

Graphics applications have come a long way since the dawn of computers. Early pro-grams provided you with a virtual pen and allowed you to change only the color of the ink and thickness of the virtual pen's tip. Later versions included functionality such as adding basic (and perfect) shapes, as well as features such as textures and the ability to copy, rotate, and resize objects.

Today, graphic design applications allow artists to do things with their art that would have been impossible—or at least extremely difficult and time-consuming—only a few years ago. These abilities include morphing, blending textures, adding metal/chrome effects, and more.

Graphics applications are similar to photo editing applications (discussed in Chapter 7). You can import digital photos and modify them in an infinite number of ways. But these graphics programs have the added benefit of allowing you to create something from nothing on the "canvas" (the blank screen). While these applications have typically been out of reach of the typical computer user—usable only by the highly skilled graphic artist—that is chang-ing. Today, there are graphics applications that are user-friendly but don't skimp on features. This chapter introduces you to two of them. One is Adobe Illustrator, which is likely to be found on every professional graphic artist's computer and comes with a professional price. The other is Inkscape, which can easily be downloaded and installed on your computer, and comes with a price you'll love: free.

The Defender

As a writer, I frequently work with graphic artists. While I'm writing the words that will appear on a web site, in a brochure, or in a book, the graphic artist is concerned with creating the eye-catching images, icons, and layout that share the page with my text. When I inquire about the application the artist is using, the answer I get almost every time is Adobe Illustrator.

Adobe Illustrator, shown in Figure 8-1, seems to be the application of choice for most professional digital artists. It's a powerful application, with tools and options that I have absolutely no clue how to use (or even what they do). But my graphic artist friends tell me that they use feature x every week and feature y once a month, and can't live without them. With Illustrator, an artist can create original art as well as modify existing items.

Figure 8-1. *Adobe Illustrator is the professional graphic artist's application of choice.*

Whether you're using a mouse or a specialized tool such as a tablet with a digital pen (see Figure 8-2), Illustrator provides a collection of tools such as brush shapes, textures, and colors to create graphics. Another collection of features can be used to twist, tweak, distort, blend, shrink, and so on. If you can envision what you want to do to an image or photo, Illustrator can probably make it a visual reality. (A complete list of the features found in the latest version of Adobe Illustrator can be found at http://www.adobe.com/illustrator.)

Figure 8-2. *Many graphic artists use a digital pen and tablet instead of a mouse.*

At its heart, however, Illustrator is a vector graphics application. What does that mean? Well, there's a complicated definition that I'll spare you. Instead, I'll give you a simple explanation using the few simple elements shown in Figure 8-3.

Figure 8-3. *The difference between vector graphics and standard bitmap graphics*

For most graphics, when you enlarge or shrink an item, you get a distorted image. It is most noticeable when enlarging a photo or graphic. Figure 8-3 shows a simple graphic image in the upper-left corner created using Microsoft's Paint program and saved as a bitmap (.bmp) file. The lower-left corner shows that same graphic image after I've enlarged it by 100%. Doubling it in size has ruined the smooth edges of the original circle. In the upper-right corner, I've drawn another simple image using a vector graphics application and enlarged it in the lower-right corner. Can you see the difference?

▨**Note** Some typical graphic image file formats are bitmap and JPEG. Bitmaps are uncompressed image files with a .bmp extension. JPEG stands for Joint Photographic Experts Group format. JPEGs are compressed images.

The large smiley face looks jagged and has lost all its smooth edges. This is called *pixelation* and occurs when you resize images in most standard graphics applications. It happens because the application is simply unable to determine what must be added to the original image (or taken away) in order for the proportions, colors, and other qualities to appear properly in the new size.

A vector graphics application doesn't suffer from this problem. These types of applications use a type of math, called *vector math*, to assist in keeping the qualities of a modified graphic the same as the image is enlarged, shrunk, or otherwise modified. It's complicated, but all you really need to know is that the vector graphics you create can be easily modified without pixelation.

Vector graphics are drawn with lines that can be redrawn to different scales. Bitmap graphics are laid down as collections of bits that the computer no longer can recognize as lines and circles and such. When you resize a vector graphic, the computer redraws all the lines. When you resize a bitmap, the computer must expand the number of pixels without knowing what each pixel represents in the image, and the enlarged bitmap image gets that jagged look. (If you wish to learn more about vector graphics and how they work, visit http://en.wikipedia.org/wiki/Vector_graphics.)

I've seen some amazing artwork created using Illustrator. However, Illustrator's price is simply out of range for most computer users. I occasionally need to create some original graphics for presentations or chapters (such as Figure 8-3), but that doesn't warrant my purchasing Illustrator. I needed to find a vector graphics application that has many or all of the standard graphic tools available in Illustrator, but at a much-reduced price. Let me tell you what I found during my search.

GIMP OR INKSCAPE?

Both GIMP (covered in Chapter 7) and Inkscape are capable of working with photos, and both applications can also be used to create original graphic art. Each application has a collection of tools that allow you to draw lines, add shapes, change colors, and more. So, do you really need both? Maybe.

GIMP has much more powerful capabilities for photo editing than Inkscape, including a multitude of effects that can be applied to photos, including lighting changes and texture formatting (such as changing a photo to look as if it were painted or drawn using pen or pencil). However, GIMP is not a vector graphics application. It can enlarge and shrink photos to a point, but there are limits that, when reached, will cause photo distortion.

While Inkscape can import photos and has a variety of tools to modify them, it lacks the photo manipulation controls of GIMP. Its ideal use is for creating original graphics (as well as adding them to photos) that can be enlarged and shrunk with no visible distortion.

In a nutshell, use GIMP when doing any type of work on digital photographs (or other image files) and GIMP when you need to create some original artwork. For something in between, use the application that you find has the most comfortable interface and that you enjoy.

The Contender

Say hello to Inkscape, a 100% free, open source, vector graphics application that is extremely easy to download, install, and use. Inkscape comes with a ton of online support, tutorials, and even a free online book.

Inkscape has a clean, uncluttered user interface. Tools are found along the left and top edges of the screen. The workspace is in the center, menus along the top, and color selections along the bottom edge. Figure 8-4 shows that my default workspace is an 8.5 × 11-inch document with a white background, but I can change that easily enough (as you'll see in the "Adjust Your Screen Settings" section later in this chapter).

As a vector graphics application, Inkscape allows you to design new images (or modify existing ones) without losing visual quality as you shrink, enlarge, and perform modifications. Whereas Illustrator saves files using the file type .ai, Inkscape's developers elected to have their application save files using the .svg file type. Scalable Vector Graphics (SVG) is a specification being developed as an industry standard for graphics applications. Among other things, this specification defines the standards for certain types of graphic files, including making certain the graphics are compatible with as many graphics applications as possible. Illustrator supports the .svg format, so images created in Illustrator and saved using the .svg file type can be opened and modified using Inkscape and vice versa.

Inkscape is evolving, and its developers are committed to improving this open source application, adding new features while still making it available for free distribution and use. The remainder of this chapter will show you where to get the software, how to install it, and how to perform some basic functions using this outstanding vector graphics application.

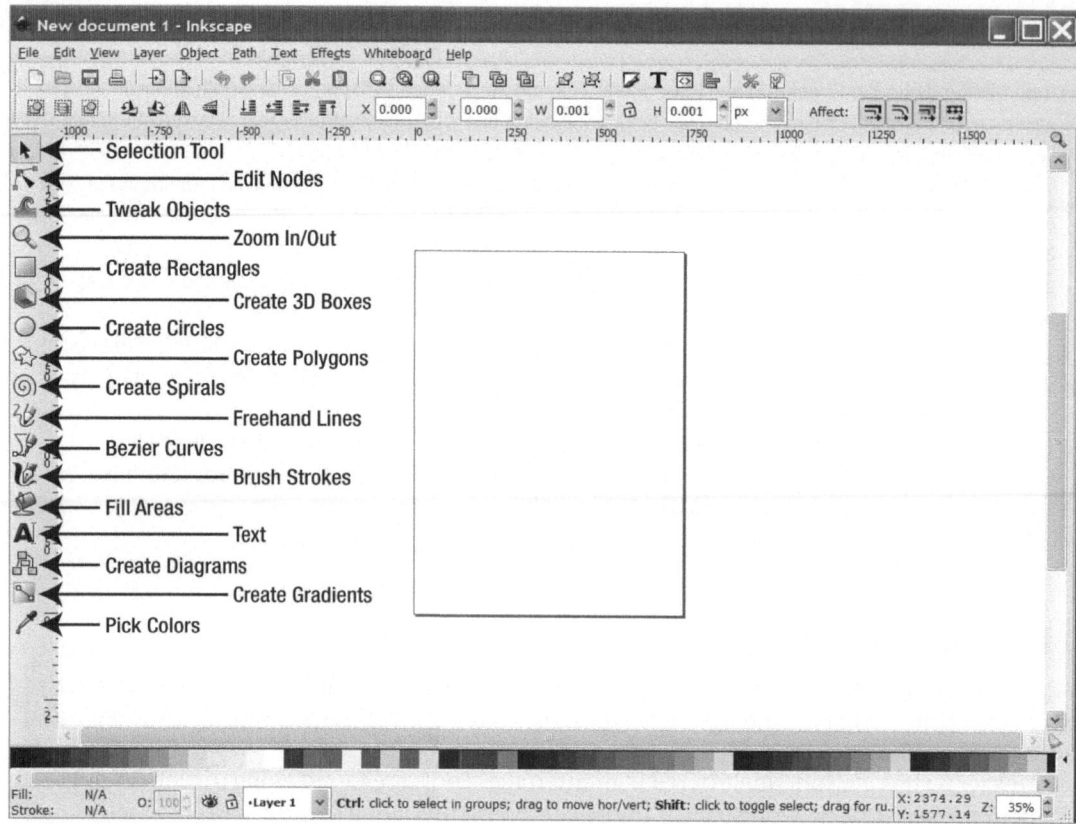

Figure 8-4. *Inkscape's user interface makes most of its tools available with a single mouse click.*

Where to Get the Software

You'll need to download a software installation file that will be used to install Inkscape on your computer. To get the software, perform the following steps:

1. Visit http://www.inkscape.org/.

2. Click Download in the list in the column on the left side of the screen.

3. Look under the Official Release section and download the latest version of Inkscape by clicking the link that corresponds to your operating system. (As I write this chapter, the current version is 0.46).

■**Note** Why isn't the current version of Inkscape 1.0? The Inkscape development team has decided that the 1.0 status will not be awarded until certain key features are implemented in the application. One of the most important implementations the team is working toward is 100% compatibility with the SVG 1.1 industry specification. Inkscape is feature-packed, and its current version is 100% usable and stable for the typical computer user.

Notes on Inkscape Installation

To install Inkscape, double-click the installation file you downloaded and follow the on-screen instructions. When you are given the opportunity to check or uncheck components for installation, uncheck the Translations box, and only the English translation will be installed. This will save you approximately 45MB of hard drive space, and Inkscape's installation will take up 170MB. But if you wish to install any other languages for Inkscape, place a check in the box besides the language(s) you wish to include.

Basic Inkscape Tasks

To use Inkscape, you'll need a basic understanding of the various tools available in the application. I encourage you to consult the online documentation and tutorials mentioned in the "Investigate Further" section of this chapter to learn more about the application. Here, I'll show you how to perform some basic tasks to introduce you to how Inkscape works.

To get started, double-click the Inkscape icon on your desktop (or select it from the Start menu).

Adjust Your Screen Settings

When you first open Inkscape, your screen opens with some default settings such as using pixels (instead of inches or millimeters) and the A4 paper format (instead of Legal or Letter). The default setting of A4 is an odd paper format used in European countries, not in the United States, and measurement in inches (or millimeters) is easier to visualize than pixels. Also, the default workspace size is quite small (see Figure 8-4). Here's how you can change these settings:

1. Select File ➤ Document Properties. The Document Properties window will open.

2. On the Page tab, select your desired paper size from the Format section. Choose Landscape or Portrait orientation. Select your default units from the drop-down menu at the top of the window, or enter a custom size for your document in the Custom size section. Figure 8-5 shows that I've selected inches (in) and a landscape orientation for my letter-size workspace. The changes are made automatically as you select them. Click the Close button when you're finished.

3. To enlarge the workspace, select View ➤ Zoom and select Page from the fly-out menu, as shown in Figure 8-6. Your workspace will expand to almost full-screen size, allowing you to see more details in your drawing.

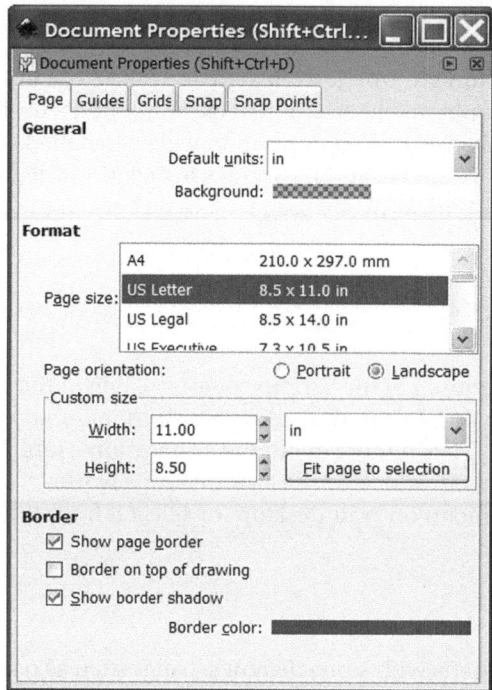

Figure 8-5. *Define the size of your workspace and the default units or create a customized workspace.*

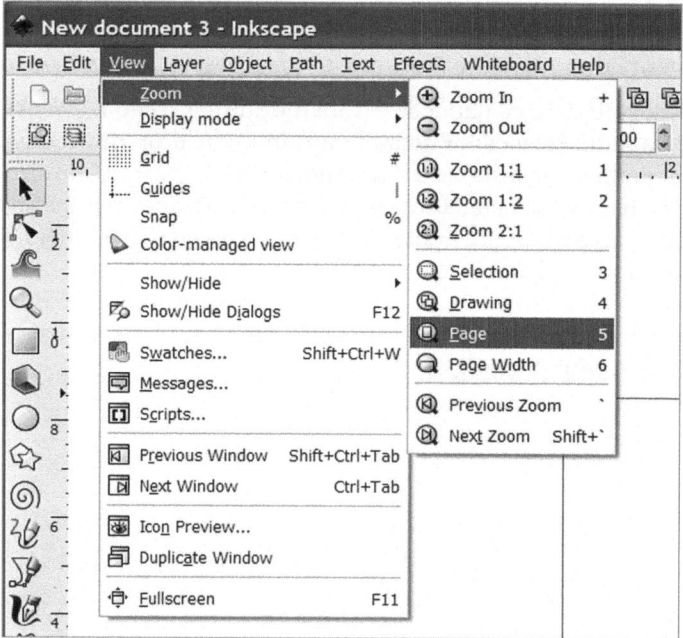

Figure 8-6. *Enlarge your workspace a bit so you can see more of your drawings.*

Add Basic Shapes

Before you can walk, you must learn to crawl, right? Learn to add simple shapes like squares and circles by following these steps:

1. Select the Rectangle tool (see Figure 8-4), and then click in the workspace where you wish to place a corner of the rectangle while holding down the mouse button. Drag the mouse, and you'll see your rectangle grow (or shrink) as you move the mouse around. Release the mouse when you're satisfied with the rectangle's size. The rectangle will be added to the workspace, as shown in Figure 8-7.

Figure 8-7. *Drawing rectangles is simple using Inkscape's Rectangle tool.*

2. To make a perfect square, use the Rectangle tool, as in step 1, but hold down the Ctrl and Shift keys while dragging the mouse. The sides will be kept to an identical size, allowing you to create a square, as shown in Figure 8-8.

3. Select the Circle tool (see Figure 8-4), and then click in the workspace while holding down the mouse. Drag the mouse around the screen, and you'll see your oval shape form. Release the mouse, and your final shape will be added to the drawing, as shown in Figure 8-9.

Figure 8-8. *Drawing squares is also easy when you use the Ctrl+Shift-drag technique.*

Figure 8-9. *Draw round shapes using the Circle tool.*

4. To create a perfect circle, use the Circle tool as in step 3, but hold down the Ctrl and Shift keys while dragging the mouse. Release the mouse button to complete the circle, as shown in Figure 8-10.

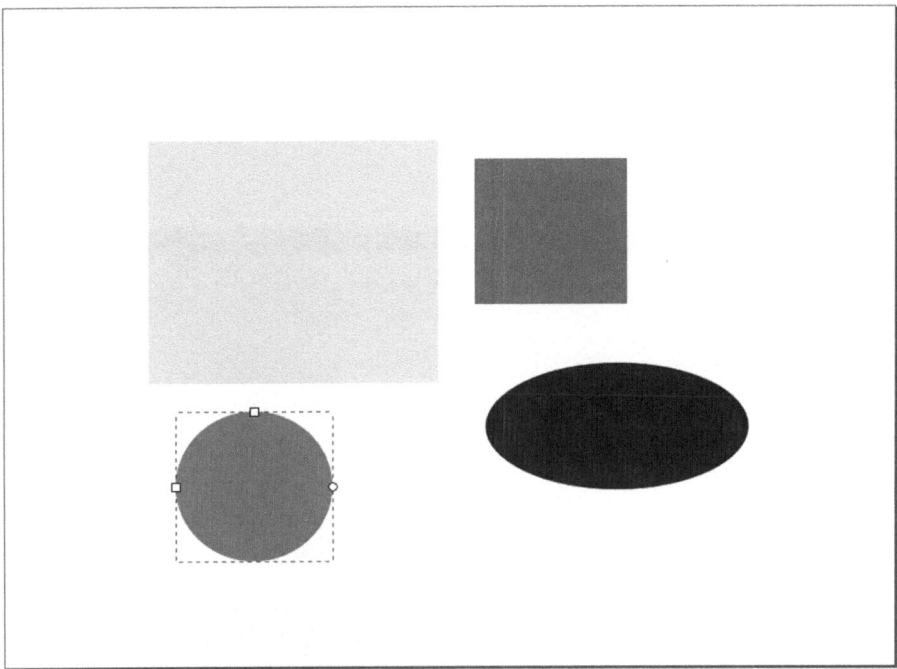

Figure 8-10. *The Ctrl+Shift-drag technique creates a perfect circle.*

5. Notice the small squares and circles on the dotted line surrounding the shapes you draw. These appear when the shape is selected. Try clicking and dragging them around. This is how you can modify the shape of the selected item.

6. Click one of your shapes, and then click a color in the color bar at the bottom of the screen. This changes the color of the item.

Free Drawing

Sometimes you don't need a standard shape like a circle or square. Free drawing options such as the Freehand Line tool, Bezier Curve tool, and Brush Stroke tool are fun to use and give you the ability to create some interesting shapes, lines, and other effects. Try these steps:

1. Select the Freehand Line tool (see Figure 8-11). Click and hold down the mouse button as you drag the tool on the workspace. It works just like a pen or pencil. In Figure 8-11, I've used this tool to write "Inkscape" on the rectangle.

Note With a mouse, the Freehand Line tool doesn't provide the nicest looking results. With a tablet (like the one shown in Figure 8-2), the tool will give better results.

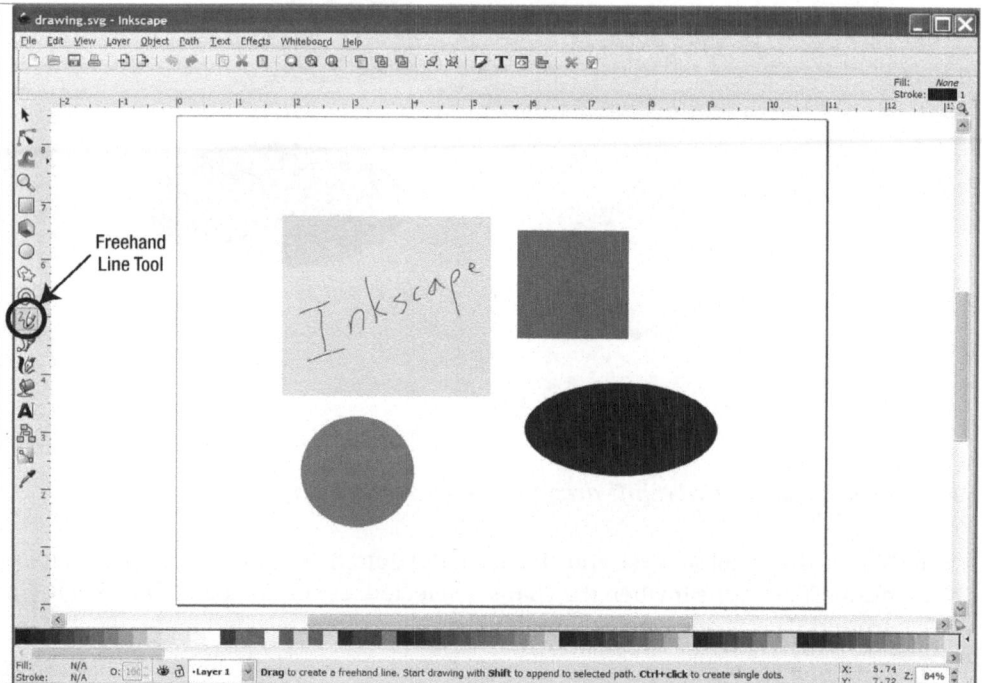

Figure 8-11. *Use the Freehand Line tool to draw or write on the workspace.*

2. Select the Bezier Curve tool (see Figure 8-12). Click in your workspace where you wish to place one end of a curve, as shown in Figure 8-12. Don't release the mouse button.

3. While still holding down the mouse button, drag to different point on the workspace. Then release the mouse button. This will create the second point of your line. Figure 8-13 shows the second point placed.

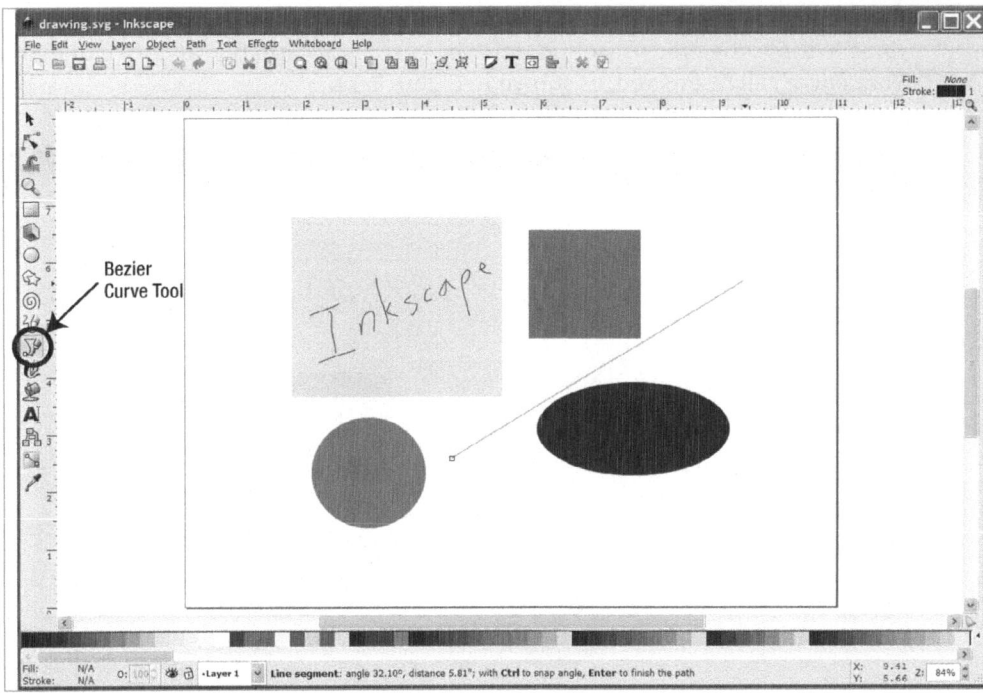

Figure 8-12. *Use the Bezier Curve tool to create specialized curves for your drawings.*

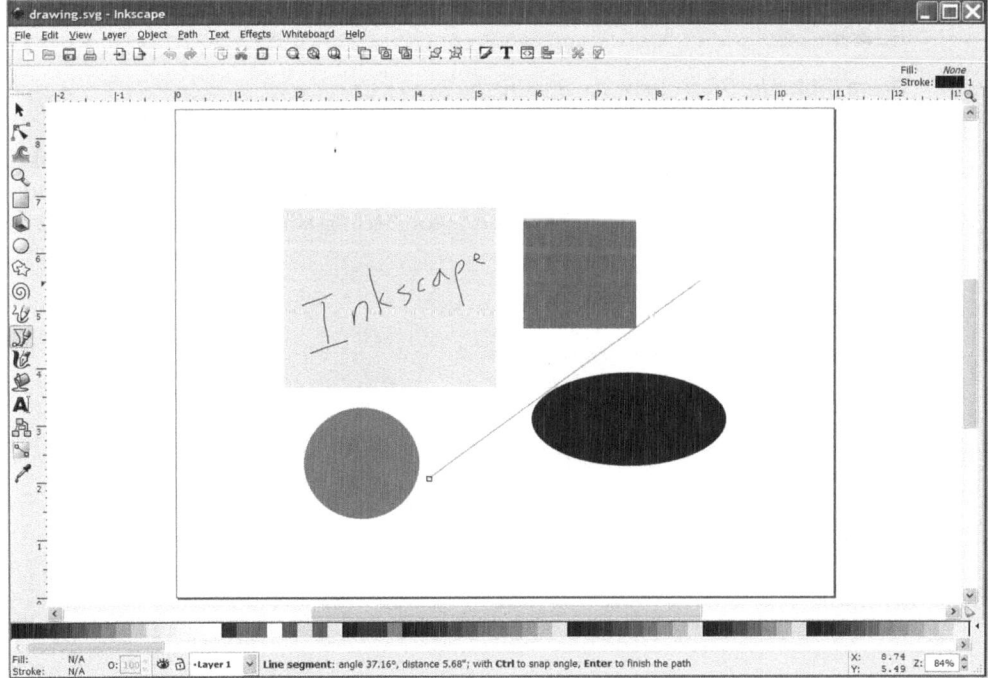

Figure 8-13. *The second point created by the Bezier Curve tool defines the length of the curve.*

4. Drag your mouse around (do not click), and you should see a curve take shape. Continue to move the mouse around until the curve is acceptable, and then double-click. Your curve will be created, as shown in Figure 8-14.

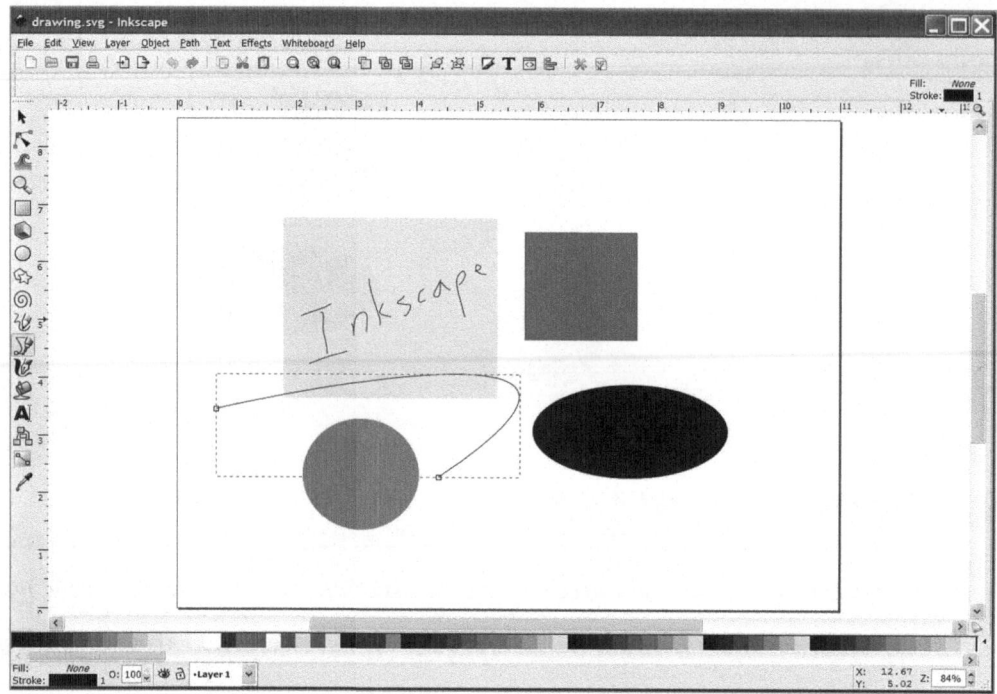

Figure 8-14. *The final curve created by the Bezier Curve tool*

5. Select the Brush Stroke tool (see Figure 8-15). Click in the workspace and hold the mouse button while dragging. The results are nicer than with the Freehand Line tool, as shown in Figure 8-15. You can use this tool to add some calligraphy or nice flourishes to your drawing.

Figure 8-15. *The Brush Stroke tool creates eye-catching flourishes.*

Use Layers

Like the GIMP application covered in Chapter 7, Inkscape uses layers. Layers allow you to work on an individual element or collection of elements—image, shape, text, and so on—without worrying about deleting, erasing, or otherwise changing any other elements. Layers are a virtual "stack," allowing you to work only on elements stored on a single layer without changing any other layers. Refer to Chapter 7's discussion of layers (in the "Basic GIMP Tasks" section) for more details.

To view and edit any layers currently being used in Inkscape, perform the following steps:

1. Select Layer ➤ Layers, as shown in Figure 8-16. The Layers window will appear along the left edge of the Inkscape screen, as shown in Figure 8-17. In this example, only one layer (named Layer 1) currently exists.

2. Click the + button in the Layers window to add a new layer.

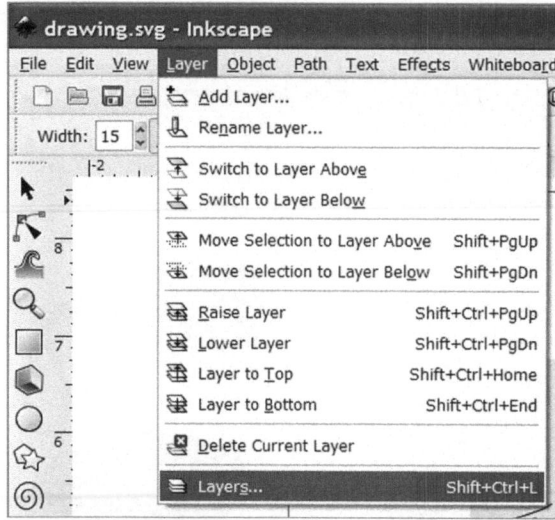

Figure 8-16. *Select Layers from the Layer menu to open the Layers window.*

Figure 8-17. *The Layers window takes up little space but is a very useful tool to get to know.*

3. In the Add Layer dialog box, give your layer a name, as shown in Figure 8-18, and then click the Add button. In this example, I've created a new layer named Background that will appear above the existing layer.

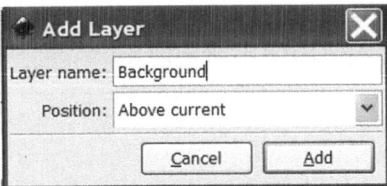

Figure 8-18. *Creating new layers is easy using the Add Layer dialog box.*

4. In the Layers window, click the new layer to select it. Now, anything you draw in this new layer will sit above Layer 1 and cover any items below it. Add a shape of your choice here. Figure 8-19 shows a large colored rectangle that I've drawn on the Background layer. Notice that it covers most of Layer 1.

Figure 8-19. *Click a layer to select it and then draw on it.*

5. To move the new layer (Background in this example) below the existing one (Layer 1), select that layer in the Layers window and click the down-pointing arrow button, as shown in Figure 8-20. (The other buttons in the Layers window allow you to raise a layer all the way to the top, lower a layer all the way to the bottom, delete a layer, and raise a layer up one level.) The Background layer is now underneath Layer 1. In the example in Figure 8-21, all of the elements from Figure 8-15 now sit on top of the large rectangle I added to the Background layer.

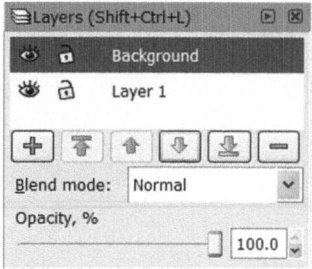

Figure 8-20. *Use the buttons in the Layers window to raise, lower, or delete layers.*

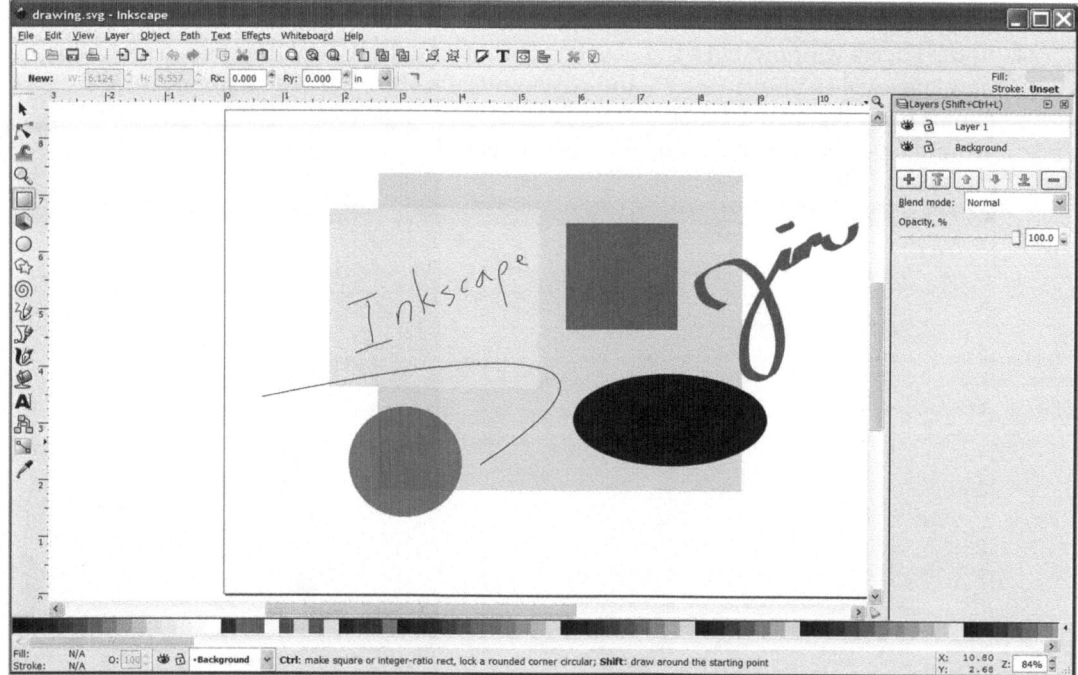

Figure 8-21. *Use layers to create overlaps and other effects in Inkscape.*

Perform Other Drawing Tasks

As you experiment with Inkscape, you'll find many other things you can do. The following are some quick instructions for a few more basic tasks. Refer back to Figure 8-4 for the tool locations.

- Click the Text tool to add text to your drawing. You have control over the font, font size, and color of your text.

- Click the Polygons tool to add stars and other interesting shapes to your drawing.

- From the Object menu, you can select options that will allow you to rotate selected items and flip them horizontally and vertically.

- Select Object ➤ Transform. From the window that opens, you can make very subtle changes in the location and size of any selected object.

Investigate Further

Sometimes, open source software suffers from a lack of documentation. Books and online tutorials tend to come later, once the application has gained in popularity. The Inkscape developers had an interesting solution to this problem. In July 2008, contributors from the United States, Australia, France, Netherlands, and Russia held a "book sprint" (a manual is written quickly by more than one individual). The project was funded by Google. The group members were asked to provide a minimum of 14 chapters. They wrote 35 chapters. The manual is freely available at `http://en.flossmanuals.net/inkscape`, and it's a great place to start for some more advanced training with this great application.

Along with the free online manual, the following are a few more useful online resources:

- Inkscape wiki: `http://wiki.inkscape.org/wiki/index.php/Inkscape`

- Inkscape tutorials: `http://inkscapetutorials.wordpress.com/`

- Inkscape forum: `http://www.inkscapeforum.com/`

Inkscape is really in its infancy. The developers are committed to improving the application and adding new features, while keeping it open source and totally free. If you like the application, join the Inkscape forum and let them know. You can also post requests for tutorials, ask questions (and provide answers), and suggest new features to be added.

Summary

My wife got me a tablet and digital pen for my birthday, so I'm having fun using Inkscape. One of the first things I did was to create a small graphic that contains my signature. I can add that graphic to letters and other documents. Next, I'm going to try to create a mascot of sorts for my company. I've got some ideas, and Inkscape is just the tool to help me put them on the page.

A good graphics application will always come in handy for the nonprofessional artist. Whether you need to create a flyer for a business event or a school sports activity announcement, Inkscape can help you add some eye-catching color and graphics to otherwise boring text.

And if you're in any kind of profession or role that requires you to occasionally (or frequently) draw or create graphics, Inkscape can potentially save you a lot of money. It's worth investigating this free application before spending any funds on a big-name graphics application. You might be surprised to find that Inkscape provides a nice collection of tools and effects that can handle all your graphic design needs.

- Adobe Illustrator: $599

- Inkscape: $0

CHAPTER 9

■■■

Virus Protection

It's an unfortunate truth that your computer is always under attack from individuals who wish to damage your hardware, corrupt your software, and delete your files.

During the 1970s, the term *hacker* was a positive one, referring to someone who enjoyed tweaking and modifying hardware and software to do interesting (and legal) things. By the 1980s, however, the meaning of *hacker* changed to refer to someone who uses a computer's hardware and software to perform malicious activities.

Of all the methods used by these bad guys, none has been worse than the digital computer virus. Like a biological virus, a computer virus spreads through contact, can cause damage (but not always), and can be difficult to remove. The first known virus attacks began back in the early 1980s and continue to occur today. They target everyone who uses a computer, including you.

Your computer can pick up a virus by opening an infected file that was downloaded over the Internet or maybe a file included on a CD that someone gave you. Viruses can infect Word and spreadsheet files, applications, and even your operating system. When your computer is infected, it can run slower, programs can crash, and your files can be corrupted and unreadable or even deleted. Many infected computers must have their operating system completely reinstalled, all the applications reinstalled, and the data files restored to the hard drive.

Besides the monetary costs involved in restoring your computer to a working state after it has been infected by a virus, there is also the issue of time. It can take hours—even days—to properly reinstall and reconfigure your computer's software. And then there's the cost (in both time and money) to restore an individual or company's reputation. Viruses are a scourge to computer users everywhere.

Fortunately, the easiest method for protecting yourself from the damage and hassles that viruses can cause involves three simple steps (which are covered in this chapter):

1. Install an antivirus application on your computer.

2. Configure the antivirus application to perform scheduled scans and download updates.

3. Use the antivirus program to scan any files downloaded to your computer.

I recommend dozens of programs in this book, but if you're going to install only one, make that an antivirus application. New viruses appear almost daily, so even if you're already using an antivirus application, you need to make certain that its virus database is being updated regularly. This usually involves downloading a file that informs your antivirus program about the latest viruses that have popped up.

In this chapter, we'll look at two antivirus programs: the commercial Norton AntiVirus application and the free Avira AntiVir Personal application.

Note Common sense is one of your best weapons against malicious viruses and software. If something sounds too good to be true ("Click here to get your $1,000 check in the mail!"), or even if it sounds remotely possible ("Your bank account may be in danger; click here to log in with your password and verify your account balance"), don't do it. Always look at the Internet with a large dose of skepticism. You'll not only increase your odds of avoiding viruses, but you'll also likely avoid the scam artists out there just waiting to pounce.

The Defender

One of the most popular antivirus applications sold today is Norton AntiVirus (NAV). The current version is NAV 2009. When installed, the application tells you how many days are left on your update subscription (access to downloadable virus updates) and provides some visual feedback on the application's impact on your computer's processor (CPU) usage. You also have the ability to run scans of your computer by clicking the Scan Now link. Figure 9-1 shows a virus scan in action.

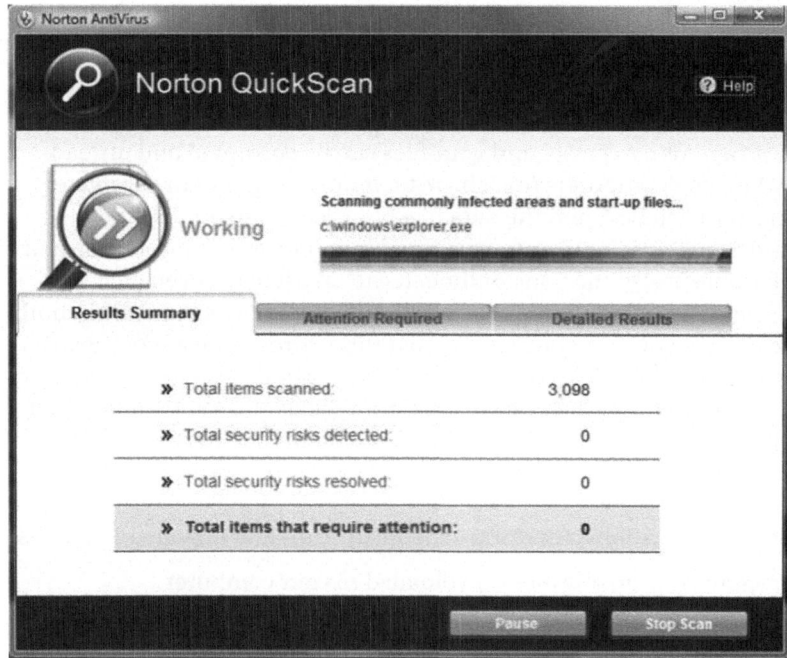

Figure 9-1. *A Norton AntiVirus scan in progress.*

WHAT IS A VIRUS SCAN?

A virus scan is simply the terminology used for when your computer's antivirus application is examining the files stored on your computer for infection by a virus. Most applications give you the ability to scan every file on your computer or select specific files or folders.

It is recommended that you always scan any files that you download from the Internet. Make a habit of saving these files into a temporary folder on your hard drive (such as a folder labeled Scan for Viruses), and then run your antivirus application and specify that folder be scanned.

You should also make a habit of scanning your entire computer's hard drive—every single file—weekly or at least monthly. Fortunately, most antivirus applications provide scheduling capabilities, so you can configure the application to perform this type of scan late in the evening (3 a.m. is when my scan is performed weekly) or on a weekend. Just be sure to leave your computer turned on when the scan is scheduled to occur. If you're not comfortable leaving your computer turned on 24/7 (some users prefer to save electricity and others believe that a running computer invites hackers, and both are legitimate concerns), then at least leave it on when the antivirus app is scheduled to run.

NAV's standard user interface gives you access to other features, such as scheduling and creating alerts. And as you run scans of your computer, NAV gives you a real-time update of any viruses caught, as well as details on whether the virus could be "cleaned" or if the infected file had to be quarantined, which means that it was moved to a safe folder on the hard drive where it can't do any additional damage. (A complete list of the features in the latest version of NAV can be found at http://www.symantec.com/norton/antivirus.)

I have a lot of problems with NAV and similar pay-to-use applications. The technology used to scan viruses is not only widely available, but it also doesn't change that often. There are hundreds of antivirus applications out there competing for your business and money. But there are also dozens of free alternatives that do just as good a job (maybe even better—keep reading) as the store-bought versions.

Another complaint I have is that users must pay a yearly (sometimes monthly) subscription fee to keep NAV updated with the latest virus database. In my opinion, once you've purchased the software, you should get the updates for free for as long as you choose to use that application. But NAV and other antivirus apps hit you up for $30 or more every year. By charging this subscription fee, the antivirus companies are basically forcing you to upgrade your software every year. Even Microsoft doesn't release a new version of Office every year!

The Contender

Antivirus applications are good only if they actually catch viruses. Antivirus programs use an internal database of existing viruses to scan your computer and its files, looking for matching viruses. But new viruses are being created every day! All antivirus programs allow you to update this virus database periodically—some monthly, some weekly, and some even daily. The important part is that your antivirus program needs to be updated constantly with information on the latest virus threats.

Note Don't be confused by those Internet pop-up ads saying "Your computer may be infected! Click here . . . ." They're just trying to sell you something. If you have a legitimate antivirus application running, let it tell you if it detects a file infection.

One of my favorite web sites is `http://www.av-comparatives.org/`. I suggest that you bookmark it and remember it for future reference. Point your web browser there and click the Comparatives tab. You'll be shown a list of comparison tests this organization performs on a variety of antivirus applications. The most recent test will be listed at the bottom, and the results can be viewed online by clicking the Online results link, as shown in Figure 9-2. The most popular antivirus applications are tested and evaluated, side-by-side, on this web site. The number one position changes now and then, but again, this is tried-and-true technology that doesn't really change from application to application.

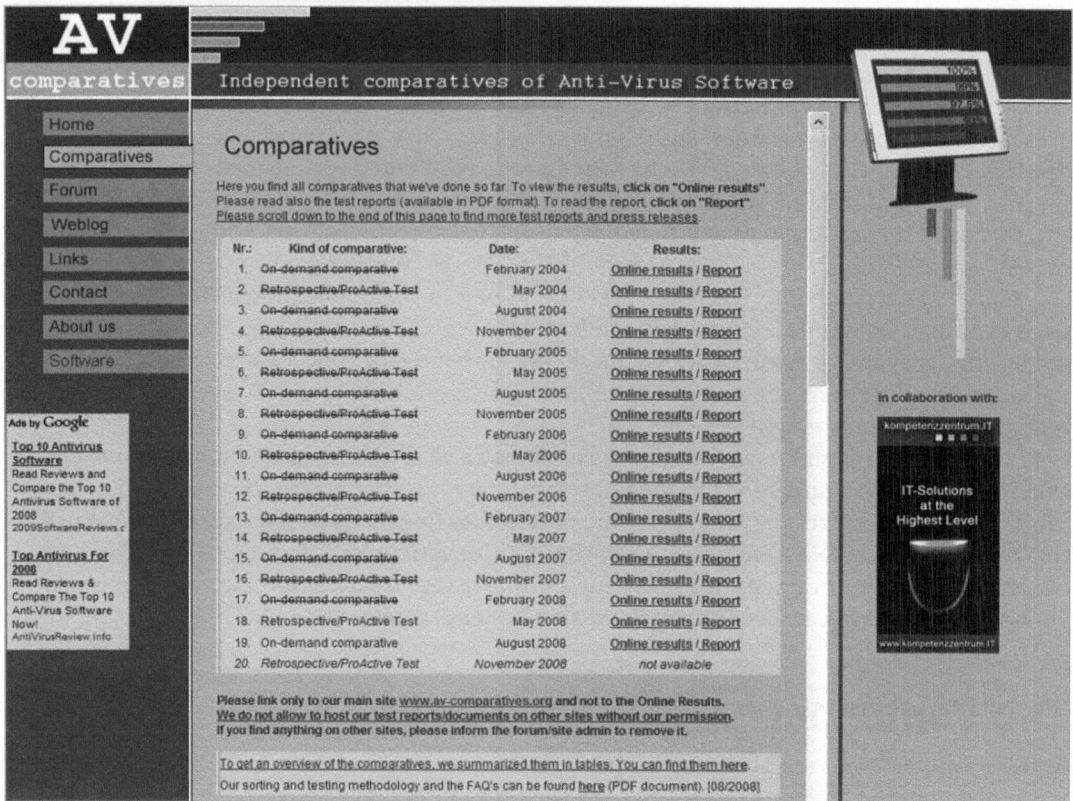

Figure 9-2. *AV-Comparatives offers comparison tests of various antivirus applications.*

As this chapter was being written, the current test (performed in November 2008 on 16 different antivirus applications) pitted the antivirus applications against one million different viruses. Can you guess which company got the overall best results? Avira, a company that provides a 100% free version of its antivirus application for you to download and install. (This ranking may have changed by the time you read this, but rest assured that Avira is likely to be near the top of the list as one of the best antivirus applications.)

Avira AntiVir Personal (AAP) is a free antivirus application for your home computer. Avira specifies that it be used for personal use, not business/commercial use. If you're a small business owner and want to play by the rules, Avira encourages you to purchase its Premium version. But I recommend that you download and install the free version first, to check how it works. If you like it, then by all means consider purchasing the Premium version to support the company and encourage it to continue the free Personal version.

Avira has a fairly simple interface, as shown in Figure 9-3, without a lot of bells and whistles. But it does what it's intended to do—find and remove viruses—and requires no purchase on your part.

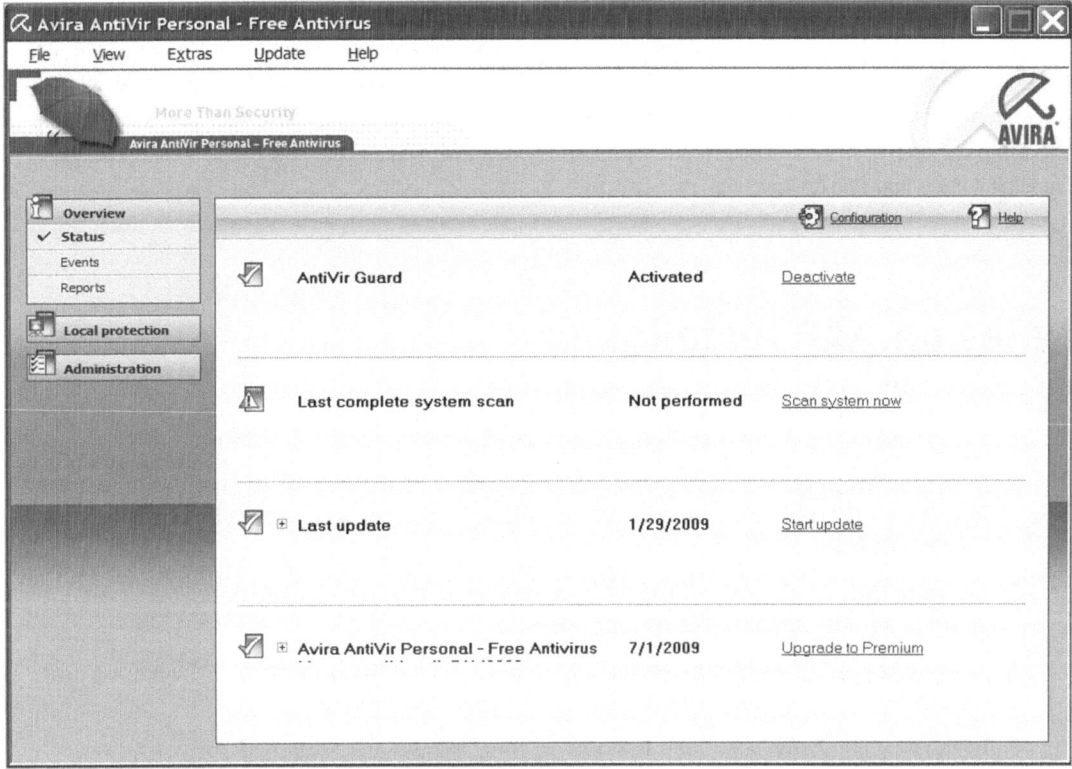

Figure 9-3. *Avira AntiVir Personal is a powerful antivirus application for your PC.*

A lot of free antivirus applications are available, but I recommend Avira because I use it, and I know it works. The fact that it always scores high in the antivirus comparison tests further proves its value and effectiveness. In the remaining sections of this chapter, I'll show you where to get AAP, how to install it, and how to use it. I encourage you to follow along and get an antivirus application installed immediately, if you don't already have one.

Where to Get the Software

You can download and install the free version of Avira by following these steps:

1. Visit `http://www.free-av.com` (or visit `http://www.avira.com`, click the Downloads link, and then click Avira AntiVir Personal – Free Antivirus).

2. Click the Download Your Free AntiVir button.

3. Avira will provide you with two or more locations to download the installation files. Pick one and click it. Then follow the instructions to download the Avira installation application.

■**Note** Why would Avira give away a free version of its software? Many companies give away a personal (or home) version in the hopes that you'll like the software and possibly recommend it to your employer or buy an upgraded version with more features. The free version of Avira also pops up the occasional sales screen that talks about its other products. Just close the window if you're not interested. Yes, this is a little annoying, but keep in mind that you're getting a top-notch antivirus application for free. You can always uninstall it if the pop-ups drive you crazy.

Notes on AAP Installation

Let's get this antivirus application installed pronto!

1. Double-click the Avira installation file that was downloaded to your computer.

2. A window pops up to tell you that this is a valid version of the software and gives you a link to visit Avira's web site to purchase other products, as shown in Figure 9-4. Click the Accept button.

3. After the files are unzipped, the Avira Installation Wizard will welcome you to the setup program. Click the Next button twice.

4. After your read through the license agreement, check the box labeled "I accept the terms of the license agreement." Then click the Next button.

5. In the next window, you need to confirm that you will be using AAP for your own personal use, and not for commercial uses. Place a check in the box indicating your agreement, and then click the Next button.

6. Next, you can choose between a complete or custom installation, as shown in Figure 9-5. The custom installation is recommended only for advanced users, so for now, just allow the complete installation to occur. Click the Next button to continue.

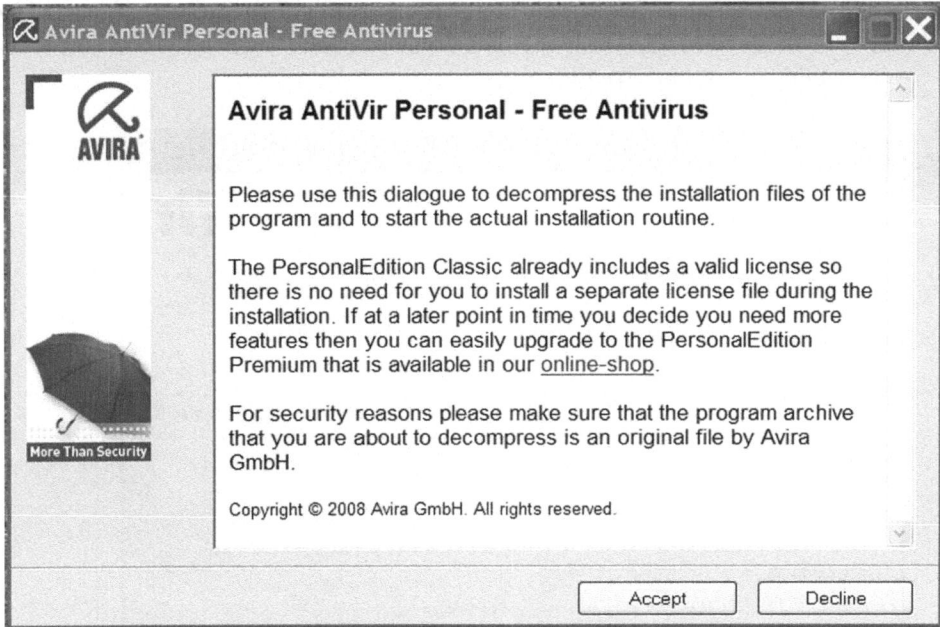

Figure 9-4. *Preparing to install Avira AntiVir Personal*

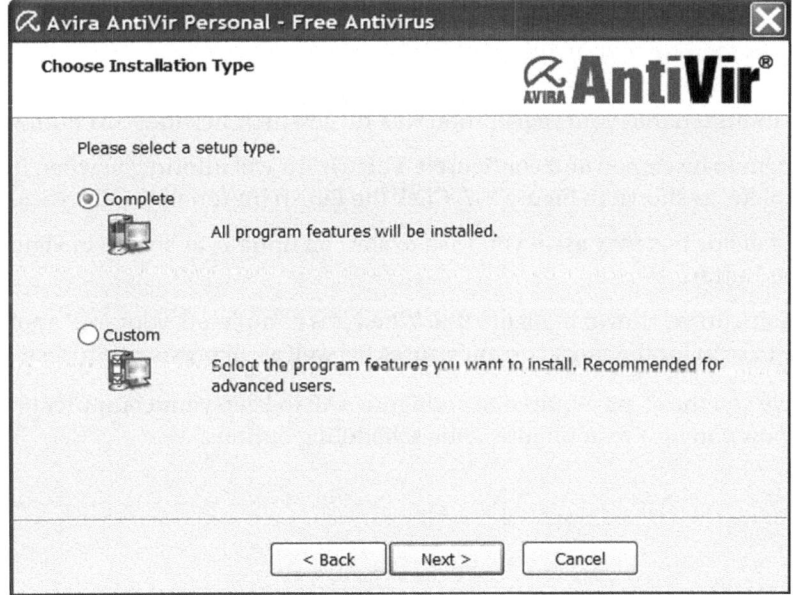

Figure 9-5. *The complete installation is recommended for most users.*

7. In the next window, provide some basic registration information, as shown in Figure 9-6. You need to fill in only the data that is starred (*). Click the Next button when you've filled in your information.

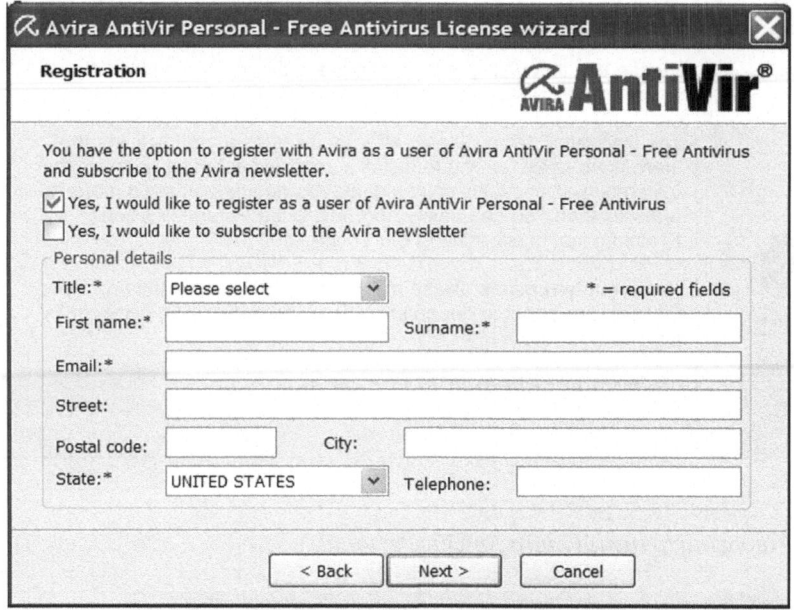

Figure 9-6. *Register your copy of Avira AntiVir Personal.*

8. You will be informed that your registration was successful. Click the Next button.

9. Files will begin to be copied and configured. The wizard will inform you when installation is complete, as shown in Figure 9-7. Click the Finish button to exit the wizard.

10. A small alert dialog box may ask if you wish to start an update, as shown in Figure 9-8. Click the Yes button.

11. Let the update run, as shown in Figure 9-9. When it is completed, your AAP application will be able to scan for the most current viruses (as well as all previous viruses).

Up next, I'll give you the steps required to configure AAP to keep your computer protected, as well as show you how to configure some scheduling options.

Figure 9-7. *Avira AntiVir Personal is successfully installed.*

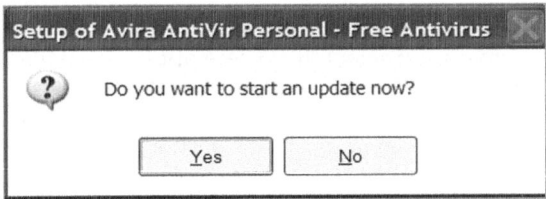

Figure 9-8. *Accept the offer to start an update to get the latest antivirus information for Avira.*

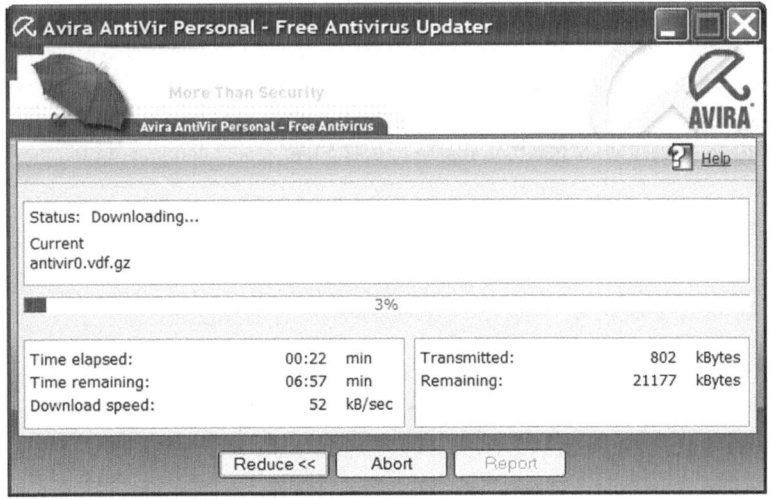

Figure 9-9. *The update is necessary for Avira to know about the latest viruses.*

Basic AAP Tasks

This section covers two important tasks that you should perform as soon as possible with AAP. Open the application by double-clicking the Avira desktop shortcut or the small *A* icon in your system tray, and follow along.

Run a Complete System Scan

The first time you run AAP, you should perform a scan of your entire hard drive. Don't be surprised if it finds a few viruses in your files. As you'll soon see, it found some on my hard drive.

Note A complete system scan could take some time, so take a break after you start it. Remember that there are thousands—possibly tens of thousands—of files on your computer that AAP must examine.

Here are the steps to follow to perform the complete system scan:

1. Open AAP and click the "Scan system now" link, as shown in Figure 9-10. AAP will begin to scan your system files, as shown in Figure 9-11.

2. If AAP finds an infected file, the scan will pause, as shown in Figure 9-12. The default choice is to "Move to quarantine," or you can select the Delete option if you definitely don't want that file on your computer. Also, you can place a check in the box labeled "Apply selection to all following detections," and any future infected files will get the same treatment.

Note What is *quarantine*? It's a special folder created on your hard drive where AAP can move files that are infected, rather than deleting them. This way, you can examine the files to possibly determine if the infection is legitimate or not. Sometimes files are flagged as infected when they're not; this is called a *false-positive*. Some users will scan potentially infected files using another antivirus application as a sort of second opinion. Quarantine is sometimes also useful for identifying a file and its creator. You can then notify this person that her computer may have a virus infection that is infecting files she is sending out to others.

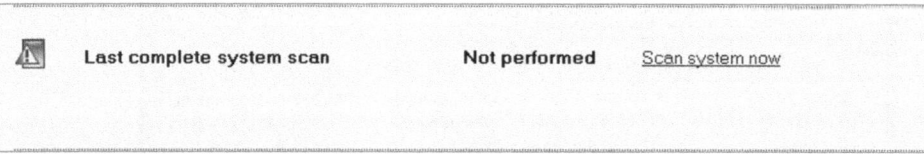

Figure 9-10. *Make your first priority a complete system scan.*

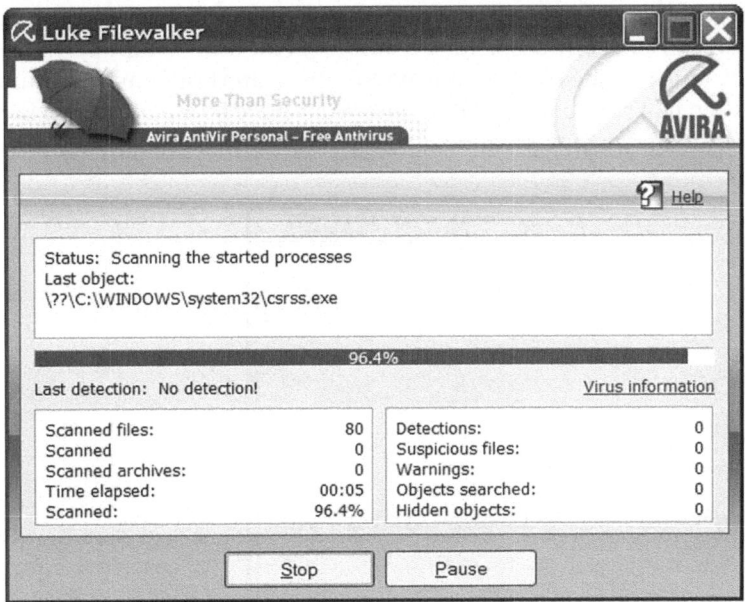

Figure 9-11. *The system scan can take some time, but be patient—it's an important task.*

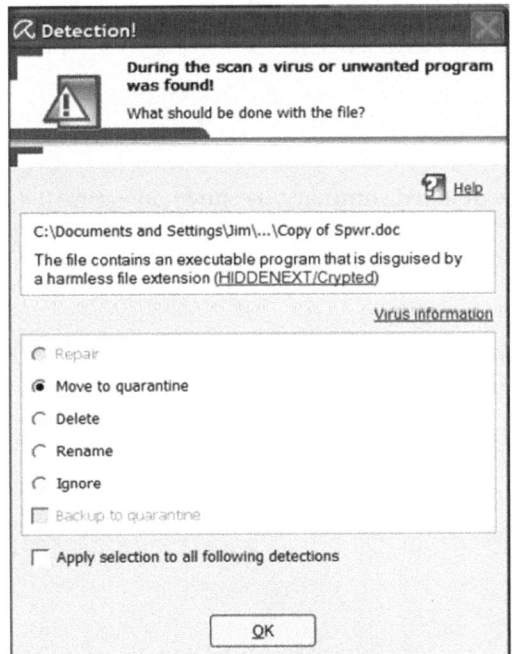

Figure 9-12. *You have options if a virus is found, including to quarantine, delete, or ignore it.*

3. After an infected file is handled, the application begins its scan again. You can click the Stop or Pause button at any time, but it's best to let the scan complete. In my case, when AAP finally finished, the complete scan took about one hour and 21 minutes and involved more than half a million files! Four infections were found, as shown in Figure 9-13. I quarantined two of them and deleted the other two.

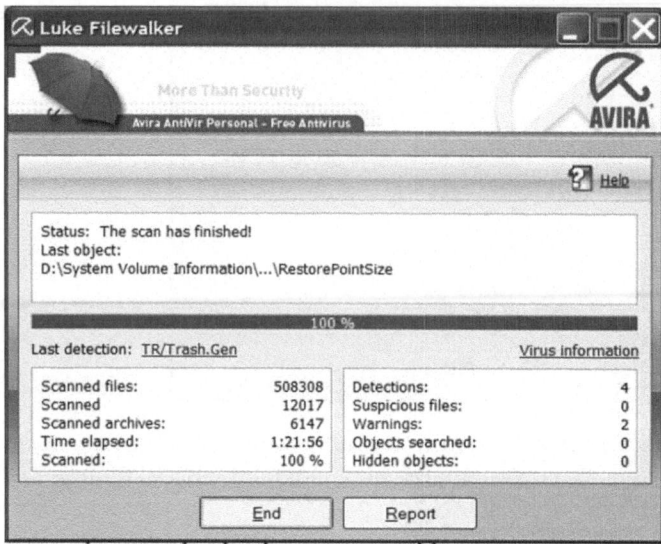

Figure 9-13. *When the scan completes, Avira AntiVir Personal displays the number of infections found and time taken.*

4. Click the Report button to get a more detailed summary, as shown in Figure 9-14.

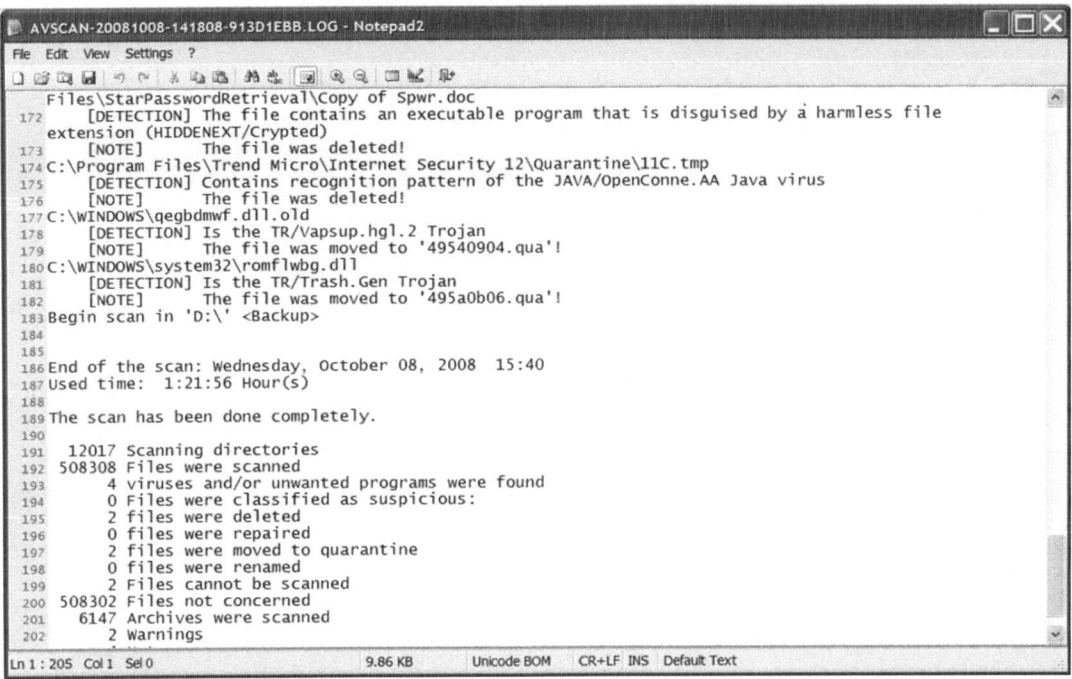

Figure 9-14. *You can view or print a more detailed scan summary.*

Schedule Routine Scans

It's a good idea to have AAP scan your computer without your intervention, possibly weekly or monthly. Here's how to schedule scans to occur on a regular basis:

1. Open AAP and click the Administration tab, as shown in Figure 9-15.

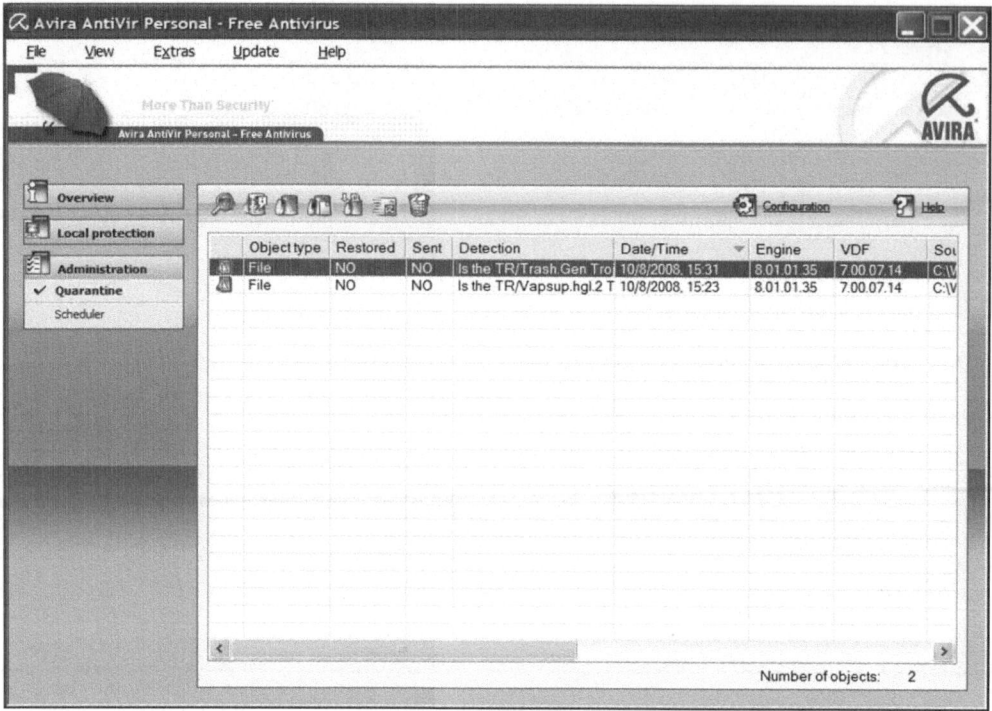

Figure 9-15. *Use the Administration tab to configure a scheduled scan.*

2. Click the Scheduler subtab, as shown in Figure 9-16. If you examine Figure 9-16, you can see that a daily update activity is currently scheduled—it has a check mark under the Activated column. This means that AAP will attempt to connect and download any updates from the company every day.

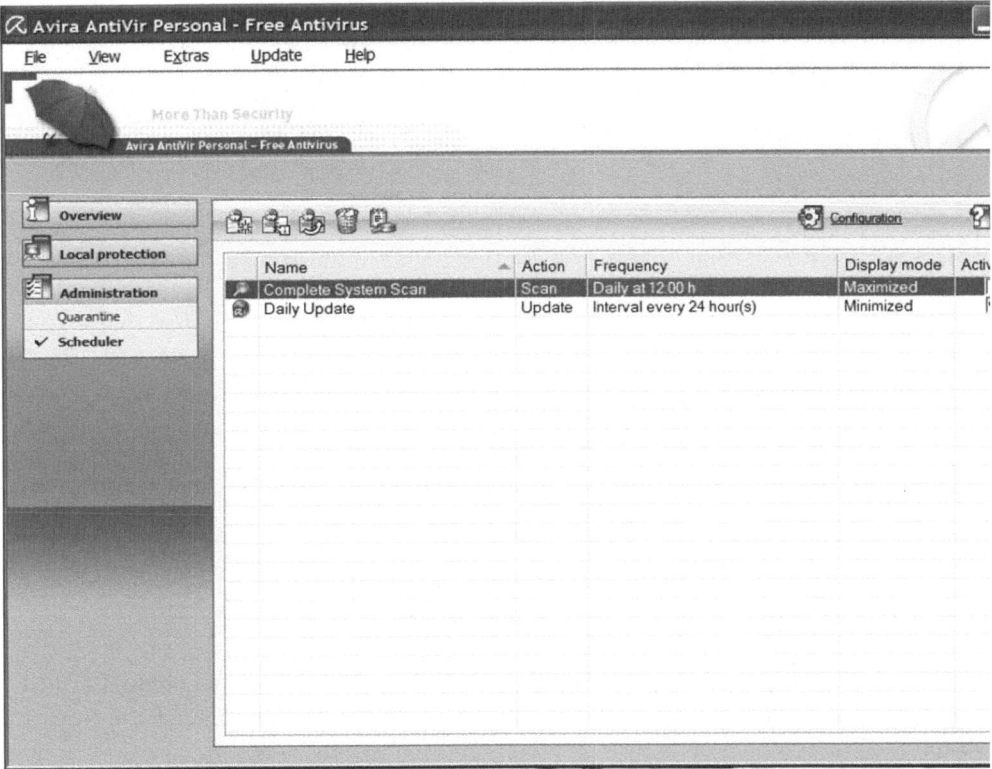

Figure 9-16. *The Scheduler tab shows the activities that have been scheduled.*

3. To schedule scans, click the Insert New Job button, as indicated in Figure 9-17.

Insert New Job Button

Figure 9-17. *Click the Insert New Job button to create a new job that automates virus scanning.*

4. A window will appear, asking you to provide information about the new job. In Figure 9-18, I've given it the name Weekly Scan and provided a description of what the scan will cover (my C: drive). Click the Next button to continue.

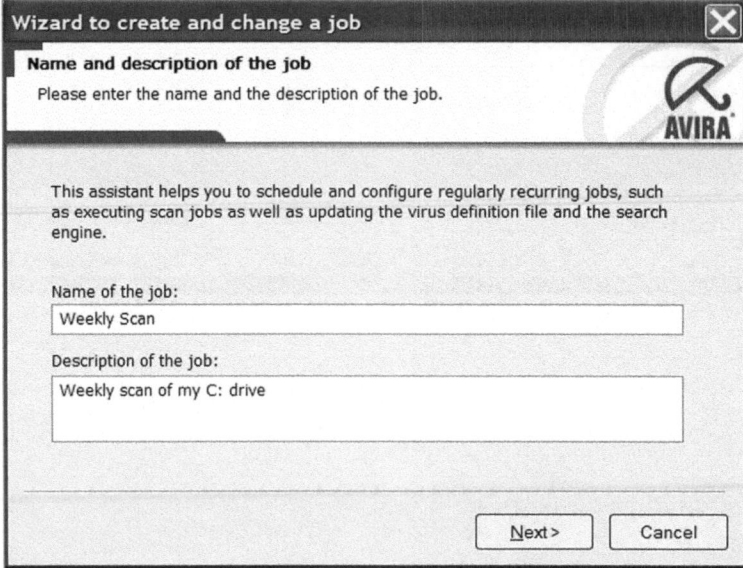

Figure 9-18. *Give your new job a name and description.*

5. In the next window, select Scan job or Update job from the drop-down menu. Because I'm creating a weekly scan, I chose Scan job, as shown in Figure 9-19. Click the Next button.

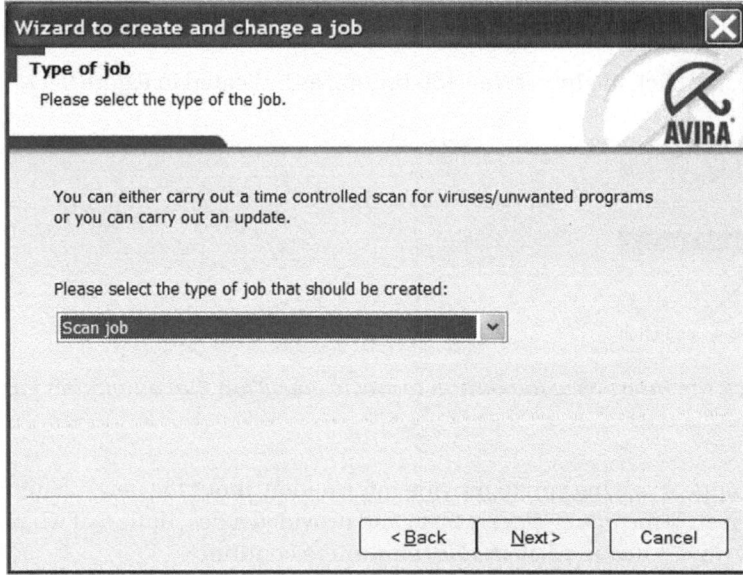

Figure 9-19. *Select the type of job you wish to schedule: scan or update.*

6. In the next window, select which files you wish to scan from the drop-down menu. You can choose My Documents, system files, hard drives, and so on. Individual files can be selected by choosing the Manual option in the drop-down menu. I selected Local Hard Disks, as shown in Figure 9-20 Click the Next button to proceed.

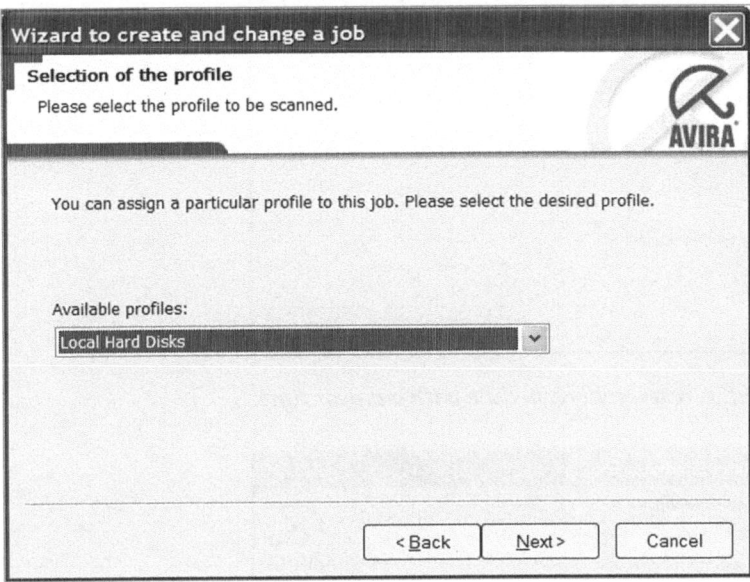

Figure 9-20. *Select the files, folders, or hard drives you wish to scan.*

7. In the next window, select the frequency of the scan. For this job, I selected Weekly. Additional options are available after you choose the schedule. For my job, I selected Sunday at 3 a.m. for my weekly scan, as shown in Figure 9-21. Click the Next button to continue.

8. Choose whether AAP runs in the background (invisible), minimized (visible as a tab on the taskbar), or maximized (visible on the screen) from the pull-down menu, as shown in Figure 9-22. You can also choose whether to have AAP shut down your computer when the scan is done by placing a check in the box labeled "Shut down computer if job is done." Click the Finish button after you've made your selections. The Scheduler now lists your new job in the window, as shown in Figure 9-23.

Now that I've scheduled the weekly scan, if I leave my computer on Sunday evening, the scanning will start at 3 a.m.—perfect! It's just like any chore: leave the trash can on the curb on Thursday morning, mow the grass on Saturday, and so on. But this one doesn't require any manual labor!

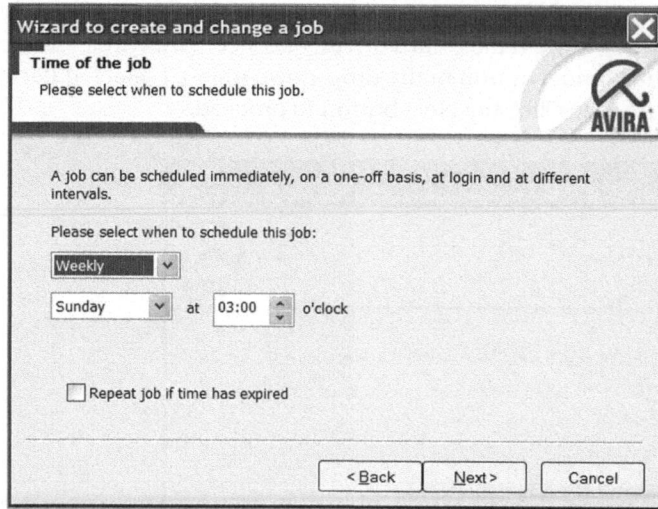

Figure 9-21. *Configure a weekly schedule with a day or time.*

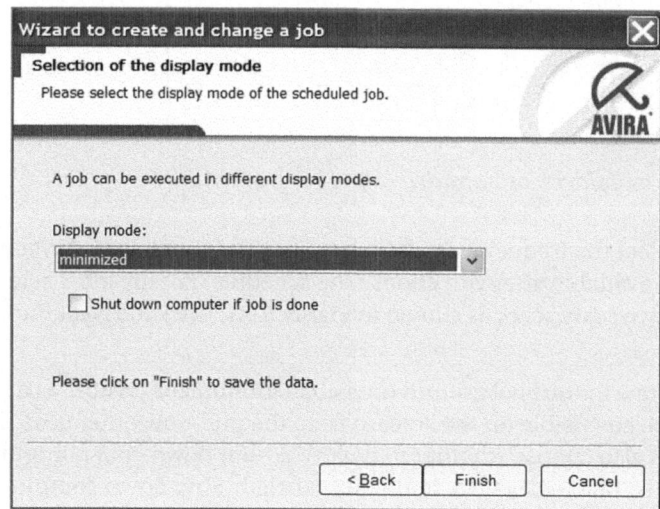

Figure 9-22. *Configure whether Avira AntiVir Personal runs invisible, minimized, or maximized.*

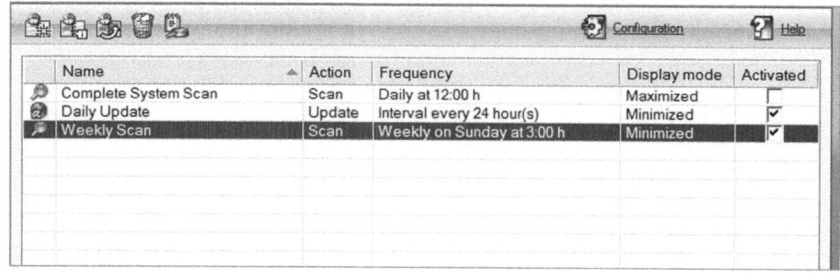

Figure 9-23. *The job is scheduled and ready to run.*

Investigate Further

Besides viruses, you also need to protect your computer from something called *spyware* (or *malware*). Spyware is typically installed on your computer without your knowledge when you install certain programs or visit specific web sites. As the name implies, the software is designed to spy on your activities—shopping habits, books purchased, clothing ordered, and so on—and report back to the company that created the software. This information is typically used to flood your e-mail inbox (or your real mailbox) with spam and junk mail. At other times, the spyware is installed for malicious reasons, such as to collect your credit card number when you order something online or store passwords you use when logging in to certain web sites.

Spyware is a major hassle, but fortunately, two of the best anti-spyware applications are 100% free:

- Lavasoft's Ad-Aware: http://www.lavasoft.com

- Spybot–Search & Destroy: http://www.spybot.info

Pick one and install it (many people install both). Both applications are designed to update regularly and block known spyware from being installed on your computer. They run in the background, invisible to you, and alert you when something unfriendly tries to install itself. (I've used both and am currently running Spybot on my own computers.)

Summary

If you're a homeowner, you most likely take regular precautions such as checking the batteries on your smoke detectors and testing the alarm system to protect your investment. With a vehicle, you change the oil regularly and rotate your tires. So why should your computer be treated any differently?

For your PC, you shouldn't be concerned about just the hardware. Your software, personal and business files, and operating system should all be protected from harm, and an antivirus application is the place to start. Even if you intend to use your computer only for browsing the Internet and exchanging e-mail, installing an antivirus application is the most important task you'll perform if you wish to have a happy, healthy computer.

AAP is free and easy to use. There's simply no excuse not to protect the valuables stored on your computer's hard drive. Set aside some time soon to download and install this great little application. Also be sure to read the next chapter, which covers another critical way to protect your computer: backing up your data.

- Norton AntiVirus: $69

- Avira AntiVir Personal: $0

CHAPTER 10

■ ■ ■

Data Backup

This is a true story. In 2002, I was working as a jack-of-all-trades computer guy for a small company. I fixed computers, debugged laptops, installed software, managed e-mail and web site servers for various companies, and everything in between. On one particular blue-sky, birds-are-singing day, my phone rang. A "high-level" employee (let's call him Tony) for one of the small businesses I supported was in near panic because some files on his computer had disappeared. He had been working all week on them, and when he left the office the previous night, the files were still there. The next morning, they were gone.

He looked in the Recycle Bin, but the files weren't there. He did a file search of his entire hard drive using a few of the file names, but the files didn't turn up. Tony was ready to flip out! I calmed him down, rearranged some scheduled appointments, got in my car, and paid a visit.

My initial search found nothing. (I had some special debugging software that would let me examine deleted files that weren't showing up in the Recycle Bin, but it was no use.) The files weren't there. But I still had one option left.

I accessed the company's file server (its shared office computer), and located a folder I had created months earlier labeled Tony Backup. As a precaution, I had installed some simple backup software on the ten computers in this office. This software automatically backed up the My Documents folder of each PC to the server at 3 a.m. (my favorite backup time). Tony's files were there, and I copied them over to his computer in about 20 seconds.

Everyone was happy, including the office manager, who promptly paid my bill (including the emergency call fee) on the spot.

I have dozens of stories like this one, from friends as well as customers, but not all of them end happily. Data losses happen, and as computers get more complex, the possibility of major mistakes gets greater, too. It's not just an event in big offices—it could easily happen to you. Fortunately, this story did end on a happy note, and all because I knew the value of performing regular backups of my customers' valuable data.

Just like a word processor used to write a letter or an antivirus application that scans files for viruses, software exists to assist you with backups. In this chapter, you'll learn about a commercial backup program that you can purchase, and a free software package that will probably take care of all your backup needs.

Your Valuable Data

Think about the types of files you have stored on your PC. These days, an increasing amount of important personal information is stored only on your PC. There are work documents and personal documents. You'll find everything from your company's confidential stock report to your grandmother's original recipe for chicken soup, photos of last year's vacation, video of your child's first steps, scanned receipts for your small business purchases, financial reports, resumes, addresses and phone numbers, e-mail, and much more.

What would you do if you were told those files would be deleted from your computer's hard drive tomorrow? Most likely, you would burn as much of it as possible to a CD or DVD, or copy it to another computer. You would do whatever you could to make sure a copy (or copies) existed, right?

Well, the bad news is that most of us are never given a warning that our data will be deleted. You might turn on your computer one day and discover a file has disappeared. Or your three-year-old son, who has carefully observed how you press keys and move the mouse, decides to take a spin on your laptop, and manages a dozen right-click-and-delete actions, including emptying the Recycle Bin. Maybe you made some significant changes to an original document yesterday (without working on a copy) and then realized that you need the original back.

Whatever the reason, if you value your data, you need to protect it. This means implementing a plan to back up your data regularly. This plan will involve using an application to back up your data to CD or a DVD, or possibly to a second hard drive. It will involve configuring the application to perform the backup, whether or not you're sitting in front of the computer. And it will require that you understand how to restore one or more files should the need arise.

BACKING UP YOUR DATA IS ONLY PART OF THE PLAN

In the previous chapter, you read about the importance of installing and using a good antivirus application. Not only can an antivirus program protect your operating system, but it can also keep your data files from becoming infected or damaged by viruses and other malicious software (or *malware*). But even if you're running an antivirus application, there's always a small chance that files can be infected, damaged, or even deleted by a virus or malware that sneaks through your defenses. That's where your data backup plan comes into play.

I suggest that you perform three tasks to protect your computer, software, and data files:

- Run an antivirus application (covered in Chapter 6).

- Create a regular data backup plan—and use it (covered in this chapter).

- Create an image (or copy) of your hard drive that backs up your operating system and applications (covered in this book's appendix). In the event of a hard drive failure, the image can be reinstalled on a new hard drive.

Of the three tasks, backing up your data is probably the most important. You can always reinstall your operating system and applications should a nasty virus (or other malware) do its worst or a hard drive fail. But if your data is damaged or deleted and you don't have a backup, it's gone forever.

The Defender

One of the larger software companies out there, Symantec, offers what many consider to be the industry-standard backup program: Norton Save & Restore. This program is a useful baseline for our comparison.

Figure 10-1 shows a backup strategy being created while installing Norton Save & Restore. Figure 10-2 shows how you can select specific file type folders to protect via backup.

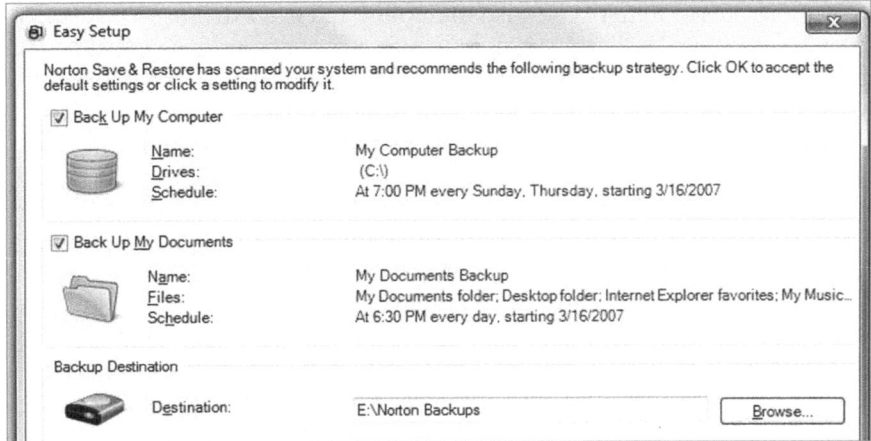

Figure 10-1. *Defining a backup strategy with Norton Save & Restore*

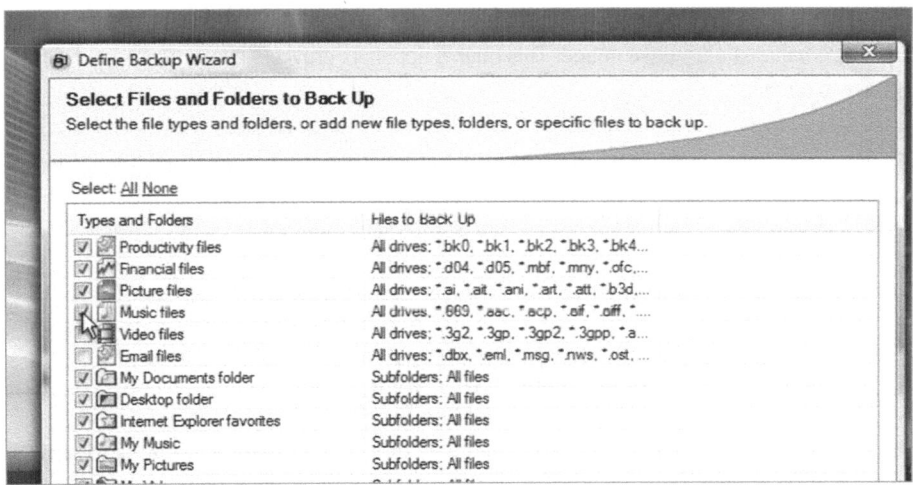

Figure 10-2. *Specifying which file types and folders to protect via Norton Save & Restore*

■**Note** A complete list of the features found in the latest version of Norton Save & Restore can be found at http://www.symantec.com/norton/save-restore.

As with most Norton products, Save & Restore doesn't skimp on the features. You are given many more options than are necessary—a lot of them clearly intended for professional computer guys like me (and not necessarily for you, the end user). This can be good and bad. You're sure to find the method you like best for backing up your data, but it can take a while to learn how to properly tune the application to get it to do exactly what you want.

Norton Save & Restore offers some key features that you'll definitely want to look for in a data backup application. These include the ability to automate your backups, as well as to select individual files and folders to be backed up. If you need to restore files, Save & Restore allows you to pick only those files or folders you wish to retrieve and leave the rest. You also have the ability to encrypt your data backups. (I don't recommend encryption, just in case you forget the password, but the option is there.) You also get the ability to back up the Windows startup files required to get Windows back to a working condition.

Finally, Save & Restore supports full, incremental, and differential backups. A full backup is just what it sounds like: everything is backed up. With an incremental or differential backup, only those files that have changed since the last full backup are backed up in subsequent backup operations. This can save space on your hard drive or other storage media where you store your backup files.

In a nutshell, Norton Save & Restore gives you the ability to create scheduled, automated backups (full, incremental, and differential) of your files, folders, and operating system, as well as the ability to restore those same files, folders, and system files. But you can already guess what I'm going to tell you next, can't you? Yes, almost all of these same features can be obtained absolutely free, and I'm going to show you the application that can do it.

■**Tip** While the ability to back up the Windows system files is a very useful feature, you can get the same functionality (for free) by creating a hard drive image. This book's appendix provides information about a free application you can use to do this.

The Contender

When it comes to data backup software, what you're really looking for is an application that will let you do both manual backups (at the time of your choosing) and automated backups (again, at a time of your choosing, but without you needing to start the process), selecting the files and folders that you wish to include in the backup. Cobian Backup is a good solution.

Cobian Backup, shown in Figure 10-3, is an open source data backup application with numerous special features built in. Rest assured, however, that if your primary goal is to simply make backups of your data quickly and easily, without a lot of messy settings to learn, Cobian Backup is all you need.

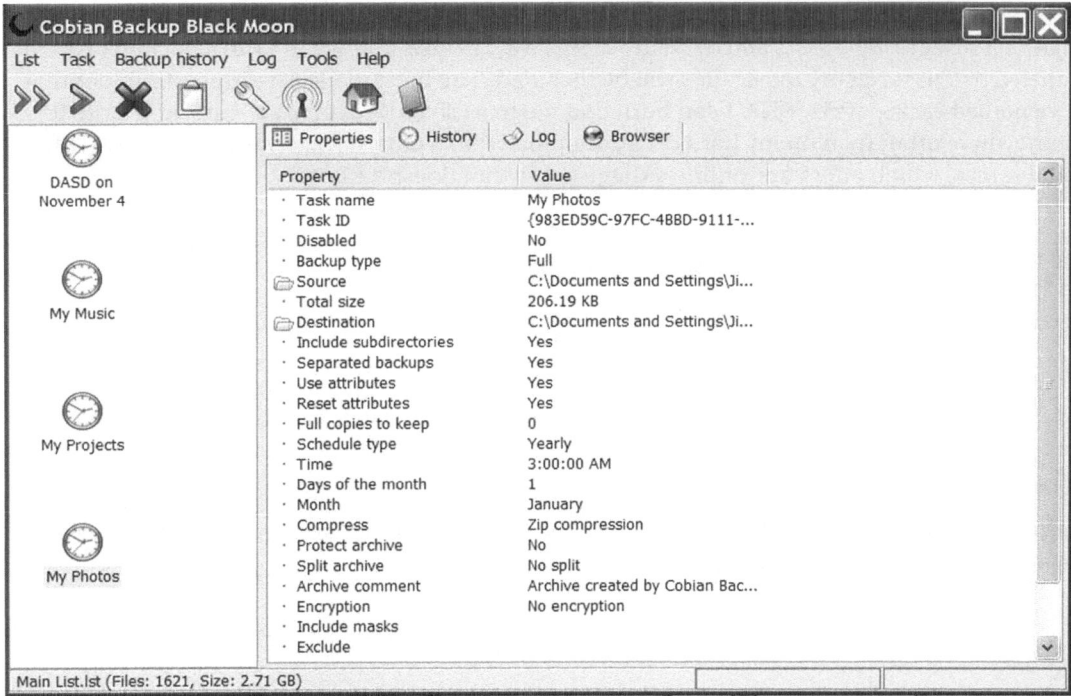

Figure 10-3. *Cobian Backup lets you create multiple backup jobs to run at any time.*

Cobian Backup can back up both files and folders. This means that Cobian Backup is ideally suited for backing up the contents of an entire folder such as My Documents or something as specific as a single OpenOffice.org spreadsheet named MyCurrentInvestments.ods, located in the subfolder My Finances of My Documents.

Cobian Backup also works great when you need to restore a complete folder or an individual file. When you find that you need to retrieve a damaged or deleted file, you simply restore that file to the original location. If you need to recover an entire folder, without overwriting the contents of the original folder (say, your My Documents folder), you can choose to restore to a temporary folder, copy the files you need to the original location, and then delete the temporary folder.

Note Cobian Backup also allows you to schedule your backups to run at a later time. This does require that you leave your computer turned on so the backup can occur, but it's a small price to pay for the ability of running a data backup at a more convenient time.

Cobian Backup is a powerful backup tool, but one with a simple-to-use interface that helps you set up quick and easy backups. What I like best about it is that I can create a handful of different backup routines (called *tasks*) ahead of time, and run them when I need them with a single click of a button. I store my personal files in dedicated folders with names like My Projects, My Music, and My Photos. This way, I know that when I run a backup task labeled My Music, all my music files will be included. The backup file is written to a folder that I've named Backup This File. I can burn that file to a CD or DVD at my leisure, and store it somewhere other than on my hard drive, or upload it to a data storage site of my choice (like adrive.com, which offers free online storage space that doesn't expire).

Where to Get the Software

To download the free Cobian Backup application, follow these two simple steps:

1. Visit http://www.educ.umu.se/~cobian/cobianbackup.htm.

2. Click the link labeled Download Cobian Backup 8 to download the installation file.

Note Cobian Backup 9 is not open source software. Of course, you can download and try it if you like. This chapter covers Cobian Backup 8, which is open source.

Notes on Cobian Backup Installation

There's nothing fancy or troublesome about installing Cobian Backup. Simply double-click the application's installation file to begin the installation and follow the on-screen instructions. When the installation asks for you to choose an installation type, change the default option to "As an application (no autostart)" and click the Next button. Click the Done button when the installation wizard completes.

Note I encourage you to uncheck Cobian Backup's autostart option, because if you're like me, seeing a dozen applications running in the system tray can be a little annoying, and they also eat up valuable RAM needed to run other programs.

After the installation, Cobian Backup will automatically start up. You will find it running in the system tray in the lower-right corner. Its icon looks like a half moon. For all future uses, you must launch the application by selecting Start ➤ Cobian Backup.

Basic Cobian Backup Tasks

The two basic Cobian Backup tasks are as follows:

Back up files and folders: This is the process in which you choose which files and folders you wish to copy to a backup.

Restore files and folders: This is the process in which you select files and folders to restore to your computer.

The most frequent task that you will perform using Cobian Backup is backing up files and folders. Cobian Backup allows you to save your backups in `.zip` format (a standardized, "compressed" file format that takes up less space). This allows you to quickly and easily examine a zipped file to find the files and/or folders you need to recover.

I'll cover both the backup and restore tasks here, and show you how easy it is to use this application. As you read through the following section, I highly encourage you to follow along and perform a backup immediately.

Back Up Files and Folders

Without a backup, there can be no recovery. First, you create a backup task that will run automatically at the time you scheduled. Then you can test that task by running it manually.

Create a Backup Task

Use the following process to create a task to back up the important files on your system:

1. Double-click the Cobian Backup icon located in the system tray in the lower-right corner (as noted, it looks like a half moon). Cobian Backup will open, as shown in Figure 10-4.

2. Select Task ➤ New Task to open the Properties window for your new backup task.

3. On the General page, enter a name for the backup task, as shown in the example in Figure 10-5. Be as descriptive as you can, including dates and folder names if possible. (Having eight different backup files named BACKUP can make life difficult later!)

4. Note the options for full, incremental, and differential backups, just as are available with Norton Save & Restore. For right now, select the Full radio button, as this will be your first backup. On subsequent backups, you can choose the Differential or Incremental option to save space.

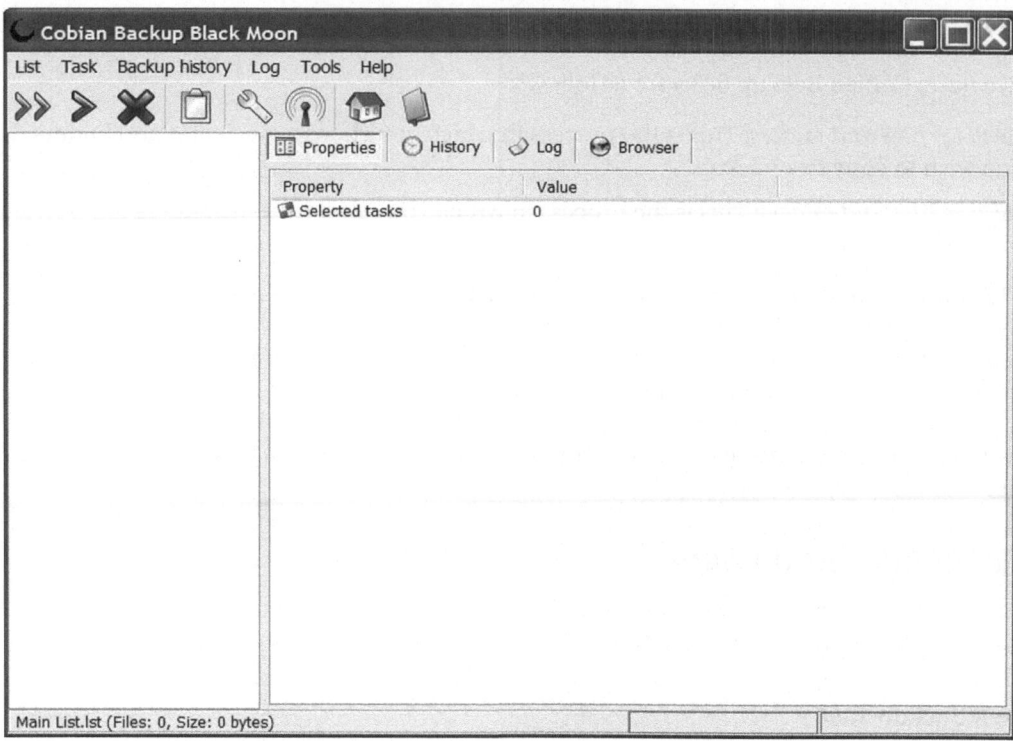

Figure 10-4. *Cobian Backup has an easy-to-use interface.*

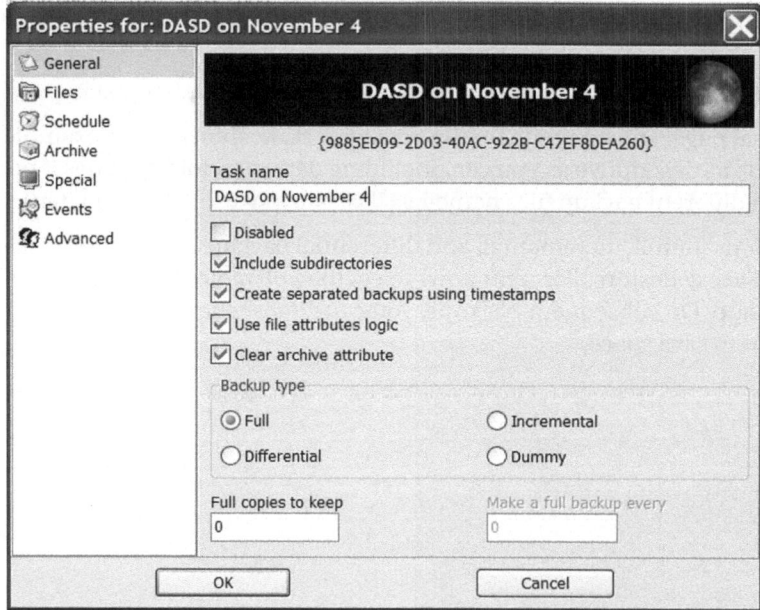

Figure 10-5. *Give your backup task a name that describes the files and folders to be backed up.*

Note Differential and Incremental backups allow you to back up files that have changed since the last full backup. For example, if you run a weekly full backup every Sunday night, you could choose to create a differential backup that runs on Wednesday of each week. This backup will consist of a smaller collection of files, because only those files that have been modified will be included in the differential backup process. The incremental backup process is useful if you want to run daily backups between two full backups and include only those files that have changed. For a more detailed discussion of the differences between differential and incremental backups, visit `http://en.wikipedia.org/wiki/Backup_rotation_scheme`.

5. Click Files in the list along the left side of the window to move to the Files page.

6. Click the Add button under the Source section and select Files, as shown in Figure 10-6.

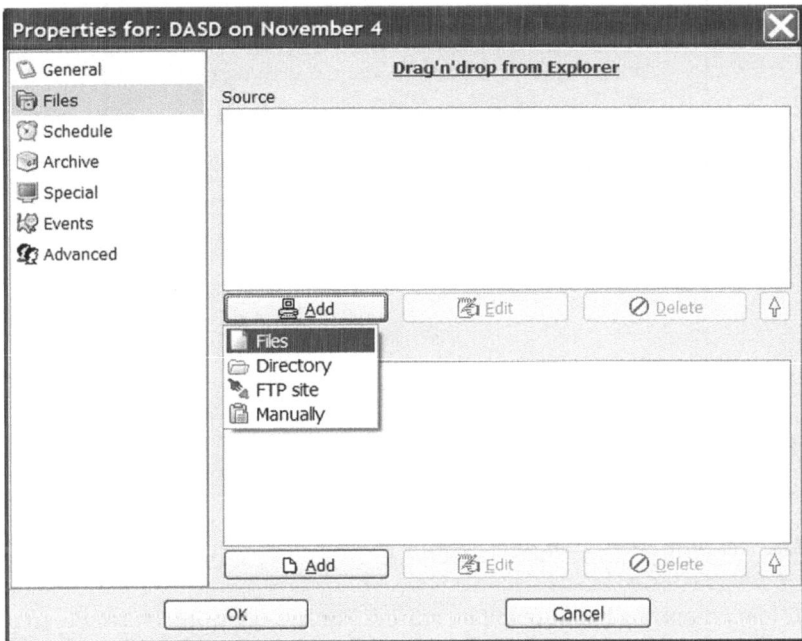

Figure 10-6. *Select the sources (files and directories) to be added to the backup.*

7. Browse to the locations of the files you wish to back up, select the files, and click the Open button. You can Ctrl-click to select multiple files at once. To back up complete folders (directories), click the Add button, select Directory, browse to the folder you wish to add to your backup, and click the OK button.

Tip Notice the "Drag'n'drop from Explorer" link at the top of the Properties page. You can simply click this link, and then drag a folder from Windows Explorer to the Source box here to add it to the list of files to be backed up.

8. Click the Add button under the Destination section and select Directory, as shown in Figure 10-7.

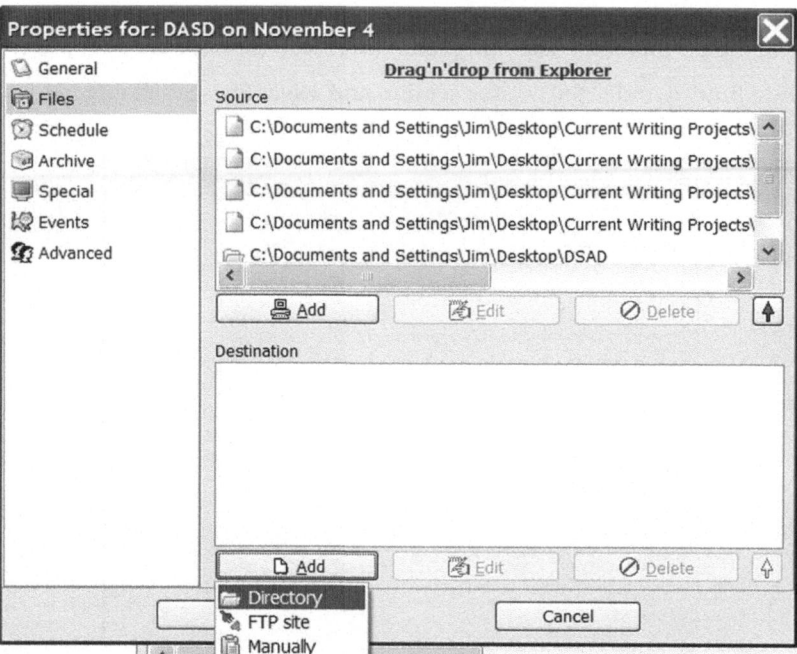

Figure 10-7. *Select the destination folder where the backup file will be stored.*

9. Specify a folder where the backup will be stored. For my example, I have created a folder on my Desktop called `Backup This File`, where my backup will be stored.

10. Click Schedule in the list along the left side of the page to move to the Schedule page.

11. From the Schedule type drop-down menu, you can choose how frequently you would like this backup to run: Once, Daily, Weekly, and other options are available. In the example shown in Figure 10-8, I've selected to run a weekly backup on Tuesdays at 3 a.m. Other options will allow you to specify the day of the month, or even a specific day of the year.

Caution Try to run your backup processes and antivirus scans (see Chapter 9) at different times or days. Both processes require accessing files on the hard drive, so scheduling these two tasks at the same time can severely task your computer's hard drive and bog down the system.

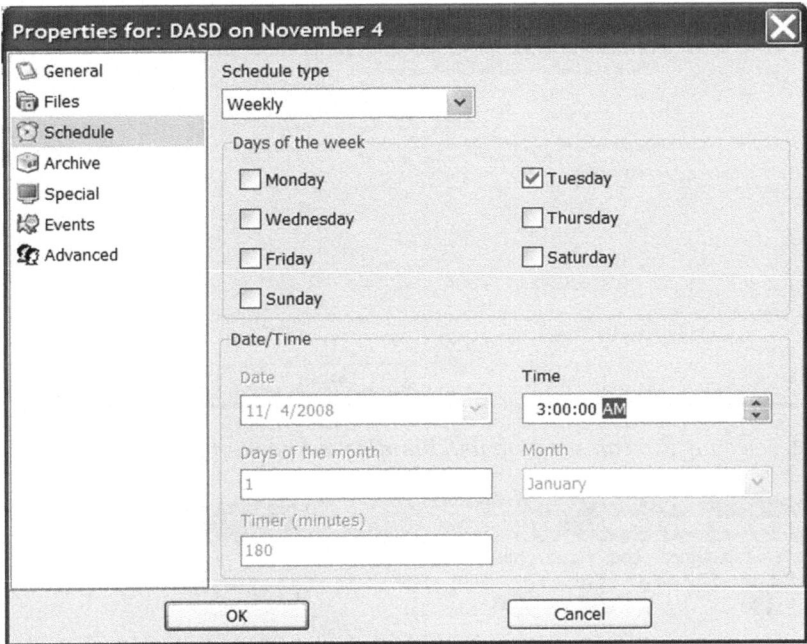

Figure 10-8. *Set a schedule for your backup to run automatically.*

12. Click Archive in the list along the left side of the page to move to the Archive page.

13. From the Compression method drop-down menu, select Zip compression, as shown in Figure 10-9. There are other options for backup file formats, but .zip is definitely one of the most convenient, as I'll explain in the "Restore Files and Folders" section.

14. Click the OK button. Cobian Backup will now create the backup task. On the left side of the window, you will see an icon that represents the new task, as shown in Figure 10-10.

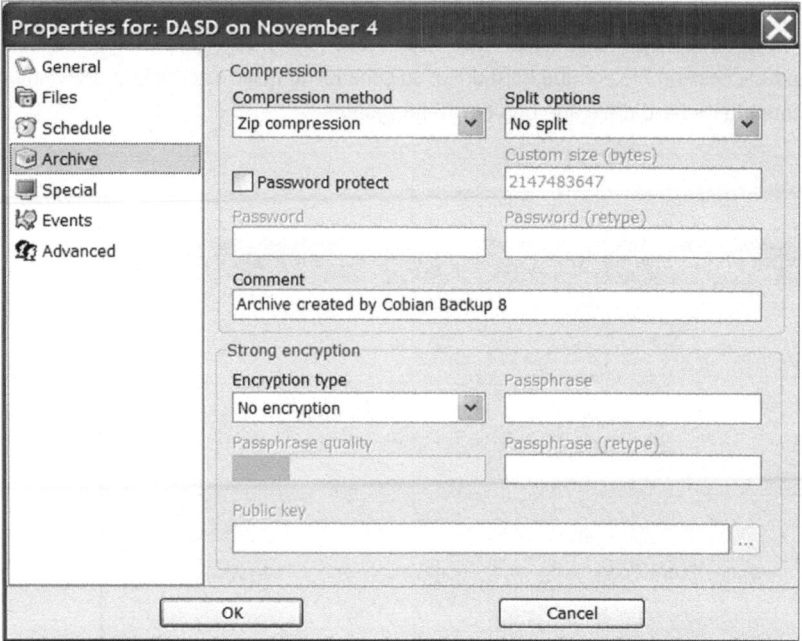

Figure 10-9. *Selecting Zip compression will bundle your backup files into a single file.*

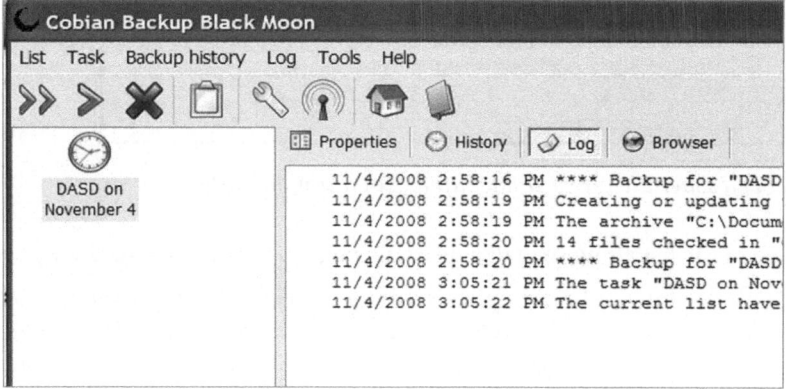

Figure 10-10. *Your backup task is represented by an icon with the name you provided.*

Run a Backup

To run a manual backup (as opposed to a scheduled backup), click the icon for the new backup task you created and choose Task ➤ Run selected tasks, as shown in Figure 10-11. Then click the OK button to confirm your choice.

Tip Why might you want to run a manual backup instead of waiting for the scheduled backup? You might choose to run a manual backup any time you are preparing to install new software or maybe to add new hardware (and the software required for the operating system to recognize it). Running a manual backup simply gives you peace of mind—you'll know that any major problems encountered during the installation of software or hardware won't affect your existing data. Another suggestion is to run a manual backup if you've recently added or modified a substantial number of files. Adding a few hundred photos from a friend's memory card or, in my case, completing two or three chapters in a few short days may warrant an immediate backup to ensure those new files are protected.

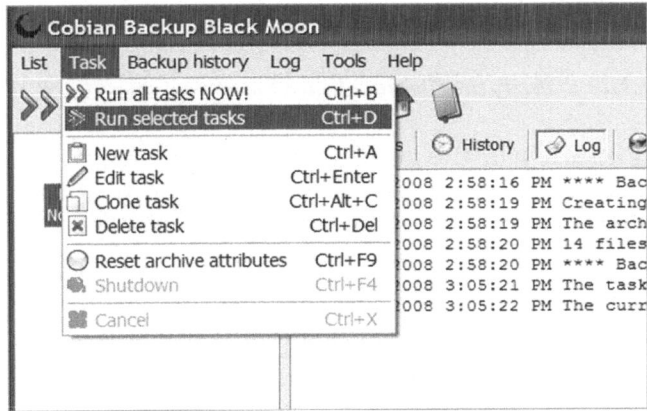

Figure 10-11. *Run your backup task manually to create a backup now.*

When the backup task has completed, you can view the log to verify that it ran and files were backed up, as shown in Figure 10-12. Notice in Figure 10-12 that the last line states:

```
Backup for "DASD on November 4" ended.
```

That's good news!

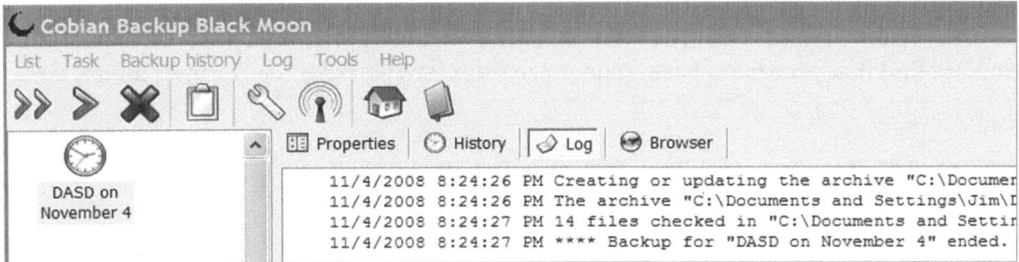

Figure 10-12. *When the backup process completes, the log will let you know.*

You can verify that the backup worked by opening the destination folder you chose. In my case, that's the Backup This File folder on my Desktop, as shown in Figure 10-13.

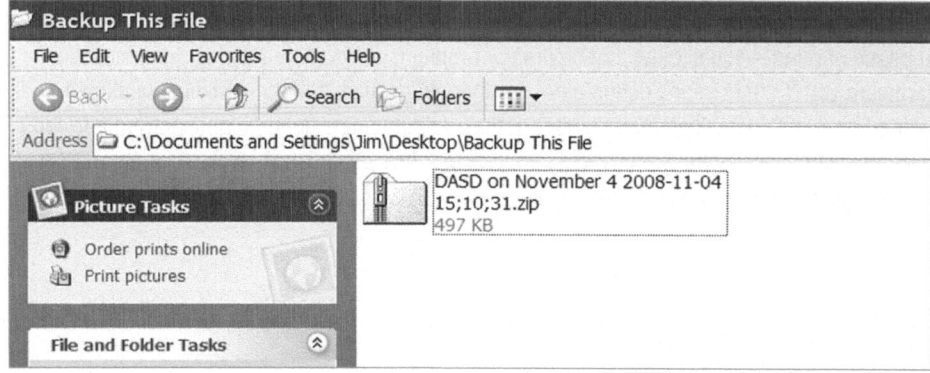

Figure 10-13. *Double-click the zipped backup to verify the files inside are the correct ones.*

Your backup is done! Now all that's left is to burn this folder to a CD or DVD, copy it to a USB flash drive, or upload it to an online storage service. After backing up the file, you can delete it from your destination folder (the Backup This File folder in my case) and wait for the next scheduled backup to run.

Restore Files and Folders

Let's assume for the moment that you've turned on your computer and found that the files and folder you backed up earlier have been deleted and are not recoverable. What you do have, however, is a small USB flash drive containing your zipped backup file. Recovery doesn't get any easier than inserting your flash drive into your computer and performing the following steps:

1. Open the .zip file by double-clicking it.

2. Locate and select a file that you need to restore.

3. Right-click the file and select Copy (or press Ctrl+C).

4. On your computer, browse to the location where you wish to place your recovered file, right-click, and select Paste (or press Ctrl+V).

You will find that your file is back. (The preceding steps work for recovering a folder, too.)

■**Caution** Try to store your file backup (whether it's on a CD, DVD, flash drive, or other media) some-where safe. If you must store it locally, consider purchasing a fire safe. Another option is to move the backup media to an off-site location such as your office (or your home for work data backups). Storing your backup file on your computer's hard drive is a common mistake. Although it may be faster and easier, it's like placing all your eggs in one basket. If your hard drive dies (or your computer is stolen), you lose your original data and your backup. It's best to be safe and store the backup separately from the original data.

You might have expected that recovery would be tricky and complex, but in fact, having a zipped file that contains your data backup provides a lot of flexibility. You can place files and folders wherever you wish, including the original location or a completely different one. You can store the zipped file on all different types of media—CD, DVD, flash drive, and external hard drive are great options. You can also store your most important working files online, then download them onto any computer you need to work from to re-create your working environ-ment on a new computer in an instant. And finally, you can take the zipped file with you and open it on another computer if you wish.

Investigate Further

I didn't cover backing up your e-mail and address book in this chapter. That's because there are many different e-mail applications out there, and each one has a slightly different method for backing up those files that contain your e-mail messages and address book. Yes, your e-mail messages and address book are stored as files on your computer. This means that you can back them up, too. You don't need to buy a program that advertises specifically "Backs up your e-mail and address book!" It's incredibly simple just to back up those items yourself with Cobian Backup, for free.

The following are some web links that provide step-by-step instructions for locating and backing up those files that contain your e-mail and address book for the most popular e-mail applications:

- Microsoft Outlook: http://office.microsoft.com/en-us/outlook/HA010875321033.aspx

- Microsoft Outlook Express: http://support.microsoft.com/kb/270670

- Eudora: http://www.eudora.com/techsupport/kb/1602hq.html

- Thunderbird: http://kb.mozillazine.org/Archiving_your_e-mail

If your e-mail program isn't on this list, a simple Google search using the keywords "backup e-mail" and your e-mail program name should provide instructions.

The key point to understand is that once you locate the folder or folders that contain your e-mail and address book, you can add those folders and files to your backup routine. Just make sure to close your e-mail application before backing up the files—that's the safest way to make certain you get a good backup.

Summary

Only you know the value of your data. The cost to pull data off of a failed hard drive typically runs between $1,000 and $5,000, and there's no guarantee that a data-recovery company will be able to retrieve it all. Even if you think your data has no monetary value, consider the time it might take to reproduce it. If you've spent hours (or days) writing a document or creating a detailed spreadsheet, remember the old adage "Time is money." The effort you would need to put into re-creating lost data will take time, and that's going to cost you (or your business or family) time that is better spent doing something else.

Come up with a data backup strategy, and implement it! Do it once a week or once a month, but set aside some time to create an automated data-recovery process that will run when you're away from your computer. The few minutes you spend setting up a data-recovery plan may very well save you hours—maybe even days—of work, as well as eliminate the stress you will encounter if you should suddenly find your data is gone. The software won't cost you a penny.

- Norton Save & Restore: $49.99

- Cobian Backup 8: $0

CHAPTER 11

■ ■ ■

Personal Finance

One of the first things a financial advisor typically will tell a new client is, "If you wish to improve your financial situation, you must know your current financial status." This means knowing how much money you have coming in (your paycheck, for example) and how much money is going out (such as your bills). My financial advisor, Blair, told my wife and me that we were going to be shocked the first time we saw a pie chart showing the breakdown of where our money was being spent. Dining out, a weekly movie rental or two, that daily coffee shop visit—they all add up.

One of the very first instructions I received from my financial advisor was to install a money management application on my computer. Blair told me that the software would allow us to see where our money was going and help us to develop a budget to keep our spending under control. He also said that the software would help us manage our funds so we could increase our investments, pay down debt faster, and build up that mythical six-months-of-expenses safety fund that we're supposed to have.

All of that sounded great, but then Blair told me to do something that surprised me: buy a $60 piece of software. You would think that the financial industry would have some sort of free application that customers could download and install, right? But it appears that the advisors have fallen into the same trap as most computer users, and go with the big-name software because that's what everyone uses, or maybe they just don't realize there are other options when it comes to financial software.

The story doesn't end there, though. After purchasing the software (I'll tell you its name shortly) and installing it, I found that it was not that intuitive to use. Not only did I need to buy a book to learn how to use it ($20 extra), but I also needed to call my bank and sign up for a service ($4 per month) that would allow this software to communicate with my bank and update my financial information. Yes, it's nice that the software talks to my bank each week and downloads my latest transactions, but if I could save $48 per year and download the transactions in a spreadsheet format myself, I sure would prefer that method.

After about three months of using the big-name software, I began my search for a free financial management application, and—wouldn't you know it—I found a great one. It's open source, free (with no strings attached), and so easy to use I couldn't believe it. I download my transactions from my bank in a standard format, and then this financial application imports the file in less than 30 seconds, so that saves $48.

In this chapter, I'll introduce you to two applications for your financial management needs. Intuit's Quicken is considered the industry standard. Money Manager Ex is quickly becoming a word-of-mouth, open source success story.

The Defender

The biggest name in personal finance management software is Intuit's Quicken. If you've never heard of it, you're in an extreme minority. Intuit advertises its flagship product on TV and radio, and in every newspaper and magazine imaginable. Quicken's primary purpose is to gather your financial data and organize it in an easy-to-follow and easy-to-search manner. Versions of Quicken can be found for personal use and business use, as well as to track investments.

Quicken's user interface, shown in Figure 11-1, seems to change year to year, but the basic idea is the same: your data is broken into the three areas of Money In, Money Out, and What's Left. You can configure Quicken to communicate with your bank and grab transactions such as deposits (Money In) and bills paid (Money Out). You can also configure the frequency with which Quicken logs in to your bank and grabs this information. The What's Left section performs the calculations and shows you the balance of funds you have remaining.

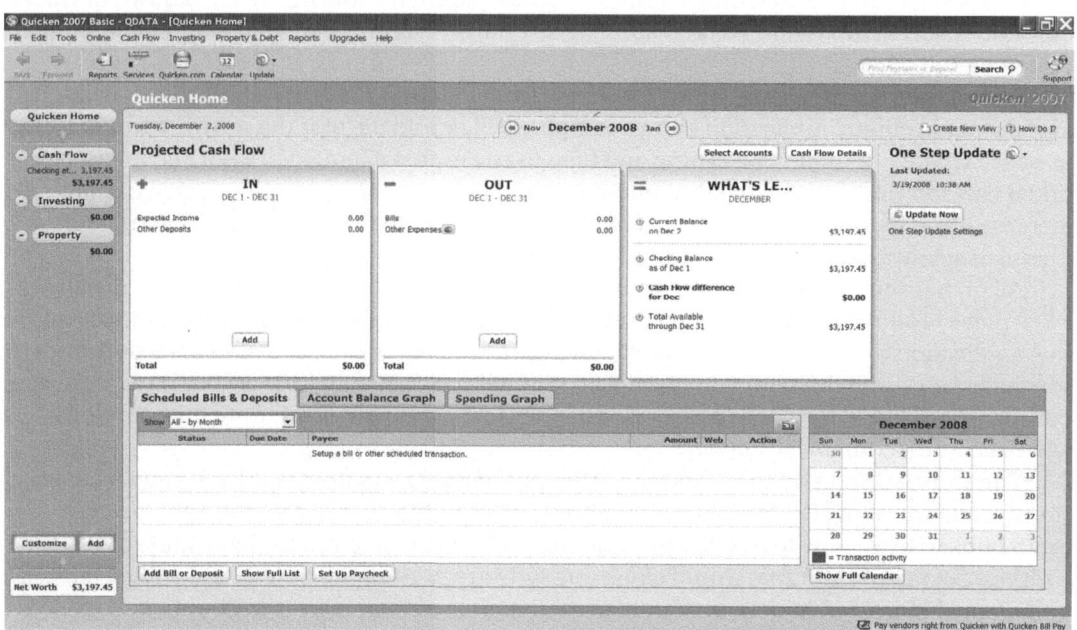

Figure 11-1. *Intuit's Quicken is the most popular personal finance management application.*

Quicken keeps the details hidden until you decide to view them. Features allow you to burrow deeper, looking at individual transactions. Quicken also organizes your transactions using predefined labels such as Mortgage and Fuel, but you can create custom labels, such as Babysitter and Bookstore. When you assign a transaction a label, you are able to use Quicken to filter your transactions. This allows you, for example, to see how much money you spend per month on books and how much filling up your car's tank is costing you per year. (A complete list of the features found in the latest versions of Intuit's Quicken can be found at http:// quicken.intuit.com.)

> ■**Note** Although Quicken updates every year (I own Quicken 2007), you're not required to upgrade to the latest version. Older versions of Quicken will continue to work, but Intuit is always changing the user interface and adding new features. Some users are unaware of this and purchase the latest version year after year, thinking that they must have the current year's release.

However, Quicken can be a little overwhelming. A lot of features are built into this application, and many of them require customization to use. For instance, my financial planner wanted me to e-mail him reports in certain formats, and it took me some time and experimentation to get it right. As I mentioned, I ended up purchasing a book just so I could learn how to use Quicken. Ultimately, I got frustrated with the application, and I've turned down pop-up offers to upgrade the product.

But that's my experience. Quicken definitely has a large base of users who are fond of the application, which is why it continues to be the sales leader for this type of software. If you are currently using Quicken and are happy with it, then by all means, continue using it. But you might want to keep reading and learn about a free alternative that may just provide everything you need in a personal finance application. You might find, as I did, that you can take that $60 (or more) per year you saved by not purchasing financial software and put it back into your bank account.

The Contender

I enjoy introducing people to Money Manager Ex. This free, open source personal finance application is truly one of those little-known software gems, and it's definitely beginning to get the attention it deserves.

Like almost all open source applications, Money Manager Ex comes with online support, including a discussion forum where users can post questions and learn more about using this software. It's free to download, it has no advertisements, and you are most certainly not required to upgrade it every year.

Figure 11-2 shows the Money Manager Ex interface. The left window pane lets you select from multiple options that display specific types of financial data: bank account, stocks, assets, and a variety of reports. After you select an option on the left, the desired information is displayed in the larger viewing area on the right. Menu options allow you to switch back and forth between multiple types of accounts, print reports, and back up your financial data to files that can be stored on your hard drive or burned to a CD or DVD.

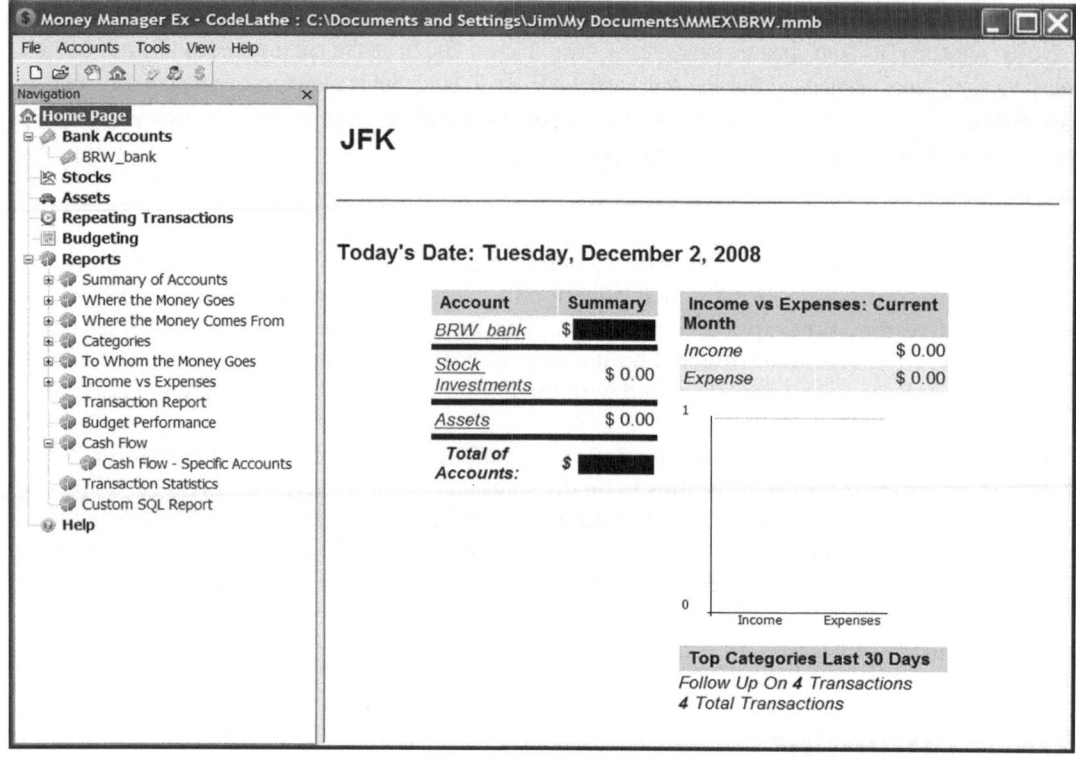

Figure 11-2. *Money Manager Ex has an easy-to-read user interface.*

Don't let Money Manager Ex's simple user interface fool you, though. It has some powerful features that I'll demonstrate after explaining how to install and download the software.

Where to Get the Software

To install Money Manager Ex, you first need to download the software for your operating system. Versions exist for Windows, Mac, and Linux. To find the correct version for your computer, follow these steps:

1. Visit http://www.codelathe.com/mmex/.

2. Click the Download link on the right side of the screen.

3. Locate the version for your computer's operating system, and click the Download link.

Notes on Money Manager Ex Installation

To install the software, double-click the Money Manager Ex installation icon. Follow the on-screen instructions, including accepting the license agreement and selecting whether Money Manager Ex places a shortcut icon on your desktop and/or a Quick Launch icon.

To run Money Manager Ex, double-click the desktop shortcut icon, or start the application from the Start menu. The first time you run the application, you'll be asked to select your language from a list. Select your language and click the OK button. The next dialog box prompts you to create or open a database, as shown in Figure 11-3. After you create your first database (as described in the next section), this dialog box will not appear again unless you place a check in the box labeled "Show this window next time Money Manager Ex – CodeLathe starts."

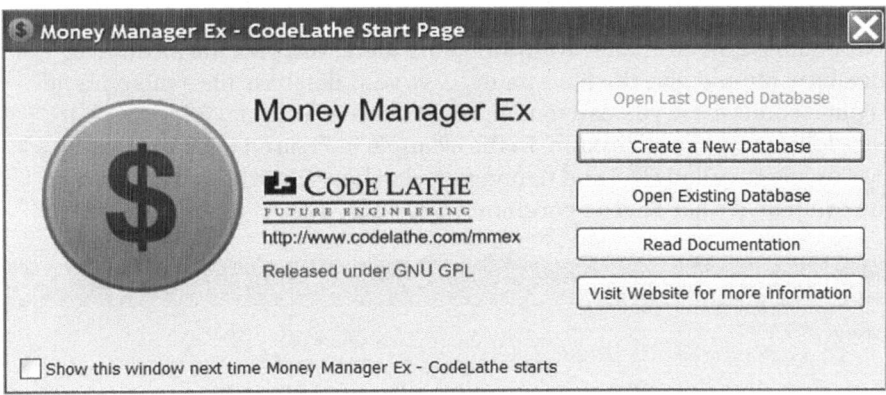

Figure 11-3. *Money Manager Ex will prompt you to create a new database.*

Basic Money Manager Ex Tasks

Before you start using Money Manager Ex, you must create a database where your financial data will be stored. Here, I'll show you how to create a database, import financial transactions, and examine your personal finances.

Create a Database

All of your financial data will be stored in a single database file stored on your computer. To create this database, follow these steps:

1. Start Money Manager Ex by double-clicking the desktop shortcut icon or from the Start menu. Select your language and click the OK button. In the next dialog box, click the Create a New Database button, as shown in Figure 11-4.

Figure 11-4. *Create a new database to hold your financial data.*

2. The "Choose database file to create" window opens. Here, you pick the location to store the database file and give the file a name. Give your database file a memorable name, and put it somewhere you can remember, such as in a special folder in your My Documents folder or on your desktop. In the example in Figure 11-5, I'm creating a folder in My Documents called MMEX and naming my database file BRW (for Blue Rocket Writing, my company). Click Save to continue.

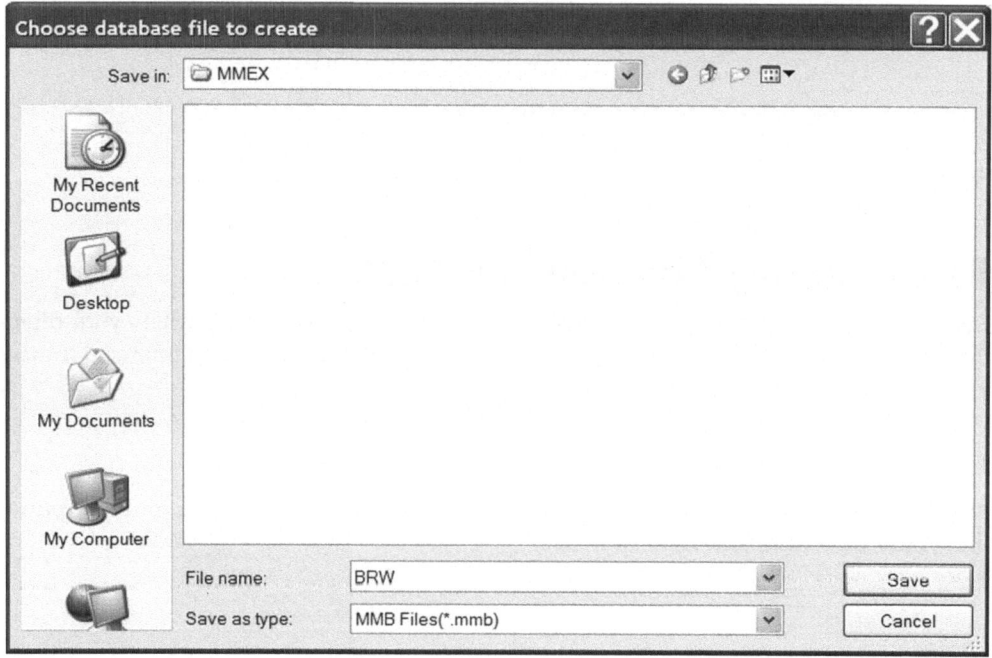

Figure 11-5. *Pick a location for your database file and give it a name.*

3. The New Database Wizard starts, as shown in Figure 11-6. Click the Next button to continue.

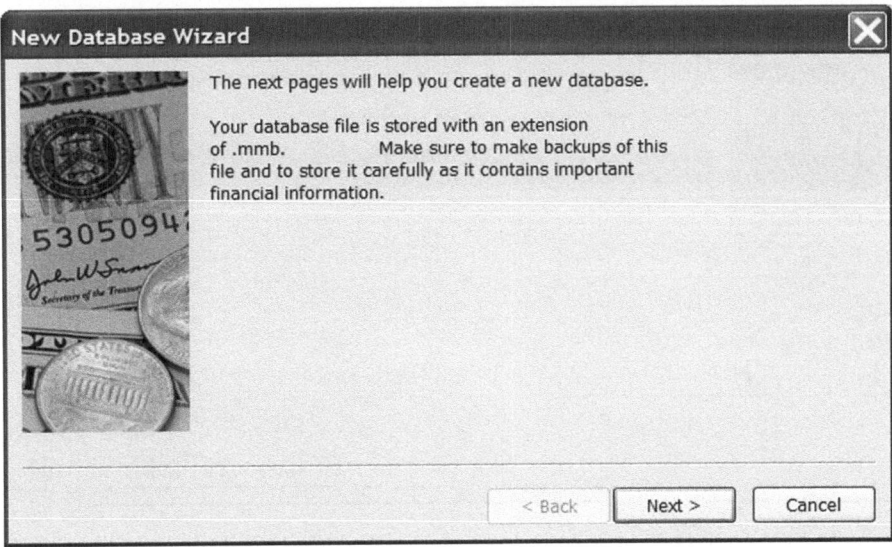

Figure 11-6. *The New Database Wizard will walk you through setting up your database file.*

4. Click the Set Currency button and select the type of currency used in your financial data. In Figure 11-7, I've selected US Dollar. Enter a username, and then click the Finish button.

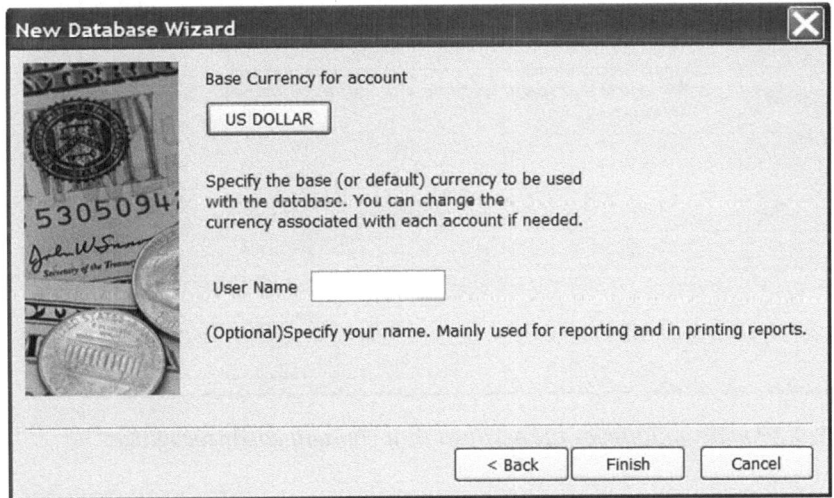

Figure 11-7. *Provide a currency type and username for your database file.*

5. Next, you need to create an account using the Add Account Wizard, as shown in Figure 11-8. Click the Next button.

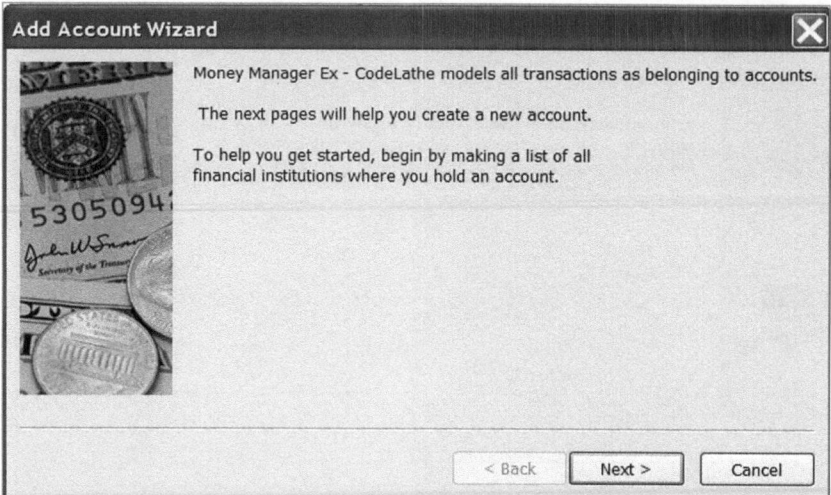

Figure 11-8. *You must create an account that will be used to access the financial data.*

6. Provide a name for the account. In the example in Figure 11-9, I've given my account the name BRW_bank. Click the Next button.

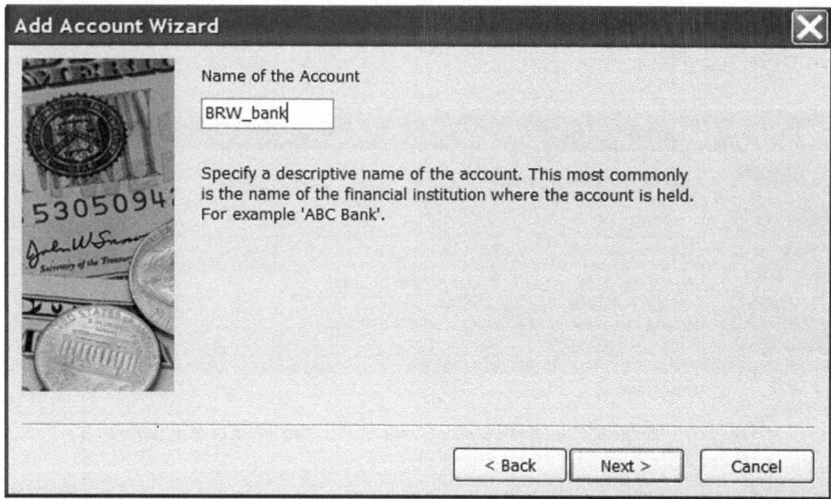

Figure 11-9. *Provide a name for the account that you will easily recognize.*

7. In the next window, select the type of account from the drop-down menu. Your choices are Checking/Savings or Investments. In Figure 11-10, I've selected Checking/Savings. Click the Finish button.

8. Finally, you can provide helpful details about your account. In the example shown in Figure 11-11, I've entered some information about my account, including the web address and contact name. (I've obscured my bank account number for obvious reasons.) Click the OK button when you're finished.

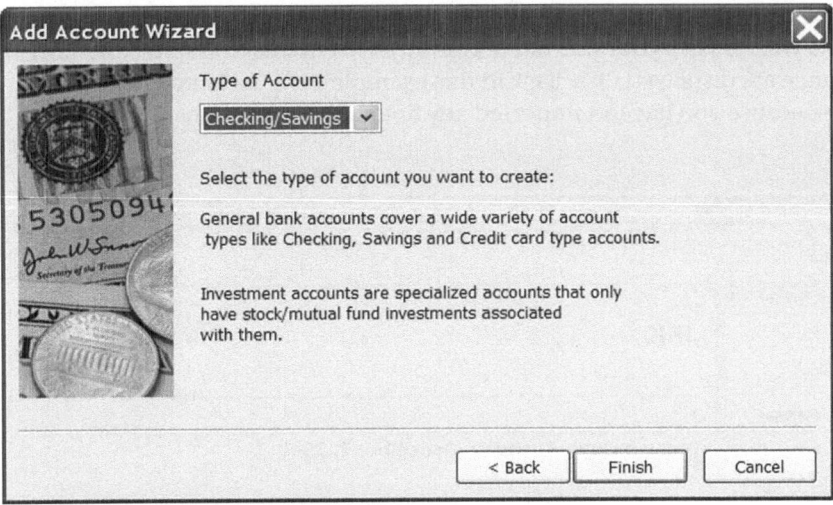

Figure 11-10. *Select the type of account that represents the data stored in the database file.*

Figure 11-11. *Enter additional data about your account.*

Tip You can create multiple databases to use with Money Manager Ex. This is useful if you're married and have separate bank accounts, for example.

Figure 11-12 shows the starting window for Money Manager Ex after you've created your database file. As you can see, your username is shown (JFK in this example), and the account name and balance are displayed (BRW_bank in this example). It's not much to look at yet—it's blank, in fact—because you haven't imported any financial transactions. I'll show you how to do that next.

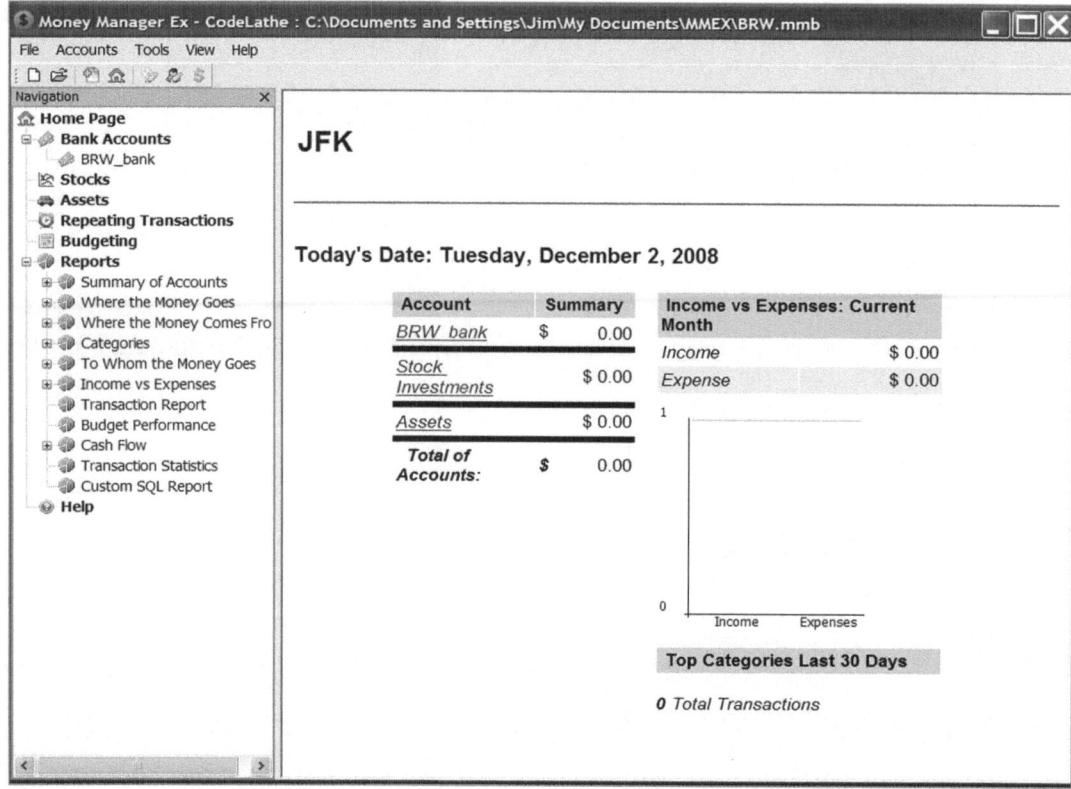

Figure 11-12. *Your account is created and is now ready for financial transactions.*

Import Financial Transactions

Money Manager Ex isn't going to be of much use to you without actual financial data. Figure 11-12 shows a basic Money Manager Ex database, ready to be loaded up with transactions. How the application does this involves importing what's known as a comma-separated value (CSV) file. A CSV file stores data using commas to separate each piece of information. CSV files can be opened and viewed using a spreadsheet application or even a basic text editor like Notepad.

The following is an example of a portion of the text from the CSV file I've downloaded. (I'll show you how this is done shortly.)

```
Date Posted, Transaction Type, Check No., Description, Transaction Amount
11/11/2008, CREDIT, , *Customer Deposit, xxxx.xx
11/10/2008, DEBIT, , AMERICAN EXPRESS ELEC REMIT, -xx.xx
11/3/2008, DEBIT, 1116, 1116, -xx.xx
```

If this file is viewed in a spreadsheet, the first line provides the column names, including the order that the data will be provided. The date of a transaction is listed first, followed by a comma, then the type of transaction (credit or debit), another comma, and so on. This is the format that Money Manager Ex will import using a CSV file that you specify.

Download and Prepare Your Financial Data

Most banks offer customers the ability to download their financial data in CSV format. The only difference is in how a bank customer obtains the file. If you do any type of online banking, look for a link with a label such as "Download transactions" or "Download your account info." If you're unable to find a way to download a CSV file, you'll need to contact a bank representative and inquire how to download your account information.

■**Note** If you haven't signed up for online access to your bank account, you should do so! Many banks offer preferential treatment—such as reduced fees, free transactions, or reduced monthly fees—for signing up for online access. Most banks do not charge for online banking services. However, there are always exceptions. It is possible that your bank may charge you a fee of some sort to access your account information online. It's up to you to decide if that's worth the price. My suggestion is to change banks if you're being charged for this type of service.

To show you how to download your financial data and prepare the CVS file, I'll walk you through how I do it. Your steps will be similar.

1. I log into my bank account using my bank's online access.

2. Along the left side of my bank's access screen is a link labeled Download transactions, as shown in Figure 11-13, which I click. Your bank may put the access options in a different location or format, but an option to download transactions should be there.

■**Caution** Be certain you're logging in to your bank's official web site and not a fake web site created by phishers. Read more about phishing at http://en.wikipedia.org/wiki/Phishing.

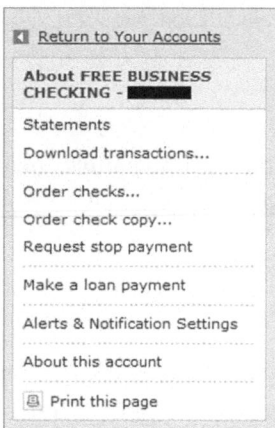

Figure 11-13. *Use the appropriate link from your bank's online banking web site to download transactions.*

3. I'm presented with a window like the one shown in Figure 11-14. I enter dates in the From and To fields to indicate the financial data I want. In this example, I've selected November 1, 2008, through December 8, 2008. I've also selected CSV from the Software drop-down menu as the format for the data. (Other options offered by my bank are Microsoft Money, Quicken, and QuickBooks formats.) Then I click the Next button.

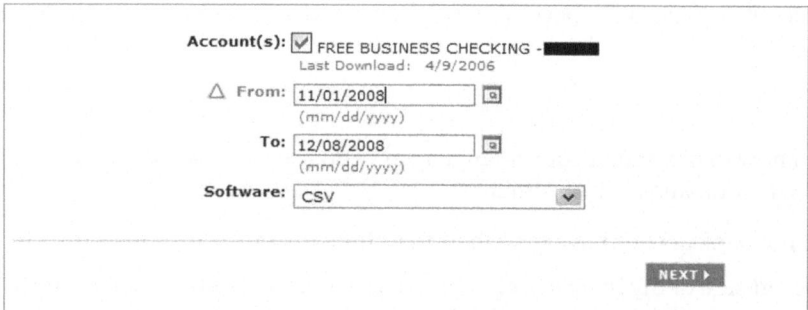

Figure 11-14. *I've selected dates and the CSV format for my financial transactions.*

4. On the next screen, I click the Download button, and the file is downloaded to my desktop, shown in Figure 11-15. (My default spreadsheet application is OpenOffice.org Calc, so the icon looks like an OpenOffice.org Calc sheet; see Chapter 4 for more information about Calc.)

Figure 11-15. *A CSV file appears on my desktop.*

5. I open the downloaded CSV file. You can open this file using a spreadsheet or text editor application such as Notepad. Figure 11-16 shows how the data appears (with some of my personal data censored) in a spreadsheet (top) and a plain text editor (bottom).

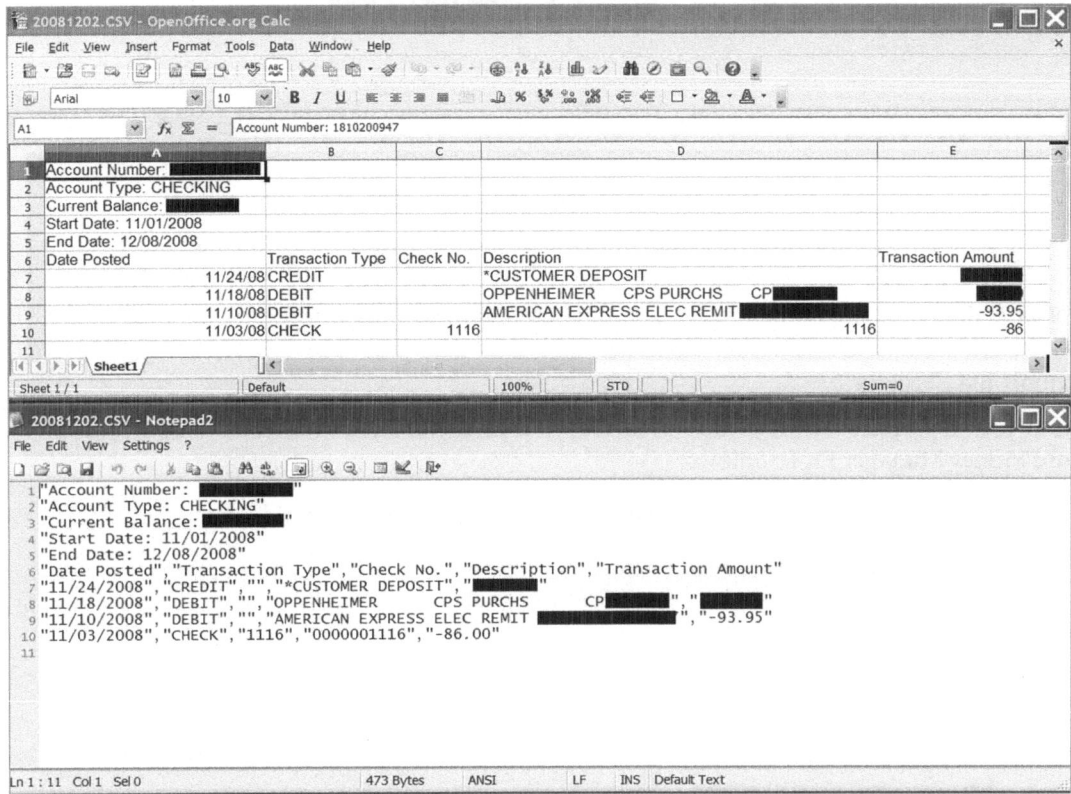

Figure 11-16. *A CSV file can appear differently, depending on the application you use to open it.*

6. Money Manager Ex doesn't care about any data (including column names) other than the transaction information. This means I need to edit this CSV file and delete that extra information at the top showing headings like Account Number and Account Type, as well as the column names like Date Posted and Transaction Type. I don't need the headings, because I'll tell Money Manager Ex what each comma-delimited field means when I import the data. I note the order of the headings, as this is also important when I import the data. In Figure 11-17, you can see that I've deleted the extra information (compare it to Figure 11-16).

7. I save the edited file. Now I'm ready to import it into Money Manager Ex.

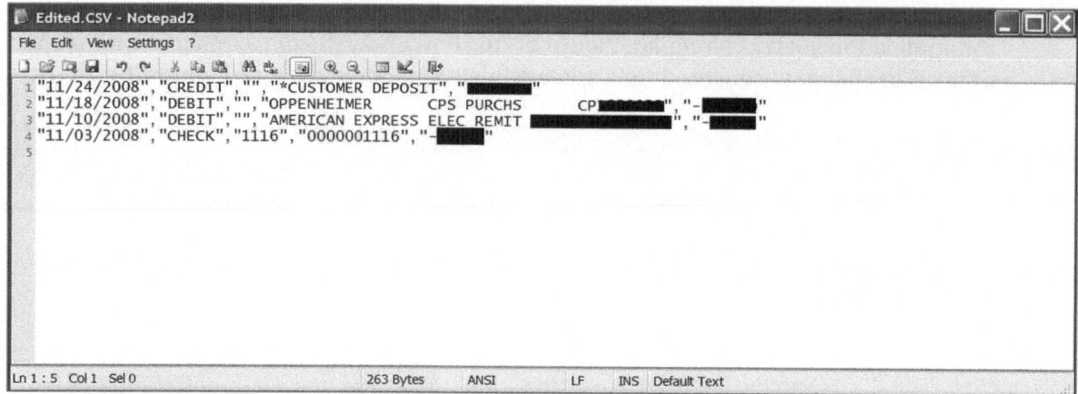

Figure 11-17. *You may need to edit the CSV file to remove unwanted data.*

Import the CVS File

After you've prepared the CVS file containing your financial data, you need to import this file into Money Manager Ex, as follows:

1. Select File ➤ Import ➤ Universal CSV Files, as shown in Figure 11-18.

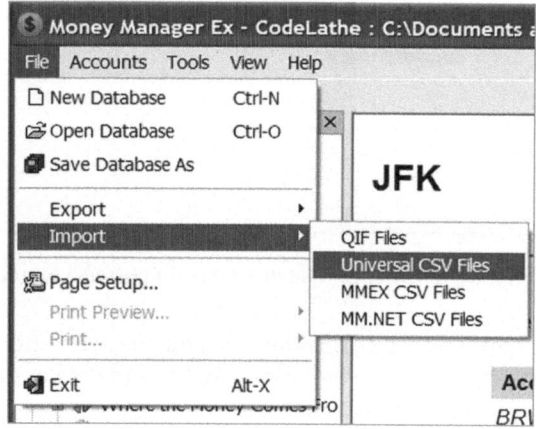

Figure 11-18. *Choose to import the CSV file into Money Manager Ex.*

2. The Universal CSV Importer Dialog box appears, as shown in Figure 11-19. In this dialog box, you define what each field in your CSV data file means. This is how you tell Money Manager Ex that the text "11/24/2008" is a date, or that the number 1116 is a check number. Money Manager Ex also must be told the order of the transaction data. Click the Add button to see the fields available.

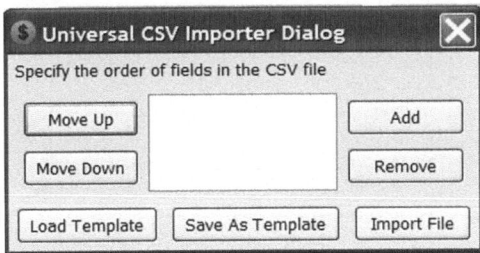

Figure 11-19. *Each type of CSV data will need to be defined.*

3. The CSV dialog box lists the fields in your file, as shown in Figure 11-20. In some instances, the names may not match exactly. For example, the headings from my CSV file use Description instead of Payee, and Check No. instead of Transaction Number. Select a field and click OK to add it into the Universal CSV Importer Dialog box list.

4. Repeat steps 2 and 3 to add the fields from your CSV file. Order the fields in this list by using the Move Up and Move Down buttons. I added the five fields you see in Figure 11-21. I used the Move Up and Move Down buttons to reorder the fields to match the headings from my CSV file. As you can see, I've selected the order as Date, Category, Transaction Number, Payee, and Amount (+/−) to match my CSV data fields of Date Posted, Transaction Type, Check No., Description, and Transaction Amount.

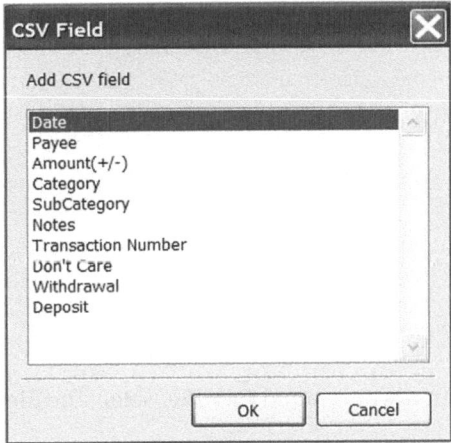

Figure 11-20. *Select the field names for your CSV data.*

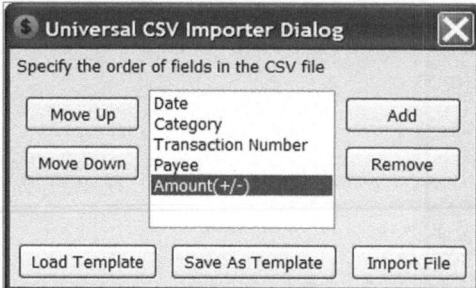

Figure 11-21. *Reorder the field names to match the order of your CSV data.*

5. When you're finished adding and arranging fields, click the Save As Template button. This saves the information to a file, so you don't need to re-create this CSV structure.

6. Click the Import File button. You'll be asked which account the data will be imported into, as shown in Figure 11-22. Select an account, and then click the OK button.

Figure 11-22. *Pick the account where the imported data will be added.*

7. In the next window, browse to the location of your edited CSV file. Select the file and click the Open button.

8. The data will be imported, and a dialog box similar to the one shown in Figure 11-23 will appear. Click the OK button.

9. In the Money Manager Ex main window, click your account name in the left column, and you'll see the newly imported transactions, as shown in Figure 11-24.

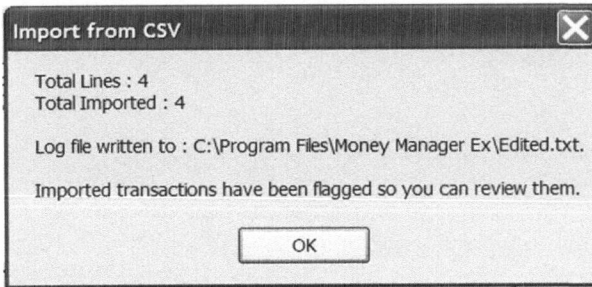

Figure 11-23. *The CSV file's data has been successfully imported.*

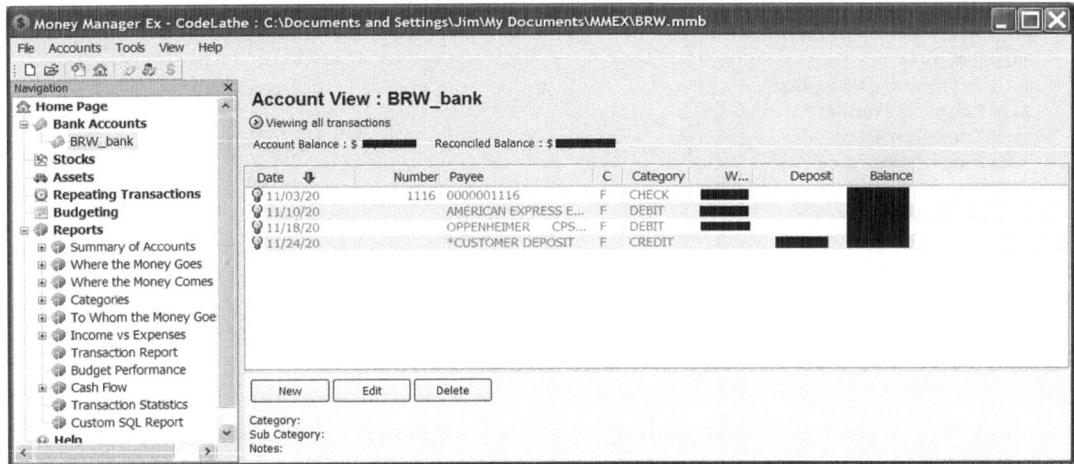

Figure 11-24. *Your imported transactions now appear in the proper account.*

Now that the data has been imported, you can use the features of Money Manager Ex.

Examine Your Personal Finances

It's time to let Money Manager Ex help you understand your financial situation. The application does this by using a set of reports, which are accessible from the left side of the main window, as shown in Figure 11-25.

Figure 11-25. *Reports provide assistance in interpreting your finances.*

Suppose you want to see a breakdown of where your money is being spent. To do this, click the report labeled Where the Money Goes. You'll see a pie chart and list, as shown in Figure 11-26.

If you want more details, such as exactly who or what business is getting your money, click the To Whom the Money Goes report. You'll see another pie chart plus the descriptions of your payees, as shown in Figure 11-27.

There are many more reports available, and I encourage you to play around with all of them. Don't worry about making mistakes. Money Manager Ex doesn't have direct access to your funds, so you won't suddenly find your bank account empty.

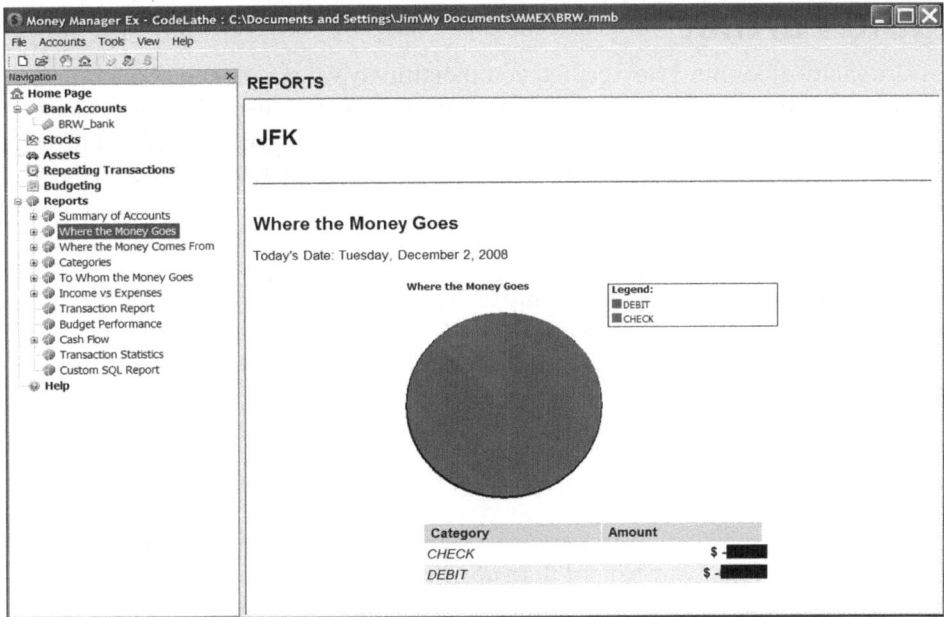

Figure 11-26. *Money Manager Ex shows me my spending habits.*

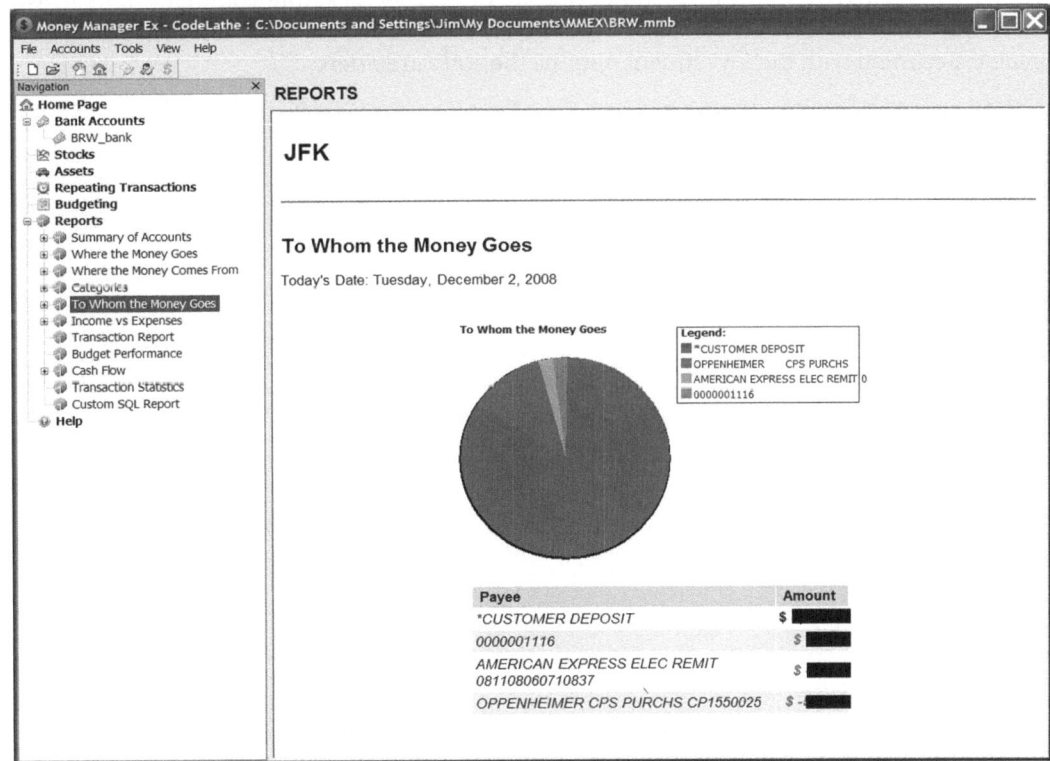

Figure 11-27. *Money Manager Ex also shows me who is getting my money. Apparently I'm making more deposits than I'm paying out—great news!*

Investigate Further

If you like the simplicity of Money Manager Ex, you'll definitely want to spend some time learning more about its features. Use the built-in manual by clicking the Help menu. Consider learning how to use Money Manager Ex to create a budget. You might also want to investigate setting up repeating transactions (such as a monthly gym membership), as well as adding in the ability to track your stock portfolio. Remember that Money Manager Ex has a growing community of users who often post questions on the official forum at `http://www.codelathe.com/forum`.

While I prefer to keep my financial data on my own computer, if you're looking for software that fits the SaaS category, you might want to check out Buxfer, an online personal finance application. A lot of people recommend it, and the application definitely looks user-friendly. You can find it at `http://www.buxfer.com`.

Summary

Why pay for software to help you with your personal finances? If you're trying to get control of your spending, what better way to start than downloading and using a free, open source personal finance application? Money Manager Ex is simple, without a lot of bells and whistles—but then again, you may not want more than that from your financial software.

Money Manager Ex shows you how much money you have in the bank, where you're spending it, and what's coming in. It allows you to import CSV files from your bank, and gives you a simple list of reports that are easy to understand. And if you're doing some investing, you can experiment with the investment options the software offers.

- Intuit Quicken: $59
- Money Manager Ex: $0

CHAPTER 12

∎∎∎

Gaming

The applications I cover in this book can make your life easier or more efficient, but most people wouldn't label them as entertaining. Okay, maybe some of you actually laugh out loud when you use a word processor, and I'm sure that one or two readers design spreadsheets as a hobby. But let's be honest—for many of us, computers are all about the games.

The advances made in graphics and sound technology, combined with the lightning speeds of today's processors, memory, and hard drives, have transformed gaming into a powerhouse industry. The money you save on software by using the applications covered in this book can buy you more of that advanced hardware, which means more advanced game playing!

New games are released each year for every interest. Enjoy racing cars? There are Formula 1 simulator applications that put you behind the wheel. Wish you could pilot your own X-Wing Fighter and take out the dreaded Death Star? Dozens of games for your computer are based on the wildly successful Star Wars movie franchise. And the list doesn't end there: board games (try winning Monopoly against the computer—good luck!), strategy, shoot-'em-up, and role-playing games are just a sampling.

Thousands of free games are available for download over the Internet. If you have a favorite type of game, it's out there and just a few clicks away. Just do a search for "Free computer games," and be prepared to spend hours sifting through all the available options. Sure, many of these are low-quality games, but you can also find plenty of high-quality games, too. You don't need to spend money for great games. Are you doubtful? In this chapter, I'll recommend a game that will convince you that free games are just as fun as their pay-to-play counterparts.

As usual, let's begin with the commercial software to compare with the free version. In this case, that's World of Warcraft.

The Defender

In the world of computer gaming right now, one game stands out among them all: World of Warcraft (WoW). WoW is legendary in the gaming community. If you don't know someone who plays this game and have never heard of it, continue reading for a brief description.

WoW is a fantasy-based, role-playing, massively multiplayer online (MMO) game. This means that the game takes place in a fantasy world (named Azeroth) filled with wizards, warriors, priests, elves, dungeons, treasure, dragons, orcs, gold-laden chests, magical swords, and more. (So much more that entire books have been written about WoW.) Figure 12-1 shows one view of WoW.

Figure 12-1. *One view of World of Warcraft showing many players running from a monster*

Players of the game create what is called a character (the role-playing portion of the game), an in-game persona that interacts with other players, fights monsters, collects treasure, and increases in power and skills the more you play. All characters start at Level 1, which gives you some basic skills (such as sword-wielding or spell-casting) and health (how much damage you can take from monsters before your character is killed and then resurrected). Your character's skills and health increase (as do the values of treasures and the hazards from monsters) as you ascend through the levels. All of this happens in a shared-world environment, where other players appear on the screen when they are in your vicinity. You can talk to other players (via the keyboard or a microphone), fight with them, and band together with them to fight a common enemy. You can also buy, trade, and sell in-game items such as swords, armor, and healing potions. (For more details on WoW, visit its official web site at http://www.worldofwarcraft.com.)

WHAT'S AN MMO?

A massively multiplayer online (MMO) game is *massive* because it usually consists of a virtual world you can explore. The *multiplayer* part means that you're sharing the world with other game players. While you're exploring the virtual world, you'll see other players on the screen when they are in the same area as your character (inside a castle, for example). And *online* means that all of this happens while you are logged in to a game via an Internet connection.

Combine all these elements, and you have a game with a large explorable world, inhabited by fellow game players, that is always "running." It's not uncommon for you to log in to your game during the day and find that it is nighttime in the virtual world. Likewise, most games continue to operate even when you're not logged in, so your character is typically considered to be sleeping or practicing skills while you are away.

MMO games have a variety of themes. There are superhero MMO games, where you create a hero who dodges bullets, jumps skyscrapers, and saves the day (or where you create a villain who is never up to any good, robbing banks and building evil robots to terrorize the city). Many MMO games are fantasy-based. Others take place in the far future with star travel, planetary bases, and space battles. If you can think of a specific type of MMO game, there's a very good chance it exists, and you can join the game, where you will find other players who share your interests.

WoW is huge, with more than 11 million players. Yes, you read that correctly. And those players all pay a monthly fee to play. By charging approximately $15 per month to play, WoW is generating over $165 million dollars per month in revenue (although many people think it's even higher with tie-ins like posters, books, and figurines). WoW brings in the money because it's a lot of fun, with plenty of activities in the game.

Players particularly enjoy WoW because it continues to expand and grow. The software developers are always adding new content, such as quests for players to accept, treasures, monsters, and territories to explore. As of this writing, a new expansion pack (selling for around $40) adds an entirely new continent, and characters can grow to Level 80!

There's no denying the popularity of WoW, but the recurring cost to play has prompted some players to leave the game. If you play a few hours each day, the monthly cost is probably not unreasonable. But for more casual players, spending $180 or more per year to play a single game probably seems a little crazy. And that's why, after a few months of play, I canceled my subscription and said good-bye to my Level 17 wizard. Then I began my search for something that would allow me to continue my battle against evil and give me some deep, dark dungeons to explore with friends from around the world.

My search was not in vain. I found a small company in Germany named Frogster that offers an MMO game very similar (some might say extremely similar) to WoW. Not only is this game completely free, it's also just as much fun as WoW.

The Contender

The gaming alternative I found is called Runes of Magic. It has many of the same features I enjoyed in WoW, along with some new ones.

Runes of Magic takes place in the land of Taborea. You, as the player, begin your journey by creating a character and selecting a single class (sort of like a career)—Warrior, Mage, Rogue, Scout, Priest, or Knight—with which to play, fight, and explore.

The first time you open Runes of Magic, you'll have the opportunity to select your character's gender and body design, such as hair, face, arm, and leg sizes. You drag the small bars left and right to decrease or increase sizes of body parts (such as the legs). The pull-down menus allow you to select your class, gender, skin color, and hair color. The clothing you start with is very basic, but as the game progresses, you will be given the chance to add more colorful items, such as magic robes, leather and plate armor, and more. Figure 12-2 shows a Runes of Magic character being created.

Figure 12-2. *You can customize your character's look any way you like.*

After creating your character's look, provide a name, and click the Confirm button. You will then see your character on screen above a button labeled Enter World. Click the button, and you're ready to begin.

If you think creating the look of your character is fun, wait until you play the game! This game has an overall story about the land of Taborea and many subplots that you can investigate with your in-game character. You'll fight horrible monsters, join with fellow adventurers to explore ominous dungeons, and collect treasures. Along the way, you can acquire more powerful armor, stronger spells, and more potent potions and weapons.

And because Frogster releases periodic updates to the game (for free), you'll always find new lands to visit, new skills to acquire and use, and much more. There's enough entertainment in Runes of Magic to keep you occupied for a long time.

Note How can a company like Frogster make a game like Runes of Magic free? They do it by offering what is called an online mall. As you fight monsters and complete quests, you'll gain treasures—armor, weapons, and potions are just a few of the items you can find. But if you would like to get that super-powerful sword without all the work, Frogster gives you the ability to purchase such items using real-world money. Frogster states that any item that can be purchased from the online mall is also attainable by performing certain quests or defeating special monsters in the game. You can spend the time in the game to find the treasure, or spend some money to have that treasure now. If you want that fancy, glowing Sword of Infinite Tuchus-Kicking, you can just buy it, rather than spend hours fighting random monsters in the hopes of finding it hidden in an old treasure chest. The money from the online mall pays for salaries and improvements to the game. Frogster claims it will always keep Runes of Magic free to play.

I must be careful not to reveal too much about the game, because it might spoil some surprises for you. Later in the chapter, I'll show you some basic activities you can perform in the game, but the real fun is simply playing. The next sections explain how to download and install the software so you can get started.

Where to Get the Software

Follow these simple steps to download Runes of Magic:

1. Visit http://www.runesofmagic.com.

2. Click the Register Here Now button to sign up and download the latest version.

Note Runes of Magic is a large download—more than 5GB! You need a broadband Internet (DSL or cable) connection to get it. Don't even attempt to download this game using a dial-up connection.

Notes on Runes of Magic Installation

Installing Runes of Magic is quite easy. Here's the procedure:

1. Double-click the RoM icon to start the Setup Wizard, as shown in Figure 12-3. Click the Next button to proceed.

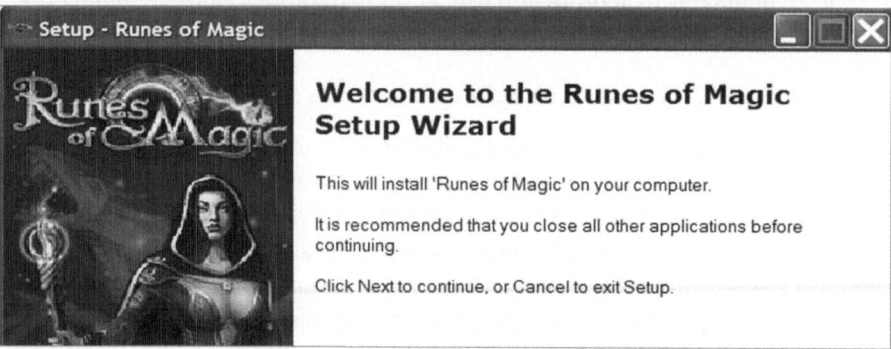

Figure 12-3. *Install Runes of Magic on your PC.*

2. Read through the license agreement, select the option labeled "I accept the agreement," and click the Next button.

3. On the next screen, you will be shown the location on your hard drive where the game will be installed. Click the Next button, and the installation will begin.

Once the game installation is complete, either double-click the shortcut placed on your desktop or select Runes of Magic from the Start menu. When you see the startup screen shown in Figure 12-4, click the Start Game button, and you're ready to begin.

■**Note** Don't let the "Beta" in the figures in this chapter worry you. As I'm writing this chapter, the game is still in beta testing, but an official release will be available by the time you're reading this book.

The first time you play, you'll be offered entrance to a beginner's instruction zone. Click the Enter into button, and follow the on-screen instructions to learn how to walk, run, pan the camera around, and accept quests.

Figure 12-4. *Click the Start Game button, and you're ready to play.*

A Sampling of Runes of Magic Activities

Here, I'll go over a handful of Runes of Magic activities. These are fairly basic because, well, I just don't want to give away any big secrets. It's a fun game, and there are many surprises in store for you.

Accept a Quest

Quests are one of the key activities you'll be performing in Runes of Magic. Quests are typically special actions that are given to you by nonplayer characters (NPCs). These are characters in the game who push the game's overall story forward. Your quests are frequently smaller bits of a larger story, which you will learn more about as you progress in the game.

During the first-time user's tutorial, you'll be instructed how to accept, fulfill, and finish quests. Every time you complete a quest, your character earns experience points (XPs). When you've obtained a sufficient amount of XPs, your character will increase in level. This will increase your hit points (HPs, or health) and your mana points (MPs), which are used for casting spells and performing special actions other than fighting. You'll need those increases in HPs and MPs in order to accept more challenging quests and to explore lands farther away from home.

Thousands of quests exist in Runes of Magic, and they run from the extremely easy (deliver this note) to the unbelievably difficult (slay the dragon using only this magic dagger). You can accept multiple quests and attempt them in any order you like.

Tip Try to find quests that require defeating monsters. This way, you'll get XPs from them, as well as from finishing the quest.

Follow these steps to be assigned a quest and collect your reward upon completing it:

1. Approach an NPC with a large yellow exclamation point over his or her head, as shown in Figure 12-5.

Figure 12-5. *NPCs with quests are easy to find—look for the exclamation point.*

2. Double-click the NPC, and a list of available quests will be provided, as shown in Figure 12-6.

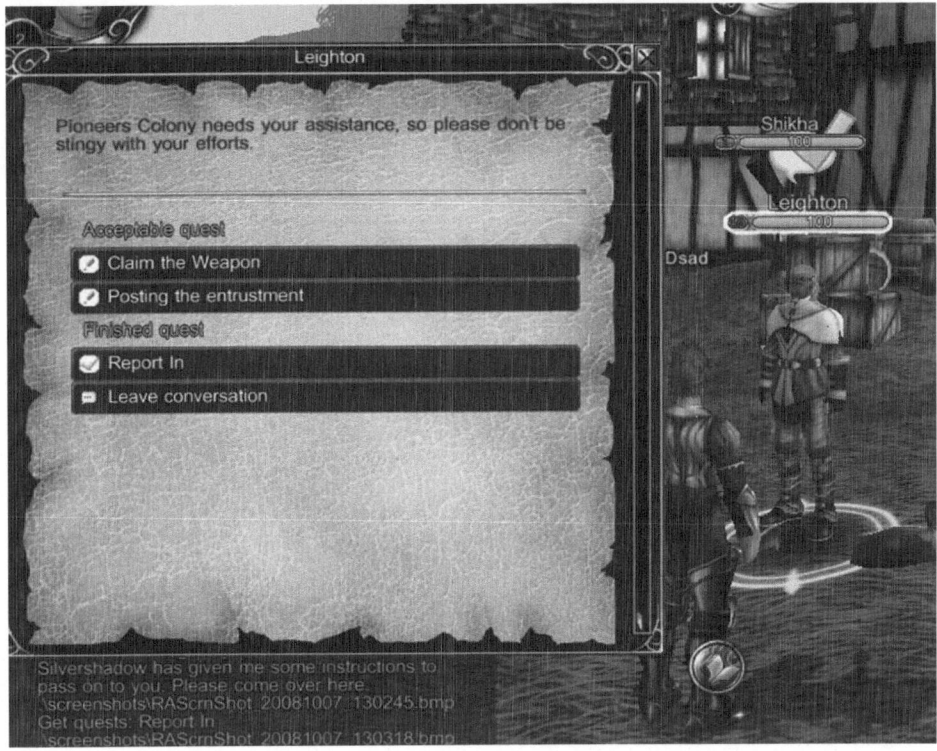

Figure 12-6. *Some NPCs have more than one quest for you to accept.*

3. Click an available quest to read details about it. If you wish to accept the quest, click the Accept Quest button, as shown in Figure 12-7. You can view your accepted quests by pressing the L key. Checking the box next to a quest will put the status of the quest on the screen to the right of your character, as shown in Figure 12-8.

4. Go and perform the quest.

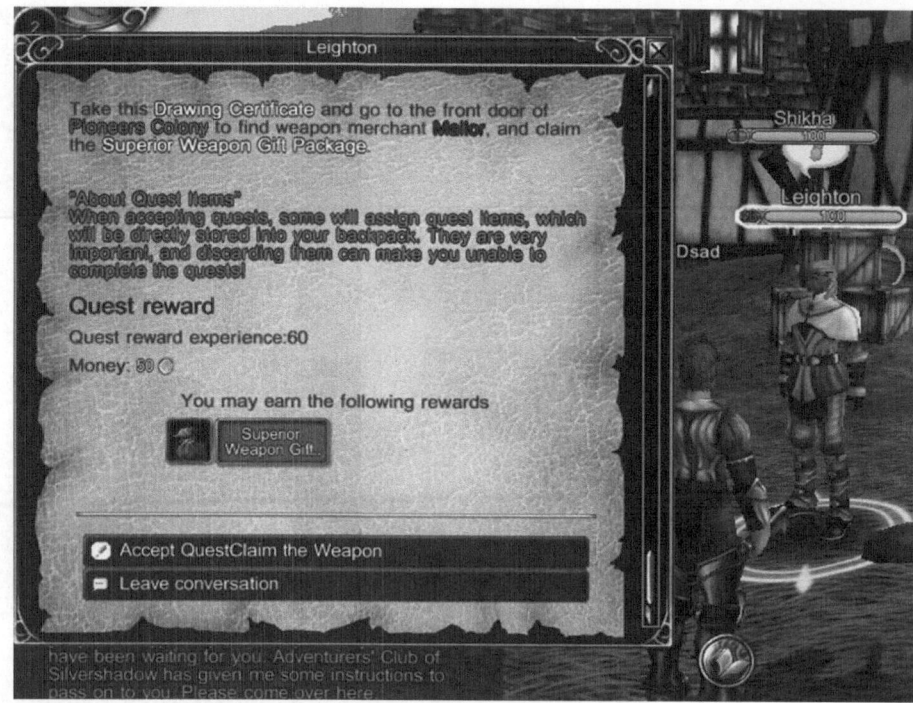

Figure 12-7. *Accept a quest to find treasure and gain experience.*

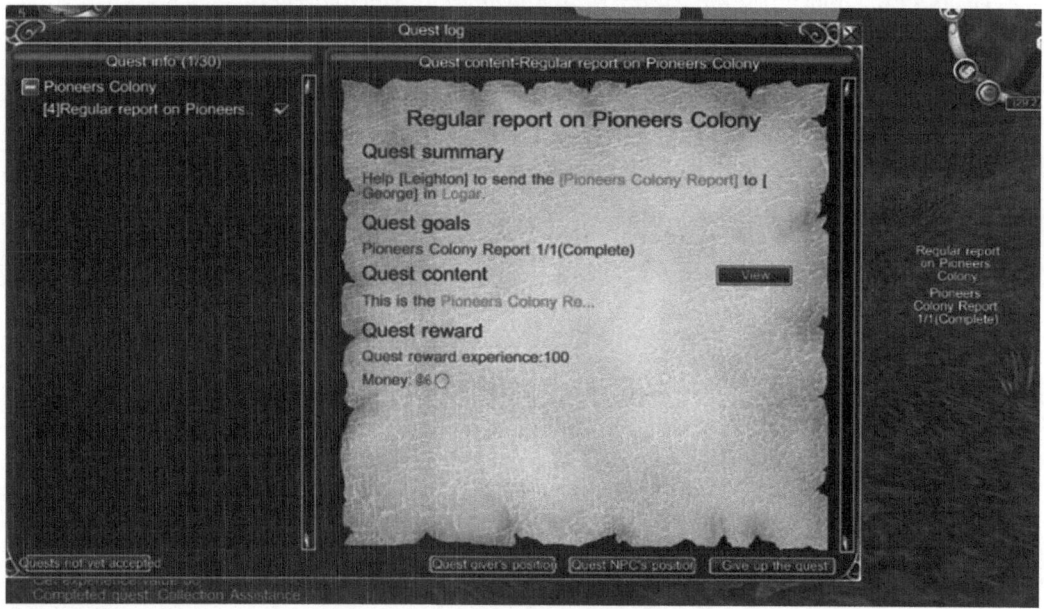

Figure 12-8. *View the requirements of a quest and the quest's rewqrds.*

5. After you have completed a quest, look for an NPC with a yellow check mark over his or her head, as shown in Figure 12-9.

Figure 12-9. *Complete a quest by finding the NPC with a yellow check mark. Get your experience points (XPs) and gold.*

6. Double-click the NPC, and then click the Complete Quest button. The NPC will award you XP, gold, and possibly a treasure item or two, as shown in Figure 12-10.

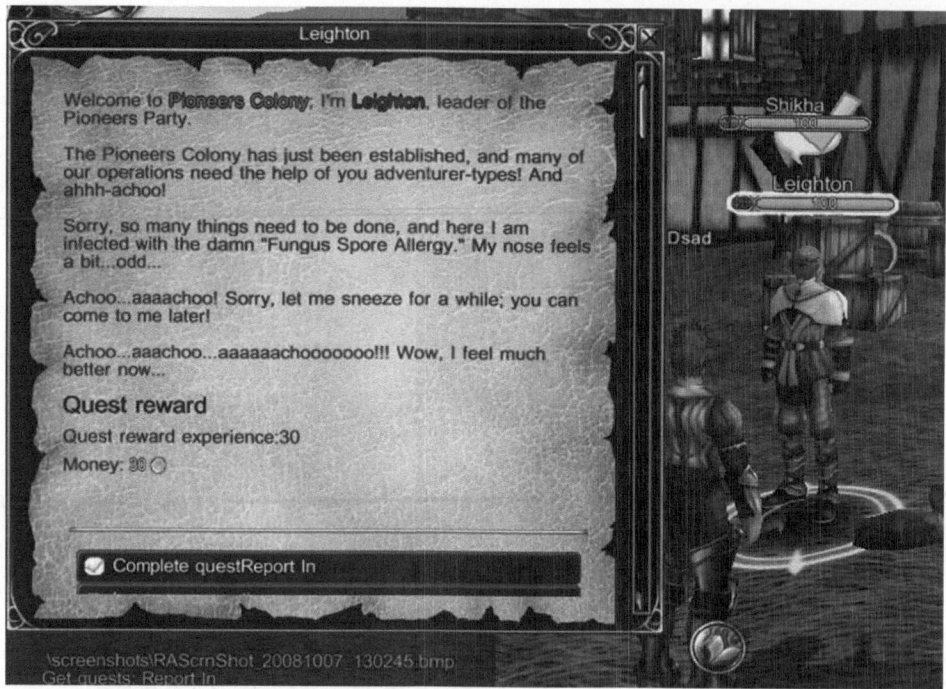

Figure 12-10. *After completing a quest, sometimes the NPC will have additional quests.*

Rent a Mount (Horse)

While your character can run and walk, a faster option to get where you're going is to rent a horse. Most towns have a stable master who will rent you a horse for 900 gold pieces, as shown in Figure 12-11. It's a bit pricey, but consider that using a horse saves time as well as helps to get you past nasty monsters quickly, so they're less likely to attack you.

Once you've rented the horse, press the B key to view your bag. Right-click the saddle icon, wait a few seconds, and you'll find your character on a fast mount, ready to go, as shown in Figure 12-12.

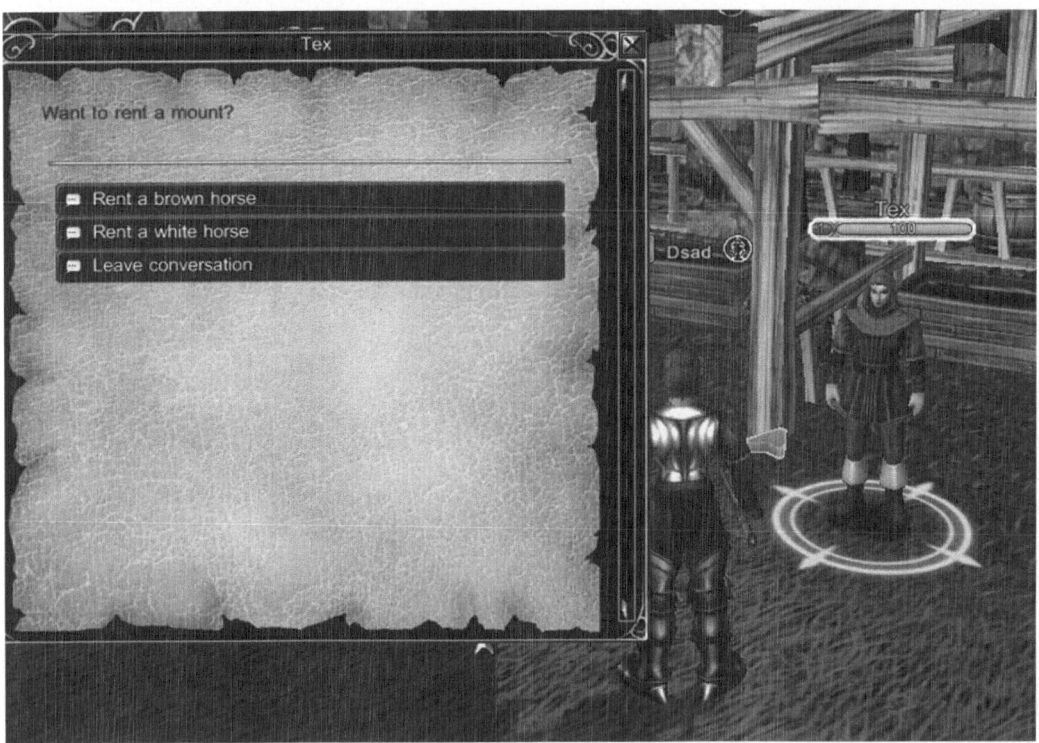

Figure 12-11. *Rent a horse to move faster around the world of Taborea.*

Figure 12-12. *You'll find a saddle in your bag that you can use to mount your horse.*

Change Weapons

Sometimes, after defeating a monster, you will obtain a new weapon or more powerful armor; other times, you'll find healing potions and other items. If you find a new weapon that your class can use (wizards, for example, cannot use swords), click the C key to view your character's equipment, and then click the B key to open your bag. This brings up your character sheet, as shown in Figure 12-13. Here, a check indicates your character can use a weapon, armor, or item in that slot.

Figure 12-13. *Open your character sheet and bag to view your equipped and carried items.*

In the example in Figure 12-14, my character has found a new sword in his bag. If I move the mouse over the sword, I can see its details (how much damage it does, for example) and the details of my currently equipped weapon. Because this new sword does slightly more damage, I simply drag and drop it over the old sword, and the items switch positions.

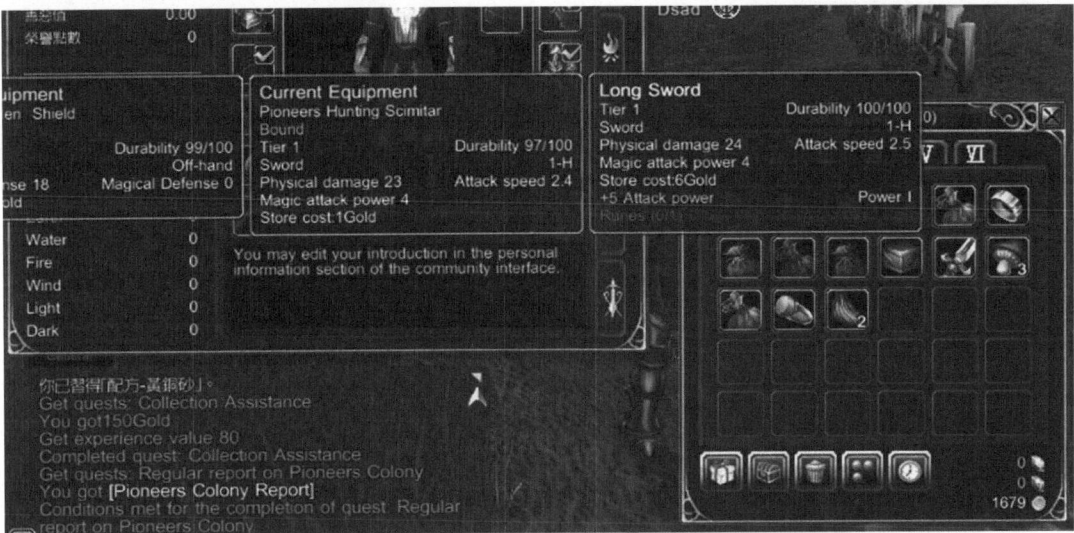

Figure 12-14. *Exchange old armor and weapons for newer, more advanced items.*

Investigate Further

Runes of Magic isn't the only free MMO game available. Here are some others that you might enjoy:

- *Crime Craft* (`http://www.crimecraft.com/`): Maybe you have a bit of bad guy in you. If so, you might like Crime Craft. This is a new, free-to-play MMO game that puts you in the shoes of some not-so-nice characters. Your character may be a thief or gang leader, so you can see where this is going. It's not for everyone, but if you would like to knock over a virtual bank, give Crime Craft a shot.

- *Shaiya* (`http://shaiya.aeriagames.com`): Similar to Runes of Magic, this game lets you create a character that fights, explores, and collects. And just like Runes of Magic, it also offers an online mall, where you can purchase some items without the hassle of fighting a bunch of monsters for them.

And if MMO games are just not your thing, check out this web site:

`http://www.gamesradar.com/f/365-days-of-free-games/a-2008071714293190000`

Yes, it's a long address to type, but you'll find 365 free games to play (a huge variety with some played online and some requiring a download)—plenty to keep you busy for a year!

Summary

I showed you just a few things you can do in the Runes of Magic game. There are thousands of quests and activities you'll encounter as you play. You'll team up with other players to take on large, menacing monsters (as well as obtain powerful treasures if you defeat them). You'll explore deep dungeons and learn more about the ancient evil that has awakened in the land, and that you (and other players) must fight to purge.

Along the way, you'll discover mysteries to solve, NPCs to deal with, and monsters to fight (or run from if they're too powerful). Skills you'll learn early in the game include how to communicate with other players using the in-game text window, how to navigate the world of Taborea using maps that can be called up simply by pressing the M key, and how to upgrade your fighting or spell-casting skills so you can take on meaner, more powerful foes.

MMO games are not going away. Players enjoy the ability to escape the real world for a while and join in a common goal of fighting monsters; exploring ancient castles; and collecting magical weapons, armor, and potions. Have fun!

- World of Warcraft: $19.99 (plus $15 per month subscription fee)
- Runes of Magic: $0

■ ■ ■

CHAPTER 13

Photo Management

Ilove my digital camera. I'm not a professional photographer, so I gave up using film a long time ago. Instead, I purchased a large capacity memory stick/card (1GB of storage), so I can take pictures all day without worrying about running out of film or storage space. And with software such as GIMP (see Chapter 7) and Inkscape (see Chapter 8), I'm able to make all kinds of interesting modifications to my photos.

But there is one big problem I have with my digital photos, and maybe you have it, too: organizing all those photos and keeping track of them. When I'm looking in the My Pictures folder on my PC, with more than 2,000 digital pictures, I would sure like to be able to quickly find only those that have my son in them from last month's vacation at the beach. Unfortunately, I must rely on looking at thumbnails (those small icons that you have to squint at to see any details) or resort to opening and viewing each photo file to locate particular pictures.

Wouldn't it be nice to be able to search through all your digital photos the way you search for keywords using Google? Well, you're in luck. A great application named Picasa can help you organize your photos, plus a whole lot more. And it's 100% free.

What Is Picasa?

Picasa allows you to organize, edit, and share your digital photos. You can also rate photos (using a star system), add tags (keywords for searching), and even create gift CDs for friends and family. And that's only the tip of the iceberg when it comes to built-in features. For example, one feature I use almost every time I upload photos is red-eye reduction (which I'll cover in this chapter). Picasa is an extremely easy-to-use application, and you'll appreciate it more and more as your digital photo collection grows.

Picasa is owned by Google and is currently free to download and use. It's available in more than 35 languages for Windows, Linux, and Mac systems.

Where Can I Find Picasa?

Picasa is an application that you download and install on your computer. It takes up about 45MB of hard drive space. Here are the steps to follow:

1. Visit http://picasa.google.com/ and click the Download Picasa 3 button.

2. Download the setup file and double-click it.

3. Click the I agree button after reading the license agreement.

4. Leave the default installation location, or change the folder by clicking the Browse button. Click the Install button to begin the installation.

5. You may want to uncheck some of the boxes (such as creating a desktop icon or adding a Quick Launch icon) on the final installation screen. Read through the options and decide what to leave checked before clicking the Finish button.

How Do I Use Picasa?

The first time you open and run Picasa, you're asked to allow Picasa to perform a complete scan of your computer or just your desktop, My Documents, and My Pictures folders. It's looking for photos that include the following formats: JPG, BMP, GIF, TIF, PSD, and TIF. Be aware that a complete scan can take a while (on my computer, this initial scan took almost 25 minutes).

The first time you open and run Picasa, you'll also be asked if you would like to use the Picasa Viewer application to view all images files. You can configure Picasa Viewer to automatically open files by selecting any or all of the following formats: JPG, TIF, BMP, GIF, TGA, and RAW. If you choose not to configure Picasa Viewer, double-clicking a file will open it in whatever default application is assigned.

Next, you'll be presented with a window similar to the one shown in Figure 13-1. Along the left edge is a list of the folders on your hard drive that contain digital images. When you click a folder, the photos in that folder are displayed in the area on the right.

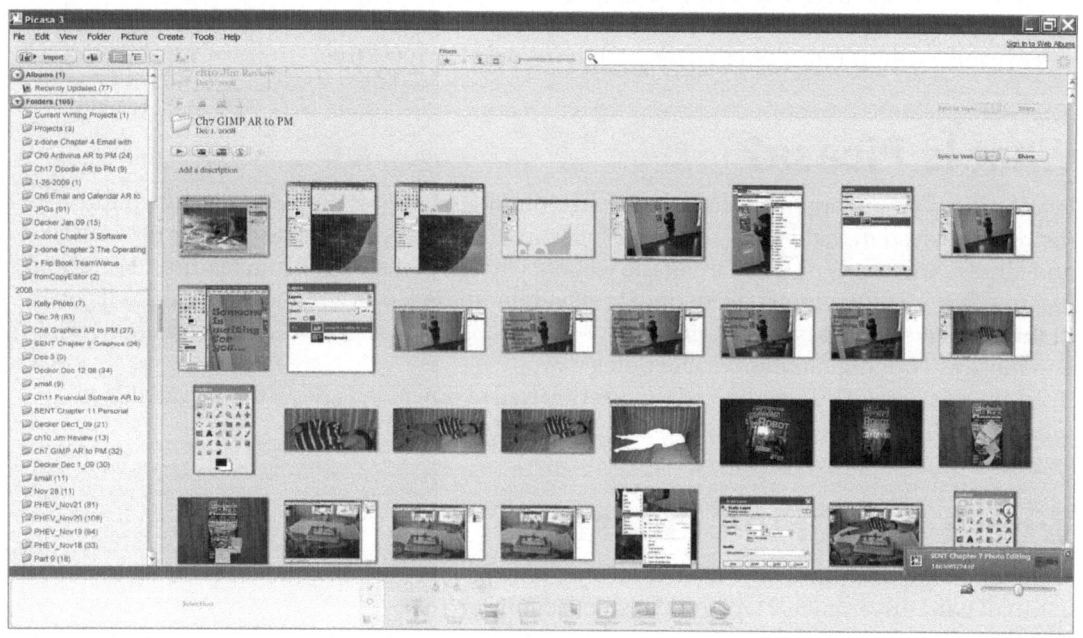

Figure 13-1. *Picasa organizes your images using folders.*

To view a larger version of a picture, simply double-click the photo. The photo will appear on the right, and tabs with specialized tools for editing are presented on the left, as shown in Figure 13-2. Using the tools on the Basic Fixes tab, you can crop photos, reduce red eye, and experiment with different color settings. The Tuning tab and the Effects tab offer even more tweaks for you to perform on your photos. And don't worry about making a mistake while you're making changes to your photos, because you can always click the Undo button to get back your original photo!

Tip You might want to click the I'm Feeling Lucky button in the Basic Tab immediately. It can do some amazing cleanup on a photo, including fixing lighting issues and sharpening details.

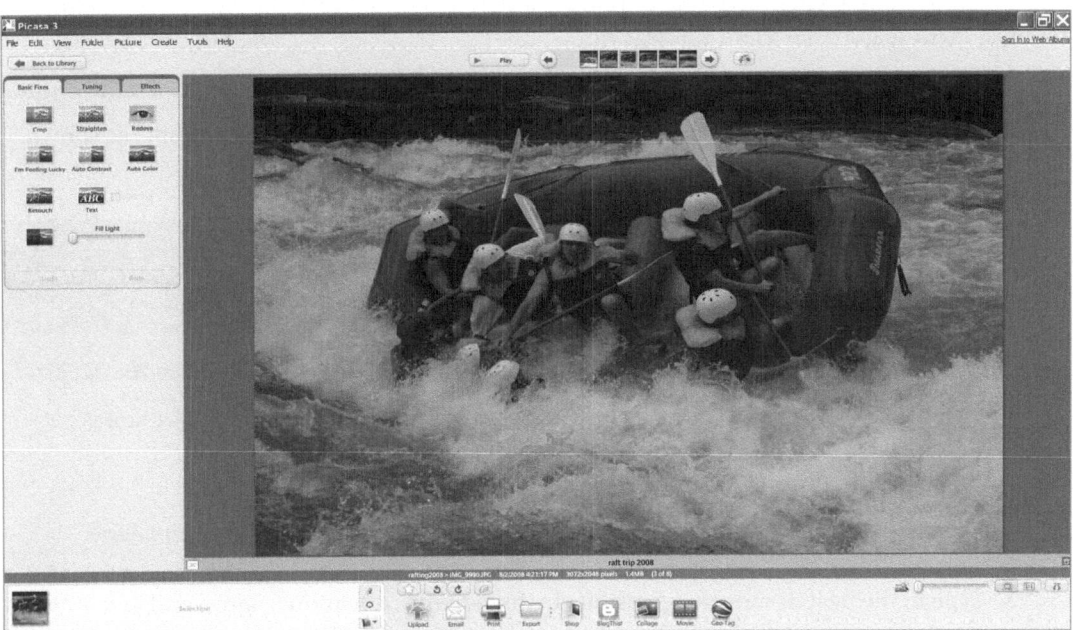

Figure 13-2. *Picasa offers numerous editing options.*

Use the Photo Tray

Picasa has something called the Photo Tray, which appears in the lower-left corner of the window. It allows you to build a virtual album of selected photos.

When you click a photo, it will be added to the Photo Tray; you can jump from one photo in the Photo Tray to the next, without hunting through the Picasa database again. This is a nice feature when you have hundreds, or even thousands, of photos on your hard drive and wish to keep a small batch together for sharing, printing, or e-mailing.

After you've added photos to the Photo Tray, you can use the buttons along the lower-right edge of the Picasa window to do something with the group, as shown in Figure 13-3. For example, if you click the Email button, Picasa will allow you to e-mail the collection of photos in your Photo Tray. It adds the photos as attachments using your default e-mail application.

Other options for the Photo Tray include creating a separate photo album, burning the photos to a CD/DVD, printing the photos on your printer, and ordering prints online.

Figure 13-3. *Use the Photo Tray to print, e-mail, and order collections of selected photos.*

Tag Photos

An important task that you can (and should) do for all your photographs is to tag them. *Tagging* is simply adding keywords to your photographs (they won't actually appear on the image) to make them searchable. Here's how it works:

1. Select a photo by double-clicking it in the folder list in Picasa. This will open the photo.

2. Directly underneath the photo, you should see the words "Make a caption," as shown in Figure 13-4. Click these words.

Figure 13-4. *Tagging your digital photos will make future searches quick and easy.*

3. Type in the best description possible. Include names, locations, dates, and any other words you can think of that describe the photo. In Figure 13-5, you can see that I've entered details about the event, plus the year and the location (haircut, 2009, Atlanta).

4. When you're finished, repeat steps 1 through 3 to tag your other photos (there's no Save button to click). You can also click the Next button to move to the next photo, or select a photo from the main window and press Ctrl+K to tag it.

Figure 13-5. *Use as many descriptive words as possible when adding a caption.*

Now, the next time my in-laws come for a visit and my wife asks me to show them photos of our son's latest haircut, I can simply open Picasa and type in a keyword such as "haircut." Then only those photos that contain that word will show up, as shown in Figure 13-6. This is much easier than flipping through a directory of hundreds of photos named something like DSCN00010.JPG, which digital cameras have the tendency to create.

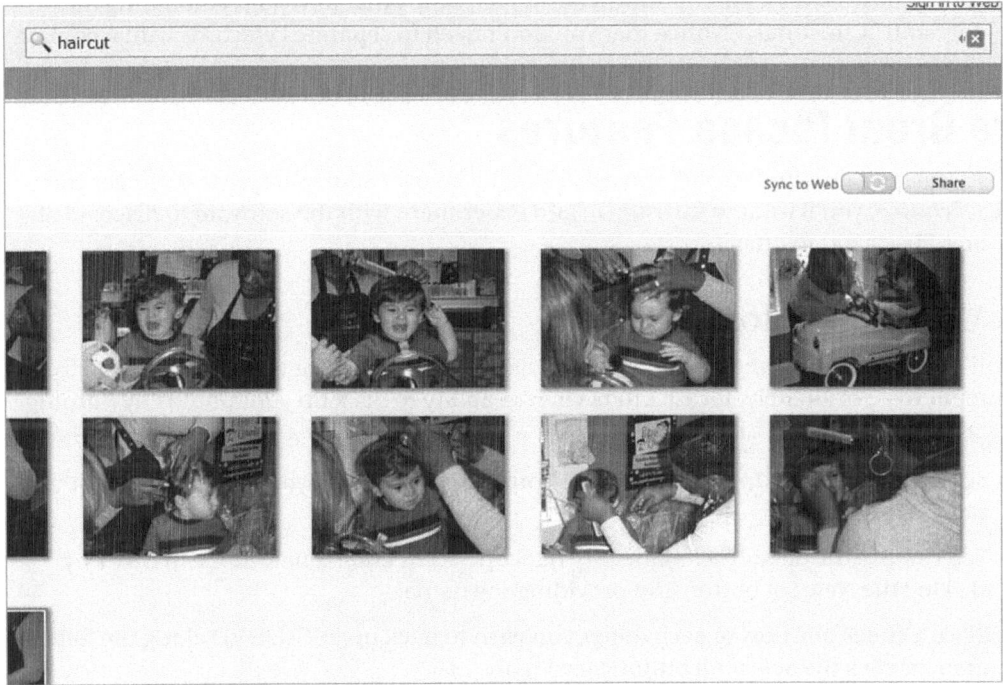

Figure 13-6. *Use keywords to search through your digital photos.*

Yes, tagging can take a while as you go through a large collection of digital photos, but the good news is that you don't need to do it all at once. Just set aside a few half-hour blocks of time, and tag as many photos as you can. (My editor suggested having a "tagging party" by letting family members view and tag photos as they take a trip down memory lane—a nice way to share the work!) Eventually, you'll end up with captions added to all your digital photos.

You should also develop the habit of opening Picasa after uploading a collection of photos to your computer and immediately adding captions. Staying on top of your tagging will pay large dividends later when you're looking for that single photo buried on your hard drive.

Tip You can tag multiple photos by selecting one photo, selecting additional photos with Ctrl-click, and then clicking the Tag button or pressing Ctrl+K to tag them all with the same text. This also works for selecting multiple photos for printing.

Once you've tagged a good array of photos, you can see how powerful the search feature is. For instance, suppose you want to find pictures of your dog during holidays. You can search for "dog Christmas," and Picasa will show you all the photos that have tags containing the words "dog" and "Christmas." Notice that you don't need to separate keywords with a comma.

More Great Picasa Features

"What else can you do with Picasa?" you ask. Here, I'll go over some sample tasks to get you started. Of course, you'll want to investigate and experiment with the software to discover all the features Picasa has to offer.

Back Up Your Photos

After you've spent all that time organizing and tagging your photos, it would be a shame to lose your photos. Fortunately, Picasa offers you the ability to back up your photos by burning them to a CD or DVD. Here's how:

1. Select Tools ➤ Backup Pictures. At the bottom of the screen, you'll see the backup steps, as shown in Figure 13-7.

2. You can use the default set name (My Backup Set) or enter a new name in Box 1 by clicking the New Set button and providing the name.

3. Place a check box next to each folder you wish to back up to CD/DVD along the left column, or click the Select All button (see Figure 13-7).

4. Picasa will add up the storage space needed and display how many CDs or DVDs will be required. Click the Burn button when you're ready to start (and have your CDs or DVDs ready).

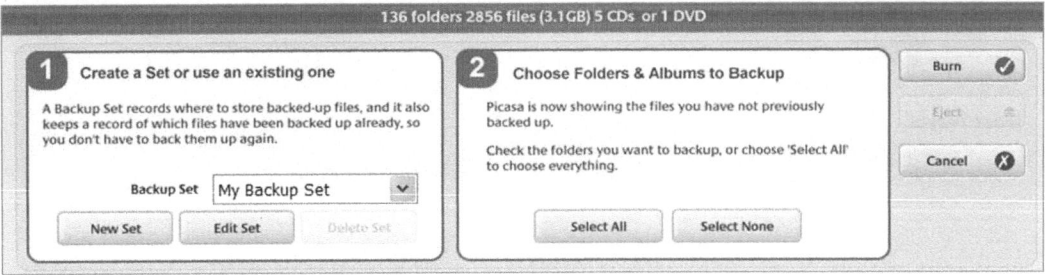

Figure 13-7. *Back up your photos to CD or DVD to prevent loss of your pictures.*

Tip If you would prefer to keep a backup of your photos somewhere other than on a CD/DVD, here's a suggestion: select Tools ➤ Upload ➤ Upload to Web Albums. You will be asked to provide your Google account name and password (or create one) before you can use the free service. Web Albums allows you to upload your photos for viewing over the Internet. You can limit who can view your photos, so consider this an option for not only backing up your photos, but also for making them available to friends and family.

Eliminate Duplicate Photos

Over time, I've copied photos from one folder to another, and I've also occasionally imported photos from old memory cards that are already on my hard drive. Besides taking up hard drive space, having duplicates also takes up my time as I sift through photos before tagging them. If you've also ended up with more than one copy of a photo, you will appreciate Picasa's duplicate photo search capability. Here's how to remove duplicates:

1. Select Tools ➤ Experimental ➤ Show Duplicate Files, as shown in Figure 13-8.

2. Picasa will display the duplicate photos it finds. For example, in Figure 13-9, the rightmost picture in the folder called `Kelly Photo` and the rightmost picture in the folder called `Dec 28` have the same file name and are duplicates. If you truly need both images, you can just leave them on your computer. Otherwise, right-click one of the images and choose Delete from Disk to eliminate the duplicate.

3. When you're finished clearing out duplicates, click the green Exit Search button at the top of the photo display.

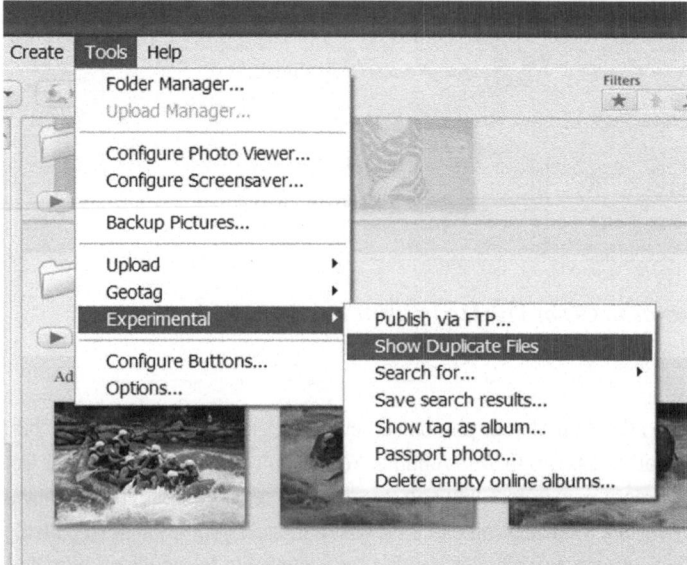

Figure 13-8. *You can have Picasa display duplicate photos that exist on your hard drive.*

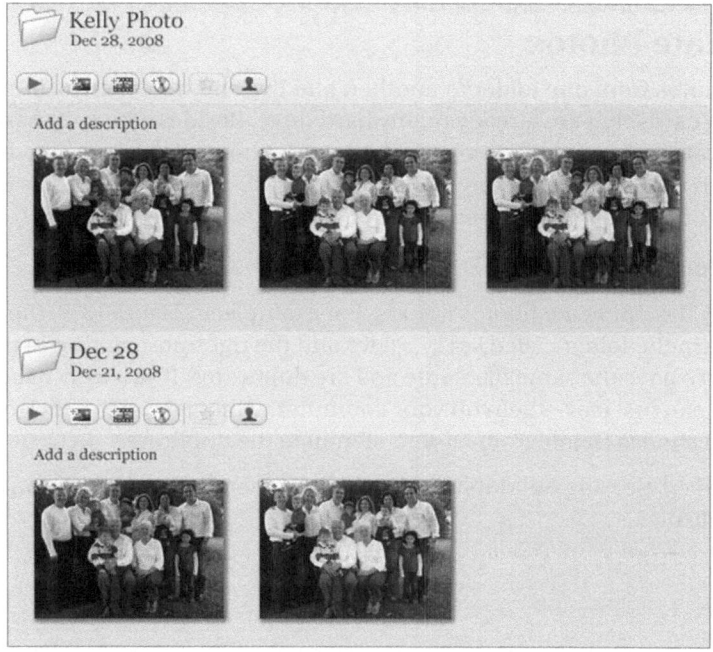

Figure 13-9. *When you find duplicate photos, delete one to free up hard drive space.*

Create Your Own Screen Saver

Picasa has a nice built-in screen-saver ability that lets you add and remove photos as often as you like. As shown in Figure 13-10, Screensaver is an album in Picasa's Albums list. You can add photos to this album and display them as your screen saver as follows:

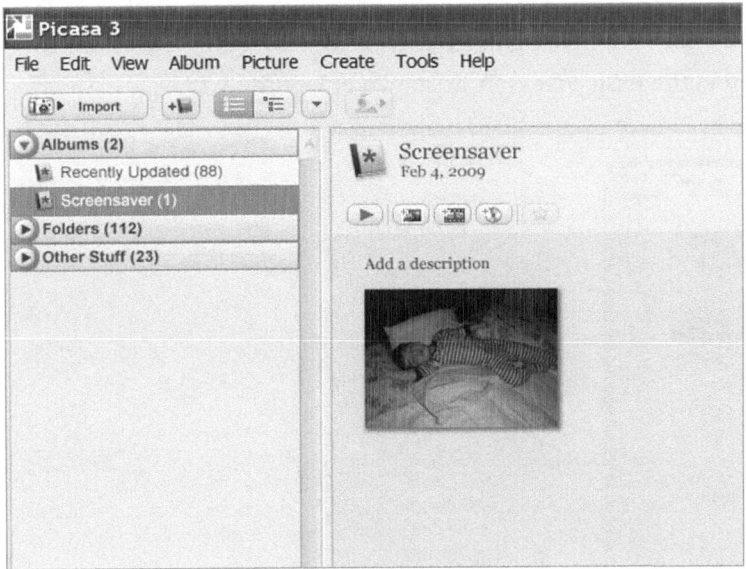

Figure 13-10. *The Screensaver album will hold photos for your screen saver to display.*

1. Right-click a photo and select Add to Album ➤ Screensaver, as shown in Figure 13-11. Your photo will be added to the Screensaver album.

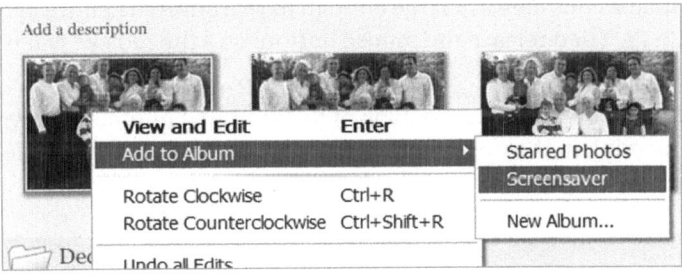

Figure 13-11. *Select the photos to include in your screen saver.*

2. To set your screen saver to use your Picasa Screensaver album, select Create ➤ Add to Screensaver.

3. Your computer's screen saver control window will open. Configure the screen-saver settings, such as time to wait and how fast it cycles through your photos.

Remove Red Eye from a Digital Photo

One of the biggest problems I have with my photos is red eye. My camera has a red-eye removal feature, but sometimes I forget to use it. Fortunately for me, Picasa has an easy-to-use feature for reducing red eye, which works as follows:

1. Open a picture that contains a red-eyed monster—maybe a picture of a mother-in-law (just kidding!).

2. Click the Redeye button in the Basic Fixes tab, as shown in Figure 13-12.

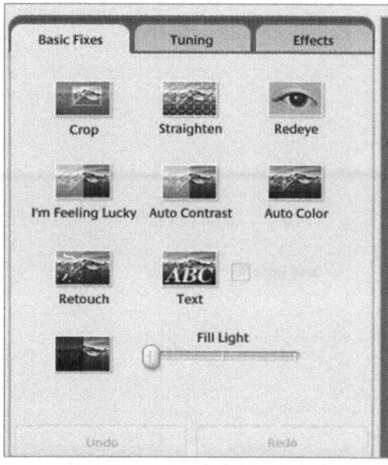

Figure 13-12. *Use the Redeye tool to clean up red eye.*

3. Hold down the mouse button and drag a small box around the offending eye. Try to make the box as small as possible but large enough to surround the entire eye, as shown in Figure 13-13. Then release the mouse button, and the red eye will be removed.

4. Click the Cancel button if you don't like the look of the modified photo. Otherwise, click the Back to Library link in the upper-right corner to save the change and return to your photos.

Figure 13-13. *Drag a box around the red eye.*

Investigate Further

In addition to Picasa, another free digital photo management tool worth mentioning is Flickr (http://www.flickr.com). Flickr is an online management service, with features similar to Picasa's. Because it's online, you'll be storing, editing, tagging, and performing other tasks using your web browser.

Flickr does offer a downloadable tool that makes uploading your photos easy, but its real power resides in its ability to share photos. You control who has the ability to view individual pictures or groups of images.

Flickr is a nice alternative to Picasa, especially if you're running out of hard drive space. It offers a free membership with a maximum storage size of 200 images. If you want to store more, you'll pay a small yearly fee for the Pro Membership, which allows unlimited storage and uploads.

Summary

Picasa is one of the most powerful little applications I've ever used, and the fact that it's free makes it even better. It makes organizing and tagging your digital photo collection easy. I suggest that you take advantage of this great tool and get control of your photos, so you can always find what you need in a hurry.

And don't think that Picasa's only useful for removing red eye and tagging your photos. It has many other features you should try. Click the Create menu, and you'll see that you can make a poster to print, order prints online, and even publish photos to a blog.

CHAPTER 14

■ ■ ■

Internet Phone Calls

I have friends all over the world, and e-mail has been a blessing when it comes to staying in touch with them. Yet, sometimes an e-mail message is just no substitute for picking up the phone and calling someone to say hello.

But then the confusion sets in. What time does my unlimited long-distance service start in the evening? How much does it cost to call Europe during business hours? Is Dan part of my mobile phone network so I can call him for free? Trying to keep up with all the rules, limitations, and costs can drive a person crazy.

To the rescue comes this great little piece of software called Skype, which allows you to talk for free, at any time and anywhere you have Internet access. All you need is a headset, the free software installed, and a friend who uses Skype as well.

What Is Skype?

In a nutshell, Skype is software that allows you to talk to anyone in the world over your Internet connection. Skype is free, easy to download and install, and simple to use. You can talk with another Skype user freely for as long as you like. There are charges if you want to call a mobile phone or landline phone, but those costs are low, and you can pay as you go.

Other features include the ability to send instant messages to other Skype users, have a conference call with up to 24 other people, place a video call if you have a webcam, and import your contacts from other address books.

Skype offers plenty of additional pay-to-use features, but the basic, free service is all that most people will ever need. It's available for Windows, Linux, Mac, and other platforms (such as your mobile phone).

OF HEADSETS AND MICROPHONES

To use Skype, you need a headset. You can purchase one at a local computer store or find plenty of options online. If you're just using it for Skype, you don't need to spend a lot of money on a headset with bells and whistles. Just make sure it has jacks that fit into your computer's microphone and headphone ports. Headsets typically have two jacks: one for the microphone port and one for a speaker/headphones port, like the headset in this photo:

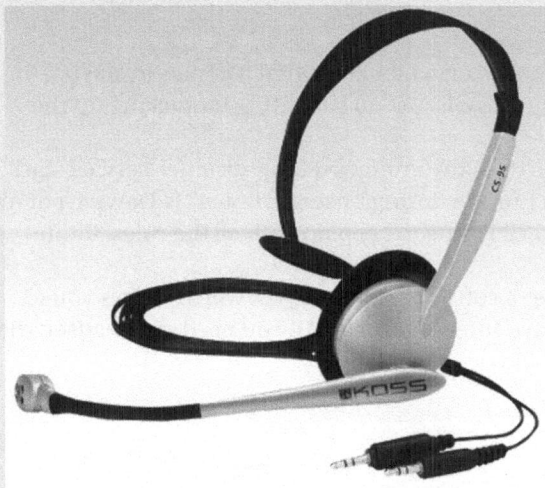

Laptops with built-in speakers also sometimes come with a built-in microphone. You'll need to check your hardware to determine if you already have a microphone. Built-in microphones are often muted by default. To check and change this setting, open the Sound/Audio applet in the Control Panel, select the Volume tab, and click the Advanced button. If the Mute box is checked for Microphone, simply uncheck it.

Where Can I Find Skype?

Skype is free to download but does require a high-speed Internet connection to use. You can obtain the software by following these steps:

1. Visit `http://www.skype.com/newtoskype/` and click the Download Skype button.

2. Follow the instructions to download the setup file and double-click it to install the software.

3. Select your language, place a check in the box to acknowledge your agreement to adhere to the license agreement, and then click the Install button to begin the installation.

4. After the installation is completed, click the Start Skype button.

How Do I Use Skype?

When Skype opens for the first time, you'll be asked to create a new Skype account. This is a simple procedure:

1. In the first Create account window, enter your full name, a Skype name (this will be what you provide other Skype users), and a password, as shown in Figure 14-1. Place a check in the box to acknowledge that you accept the license agreement, and then click the Next button.

Figure 14-1. *Create your Skype account by providing a few pieces of information.*

2. In the next window, shown in Figure 14-2, provide an e-mail address, select your country or region, and enter your city name. If you leave the "Sign me in when Skype starts" box checked, Skype will always log you in when you start the program. If you uncheck the box, you'll need to log in to start using Skype. Click the Sign In button when you've filled in the information.

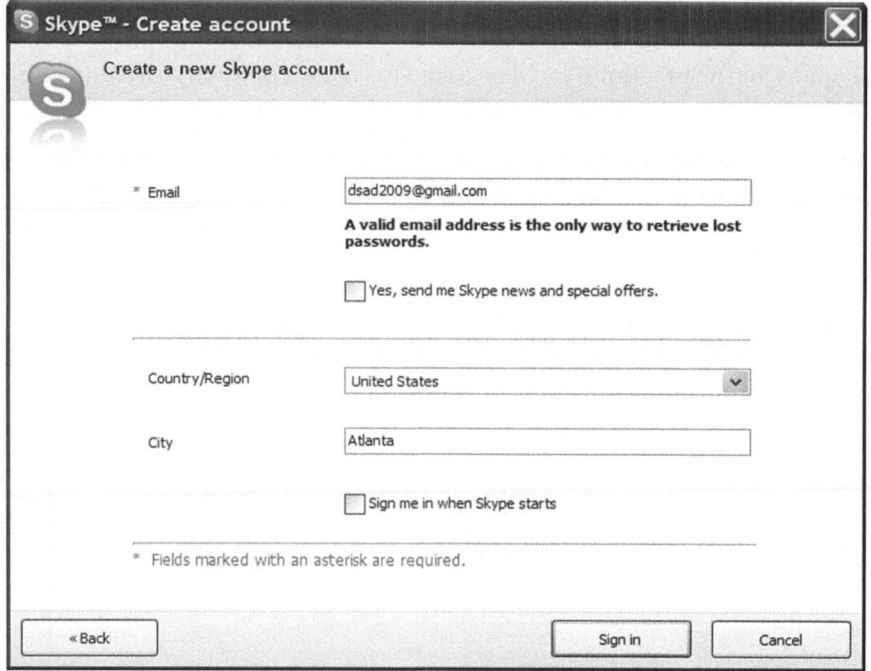

Figure 14-2. *Provide e-mail and location information, and you're ready to start Skype.*

3. Skype will take a few moments to create your account. When it finishes, plug in your headset, and then click the Start button to take a tutorial on using Skype and make a test call.

4. During the test call, you'll be asked to record a short message that will be played back to you. If you're able to record and hear the message, you're ready to start using Skype.

In order to use Skype, you'll need someone to call. This means adding someone to your Contact list.

Add Contacts

The people who you call with Skype must also be using Skype if you wish the call to be free. (Skype charges a small fee to call landline and mobile phones.) If you don't know anyone who uses Skype, you'll need to encourage friends and family members to download and install Skype. Once they've done this, just ask them for their Skype name (refer back to Figure 14-1). With that information, here's how you add them to your Contact list:

1. Start Skype and log in.

2. Click the New button and select the New Contact option, as shown in Figure 14-3.

3. The Add a Contact window will open, as shown in Figure 14-4. Enter the Skype name for your contact in the text field and click the Find button.

Figure 14-3. *Click New Contact to begin building your Contact list.*

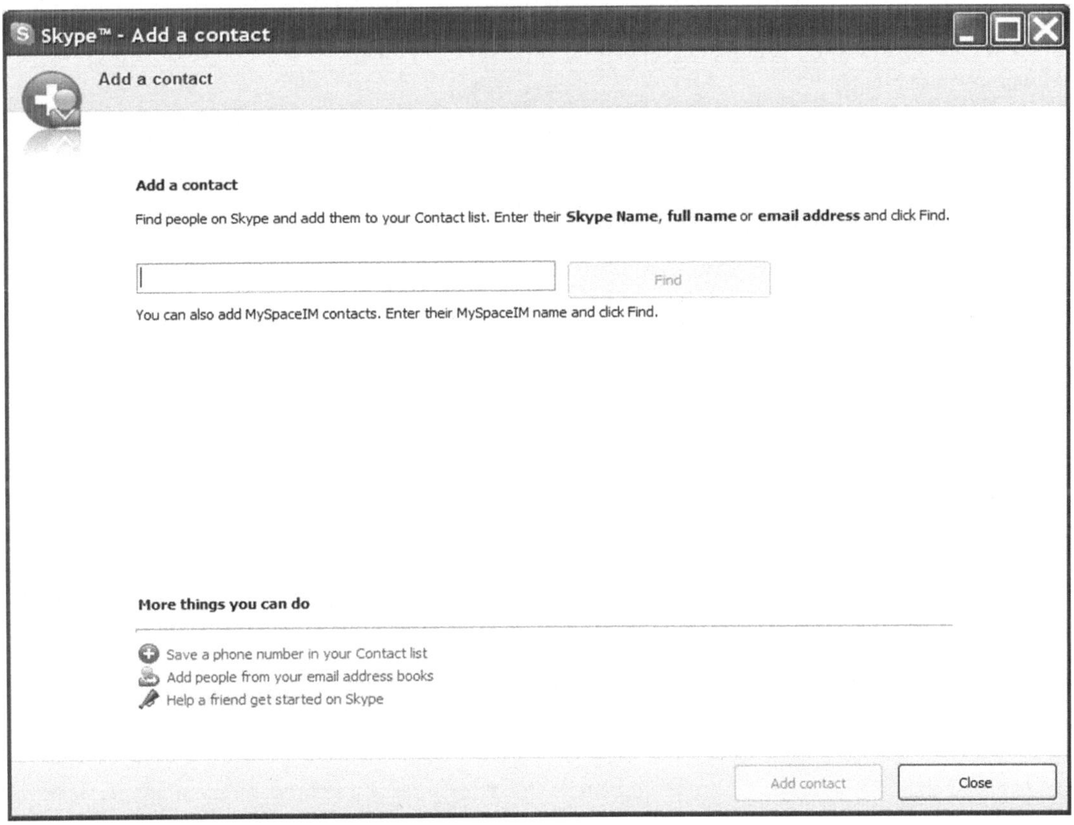

Figure 14-4. *Search for the Skype name and add that person to your Contact list.*

4. If the name is a valid Skype name, it will appear in the search results list. Click the correct name (if there are multiple names, use the location to find the proper person), and then click the Add Skype Contact button.

5. Optionally, you can enter a message to let your new contact know that you've added him to your Contact list, and then click the Send button to send it. Click the Close button to add the contact without sending a message.

Your new contact should appear in the Skype application's Contact list, as shown in Figure 14-5. Now all that's left is to make a phone call.

Note Your contacts have their own Contact lists, which can also be made available to you. This is useful in a large work environment when you need to reach someone but don't have them in your own Contact list.

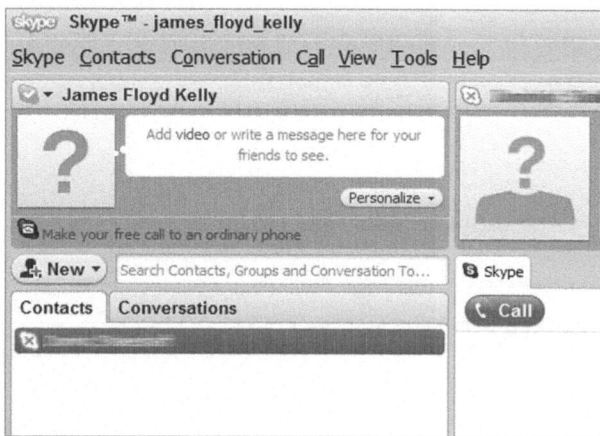

Figure 14-5. *Your contacts are listed in the Contact list.*

Make a Call

To make a call, start by locating the person you wish to call in your Contact list. To the right of the person's name, you'll see a small green Call button (with an icon representing a phone). Put on your headset, and then click that button.

You'll hear some beeps at first. When the person you are calling answers, just start talking. You're having an Internet phone call!

Caution Some Skype users consider it rude to be contacted via Skype without a text message, chat message, or e-mail notice first. Because Skype requires you to be sitting in front of your computer, it's best to give your contact a heads-up and ask her if it's a good time to call.

More Skype Functionality

In case you're wondering, Skype does more than provide free phone calls. Here, I'll introduce you to a few of the other free services built into this application.

Send Text Messages to Your Contacts

You're already familiar with the little green button you click to make a call. Now look in the lower-right corner of the window, and you'll see a little text box that allows you to send an instant message to a contact. Type your message, as shown in Figure 14-6, and then press the Enter key to send it.

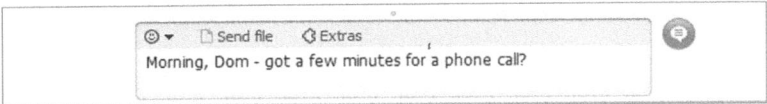

Figure 14-6. *The Chat window*

Messages between persons will queue up on the screen, with the most recent message at the bottom, as shown in Figure 14-7. If the recipient is logged in to Skype, he can respond to your message immediately by typing in a response. If the recipient is not available at the moment, the message will be waiting for him to read when he next logs in to Skype, and he can reply with his own message.

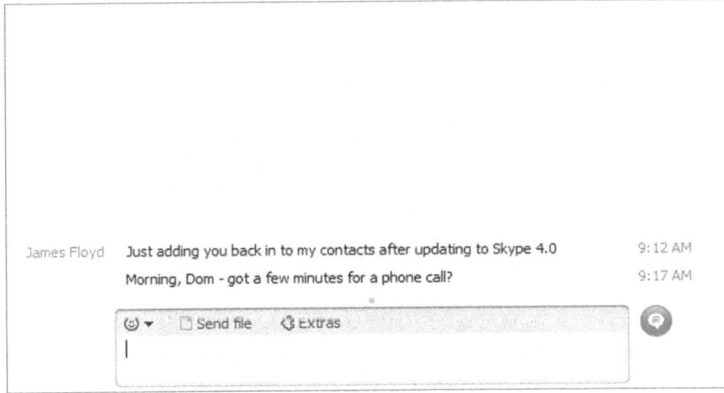

Figure 14-7. *If your contact is away or busy, the instant message will still be delivered.*

Set Your Status

To set your status from Online to Away to let others know you're unavailable for a call or chat, click the small down arrow next to your Skype name, as shown in Figure 14-8. This list offers Away, Do Not Disturb, and other status options. After you make a selection, anyone trying to call or send you a message will see your status.

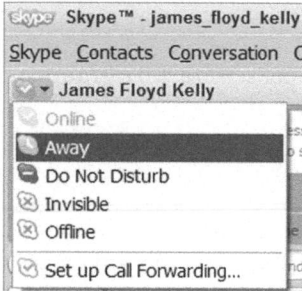

Figure 14-8. *Set your status with Skype so your contacts can see if you are busy or available.*

Make a Video Phone Call

If you have a webcam in addition to your headset, you can provide a live video of yourself to whomever you call with Skype. It's even better if the person you're calling also has a webcam so the two of you can talk face to face, but that's not required.

To set up Skype for video calls, plug in your webcam, and then open Skype. Select Tools ➤ Options. In the Skype Options window, click the Video Settings tab, as shown in Figure 14-9.

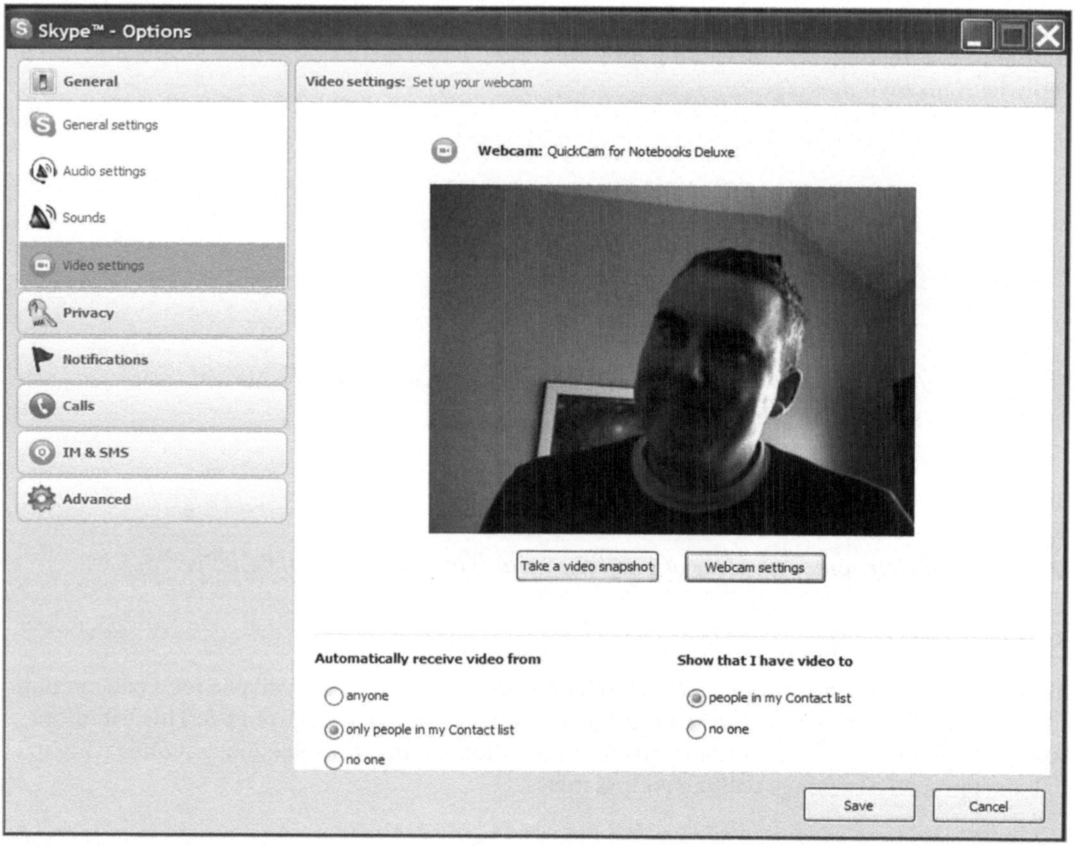

Figure 14-9. *Configure Skype to use your webcam using the Options window.*

If your camera is working properly, you should see an image of yourself. Beneath that image are settings for who you can automatically receive a video call from, as well as who knows you have video capabilities. I suggest accepting the default of receiving video only from your known contacts. (You don't want strangers calling you up with their webcams turned on and doing who knows what, right?)

Once you've made your selections in the Options window, click the Save button. A new Video call button will be added in Skype, as shown in Figure 14-10.

Tip You can also block anyone but those in your Contact list from placing phone calls to you. Select Tools ➤ Options. In the Options window, click the Calls tab along the left edge of the window. Make sure the option labeled "Only allow people in my Contact List to call me" is selected.

Figure 14-10. *When a webcam is detected, a new Video call button is available.*

Click the Video call button for a contact, and when the call is connected, that person will be able to see your shiny, happy face. If you didn't initially make a video call, click the Turn on Video button during a regular phone call to start the video, and keep talking.

Making a video call is a lot of fun. Just change out of your pajamas if it's a business call, okay?

Investigate Further

Once you understand the basics of using Skype, you'll also want to investigate some of the add-ons that are available for it. Your first stop will be https://extras.skype.com/, where you can read reviews of various expansions to Skype. There are whiteboard tools, translators, and games that you can play with those you are calling. To find other add-ons, just do a Google search for "Skype add-ons." You'll find more extra features than you'll have time to test—but that's part of the fun of Skype.

Other Skype users have found that the application makes a nice monitoring tool for your home or office. You can read the article at http://www.makeuseof.com/tag/how-to-use-skype-as-a-covert-snooper/ to learn how to configure Skype for this kind of activity.

In addition to the Skype application, you might also consider faxing from your computer. Dozens of free services allow you to send and receive faxes. Unfortunately, some of them are limited to specific countries (for example, FaxZero allows you to send only within the

United States and Canada). Others will allow you to only receive faxes for free, and will charge to send faxes. Here are a couple United Stated–based options:

- *FaxDigits* (`http://www.faxdigits.com/`): This service lets you receive unlimited faxes using a free fax number provided to you at sign-up. However, the number assigned might not be a local area code.

- *FaxZero* (`http://faxzero.com/`): This service allows you to send a maximum of two faxes per day (three pages per fax limit) anywhere in the United States or Canada. The cover sheet does contain an advertisement, but if you just need to send the occasional quick fax, this is a great free service.

If you need a faxing service that works outside the United States, a Google search should help you locate one.

Summary

If you like to talk to friends and family often, you should definitely encourage as many as possible to download and install Skype. The ability to speak for free, locally or internationally, is one of the unique features the Internet offers. If you have a high-speed Internet connection, the sound quality is excellent. And the ability to use a webcam lets you wave hello and say it at the same time!

CHAPTER 15

■ ■ ■

Web Logs

You don't have to write for a major newspaper to have your opinions shared with the world. And you definitely don't need to come up with 300 pages for a best-selling book covering your favorite hobby. I could have titled this chapter "Become Famous Using Web Logs." You might be surprised by the number of people who have built a reputation (and a fortune) by creating and writing a web log (or *blog* for short) of their own. Do a Google search for Matt Drudge, Paul Kos, and Glenn Reynolds to see how a few individuals turned their opinions into fame and fortune.

Blogs are everywhere. For some, a blog is an online diary, documenting thoughts and experiences for sharing with the world or keeping private. Businesses use blogs to share information with customers and their employees in an informal way. Many people use blogs to track their favorite hobby, sports team, or whatever subject strikes them as possibly interesting to other people. While blogs can be kept private, they really shine when blog writers allow the general public to read their material and then add comments. In a sense, a blog writer provides something to talk about.

Gone are the days when you had to register a domain name (such as `www.jamesfloydkellythoughts.com`) to maintain a web log; you don't need to create an entire web site just to provide insightful commentary. The best part is that blogs are free, requiring no registration fees or hosting fees.

Maybe you have a hobby that you feel the world must know more about, or maybe you think that the media is overlooking some key position held by a political figure. The point is that if you have an opinion and want to share it with the rest of us, it's a lot easier to create a blog for that purpose than to get your own TV show or publish on the back page of your favorite magazine. And it all starts with a short visit to Blogger.

What Is Blogger?

Blogger is an online tool that will allow you to create a professional-looking web log, post your opinions and news, share pictures and video, accept reader comments, and more. Blogger falls into the Software as a Service (SaaS) category, because you'll be doing all your writing using your web browser and the online tools made available to you by Blogger.

Blogger assigns you a web address (URL) in the form of http://*your-blog-name*.blogspot.com, and this is the web site that readers will use to read your latest additions (called *posts*). Blogger also offers the ability for fans of your blog to "subscribe" to your blog. When you add a new item to the blog, subscribers will receive your latest post in their e-mail or newsreader.

Blogger is owned by Google and is free to use. All it requires is an Internet connection and a web browser. You provide the words, pictures, and video, and Blogger handles publishing it all for the world to see.

Note How is Blogger able to provide its services to you at no cost? Google is covering the cost of Blogger by selling advertisements that appear on its search engine and other tools such as Gmail (see Chapter 6). Blogger will not display advertisements unless you choose to participate. If your blog becomes popular, you can elect to allow businesses to place small advertisements on your blog. Then you will get paid when visitors to your blog click the advertisements.

Where Can I Find Blogger?

Because Blogger is a SaaS, you don't need to install anything to use it. Instead, you do everything over the Web. Here's how:

1. Visit http://www.blogger.com and click the Create a Blog button.

2. If you already have a Google account, click the "sign in first" link; otherwise, enter the required information (e-mail address, password, and so on). Read through the Terms of Service, and then check the box to acknowledge your agreement to those terms, as shown in the example in Figure 15-1. Then click the Continue button.

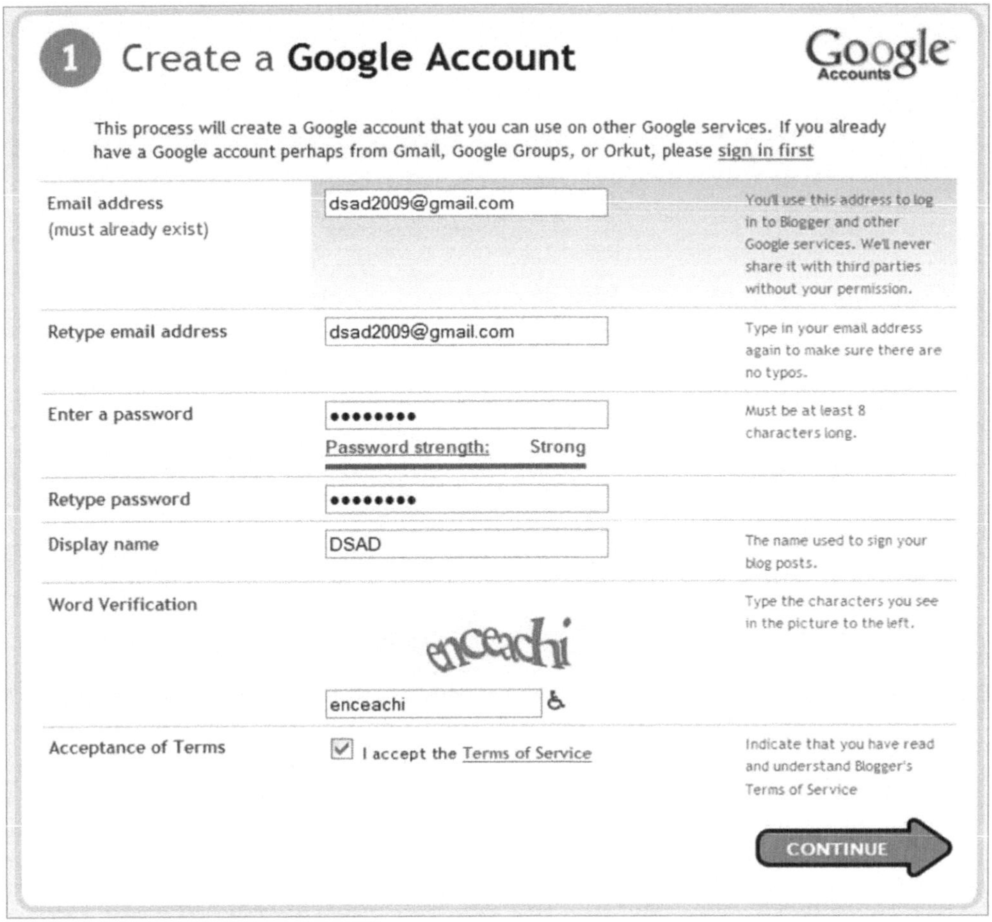

Figure 15-1. *Registering for Blogger is free and easy.*

3. Next, you need to create a name for your blog and the blog address (URL). Enter your information, as shown in the example in Figure 15-2. Then click the Check Availability link to make certain your blog address is available. Once you have entered the required information, click the Continue button.

Figure 15-2. *Pick your blog's name and give it an address that people can use to find your blog.*

4. The final step in the blog-creation process allows you to choose a template style (design) for your blog, as shown in Figure 15-3. You can click the preview template link to see a larger version on your screen. Your template selection can be changed any time you like, so don't worry about being locked into a design forever. Choose your template, and then click the Continue button.

5. Your blog has been created. Simply click the Start Blogging button to begin.

For some crazy reason, when you start Blogger for the first time, you're presented with a new screen, without any explanation of how to start. Don't worry! I'll show you the basics of using Blogger in the next section.

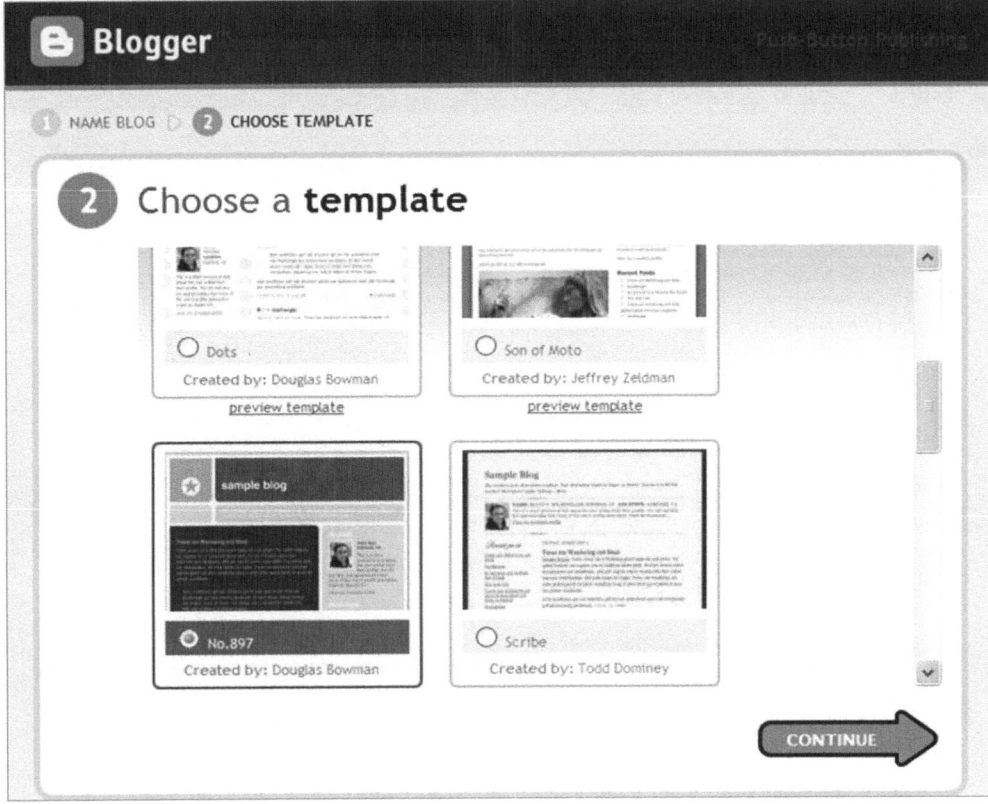

Figure 15-3. *Pick a look for your blog using the template samples provided.*

How Do I Use Blogger?

At this point, you've just created a new blog. Blogger has opened, and you're most likely seeing a screen like the one shown in Figure 15-4. It might look like a confusion of buttons to you, but trust me, it's very easy to navigate and use. I'm going to walk through the steps of creating the very first blog post for my new blog, "Don't Spend a Dime," and use a few of the buttons, so you can see how easy this really is.

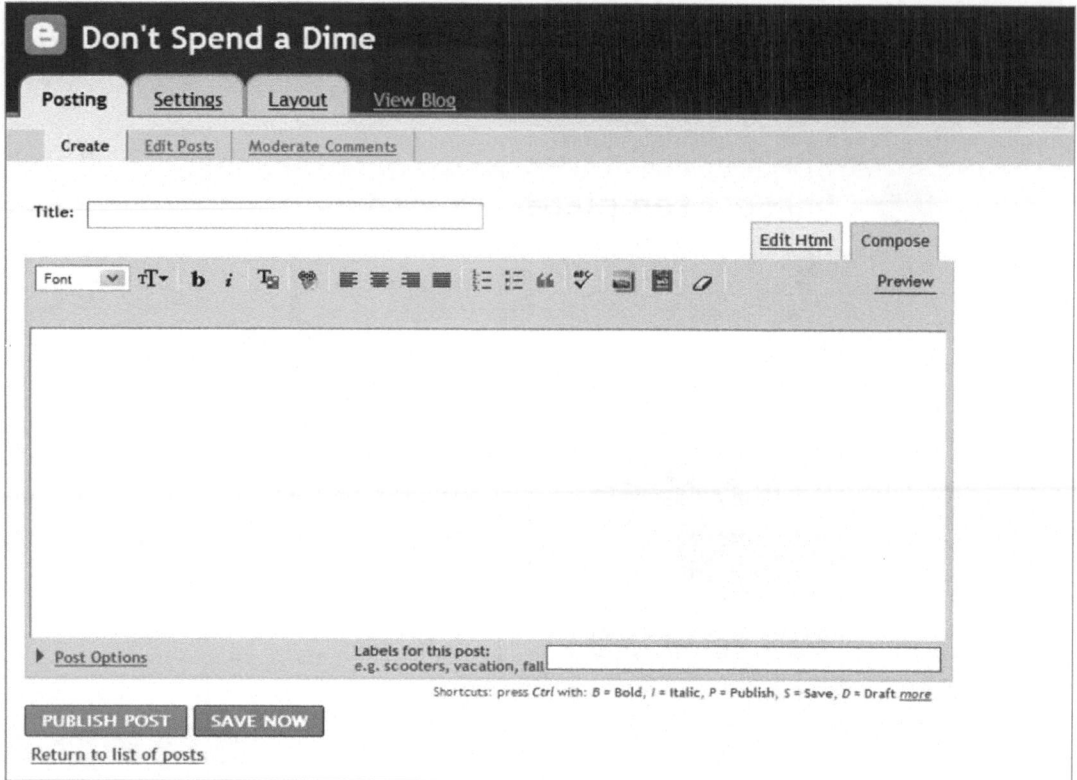

Figure 15-4. *It's time to create your first blog post.*

1. I want to welcome my readers to my blog, so I type in a bit of text, as shown in Figure 15-5.

2. It looks a little bland, so I'm going to use the first two tool buttons from the left to change the font and font size. I use my mouse to select the text, as shown in Figure 15-6, and make my selections. From the Font drop-down list, I choose Trebuchet as my font. From the Font Size (denoted by the big and small *T*'s) drop-down list, I pick Large.

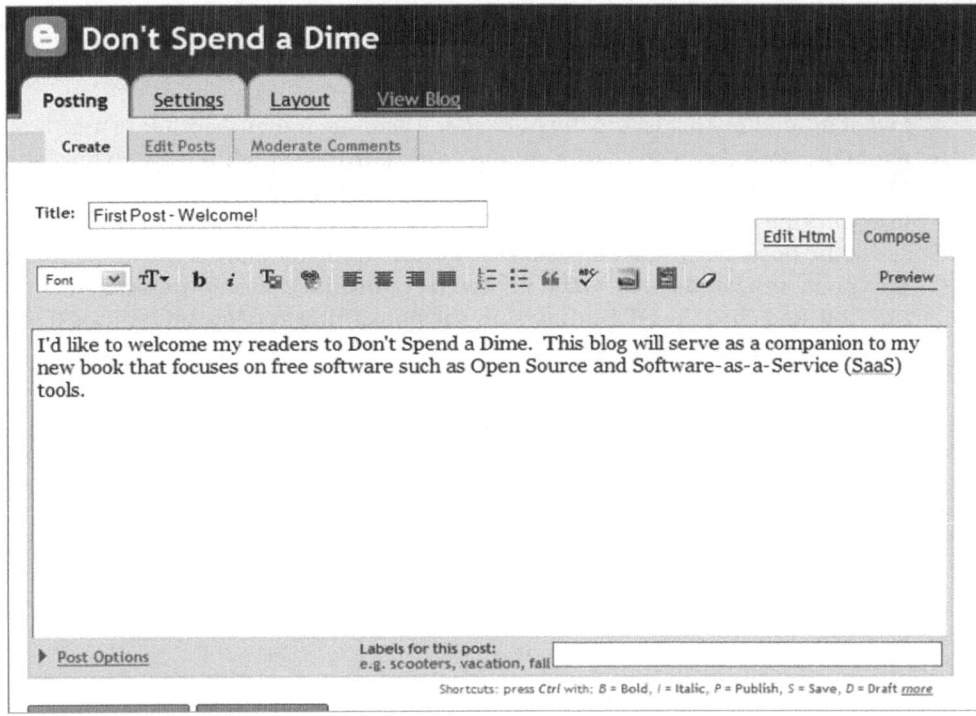

Figure 15-5. *The first post can be a welcome to your (hopefully) growing readership.*

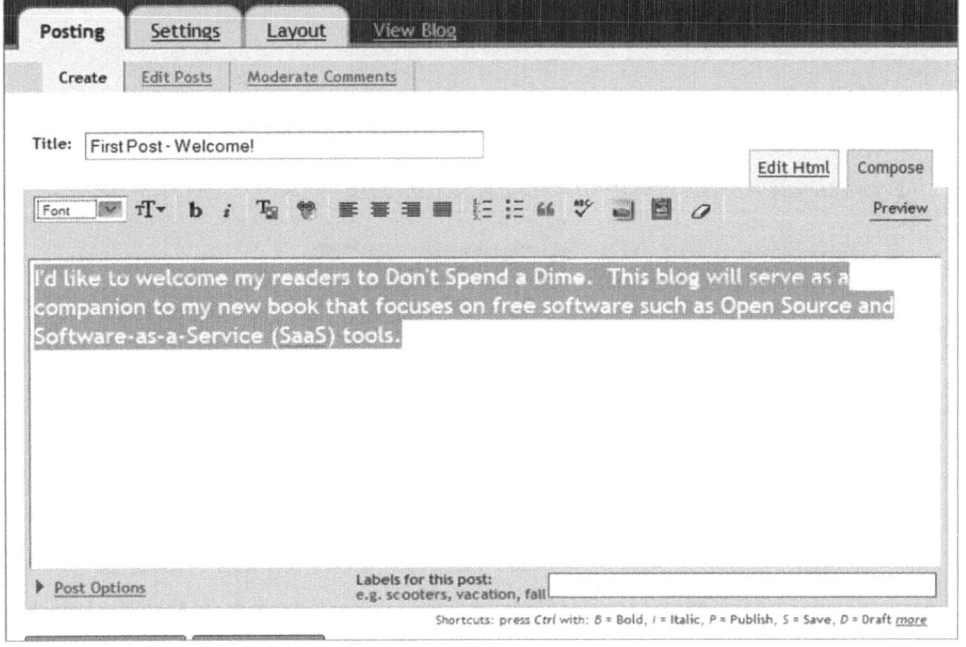

Figure 15-6. *Use the Blogger toolbar to make changes to the font and font size.*

3. The next three buttons from the left on the toolbar let you boldface, italicize, and change the color of any selected text. Just to demonstrate their use, I add some more text and apply these formats (see Figure 15-7).

4. I want to send my readers to my publisher's web site if they want more information about the book. I can do this by adding a web link (or hyperlink). A web link works just like any link found in your web browser. It typically appears as a bit of blue underlined text. Clicking the link takes you to another web page. To add a web link to my blog, I select the book's title and click the Link button in the toolbar, as shown in Figure 15-7. This pops up a window, in which I enter the publisher's web address, as shown in Figure 15-8, and click the OK button. Now the book's title appears underlined to indicate it is a hyperlink (see Figure 15-9).

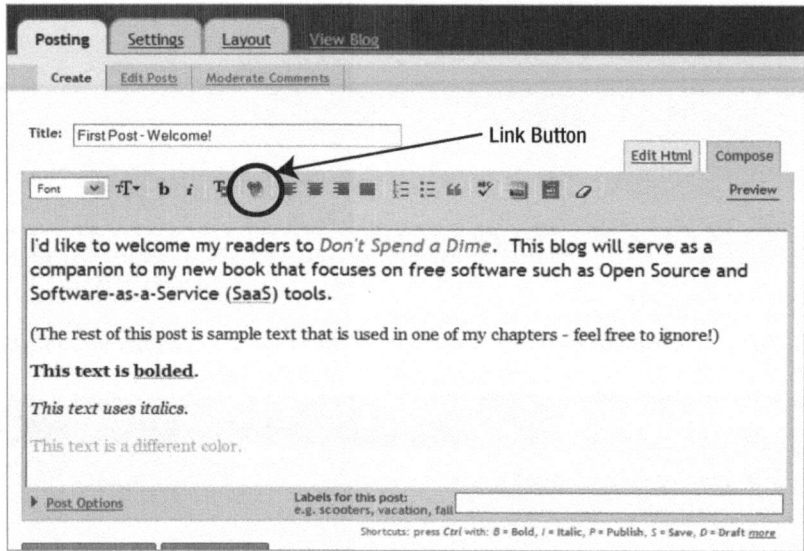

Figure 15-7. *Click the Link button to add a web link.*

Figure 15-8. *Send your readers to other web addresses by using links.*

5. A small graphic or picture is always eye-catching for a blog post. You can insert a picture by clicking the Add Image button in the toolbar and browsing to a suitable image. The image must be less than 8MB in size and contained in a `.jpg`, `.bmp`, or `.gif` file. I select an appropriate image, and it's inserted on the page. I then resize it, as shown in Figure 15-9. I could also cut and paste it to any area on the page.

Figure 15-9. *Add a photo or small graphic to your post to grab a reader's attention.*

6. I publish this post by clicking the Publish Post button at the bottom of the screen.

7. I click the View Blog link at the top of the screen, and take a look at my first blog post, as shown in Figure 15-10.

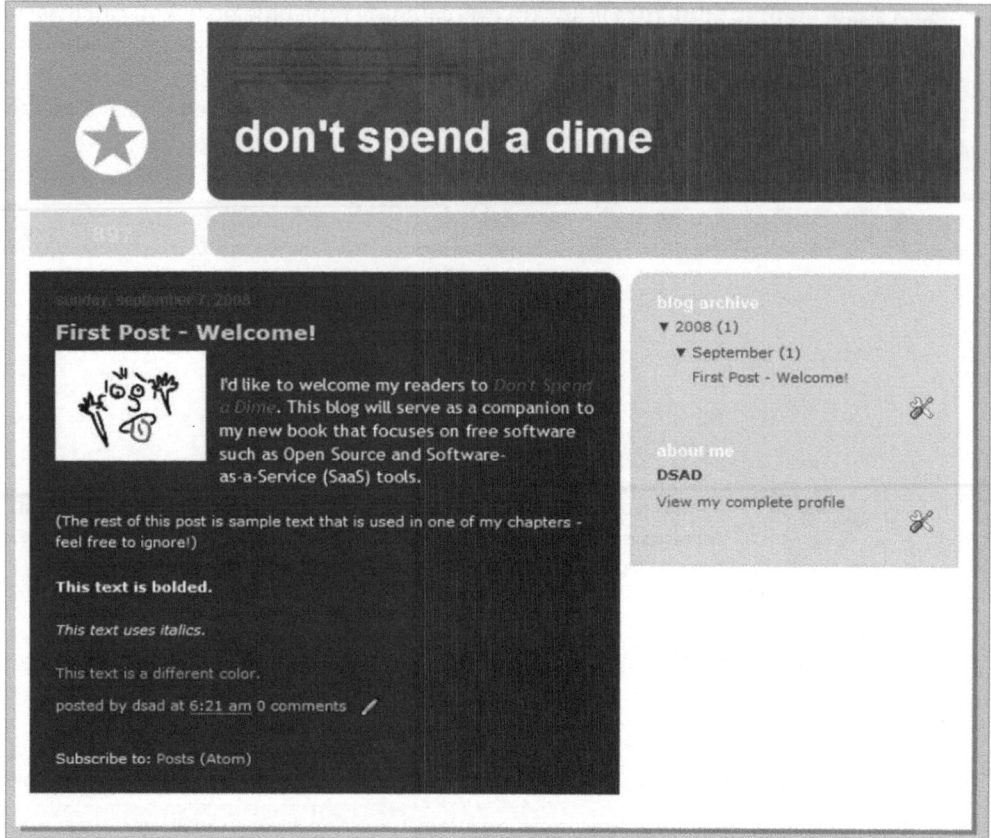

Figure 15-10. *After publishing, visit your blog address to see the results.*

Now I have a blog, and you can have one just as easily. But it gets better! Blogger offers even more features for you to investigate to make your new blog attractive (and useful) to readers. Up next, you'll discover a few more things you can do with Blogger.

■**Note** In January 2006, I started a blog titled "The NXT Step" (http://thenxtstep.blogspot.com) as a way for me to provide comments and feedback about my testing of a new LEGO product called LEGO MINDSTORMS NXT, a robot kit developed by the toy company. I provided pictures, my opinions, links to other web sites, designs, and more. The blog didn't get its first comment from a reader for almost one month. But it was a start. As of January 2009, the blog has over three years of archives, more than 2,000 posts, and 25+ contributors who I've invited to join me in adding content. The NXT Step blog consistently gets about 50,000 visitors each month who check in to read about the latest news and developments in the world of LEGO robotics.

More Blogger Details

As your blog develops, you may find yourself needing to make some changes in its look and maybe how it provides information (also known in the blogging circles as *content*). One potential change I suggest is to modify your blog's layout/design to give it more functionality and give your readers more reasons to visit your blog.

Modify the Blog Layout

Because your blog appears in a web browser, the basic template you chose when first creating your blog provides a decent design that will fit inside most web browser windows. But the templates don't lock you into that format forever. You can make a complete template change that will modify the colors and locations of items such as posts. But if you like your existing template, you can make many adjustments to add to its usefulness to readers.

First, log in to Blogger if you aren't already logged in. In the upper-right corner of the screen, click the link labeled Dashboard, as shown in Figure 15-11.

Figure 15-11. *Modifying your blog template requires a trip to the Dashboard.*

You should now see the Dashboard, similar to the one shown in Figure 15-12. Here, you can see how many posts you've made over the lifetime of the blog; the date of the last post; some buttons to modify your user profile; a button labeled New Post; and a bunch of links with names like Edit Posts, Settings, and Layout.

You'll want to experiment with all of these Dashboard items at some point, but for now, click the Layout link. It will take you to a screen that looks like the one shown in Figure 15-13. The screen will show the Page Elements tab, but there are three more tabs: Fonts and Colors, Edit HTML, and Pick New Template. Fonts and Colors is self-explanatory—simply click that tab, and you can experiment with different color schemes and see what they will look like on the sample image. Similarly, the Pick New Template tab will let you pick a completely different design. The Edit HTML page is useful, but I don't recommend playing around with these settings unless you know what you're doing and are familiar with HTML, the "language" of web pages.

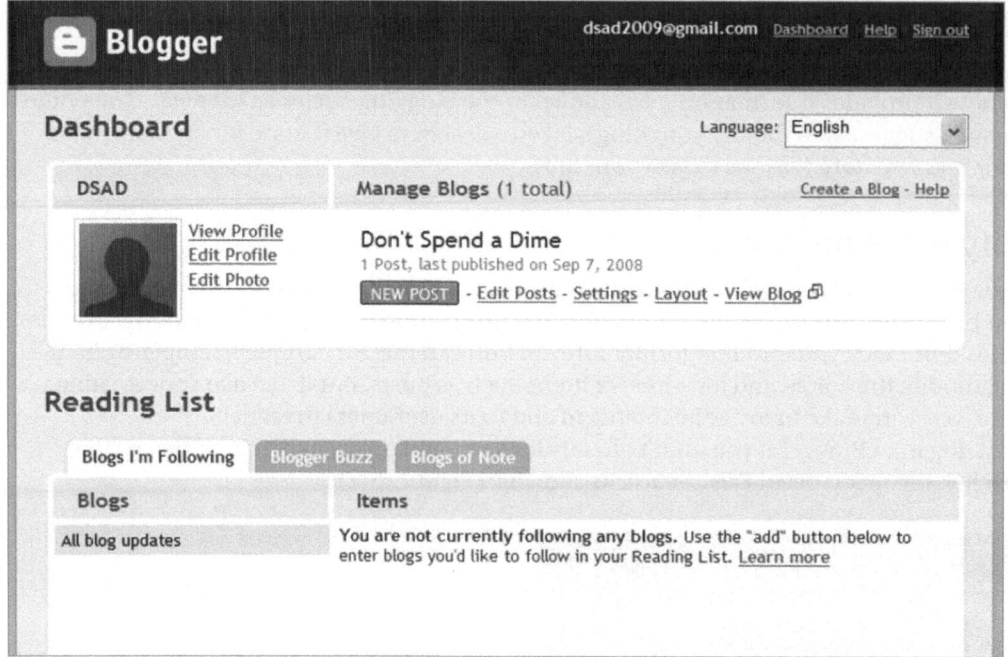

Figure 15-12. *The Dashboard is where you manage all of the blog's settings.*

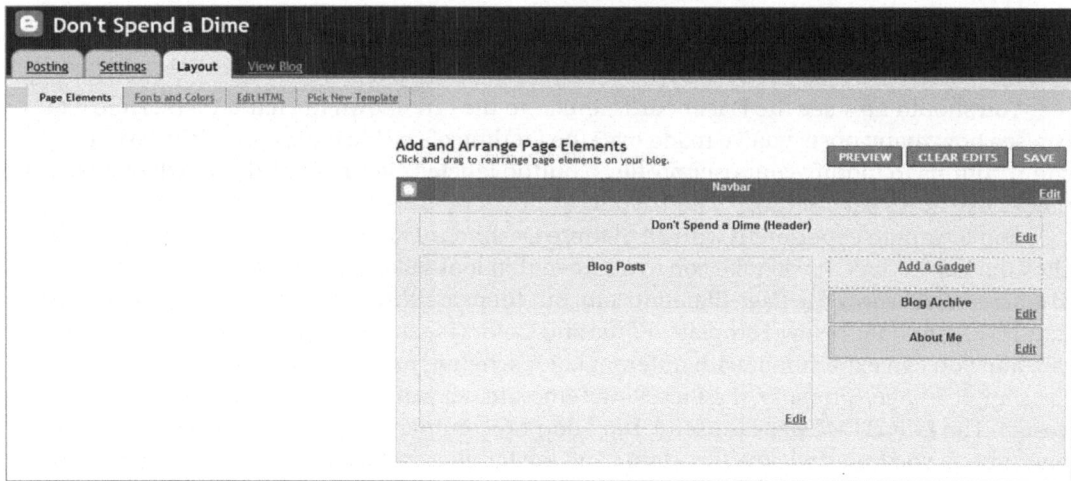

Figure 15-13. *The Layout tab will let you change the format of your blog.*

On the Page Elements tab, you will see the overall layout of your current blog, shown in a simplified form. Each area of the screen, such as Blog Posts and About Me, is defined by a box. Each box has an Edit link that will allow you to change certain things about that section. (And be sure to click the Save button often to keep your changes and additions.)

For example, clicking the Blog Posts box's Edit link opens the window shown in Figure 15-14. Here, you can make changes to the information displayed with each post, such as the date and how many comments and posts will be displayed per page.

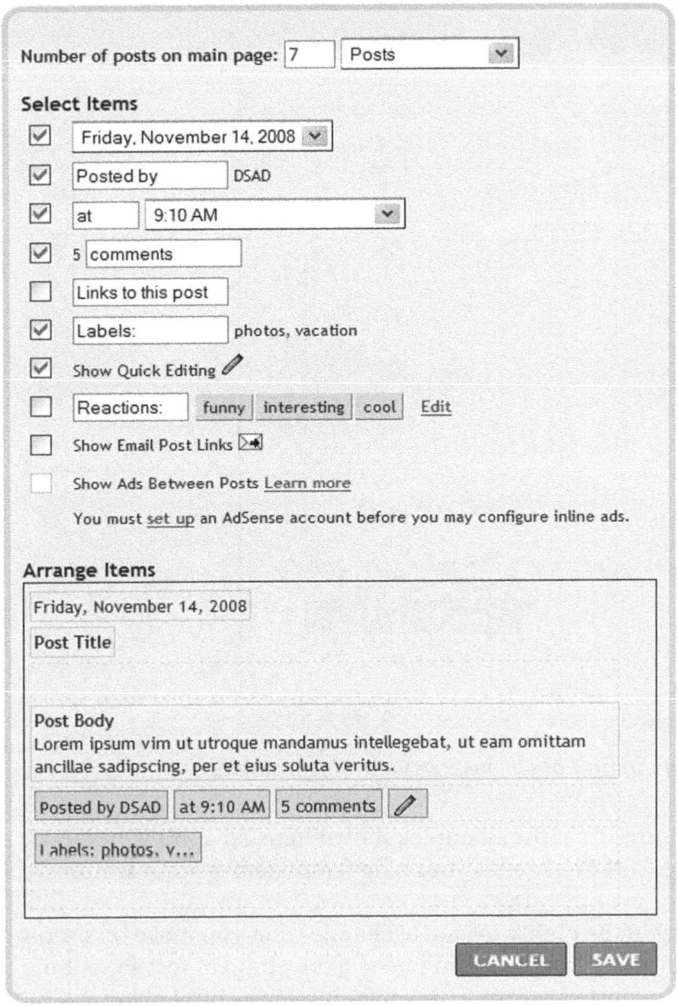

Figure 15-14. *Making changes to your posts is easy using the Blog Posts Edit link.*

As time goes by, you'll build up a large collection of blog posts (hopefully) that new readers frequently like to visit and existing readers sometimes like to reread. Allowing your blog to build an archive—a collection of previous posts—and making it easy to navigate is done by using the Blog Archive box's Edit link. This takes you to the Configure Blog Archive window, as shown in Figure 15-15.

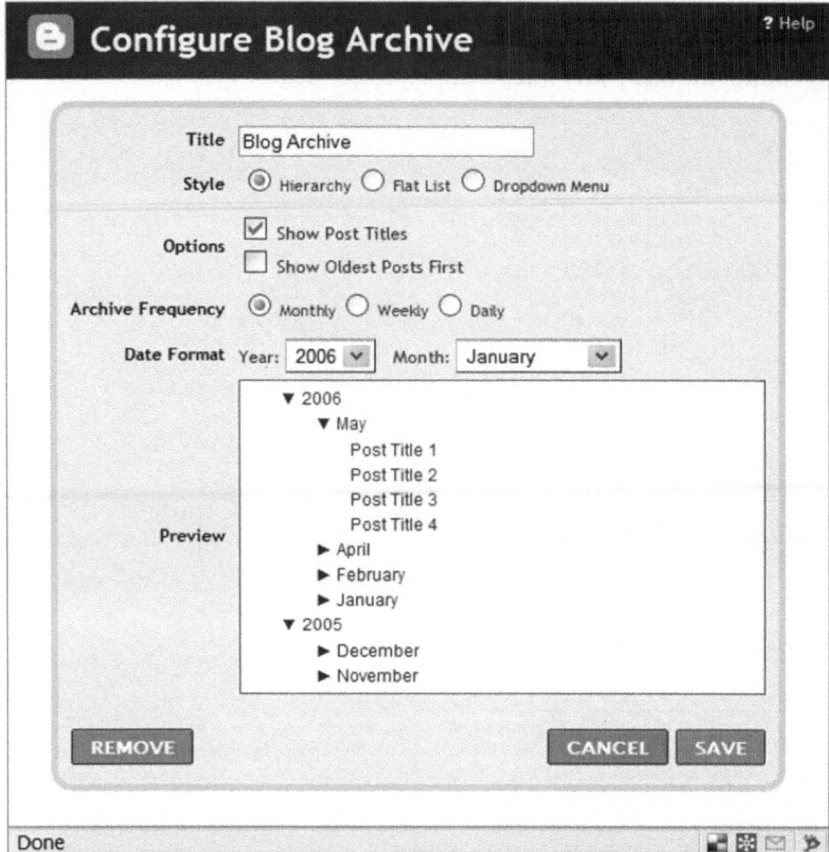

Figure 15-15. *Make it easier for readers to find older posts in your blog archive.*

Some templates have more features than the examples shown here, so don't worry if you see more boxes available for editing. This just means your blog template has other features that can be implemented.

Note that Blogger always gives you the ability to cancel changes that you make by simply clicking the Cancel button in the edit windows. You don't need to be afraid to test something and see how it looks, because you can always return to the default settings by clicking the Clear Edits button at the top of the screen (see Figure 15-13).

Turn on AdSense to Make Money

I mentioned at the beginning of the chapter that Google will let you host advertisements on your blog. If a visitor to your blog clicks one of the advertisements, you will earn a small commission!

Here's how to turn on AdSense (Google's advertisement application that pays you money when a visitor clicks a link to a paid advertiser) for your blog:

1. From your blog's Dashboard, click the Layout tab to see a screen like the one shown in Figure 15-16. Then click the Add a Gadget link on the right side of the screen.

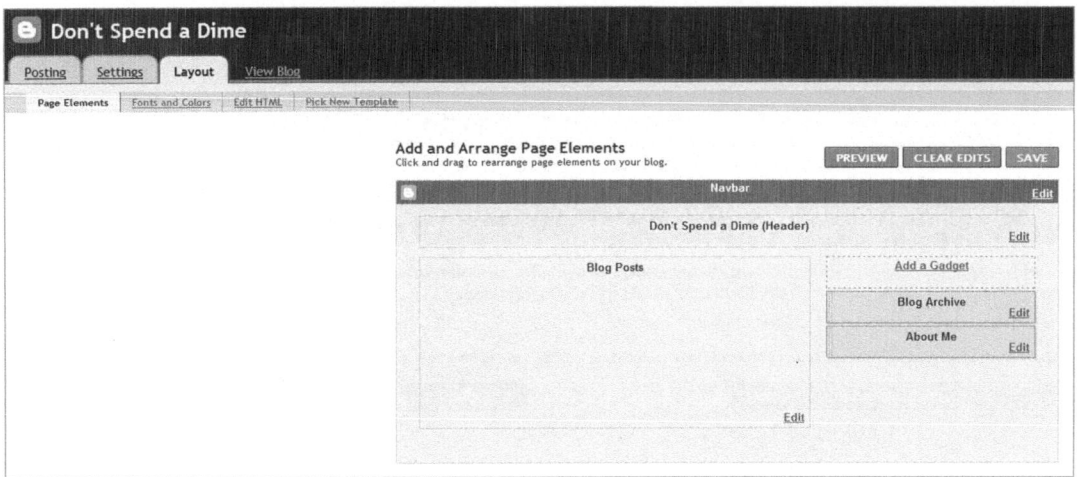

Figure 15-16. *Turn on AdSense to try to make some extra cash from your blogging.*

2. Scroll down the list that appears, as shown in Figure 15-17, and select AdSense by clicking the large + (plus sign) to its right.

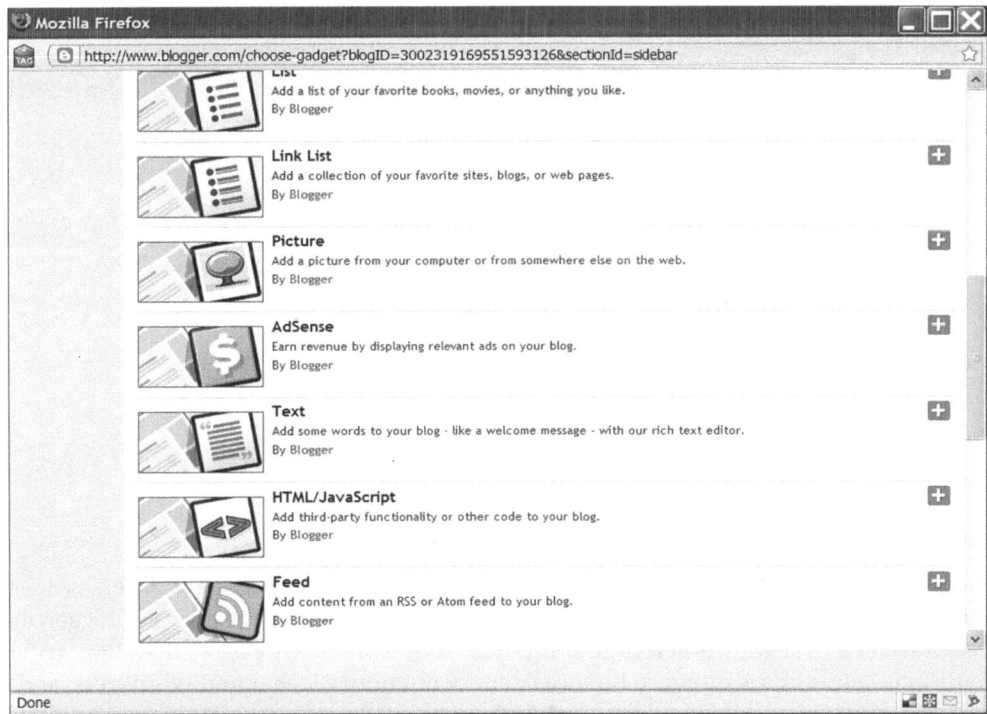

Figure 15-17. *AdSense is a gadget that you can add to your blog.*

3. If this is the first time you've ever used AdSense, click the Create a New AdSense Account button, as shown in Figure 15-18. Then follow the instructions to configure how the ads will appear (color and size), as well as to set up payment options. If you already have an AdSense account, click the Use an Existing AdSense Account button instead.

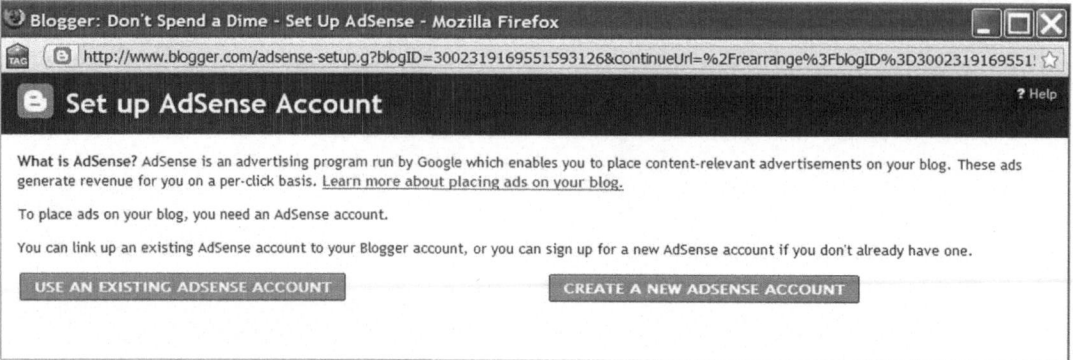

Figure 15-18. *You must create an AdSense account to receive payment from Google.*

4. After you've set up your AdSense account, check your blog. You should see one or more advertisements displayed, as shown in the example in Figure 15-19.

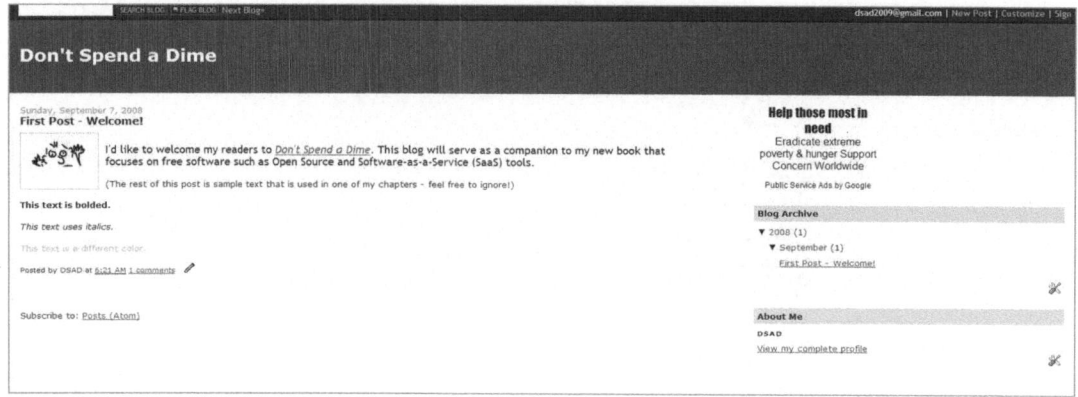

Figure 15-19. *Advertisements appear and may generate some income.*

Investigate Further

Blogger has one major competitor: WordPress (http://wordpress.org). WordPress does require a small software download, but it offers most of the same features as Blogger, and it is also free. It has a slightly different user interface, but is still fairly easy to use. Blog writers tend to be fans of one or the other, so be sure to check out both Blogger and WordPress, and decide for yourself which web blog tool works best for you.

And if you choose to use Blogger, be sure to look into the ability to use your mobile phone. Blogger offers the option to upload text and pictures directly from your mobile phone. This is a great way to document something such as a trip and provide your blog readers with up-to-the-minute reports from the road. You can find more information about this service at the Blogger Mobile page (`http://www.blogger.com/mobile-start.g`).

Summary

Blogger is a powerful and fun blogging tool. It gives you the ability to write about your favorite cause, hobby, or other subject. The fact that it's free makes it an application that you should certainly try out. Once you've become comfortable with your blog, you might want to investigate inviting others to contribute to your blog or maybe offering advertising space on your blog to generate some extra income. Blogger offers online help on these ideas and more at `http://help.blogger.com`.

CHAPTER 16

■■■

Social Networking

Our lives seem to move so fast these days that even e-mail and mobile phones can't prevent us from sometimes feeling insulated and out of touch. We take digital pictures of our vacation, but can't seem to find the time to share them with our coworkers. We shoot video, but sending DVD copies to every family member is just too time-consuming. We change jobs; we move to a different town or city; we have a bad day. How do we keep the people in our lives informed and in touch?

Building a personal web page can help you publish pictures and share information like your new mailing address. But do you really want to spend hours every day updating your web site with the latest photos and news, or would you prefer a friendlier and faster method of keeping others up-to-date on your life?

And let's flip this around. How much work is involved if you want to track down an old school friend or an ex-coworker? People change phone numbers and e-mail addresses; they move; they get married and change their names.

In this new digital world, is there something that can help us stay in touch and make it easy to share our experiences with friends and family? There is, and it's called Facebook.

Facebook has become a phenomenal success since its startup in 2004. It's 100% SaaS, so you don't need to install any software on your computer, and it's completely free to use. You're going to love it.

What Is Facebook?

Facebook can be hard to describe. It's part personal web site, mixed with a bit of e-mail and messaging type services. It has some video and photo hosting thrown in, some world-class search features for hunting down old schoolmates and friends, and it lets you post as much contact information as you care to share—phone numbers, addresses, and so on. Facebook does all this while letting you have total control over who can view your information.

Your Facebook page and all its features are available from within your web browser. There is no software to install, and you can access your Facebook account from any computer that has Internet access. This means that you can upload pictures (and video) from your vacation for your family to view—while you're still on vacation! And there's no need to e-mail everyone your new mobile phone number. You can just post your new number on your Facebook page, and all your friends and family will be notified (assuming they have Facebook accounts).

Facebook isn't a replacement for your e-mail or your personal web page. It's just another tool that can make your life a little easier and less hectic when it comes to keeping your friends and family informed and involved.

Where Can I Find Facebook?

To get started with Facebook, you need to sign up and create an account. Here are the steps:

1. Visit `http://www.facebook.com`. You'll be prompted to sign up, as shown in Figure 16-1. Fill in the basic information, and then click the Sign Up button.

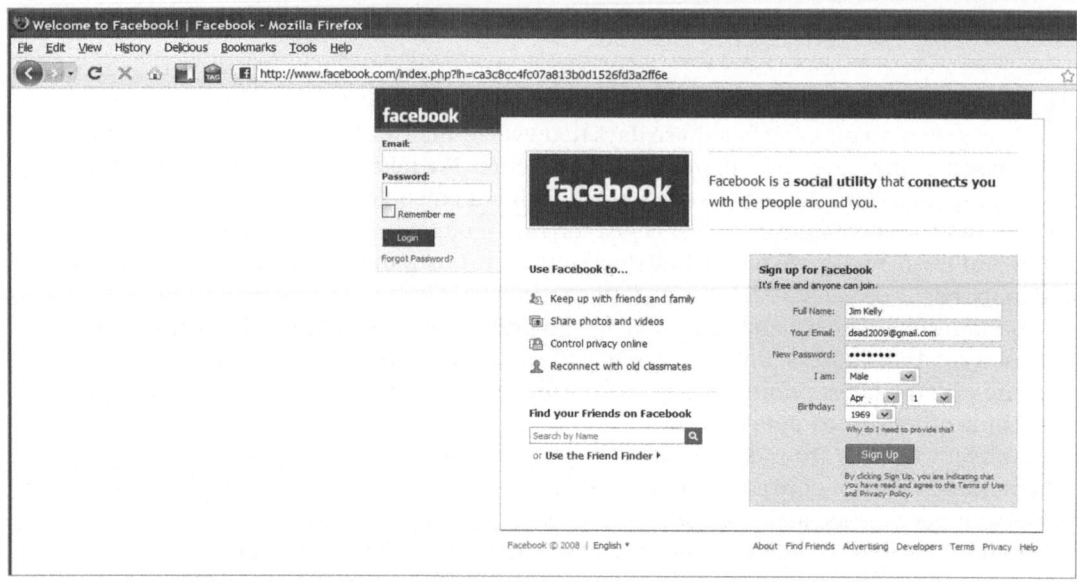

Figure 16-1. *Register for Facebook by providing some basic information.*

2. Next, you'll need to type in the words shown in a graphic, similar to what you see in Figure 16-2. Then click the Sign Up button. You'll be informed that an e-mail message has been sent to you.

3. Check your e-mail and click the link provided in the message to confirm your account. You will be taken to a web page where you can log in using your e-mail address and password, as shown in Figure 16-3.

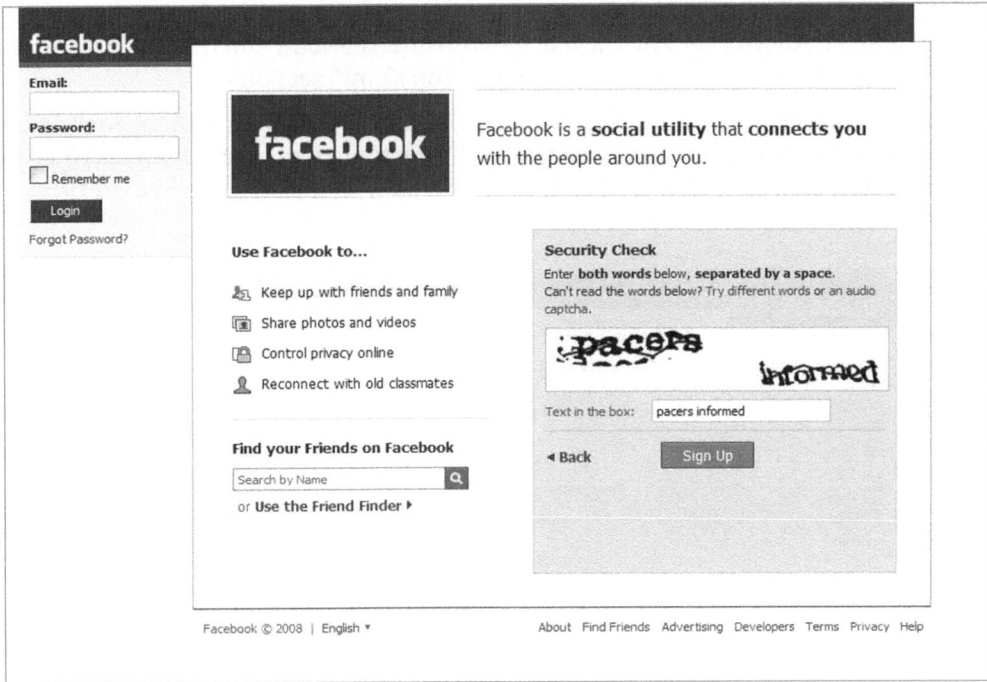

Figure 16-2. *Facebook requires you to prove you're human by typing in the words you see on the screen.*

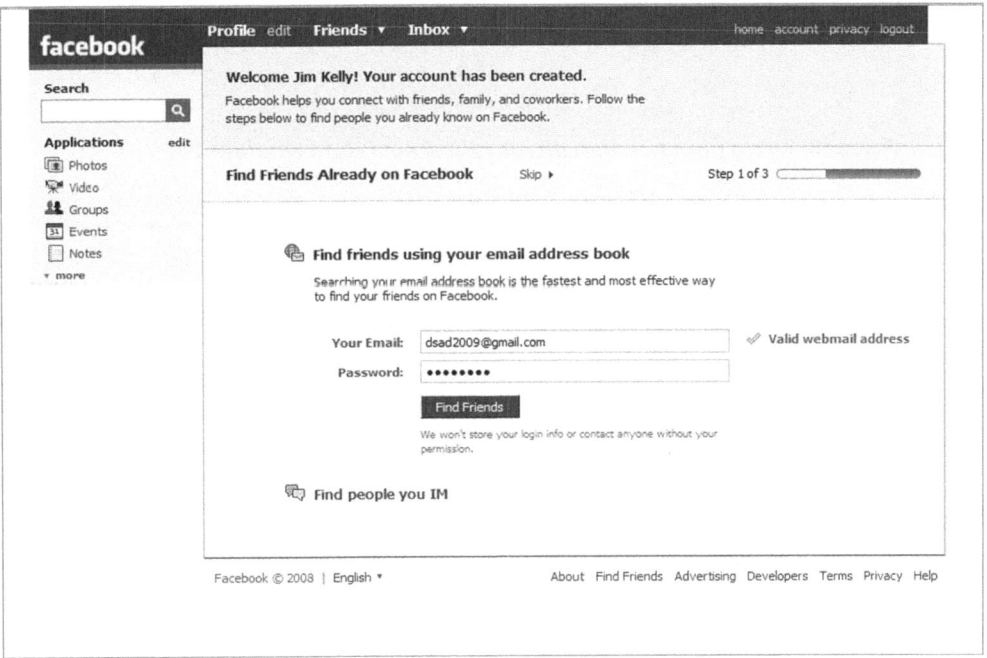

Figure 16-3. *Log in to Facebook with your e-mail address and password.*

4. Facebook will allow you to search for friends (Step 1 of 3), but I'm going to ask you to skip that step for now by clicking the Skip link. (I'll show you how to do a friend search later in the chapter, in the "Find People You Know" section.)

5. In Step 2 of 3, you can enter information about any schools you have attended, as well as your current employer. Facebook will attempt to find your schools as you enter their names (and provide you with lists to select from if your school name isn't unique), as shown in Figure 16-4. Click the Save button to continue.

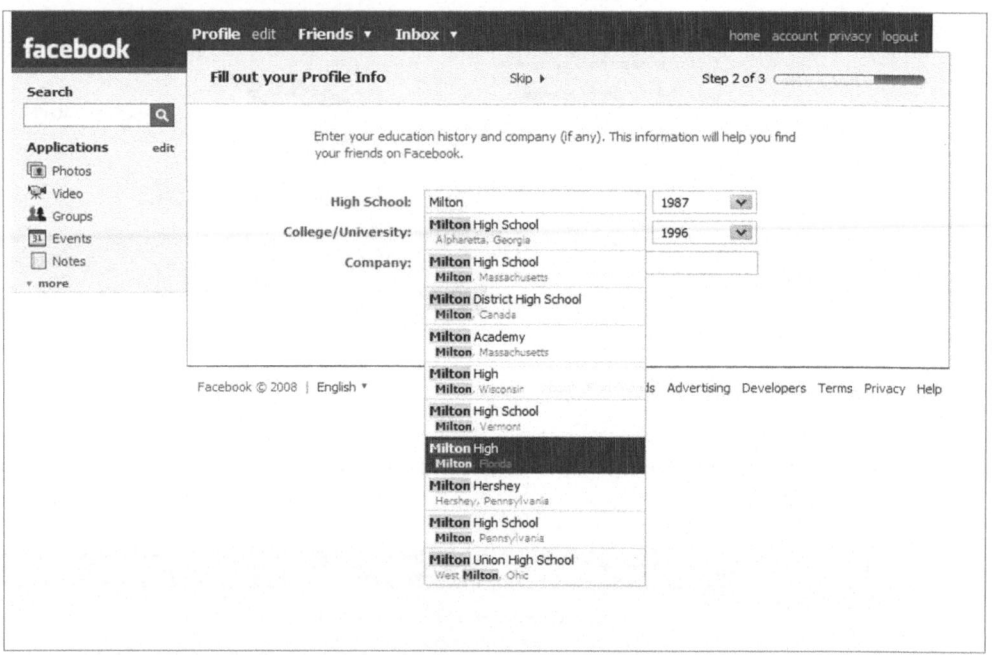

Figure 16-4. *Enter information about your schools and employer.*

6. Step 2 of 3 continues, and this is where it gets interesting. Facebook will take information about the schools you attended (and the graduation year) and your employer, and show you other Facebook users who you might know, as shown in Figure 16-5. Take the time to scroll through the list. Here, you may find some old school friends or coworkers who also have Facebook pages. Clicking a name selects that person (note the check mark on the picture) to be contacted. Each person selected will be sent a message indicating that you wish to "friend" them. In this context, *friend* is a Facebook term that indicates a relationship (friend, family, coworker, or other) exists between two Facebook users. The person contacted can accept your invitation or ignore it. After making your selections, click the Add as Friends button to continue.

7. Step 3 of 3 allows you to specify your physical location. Some towns and cities have their own Facebook group that contains users who live there. If this is true for your location, you can click the Join button to join the group or click the Skip button to ignore this option. I recommend skipping it for now. You can always join a town or city group later, after you're more familiar with Facebook.

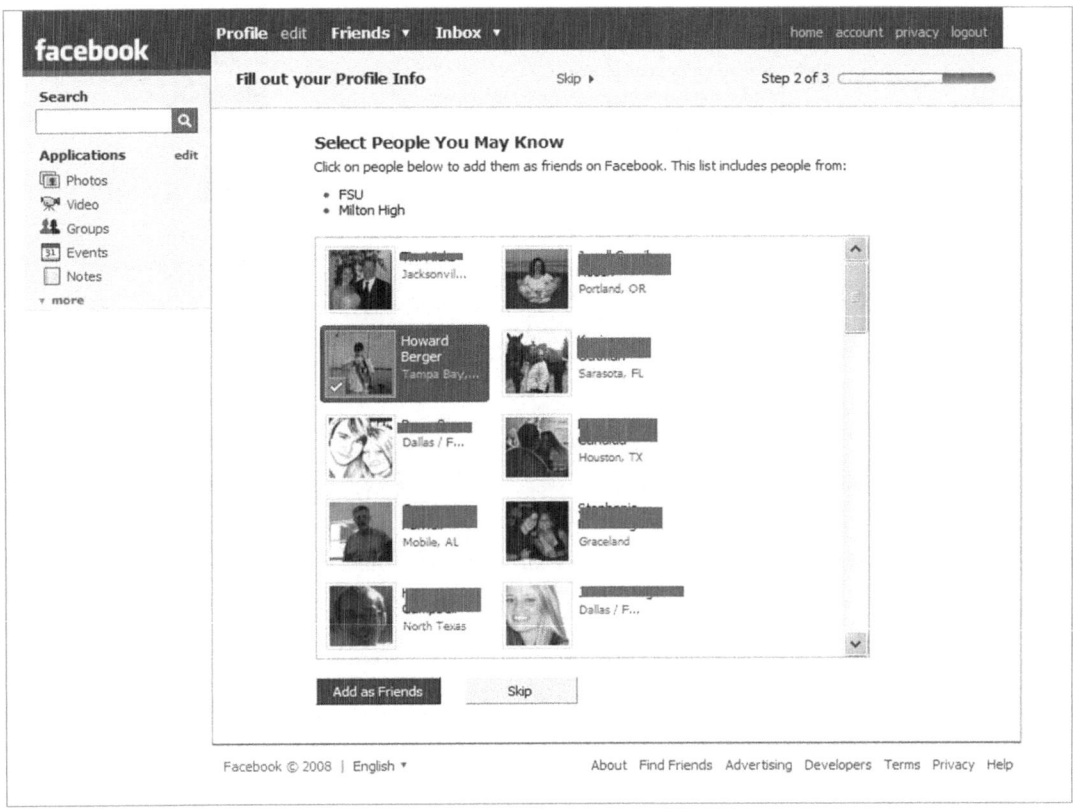

Figure 16-5. *Facebook will find other users who you may know.*

And now you're ready to start using Facebook. You begin with a fairly sparse page, as shown in Figure 16-6, but don't worry. It's easy to use, and you'll start seeing progress on your page quickly. Keep reading to learn more.

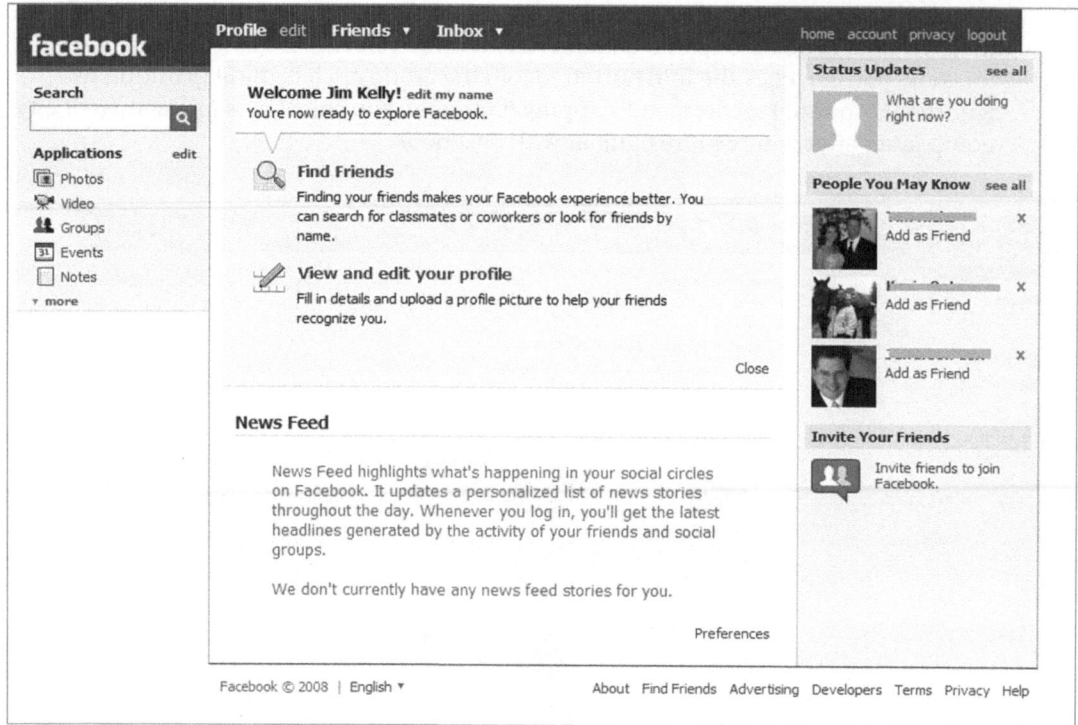

Figure 16-6. *Facebook starts you off with a blank slate, but that will change soon.*

How Do I Use Facebook?

Facebook has more features than you can imagine. You can spend hours and hours exploring and finding new tools, toys, and games to add to your Facebook page. As you become more familiar with Facebook, you'll begin to customize your page and make it more useful to you and your visitors.

Right now, your page is empty, and you have no friends (well, no Facebook friends). You might have selected some friends during your Facebook setup, but until they get the message and accept your invitation, or you get an invitation from someone else, your Friends list is blank. This is a great time to start customizing your page (sort of like cleaning your house before you have guests). So let's do some simple housekeeping and get the page ready for visitors.

Edit Your Profile

One of the first tasks you should do is to add more details to your profile. You can include items such as your hobbies, contact information, and even a place to tell the world what you're doing right this very minute. Click the "View and edit your profile" link. You'll see a page similar to the one shown in Figure 16-7.

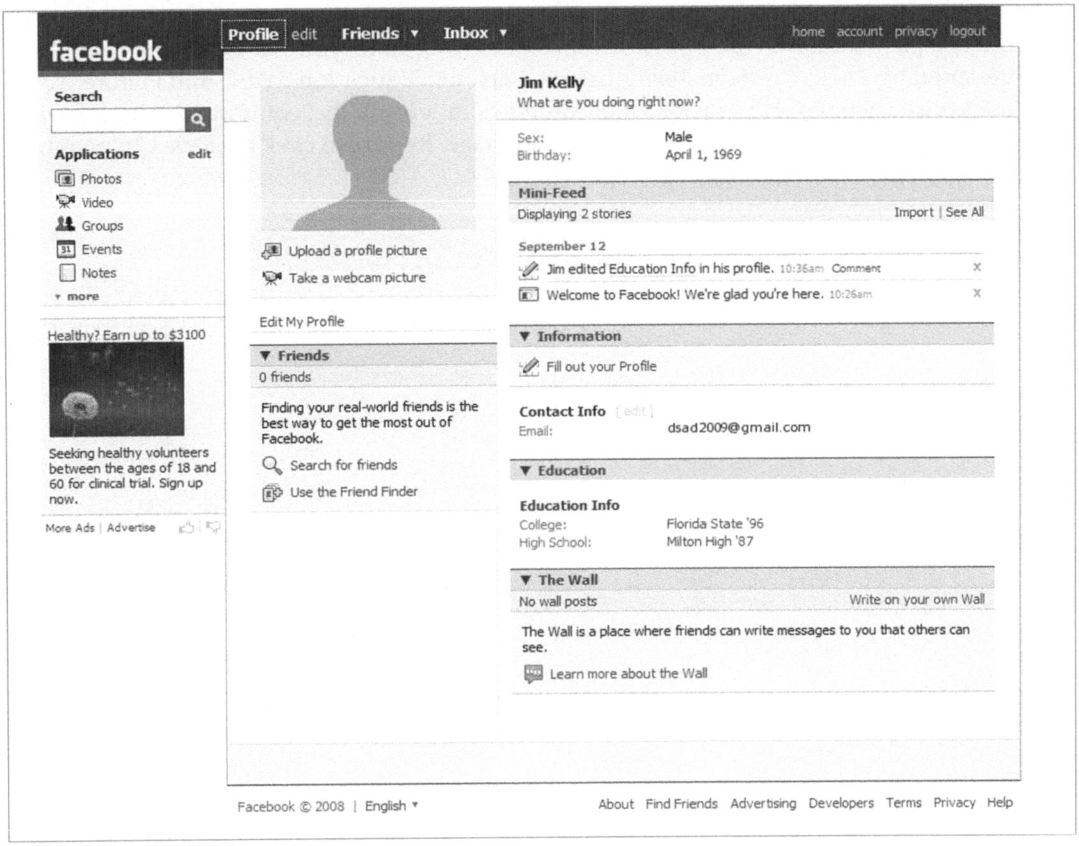

Figure 16-7. *Your new Facebook profile is ready for news, pictures, and more.*

Let's start at the top. The first thing you want to do is let your Facebook friends know what you're doing. Click the text that says "What are you doing right now?" (underneath your name), enter a description, and press the Enter key. Figure 16-8 shows a description I added to my profile. Anytime you want to update the description, just click the old one and type in a new one.

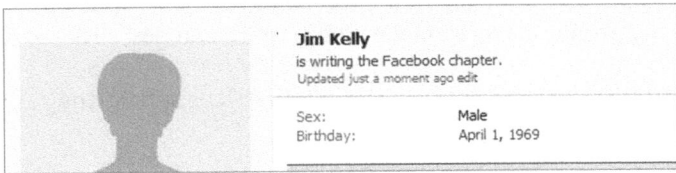

Figure 16-8. *Facebook lets you provide a description of your current mood or activity.*

Next, skip down to the Information section and click the "Fill out your Profile" link. You'll be taken to a page similar to the one shown in Figure 16-9. Here, you can enter what you like in the different tabs: Basic, Contact, Relationships, Personal, Education, Work, and Picture. Take the time to visit each tab and provide whatever information you feel comfortable sharing with those Facebook users who will have access to your page. Be sure to click the Save Changes button before you move to a different tab.

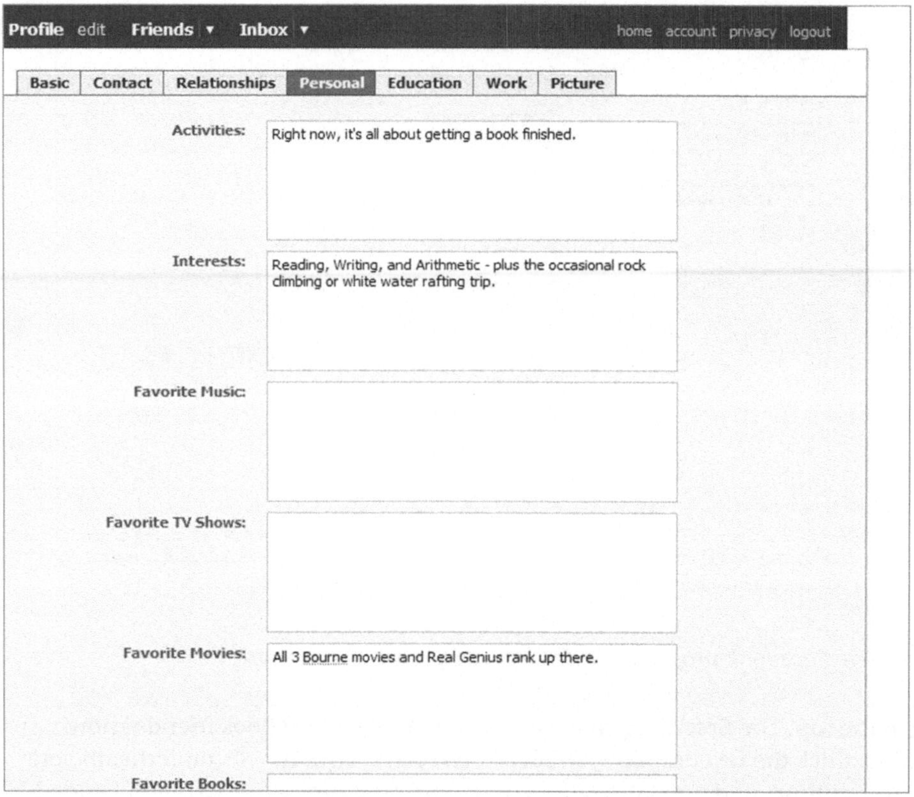

Profile edit Friends ▾ Inbox ▾	home account privacy logout

| Basic | Contact | Relationships | Personal | Education | Work | Picture |

Activities:
```
Right now, it's all about getting a book finished.
```

Interests:
```
Reading, Writing, and Arithmetic - plus the occasional rock
climbing or white water rafting trip.
```

Favorite Music:

Favorite TV Shows:

Favorite Movies:
```
All 3 Bourne movies and Real Genius rank up there.
```

Favorite Books:

Figure 16-9. *Enter more detailed information about yourself on each tab of your profile.*

When you're finished, click the Profile tab at the top of the screen to view your updated Facebook page. Figure 16-10 shows my profile so far. To make additions or changes, click the edit link to the right of the Profile tab.

I'll show you how to add and find friends in the next section, but first, let's look at one other basic task: using the Wall.

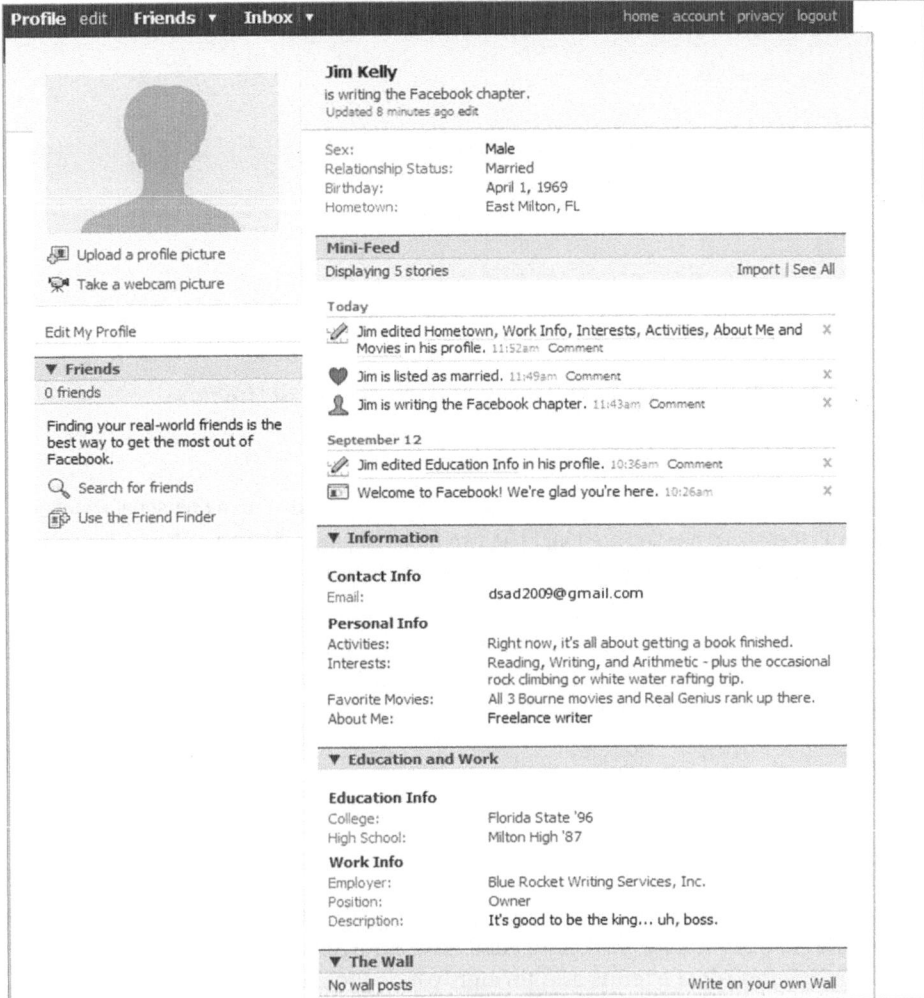

Figure 16-10. *View your updated Facebook page by clicking the Profile tab.*

Use the Wall

The Wall is found on every Facebook user's page and is a way to leave messages for that user and the user's friends who can also see that page. Users can respond to one another's Wall postings.

Because I haven't added any friends yet, I'll need to be the one to put some text on my Wall. To add text to your Wall, click the "Write on your own Wall" link. In the text box that appears, enter some text, and click the Post button. Figure 16-11 shows the Wall.

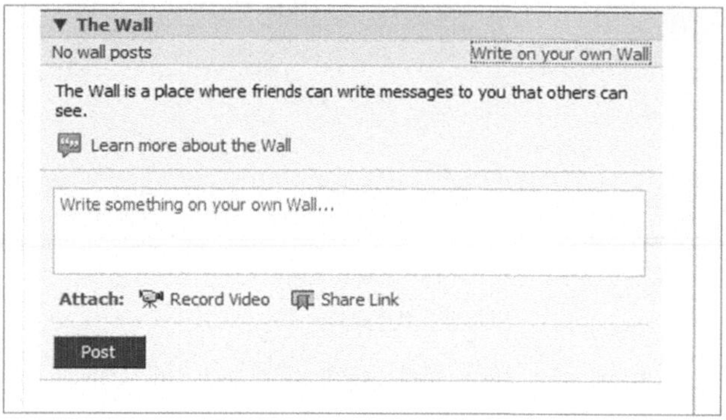

Figure 16-11. *Use the Wall feature to leave comments and greetings to your friends.*

■**Note** Facebook really has changed my life. During September 2008, I logged in to my personal Facebook page and was greeted with messages alerting me that I had two friend requests waiting. I clicked the link and was pleasantly surprised to find two of my old college friends, Howard and Janell. Howard had just joined Facebook and had located me using the school search. Janell had been a Facebook user for a while, but she had a new last name, which kept me from tracking her down. I had been looking for these two friends for some time, and Facebook allowed us to find one another, catch up on news (Janell has twins!), and make sure we don't lose touch again. I love Facebook!

More Facebook Details

Here, I'll show you a couple activities that you can do using Facebook that will increase your enjoyment of the service. The first involves using Facebook's powerful search capabilities to hunt down people such as long-lost friends and former work colleagues. The second activity is adding "mini-applications" to your Facebook page for your friends to view and enjoy. Some of these applications are games, some are organization tools, and others are hard to classify. After that, it's up to you to explore Facebook on your own. I guarantee that you'll find many fun and useful things to add to your Facebook page.

Find People You Know

You can find just those people who have a Facebook account. This is not as limiting as it may sound, because Facebook is growing by thousands of users every day. So, the odds are good that you'll locate some of your old contacts.

Let's go find an old friend or two.

1. Click the "Search for friends" link on your Facebook home page. This link is under the Friends box on the left side of the page (see Figure 16-10). You'll see a page like the one shown in Figure 16-12.

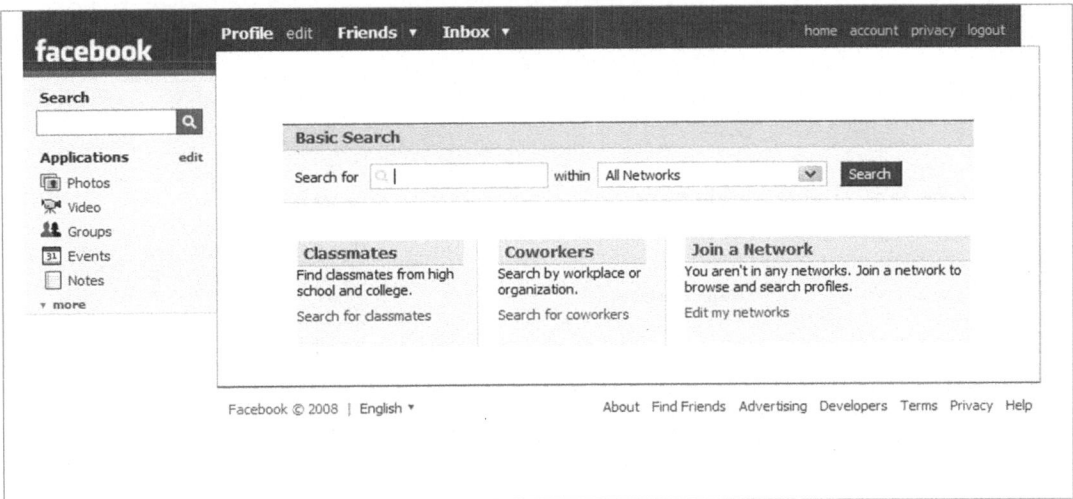

Figure 16-12. *The Search tool will let you hunt for old or current acquaintances.*

2. You could just enter the person's name in the Search for box and click the Search button, but you would likely end up with dozens (or even hundreds) of matches. Figure 16-13 shows what happened when I searched for David Thompson: more than 500 matches! Consider using other search terms, such as city/state, company name, and even birthday, to narrow down you search. You can also try the Classmates and Coworkers search options. Click either of these, and you'll see a few more fields that can be used to narrow down the search results.

3. Once you locate an existing Facebook user who you think you know, it's time to make contact (you cannot simply add them as a friend yet). Click either the Add as Friend link or the Send a Message link, as shown in Figure 16-14. I recommend using the Add as Friend link, because it will allow you send a friend request and add a personal message. The Send a Message link just lets you send a message, not a request to be friends.

4. Assuming you clicked Add as Friend, you can then click the "Add a personal message" link and type in a message. In Figure 16-15, I've added the message, "Is this the David Thompson who attended FSU in the early 1990s?" After you've entered your message, click the Add Friend button.

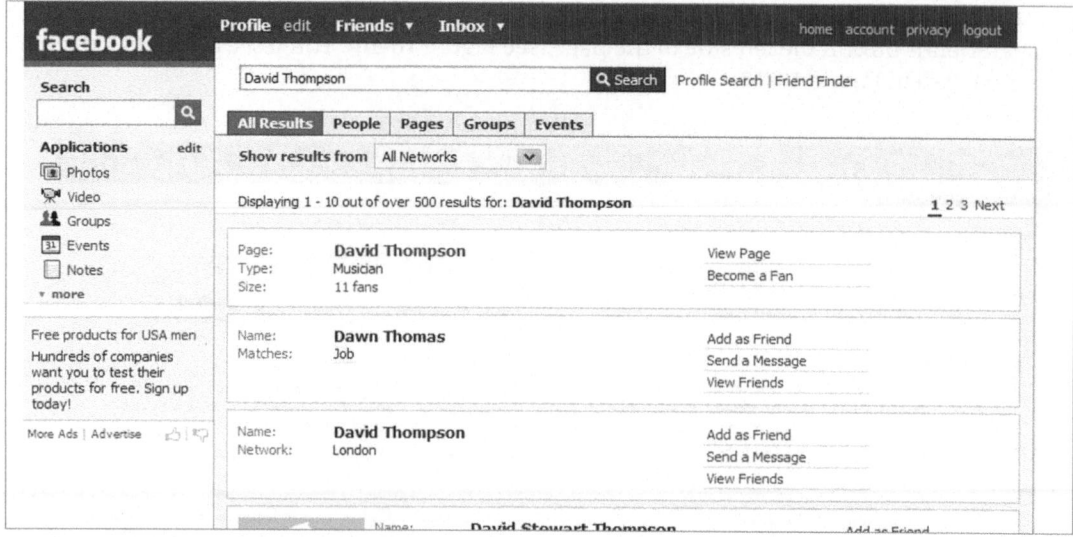

Figure 16-13. *Unless the name is unique, a basic search will not be that useful.*

---

for: **David Thompson Alabama**

Name:	**David Thompson**	Add as Friend
Network:	New York, NY	Send a Message
		View Friends

Figure 16-14. *Locate a Facebook user and make contact.*

---

friend?

David will have to confirm that you are friends.
You may only add people as friends on Facebook if you know them.

Add a personal message: Cancel

Is this the David Thompson that attended FSU in the early 1990s?

🖳 Add David to a Friend List

If you add David as a friend, he will be able to see your profile.

| Add Friend | Cancel |

Figure 16-15. *Send a friend request and wait to see if the person accepts.*

The next time this person logs in to Facebook, he will see your friend request. At that point, he can accept, decline, or send a reply message asking for additional information. If he does accept your invitation, you'll see a new friend notice the next time you log in to Facebook. This will let you view that person's Facebook page, e-mail him, and view all the information on his page that he has provided for viewing by friends.

Sometimes you'll be lucky enough that a friend or coworker will tell you her Facebook username and initiate the friend request. At other times, you'll need to do some searching for that needle-in-a-haystack friend. But in the end, the time spent locating new and old acquaintances is well worth the effort.

Tip While you're doing a search for friends, you can search for organizations, too. Do a search for that magazine that you subscribe to, that shoe company whose best product is on your feet, and even your favorite book publisher. Yes, Apress has a Facebook page where you can learn about its new book releases, and even post comments and questions. I've been assured that Apress just loves hearing from its fans, and will add you as a friend if you send a request!

Add an Application

Facebook has its own free applications! These are little bits of software that Facebook or other software developers have created that "latch on" to the Facebook user interface and are available to you and anyone else who views your profile. Here, I'll show you how to find Facebook applications and add them to your page. (These applications also have their own special location on a Facebook profile, so don't be surprised that you can't move them around to various locations.)

As you can see listed under Applications on your home page, Facebook gives you some starter applications, such as Photos, Video, Group, and Events. To add a new application, follow these steps:

1. Click the edit link to the right of the Applications list (see Figure 16-10).

2. On the new page, click the "Browse more applications" button, and you'll see a page similar to the one shown in Figure 16-16.

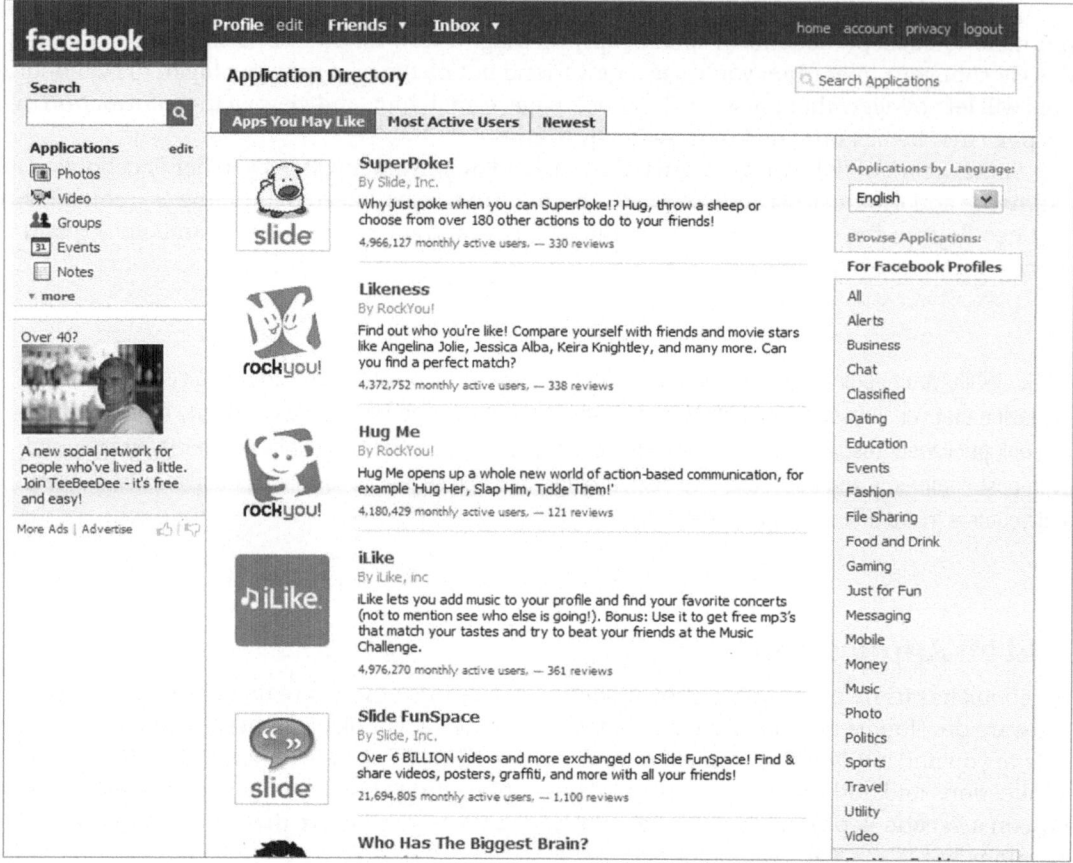

Figure 16-16. *Find new applications to add to your Facebook page.*

3. Don't let the long list of applications overwhelm you. Use the subject links listed along the right side of the Application Directory page to narrow down your search. For example, I clicked the Travel subject and found two travel-related applications, as shown in Figure 16-17.

Figure 16-17. *Use the subject list to narrow down your search for Facebook applications.*

4. When you've found an interesting-looking application, click its name to see a page with a little more information about the application and how it works. For example, I thought it might be fun to show my friends all the places I've visited, so I clicked the Where I've Been application and was presented with the page shown in Figure 16-18.

5. If you decide that you want to add the application, click the Add Application button, and accept the settings that pop up.

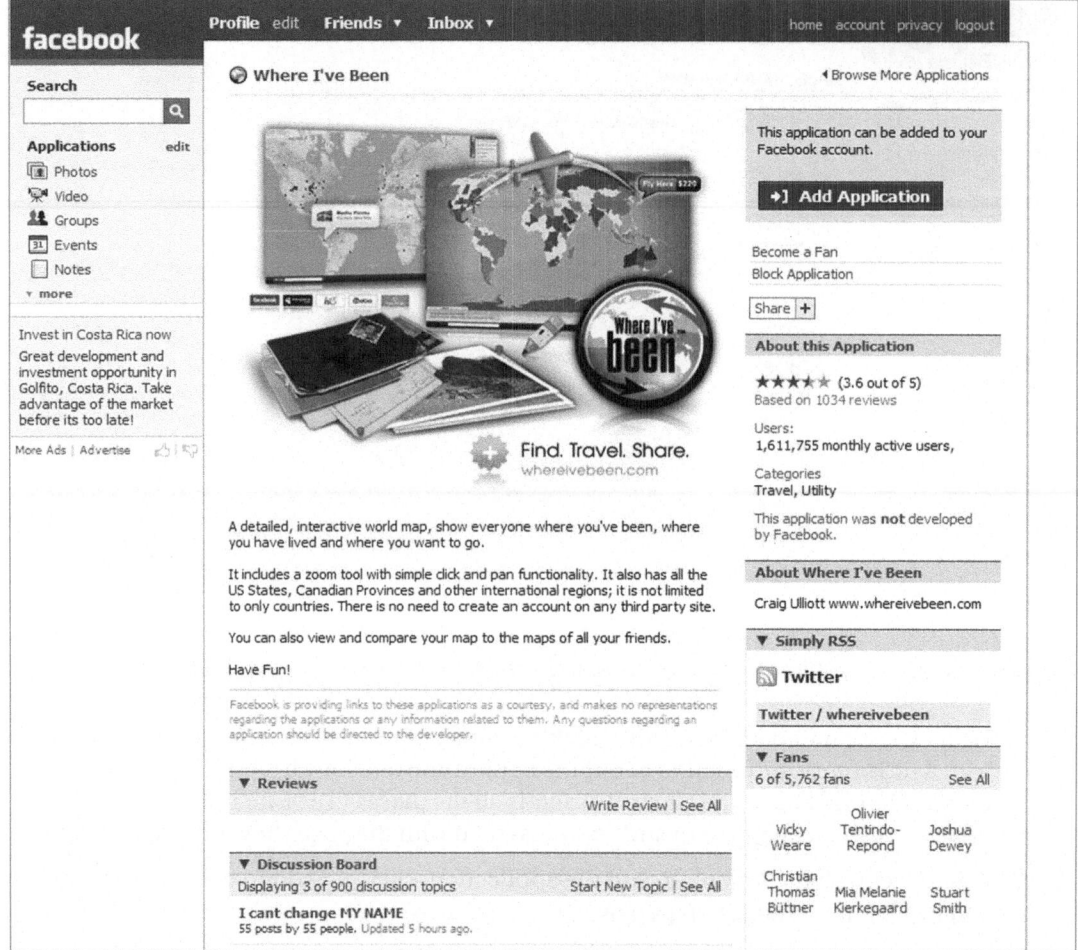

Figure 16-18. *Add the application to your Facebook page.*

After the application is installed, you can view it on your Facebook page. Figure 16-19 shows the new Where I've Been application added to my Facebook page.

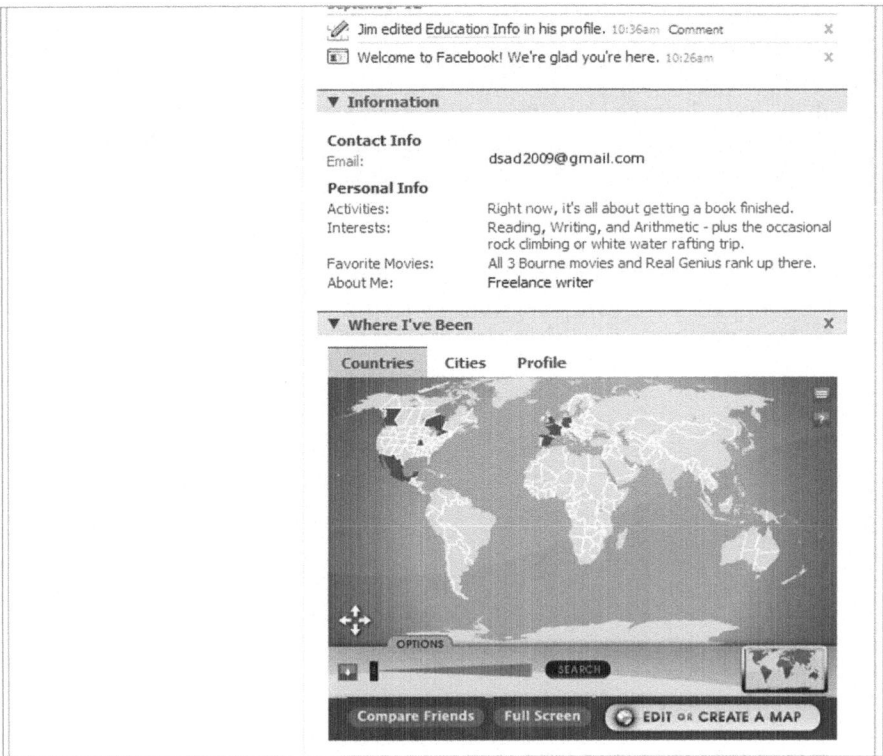

Figure 16-19. *The new application appears on your Facebook page.*

You can add and delete applications anytime you like. Spend some time browsing through the available applications, and you're sure to find one or more that would look great on your Facebook page, and give your friends something more to learn about you.

Investigate Further

Two other services that are similar to Facebook might be of interest to you. They have slightly different goals, as described here:

- *MySpace* (http://www.myspace.com): MySpace started out as a free service for musicians and bands to provide information to their fans about concerts, downloads of music samples, pictures, and interviews. Today, it's popular with just about every type of user, not just musicians. On MySpace, you can share pictures, news, and more.

- *LinkedIn* (http://www.linkedin.com): Think of LinkedIn as a Facebook for business networking. This free service lets its users stay in touch with coworkers, search for services that they require, and form networking groups for purposes of growing sales and identifying sales leads.

Summary

Facebook is one of my favorite (and *free!*) services on the Internet. I've been able to keep in touch with friends back in Texas, locate old college buddies, and track down coworkers from previous jobs. I'm able to upload pictures and video that my family and friends can view and comment on. I use an application that lets me track my participation in the Kiva.org nonprofit company. And I love to add comments to my friends' pictures and let them know I'm staying up-to-date with them.

As long as I maintain my Facebook page, I can rest assured that there is an online tool available that will let others locate me and get in touch, no matter where I live or work. Give Facebook a try, and see if you agree.

■ ■ ■

CHAPTER 17

Group Scheduling

If you've ever tried to schedule a party, night out at the movies, or other event involving more than two people, you know how difficult it can be to find a date and time that is convenient for everyone. The typical method involves a lot of phone calls or e-mail messages (or both), plus at least one negotiation with that "difficult" friend. And if your group is going to see a movie, there's the next problem of which movie to see! Typically, some time during the process, you just want to throw up your hands and cancel the entire thing.

Group scheduling will always be tricky, but fortunately. there's a free online service that will help remove some of the hassles, and allow you to pick the date and time that works best for the most people. It's called Doodle. Once you try it, you'll be hooked. Doodle is one of those "killer apps" that not only does what it's supposed to do, but also gives you new abilities and new patterns of organization that make your life better.

What Is Doodle?

Doodle is a simple and free service that allows you to turn any event (such as a birthday party) or a choice (such as between movie *A* and movie *B*) into an online poll. This is what pundits like to call a *paradigmatic change*—it's a different way of thinking about a social event. We're used to thinking about an event as something that one person determines and invites other people to join. Doodle changes that pattern. It makes event timing collectively determined by you and the people you invite.

With Doodle, you create the poll and select the options (months, days, and times, for example) from which your invitees must choose. You will be sent an e-mail message with the URL (web site address) for this poll.

Next, you e-mail the poll's URL link to all participants. Invitees click the link to go to a page where they can select the dates and times that work best for an event or make a choice from multiple options.

You are also e-mailed a private URL that takes you to a page where you can modify your poll and check the results. Doodle tracks the responses and provides you with a summary of the feedback, including the "winning" date/time (the one that has the most positive responses).

Doodle is particularly well suited when you need to invite a large number of people to an event such as a meeting, and there are multiple potential dates for that event. The alternative is keeping a complicated spreadsheet with people's preferred dates and sorting them into classes—a serious headache. With a Doodle poll, people will automatically sort themselves into the right dates. All you need to do is sit back and watch the responses roll in.

For large groups, it will be almost impossible to get one day and one time that works for everyone. Doodle lets you see which days and times have the largest number of available participants. And Doodle's ability to let you provide choices for participants to vote on is great, too.

Where Can I Find Doodle?

Doodle falls under the SaaS category, so there's no software to install. And it's such a simple little application that it's perfectly suited for using with your web browser. Follow these steps to begin using Doodle:

1. Visit `http://www.doodle.ch/`.

2. You can click the Create account link and create an account (free), or click the Schedule event button or Make choice button to create your Doodle poll immediately. Creating an account allows you to more easily manage all your polls, but is not required.

How Do I Use Doodle?

You can create either a schedule-based poll or a choice-based poll by clicking the corresponding button on Doodle's home page (`http://www.doodle.ch/`). Here, I'll walk through setting up a schedule-based poll. The process for creating a choice-based poll (the Make choice button) is similar.

1. Click the Schedule event button on Doodle's home page. You'll be presented with Step 1 of 3 for creating your poll.

2. Enter a title for your poll, as well as a simple description. This description will be helpful to your invitees when they visit the site to make their date and time selections. You'll also need to provide your name and e-mail address. In Figure 17-1, I'm creating a birthday party poll. Click Next to continue.

Caution Remember that your recipients will be getting the poll announcement as an e-mail message. You can spare yourself potential embarrassment by double-checking your description before it goes "live" in front of all your friends.

Doodle®

Schedule event: General information (Step 1 of 3)

Choose a meaningful title and provide further information in the description.

Title:

Birthday Party for D

Description (optional):

His 2nd birthday is coming quick - I hope you can attend. Please let me know the best days and times that work for you. Thanks!

Your name:

James Floyd Kelly

E-mail address (optional):

jktechwriter@gmail.com

If you supply an e-mail address, you will receive a message each time somebody participates in or withdraws from your poll. If you do not wish to receive such messages, leave the field empty.

« Back   Next »   Options   Finish

Figure 17-1. *Create your first Doodle poll by providing some basic information.*

3. In Step 2 of 3, you select the possible dates for the event. You can click the << and >> buttons to change the possible months for your event. For a particular month, click the days you wish to make available in your poll. When a day is selected, it will turn green. (Click the day again to deselect it, and it will turn dark gray.) In Figure 17-2, I have selected May 16, 17, 23, and 24 as possible days for the birthday party. As you select multiple days, those dates will be listed to the right of the calendar. You move forward and backward in the calendar to select dates in other months. Once you've selected all the possible days for your poll, click Next.

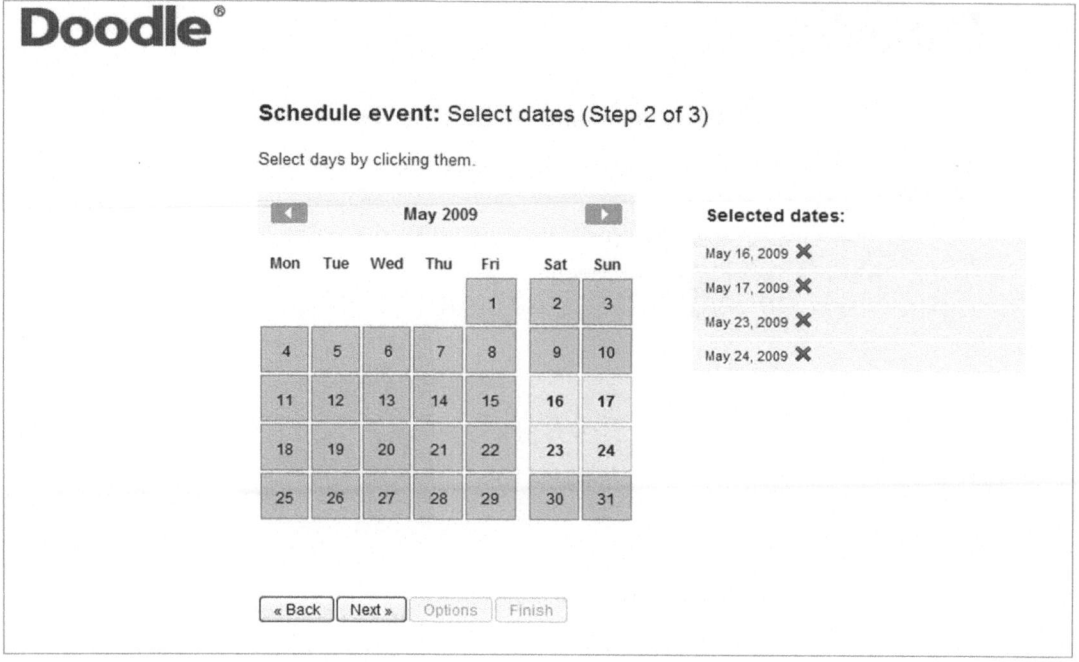

Figure 17-2. *Select the possible months and days for your event.*

4. In Step 3 of 3, you select possible times for your event. For each date that you selected, you can provide up to five possible times. If you need additional time slots, click the "Add further time slots" link. Enter your times (use am or pm to specify morning or afternoon times) in the boxes. You may also click the "Copy and paste first row" link, and the times entered for your first date will be duplicated in all subsequent dates. Figure 17-3 shows the time slots I've entered for the birthday party.

5. To complete your poll, click the Finish button. The Options button will let you make your poll results private, so only you can see them (although, generally, you will want to let your invitees see the final poll results after they provide their poll responses), and limit the number of responses from each recipient. The next page will request that you check your e-mail.

You should receive two e-mail messages: one with the poll link to send to invitees and another with a link to manage your poll. Figure 17-4 shows an example of the message you will receive to send to invitees.

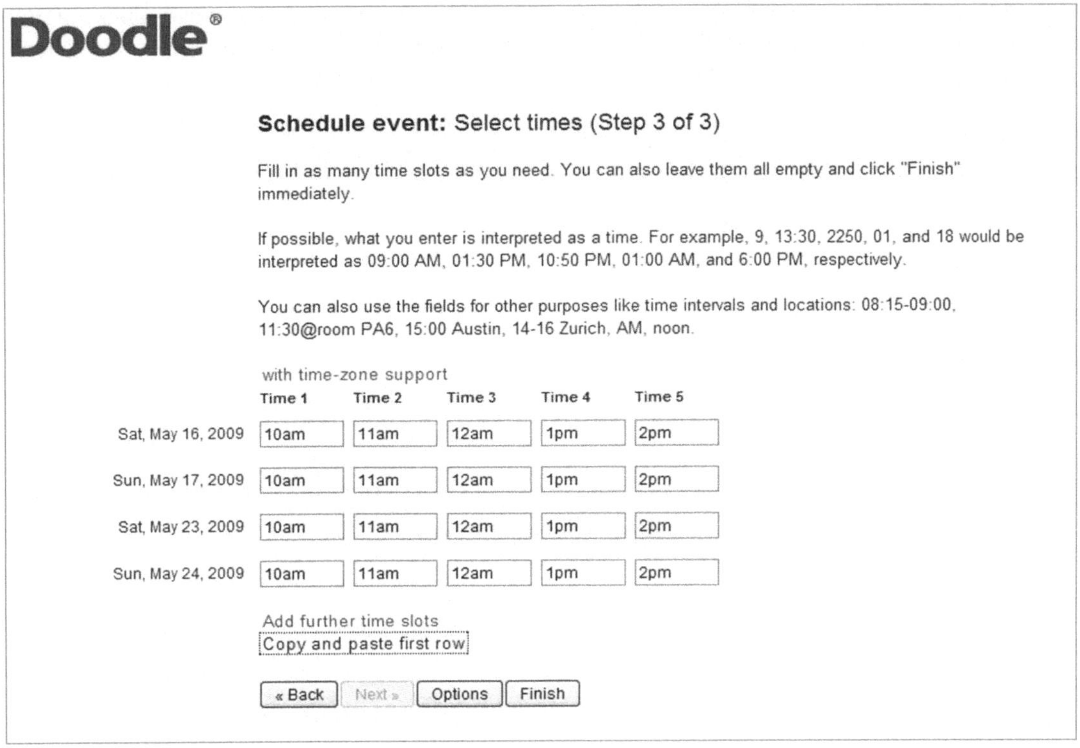

Doodle®

Schedule event: Select times (Step 3 of 3)

Fill in as many time slots as you need. You can also leave them all empty and click "Finish" immediately.

If possible, what you enter is interpreted as a time. For example, 9, 13:30, 2250, 01, and 18 would be interpreted as 09:00 AM, 01:30 PM, 10:50 PM, 01:00 AM, and 6:00 PM, respectively.

You can also use the fields for other purposes like time intervals and locations: 08:15-09:00, 11:30@room PA6, 15:00 Austin, 14-16 Zurich, AM, noon.

with time-zone support

	Time 1	Time 2	Time 3	Time 4	Time 5
Sat, May 16, 2009	10am	11am	12am	1pm	2pm
Sun, May 17, 2009	10am	11am	12am	1pm	2pm
Sat, May 23, 2009	10am	11am	12am	1pm	2pm
Sun, May 24, 2009	10am	11am	12am	1pm	2pm

Add further time slots
Copy and paste first row

[« Back] [Next »] [Options] [Finish]

Figure 17-3. *Provide times for your invitees to select.*

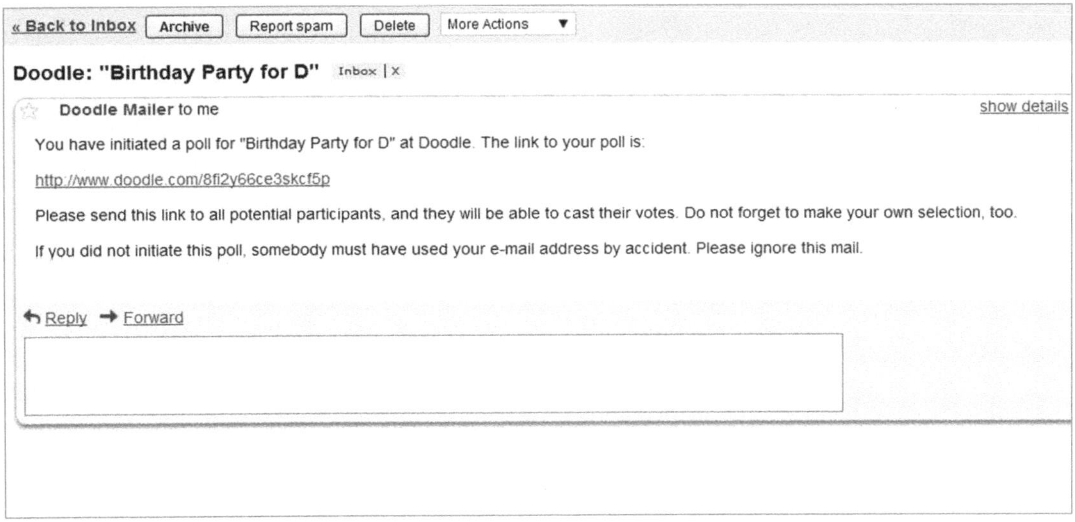

« **Back to Inbox** [Archive] [Report spam] [Delete] [More Actions ▼]

Doodle: "Birthday Party for D" Inbox | x

☆ **Doodle Mailer** to me   show details

You have initiated a poll for "Birthday Party for D" at Doodle. The link to your poll is:

http://www.doodle.com/8fi2y66ce3skcf5p

Please send this link to all potential participants, and they will be able to cast their votes. Do not forget to make your own selection, too.

If you did not initiate this poll, somebody must have used your e-mail address by accident. Please ignore this mail.

↩ Reply ➔ Forward

Figure 17-4. *An e-mail message will be sent for you to forward to your invitees.*

Figure 17-5 shows an example of the second e-mail message you will receive. Clicking the link takes you to a page where you can modify your Doodle poll, as shown in Figure 17-6. Here, you can add or remove potential dates and times. You can also click the link to add your own date/time selections to the poll.

Tip Don't forget to include yourself in the Doodle vote!

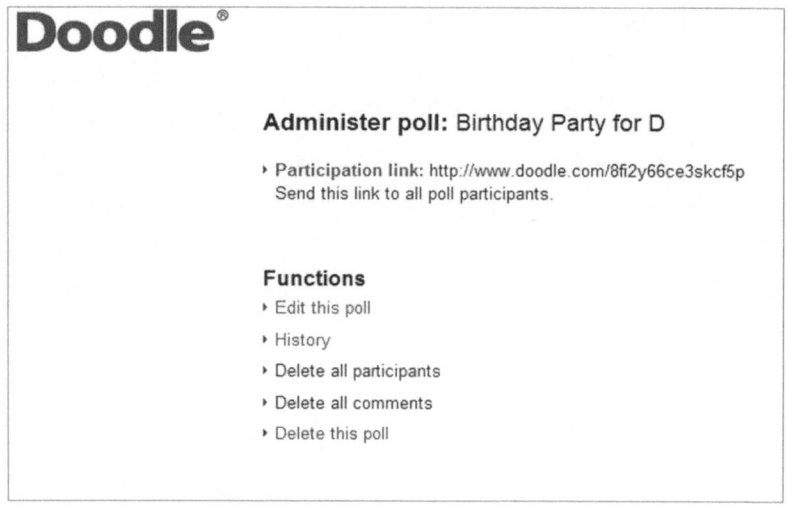

Figure 17-5. *Another e-mail message contains a link to a page for modifying your poll.*

Administer poll: Birthday Party for D

› **Participation link:** http://www.doodle.com/8fi2y66ce3skcf5p
Send this link to all poll participants.

Functions
› Edit this poll
› History
› Delete all participants
› Delete all comments
› Delete this poll

Figure 17-6. *Use the Doodle control panel to modify your poll.*

Now that the poll is created, it's time to put it to use. That means encouraging (and reminding) your invitees to use the service, all of which will be covered next.

More Doodle Details

Your Doodle poll won't be very helpful if your invitees don't use it. Before you forward the e-mail containing the poll link to an invitee, consider adding more details about your event, as well as instructions for using the Doodle poll. When using Doodle, I've found it helpful to tell invitees that they will not need to register to use the service and that the event options are easy to view and select.

Tip It never hurts to mention in your e-mail message to invitees that the event's final date and time will be selected by those who actually participate in the poll. You will be able to see the names of those who participate, allowing you to ignore the complaints from those who don't like the final date and time, but didn't vote.

When invitees receive the e-mail message and click the link, they will be taken to a page that looks similar to Figure 17-7, where they can make their selections.

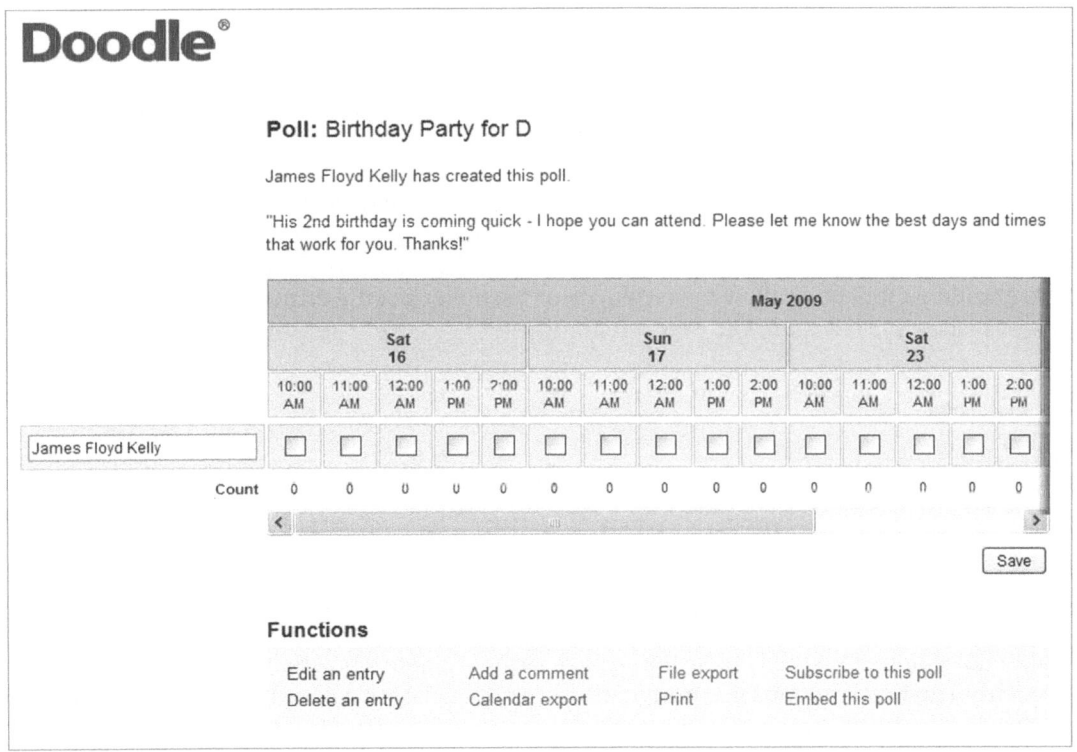

Figure 17-7. *After clicking the link in the e-mail message, invitees are taken to a page like this to choose dates and times.*

From this page, an invitee can see how many other invitees have participated in the poll, as well as their selections. The most popular date and time are also shown.

For an invitee to participate, he simply replaces "Your name" in the text box with his own name, and selects one or more of the date and time options, as shown in the example in Figure 17-8. Finally, he clicks the Save button to submit his selections.

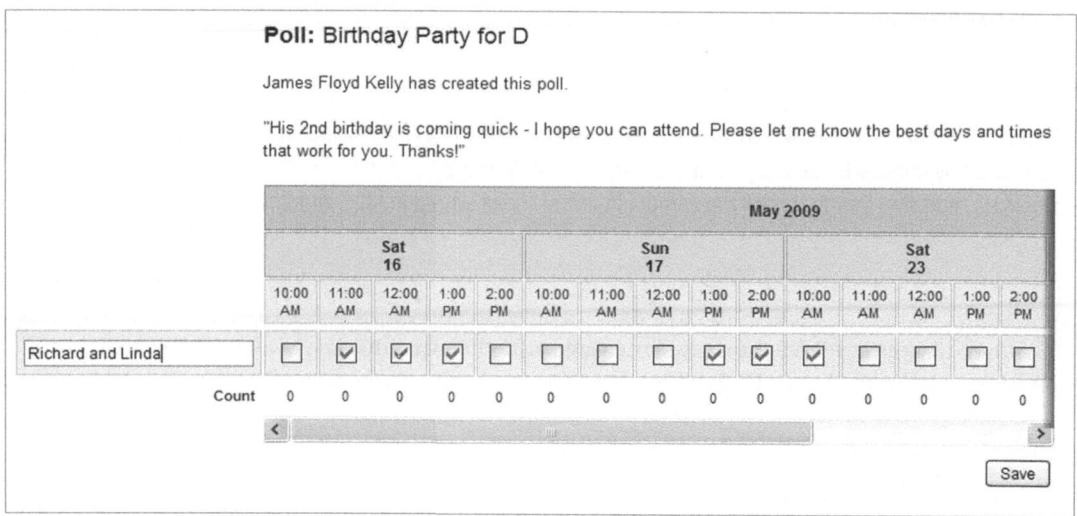

Figure 17-8. *Invitees enter their name and choose dates and times.*

Invitees can make changes to their selections at any time by revisiting the poll and clicking the Edit an entry link, as shown in Figure 17-9. Clicking the Delete an entry link removes their choices from the poll. Invitees can also leave comments by clicking the Add a comment link. Additional functions allow invitees to print the poll (click the Print link) and create a PDF or spreadsheet file (click the File export link).

Functions

Edit an entry	Add a comment	File export	Subscribe to this poll
Delete an entry	Calendar export	Print	Embed this poll

Figure 17-9. *Invitees can edit their selections at any time.*

As mentioned earlier, you can also create a choice-based poll with Doodle. Clicking the Make choice button on the Doodle home page lets you create a poll that allows participants to select from up to ten options you designate, rather than choose a month, day, and time. This is perfect for groups trying to pick a movie or a restaurant, for example.

Investigate Further

If Doodle is useful to you, you might be interested in these similar services:

- *Imagination Cubed* (http://www.imaginationcubed.com/index.php): General Electric offers a free collaboration whiteboard. You can grab the virtual marker pen and get creative, and invite others to do the same.

- *TimeToMeet* (http://www.timetomeet.info/): TimeToMeet offers a service similar to Doodle's, but also integrates with Outlook Calendar, Google, and iCal calendars. It allows you and work colleagues to find suitable meeting dates and times.

Summary

Doodle fundamentally remakes scheduling. It eliminates centralized tracking and assigning, worrying about people's schedules, and keeping track of their special requests. With Doodle, you will be sent an e-mail message each time an invitee completes the poll. You can visit the poll at any time to view the most popular date and time that works best for the largest group of invitees.

Don't let Doodle's simplicity fool you. This service can be extremely useful for any event, but it truly shines when you have a long list of invitees and can be flexible on the date and time, or have multiple meetings that your invitees can attend. The time you'll save by not having to make phone calls and handle the individual, back-and-forth e-mail can be put to use planning your event.

Appendix

I wanted to include many more free applications in this book, but time and a reasonable book length were always working against me. Rather than cut them out completely, I've listed some of my favorites in this appendix. You'll find short descriptions of each, along with the location where you can download the software or enter in your web browser to access Software as a Service (SaaS) applications.

Get Friendly Reminders

Google Calendar (see Chapter 6) can e-mail you reminders, as well as send text messages to your mobile phone so you never miss an appointment, birthday, or other important event. But if you're not a Google Calendar user, take a look at Remindr, a free web-based service that allows you to send a short description to your mobile phone, e-mail, and a few other services. It's completely free to use and requires no registration. Check it out at http://remindr.info/.

Protect Your E-Mail Address

If you frequently visit online stores and other web sites that require you to provide your e-mail address, you probably worry about that address falling into the wrong hands and being used to send you spam e-mail. Melt Mail is a nice solution.

Melt Mail is 100% free to use and completely confidential. Just visit http://meltmail.com/ and click Create. Enter your real e-mail address in the text field, and select how long Melt Mail will keep your e-mail address on record (3, 6, 12, or 24 hours). You'll be given a temporary meltmail.com address that you can provide to web sites that ask for your e-mail address. Any e-mail messages sent to this meltmail.com address during the time period you specify will be forwarded to your real e-mail address. When the time expires, Melt Mail purges your e-mail address from its database, and you won't receive any more e-mail sent to the temporary meltmail.com address you were assigned.

Brainstorm Online

How many ideas have been drawn on a napkin during a lunch or dinner meeting? Have you ever wished you could brainstorm with someone over the phone or over the Internet, and somehow share a drawing board or piece of paper when writing, drawing, or trying to explain something? If so, take a look at Dabbleboard by visiting http://www.dabbleboard.com/.

Dabbleboard allows you to collaborate with friends, business colleagues, and others using a shared drawing space. You can print whatever you create when you're finished. Your work is totally secure, and will be shared only if you choose to do so. And, even better, Dabbleboard is free to use.

Find Lost Items

I left my mobile phone sitting on a stool at a restaurant about a year ago. Later that night, I got a call on my home phone from someone who had found it, read the "Please call" information stored in the phone, and tracked me down to return my phone. Wouldn't it be nice if we could somehow tag all of our valuable items that might be lost, giving the finder the ability to track us down? Well, the nice people at SendMeHome have created an online service that can help.

SendMeHome lets you generate a code (a SendMeHome ID) for any items you wish to tag. You can write this code on the item or print out a label generated by the web site, and affix that label on the item. The labels say "If lost, please return using sendmehome.com" and also include the SendMeHome ID. If someone finds your tagged item, he simply goes to `http://www.sendmehome.com/` and enters the ID. You will receive an e-mail from SendMeHome, and the service will help arrange for communication between you and the finder.

SendMeHome is free to use, and it will never sell your information to any other organizations. The only costs you may incur are shipping charges or other costs to retrieve your item from the finder. Visit `http://www.sendmehome.com` to register and use this service.

Selective Web Page Printing

If you've ever wanted to print a web page but wished you could skip advertisements or large graphics on the page, you'll be happy to learn about PrintWhatYouLike.

To use this free service, simply visit `http://www.printwhatyoulike.com`, enter the web site address (URL), and click the Start button. Click any element on the web page that you don't want to print (such as a photo, link, or advertisement) and click the Remove button on the toolbar along the left side of the screen. You can also increase or decrease the font size, as well as remove a colored or textured background. Finally, click the Save as button, and save the edited file as a PDF or HTML document that will be saved to your computer for printing.

Send Musical Online Postcards

If you have a photo that you would like to share with someone, you can turn it into a complete package by adding some music and a personal message using Postcard.fm's free service.

Visit `http://www.postcard.fm` to begin. Browse for your photo, browse for a song in MP3 format, and then enter the recipient's e-mail address. You'll be given a chance to preview your postcard and listen to the music. Add a personal note to complete the card, and then click the Send button. Postcard.fm will deliver an e-mail with a link for the recipient to click to view the image, hear the music, and read your note.

Design a Room

If you've ever coveted that special software interior decorators use to create eye-catching room designs, you're going to love PlanningWiz. Before a single piece of furniture is purchased or placed, you can use this online application to model a room's dimensions and size, and then place furniture, rugs, and other items around the room. The application will even let you lay out multiple rooms, or an entire house or office space. Items ranging from TVs to table-tennis tables can be dropped into your floor plan, and you can drag, resize, and rotate them as desired. You can even save and print your designs (in full color if you have a color printer). Try it out at `http://v3.planningwiz.com/`.

Ship and Track Packages

If you ship and track packages routinely, you'll want to check out ShipTool. Instead of needing to visit each shipper's web site individually (UPS, FedEx, DHL, and the US Postal Service), you can visit `http://www.shiptool.com` and track all your packages from one place. Even better is the ability to get a cost estimate for shipping a package from each carrier. You provide the weight, dimensions, delivery date required, and source and destination addresses. ShipTool then gives you estimates from all four shipping companies.

Create a Web Site

Chapter 15 describes how easy it is to create your own blog. But if you have a desire to create your own web site, then you really need to check out the web design application called Trellian WebPage. It's a true "what you see is what you get" (WYSIWYG) application. You can create your own links, add pictures and video, tweak fonts and colors, and even dig deep into the actual HTML code, if you're so inclined. Download the free application from `http://www.trellian.com/webpage/` and start designing your own web site.

Hard Drive Imaging

Chapter 10 covers applications for backing up your data files, but there's another type of insurance you can obtain to protect your entire hard drive. It's called a *hard drive image*. This is a virtual photograph of your hard drive, which you can copy to a CD, DVD, or even another hard drive. If at some point in the future your hard drive should fail or catch a nasty virus, you can overwrite the entire hard drive with the image you created. It's like starting from scratch, but doesn't require you to reinstall the operating system or applications.

To create your hard drive image, you can use the 100% free application called Macrium Reflect, available for download at `http://www.macrium.com/ReflectFree.asp`. The built-in help tells you how to use it.

Child-Safe Web Browsing

Many web sites out there are simply unsafe for kids. Most parents can't sit beside their children at the computer constantly and monitor the sites they're visiting. Thankfully, applications such as K9 Web Protection provide a way for parents to lock out inappropriate content. Like an antivirus application that downloads and installs regular updates, K9 Web Protection uses a similar technology that updates its database of dangerous web sites. And it's password-protected for those budding little computer experts who might try to disable the protection. You can download this application from `http://www1.k9webprotection.com/`.

Index

A

A4 paper format, 157
AAP. *See* Avira AntiVir Personal
AbiWord word processing application, 52
Ad-Aware virus protection application, 189
Add a comment link, Doodle, 308
Add a Contact window, Skype, 258
Add a Gadget link, Blogger, 279
Add a picture link, Gmail, 117
Add Account Wizard, Money Manager Ex, 213
Add Application button, Facebook, 297
Add as Friend link, Facebook, 293
"Add further time slots" link, Doodle, 304
Add Layer dialog box, Inkscape, 167
Add Skype Contact button, Skype, 260
address books, backing up, 205
Administration tab, AntiVir Personal, 184
Adobe Illustrator graphics application, 151–154
Adobe Photoshop photo editing application, 126
AdSense advertisement application, 115, 278–280
Alienware Area-51 High-Performance Gaming PC, 20
All Mail list, Gmail, 108
antivirus software. *See* virus protection software
Application Directory page, Facebook, 296
Applications list, Facebook, 295
Archive button, Gmail, 107
Area-51 High-Performance Gaming PC, 20
automated backups, 194
Avira AntiVir Personal (AAP)
    downloading, 176
    installing, 176–178
    overview, 173–175
    tasks
        complete system scans, 180–182
        scheduling routine scans, 183–187

B

Back to Library link, Picasa, 252
Back up files and folders task, Cobian Backup, 197
backing up
    address books and e-mail, 205
    photos with Picasa, 248
backup applications
    Cobian Backup
        backing up files, 197–204
        downloading, 196
        installation, 196
        overview, 194–196
        restoring files, 196
    Norton Save & Restore, 193–194
    overview, 191–192
Banks, Michael A., 7
bare-bones PC users, 14
Basic Fixes tab, Picasa, 244, 252
Beginning Ubuntu Linux, Third Edition, 13
Bezier Curve tool, Inkscape, 161, 163
bitmaps, 154
blog address, 267
Blog button, Blogger, 266
Blogger blogging application
    accounts, 266–269
    AdSense, 278–280
    mobile phone usage, 281
    modifying layout, 275–278
    using, 269–275
blogs. *See* web logs
.bmp files, 273, 311
"Browse more applications" button, Facebook, 295
Brush Stroke tool, Inkscape, 161, 165
Burn button, Picasa, 248
business letters, OpenOffice.org Writer, 41–43
Buxfer personal finance application, 226

■C

Calc application. *See* OpenOffice.org Calc application
Calendar application. *See* Google Calendar application
calendar applications. *See* e-mail and calendar applications
Calendars tab, Google Calendar, 121
CD/DVD burners, 23
Celeron processors, 16
charts, Google Docs Spreadsheet, 73–75
chat, Gmail, 104
child-safe web browsing, 313
Circle tool, Inkscape, 159
Classmates search option, Facebook, 293
Clear Edits button, Blogger, 278
clippings, GIMP, 141
Cobian Backup application
    backing up files, 197–204
    downloading, 196
    installing, 196
    overview, 194–196
    restoring files, 204–205
column headers, OpenOffice.org Calc, 64–65
comma-separated value (CSV) files, 216–217, 220–223
Complete Quest button, Runes of Magic, 237
complete system scans, AntiVir Personal, 180–182
Compose Mail link, Gmail, 106
Compression method drop-down menu, Cobian Backup, 201
Configure Blog Archive window, Blogger, 277
Contact list, Skype, 260
contacts
    Gmail, adding to, 116–118
    Skype
        adding to, 258–260
        sending text messages to, 261
Contacts link, Gmail, 116
"Copy and paste first row" link, Doodle, 304
Corel Quattro Pro X4 spreadsheet application, 55
Corel WordPerfect word processor application, 25, 55
Coworkers search option, Facebook, 293
Create a New AdSense Account button, AdSense, 280

Create a New Database button, Money Manager Ex, 212
Create account link, Doodle, 302
Create Chart window, Google Docs Spreadsheet, 73
Create Event button, Google Calendar, 109
Crime Craft game, 241
CSV (comma-separated value) files, 216–217, 220–223
Ctrl+Shift-drag technique, Inkscape, 160–161
Custom option, OpenOffice.org Writer, 37
Custom Setup screen
    OpenOffice.org Impress, 85
    OpenOffice.org Writer, 37

■D

Dabbleboard brainstorming application, 311
Dashboard, Blogger, 275
data backup applications. *See* backup applications
Delete an entry link, Doodle, 308
Delete option, AntiVir Personal, 180
Dell Vostro 420 PC, 23
dell.com, 15
desktop shortcut icon, Money Manager Ex, 211
differential backups, 199
digital photo printers, 125
Disable radio button, Gmail, 114
do it yourself (DIY) approach, 11
.doc files, 26, 28, 63
Document application. *See* Google Docs Document application
documents. *See* word processing applications
.docx files, 27
Doodle group scheduling application
    invitees, 307–308
    overview, 301–302
    using, 302–306
Download Picasa 3 button, Picasa, 243
Download Skype button, Skype, 256
downloading
    AntiVir Personal, 176
    Cobian Backup, 196
    GIMP, 128
    Google Docs Document, 34–35
    Google Docs Presentation, 84
    Google Docs Spreadsheet, 63
    Inkscape, 156

Money Manager Ex, 210
OpenOffice.org Calc, 62–63
OpenOffice.org Impress, 84
OpenOffice.org Writer, 34
Picasa, 243–244
Runes of Magic, 231
Skype, 256
drawing tools, OpenOffice.org Impress, 82, 91–92
Dreaming in Code, 7
dual-core processors, 16
duplicate photos, eliminating with Picasa, 249
DVD/CD burners, 23

E

Edit labels link, Gmail, 111
editing profiles, in Facebook, 288–290
Effects tab, Picasa, 245
e-mail, backing up, 205
e-mail address protection applications, 311
e-mail and calendar applications
    Gmail
        contacts, adding, 116–118
        labels, 111–113
        overview, 103–104
        setting up, 105
        special options, 113–116
        using, 106–108
    Google Calendar
        appointments, creating with text messaging, 119
        overview, 105
        receiving text message reminders, 120, 311
        sharing calendars, 121–122
        using, 108–111
    Microsoft Outlook, 101–103
    overview, 101
Email button, Picasa, 245
Empty Trash now link, Gmail, 108
Enable radio button, Gmail, 114
Eudora, 205
Excel application, 56–58
Exchange Server, 102
Exit Search button, Picasa, 249
experience points (XPs), Runes of Magic, 233
Export dialog box, OpenOffice.org Writer, 44

F

Facebook social networking application
    applications, adding, 295–299
    finding people, 292–295
    overview, 283, 288
    profile, editing, 288–290
    setting up, 284–288
    Wall, 291–292
false-positives, AntiVir Personal, 180
family member PC users, 14
FaxDigits faxing service, 264
FaxZero faxing service, 264
Feeling Lucky button, Picasa, 245
file backups, 205
File Type screen, OpenOffice.org Impress, 85
file types, 27
finances, personal. See personal finance applications
Finish button, OpenOffice.org Writer, 39
Flickr photo management application, 253
folders, creating in Google Docs Document, 50
Forgotten Attachment Detector, Gmail, 104
Format Cells dialog box, OpenOffice.org Calc, 65
formulas, OpenOffice.org Calc, 68–72
free drawing, Inkscape, 161–164
free software
    hardware, 6–7
    history of, 1–2
    types of
        freebies, 5–6
        open source, 2–3
        SaaS, 3–4
Freehand Line tool, Inkscape, 161–162
freeware. See free software
friends, Facebook, 286
Friends box, Facebook, 293
Friends button, Facebook, 286
Frogster Runes of Magic. See Runes of Magic
Full radio button, 197
Function Wizard, OpenOffice.org Calc, 69
functions, OpenOffice.org Calc, 68–72

G

gamers, 14, 20
gaming applications
    Crime Craft game, 241

Runes of Magic
  downloading, 231
  installing, 232–233
  mounts (horses), renting, 238
  overview, 230–231
  quests, accepting, 233–237
  weapons, changing, 240
Shaiya game, 241
World of Warcraft, 227–229
Gateway LX series PCs, 22
Get Started button, Google Docs Presentation, 84
.gif files, 273
GIMP
  downloading, 128
  installing, 128
  layers, 129–131
  overview, 127–128
  people, adding to photos, 141–149
  text, adding to photos, 132–140
Gmail
  contacts, adding, 116–118
  labels, 111–113
  overview, 103–104
  setting up, 105
  special options, 113–116
  using, 106–108
Gmail Labs link, Gmail, 114
Gmail Settings screen, Gmail, 116
Gnumeric spreadsheet application, 77
Google AdSense advertisement application, 115, 278–280
Google Blogger. See Blogger blogging application
Google Calendar application
  appointments, creating with text messaging, 119
  overview, 105
  receiving text message reminders, 120, 311
  sharing calendars, 121–122
  using, 108–111
Google Docs Document application
  collaborating on documents, 47–49
  downloading, 34–35
  downloading files from, 51–52
  folders, creating, 50–51
  overview, 29, 31–33
Google Docs Presentation application
  downloading, 84
  inserting pictures and video, 96–98

overview, 83
  publishing presentations, 98–99
  themes, changing, 94–95
Google Docs Spreadsheet application
  charts, creating, 73–76
  downloading, 63
  overview, 59–61
  publishing spreadsheets, 76–77
Google Gmail. See Gmail
Google Picasa. See Picasa photo management application
graphical user interfaces (GUIs), 26
graphics applications
  Adobe Illustrator, 151–154
  Inkscape
    additional drawing tasks, 168–169
    downloading, 156
    free drawing, 161–165
    installing, 157
    layers, 165–168
    overview, 155–156
    screen settings, 157–158
    shapes, adding, 159–161
group scheduling applications
  Doodle
    invitees, 307–308
    overview, 301–302
    using, 302–306
  Imagination Cubed, 309
  TimeToMeet, 309
GUIs (graphical user interfaces), 26

■H
hackers, 7, 171
hard drive imaging, 192, 313
hard drives, 22
hardware needs
  identifying, 15–19
  by user type, 19–24
headphones, 256
Help Center menu option, Google Docs Document, 32
help forum, OpenOffice.org Writer, 30
hit points (HPs), Runes of Magic, 233
horses (mounts), Runes of Magic, 238
HP a6560t PC, 19
HPs (hit points), Runes of Magic, 233
HTML files, 66

I

Illustrator graphics application, 151–154
Imagination Cubed group scheduling application, 309
Impress application. *See* OpenOffice.org Impress application
Inbox, Google Gmail, 107
incremental backups, 199
Inkscape graphics application
    additional drawing tasks, 168–169
    downloading, 156
    free drawing, 161–165
    versus GIMP, 155
    installing, 157
    layers, 165–168
    overview, 155–156
    screen settings, 157–158
    shapes, adding, 159–161
Insert Picture pop-up window, OpenOffice.org Writer, 42
Insert Table dialog box, OpenOffice.org Writer, 46
Insert Video button, Google Docs Presentation, 97
Install button, Picasa, 244
Installation Wizard
    OpenOffice.org Calc, 63
    OpenOffice.org Impress, 85
    OpenOffice.org Writer, 35
installing
    Avira AntiVir Personal, 176–178
    Cobian Backup, 196
    GIMP, 128
    Inkscape, 157
    Money Manager Ex, 211
    OpenOffice.org Calc, 63
    OpenOffice.org Impress, 85
    OpenOffice.org Writer, 35–40
    Runes of Magic, 232
instant messaging, Gmail, 104
Internet phone applications. *See* phone applications
Intuit Quicken personal finance application, 208–209

J

Join button, Facebook, 287
Joint Photographic Experts Group (JPEG) format, 154, 273

K

K9 Web Protection, 313
keyboard shortcuts, enabling/disabling in Gmail, 114
kiosks, photo, 125
KWord word processing application, 52–53

L

labels, Gmail, 111–113
Labs tab, Gmail, 114
Lavasoft Ad-Aware virus protection application, 189
layers
    GIMP, 129–131
    Inkscape, 165–168
Layers window, GIMP, 135
Layers window, Inkscape, 166
Layout link, Blogger, 275
Layout tab, Blogger, 279
Layouts pane, OpenOffice.org Impress, 86
Levy, Steven, 7
Link button, Blogger, 272
LinkedIn social networking application, 299
Linux operating system, 13
logos, OpenOffice.org Writer, 41–43
Lotus Symphony Documents, 25
Lotus Symphony Spreadsheets, 55

M

Macrium Reflect application, 313
malware, 189, 192
mana points (MPs), Runes of Magic, 233
manual backups, 194, 203
massively multiplayer online (MMO) games, 227, 229
Melt Mail application, 311
memory, 20
menus, OpenOffice.org Writer, 29
microphones, 256
Microsoft Excel application, 56–58
Microsoft Exchange Server, 102
Microsoft Office suite, 26
Microsoft Outlook application, 101, 205
Microsoft Outlook Express application, 205
Microsoft Paint application, 154
Microsoft PowerPoint application, 79–81
Microsoft SharePoint Server, 47
Microsoft Word application, 25–28
MMO (massively multiplayer online) games, 227, 229

Mobile Setup tab, Google Calendar, 120
Money Manager Ex personal finance
    application
    databases, creating, 211–216
    downloading, 210
    examining finances, 223–225
    importing transactions, 216–223
    installing, 211
    overview, 209–210
Month tab, Google Calendar, 109
More Actions drop-down menu, Google
    Gmail, 112
mounts (horses), Runes of Magic, 238
Move to quarantine option, AntiVir Personal,
    180
MP3 format, 312
MPs (mana points), Runes of Magic, 233
multimedia gurus, 14, 21–22
musical online postcards, 312
My Calendars section, Google Calendar,
    122
My Contacts list, Gmail, 117
My Documents folder, 212, 244
My Pictures folder, 243–244
MySpace social networking application,
    299

N

National Association of Photoshop Profes-
    sionals (NAPP), 126
NAV (Norton AntiVirus), 172–173
network cards, 16
New Contact button, Gmail, 117
New Contact option, Skype, 258
New Database Wizard, Money Manager Ex,
    212
New Features link
    Google Docs Document, 34
    Google Docs Spreadsheet, 59
New Set button, Picasa, 248
nonplayer characters (NPCs), Runes of
    Magic, 233
Norton AntiVirus (NAV), 172–173
Norton Save & Restore, 85, 193–194
NPCs (nonplayer characters), Runes of
    Magic, 233

O

Object menu, Inkscape, 169
Office suite, 26
On the Way to the Web, 7

online banking services, 217
online coupons, 12
open source software, 2–3
OpenOffice Help menu option, 29
OpenOffice.org Calc application
    colored column headers, 64–66
    downloading, 62–63
    formulas and functions, 68–73
    installing, 63–64
    overview, 58–59
    publishing as web pages, 66–68
    user interface, 64
OpenOffice.org Impress application
    downloading, 84
    drawing tools, 89–93
    installing, 85
    overview, 81–82
    video, adding, 86–89
OpenOffice.org Writer application
    downloading, 34
    installing, 35–40
    logos, adding, 41–43
    overview, 28–31
    saving as PDF documents, 43–45
    tables, creating, 46–47
Options button, Doodle, 304
Options window, Skype, 263
Outlook application, 101, 205
Outlook Express application, 205

P

Page Elements tab, Blogger, 275–276
Paint application, 154
paradigmatic change, 301
PCs (personal computers)
    building, 11–12
    buying, 12–13
    free software, 13–14
    hardware needs
        identifying, 15–19
        by user type, 19–24
    overview, 9
    repurposing, 10
    upgrading, 10
    user types, 14–15
PDF documents, saving work as in
    OpenOffice.org Writer, 43–44
PDF Options dialog box, OpenOffice.org
    Writer, 44
per-seat licensing, 40

personal computers. *See* PCs
personal finance applications
    Buxfer, 226
    Intuit Quicken, 208–209
    Money Manager Ex
        databases, creating, 211–216
        downloading, 210
        examining finances, 223–225
        importing transactions, 216–223
        installing, 211
        overview, 209–210
    overview, 207
personal information management (PIM)
        applications, 101
phone applications
    faxing services, 264
    Skype
        calls, making, 260
        contacts, adding, 258–260
        downloading, 256
        overview, 255–256
        status, setting, 261–262
        text messages, 261
        using, 257–258
        video phone calls, 262–263
photo editing applications
    Adobe Photoshop, 126
    GIMP
        downloading, 128
        installing, 128
        layers, 129–131
        overview, 127–128
        people, adding to photos, 141–149
        text, adding to photos, 132–140
    overview, 125
photo management applications
    Flickr, 253
    Picasa
        backing up photos, 248–249
        downloading, 243–244
        eliminating duplicate photos, 249–250
        overview, 243
        Photo Tray, 245–246
        red-eye, removing, 252–253
        screen-savers, creating, 251
        tagging photos, 246–248
        using, 244–245
    Photo Tray, Picasa, 245–246
    Picasa photo management application
        backing up photos, 248–249
        downloading, 243–244

        eliminating duplicate photos, 249–250
        overview, 243
        Photo Tray, 245–246
        red-eye, removing, 252–253
        screen-savers, creating, 251
        tagging photos, 246–248
        using, 244–245
Pick New Template tab, Blogger, 275
PIM (personal information management)
        applications, 101
pixelation, 154
PlanningWiz application, 312
polls, Doodle, 301, 306
Polygons tool, Inkscape, 168
Postcard.fm application, 312
posts, Blogger, 266
PowerPoint application, 79–81
.pps files, 63, 80
.ppt files, 79
.pptx files, 79
prebuilt PCs, 15–17
Presentation application. *See* Google Docs
        Presentation application
presentation software. *See* slide show
        applications
preview template link, Blogger, 268
PrintWhatYouLike application, 312
Pro Membership, Flickr, 253
Processes tab, Microsoft Outlook, 103
processors, 20
Professional Template Pack I and II, 31
Profile tab, Facebook, 290
Properties window, Cobian Backup, 197
Publish document button, Google Docs
        Presentation, 98
Publish Post button, Blogger, 273
Publish/embed option, Google Docs
        Presentation, 98
publishing
    Google Docs Presentation presentations,
        98–99
    Google Docs Spreadsheets, 76–77
    OpenOffice.org Calc spreadsheets as Web
        pages, 66–67
purchasing hardware, 11

■**Q**

quarantines, AntiVir Personal, 180
Quattro Pro X4 spreadsheet application,
        55
quests, Runes of Magic, 233–237

Quick Add link, Google Calendar, 109
Quicken personal finance application, 208–209

R

random-access memory (RAM), 10, 22
Ready to Install Program screen
    OpenOffice.org Impress, 85
    OpenOffice.org Writer, 39
Rectangle tool, Inkscape, 159
red eye, removing, Picasa, 252
Redeye button, Picasa, 252
reminder applications, 311. *See also* e-mail and calendar applications
Report Spam button, Google Gmail, 108
repurposing PCs, 10
Restore files and folders task, Cobian Backup, 197
retirees, 33, 62
Ribbon, Microsoft Word, 26
RoM icon, Runes of Magic, 232
room design applications, 312–313
Rosenberg, Scott, 7
routine scans, Avira AntiVir Personal, 183–187
Runes of Magic
    downloading, 231
    installing, 232–233
    mounts (horses), renting, 238
    overview, 230–231
    quests, accepting, 233–237
    weapons, changing, 240

S

SaaS (Software as a Service), *see also* entries beginning with Google, *see also* entries beginning with OpenOffice. org, 3–4
Save & Restore, 193–194
Save As dialog box, OpenOffice.org Calc, 66
Save As Template button, Money Manager Ex, 222
Save Changes button, Facebook, 290
Scalable Vector Graphics (SVG), 155
Scale Layer dialog box, GIMP, 147
Scan job option, AntiVir Personal, 186
Schedule event button, Doodle, 302
Schedule type drop-down menu, Cobian Backup, 200
Scheduler tab, AntiVir Personal, 185

scheduling applications. *See* group scheduling applications
Scissors tool, GIMP, 141
screen savers, creating with Picasa, 251
Screensaver album, Picasa, 251
Security tab, OpenOffice.org Writer, 44
Send a Message link, Facebook, 293
Send Verification Code button, Google Calendar, 120
SendMeHome application, 312
Set Currency button, Money Manager Ex, 213
Settings link
    Google Calendar, 120–121
    Google Gmail, 114
Settings tab, Skype, 262
Setup Wizard, Runes of Magic, 232
Shaiya game, 241
shapes, Inkscape, 159–161
Share button, Google Docs Presentation, 98
Share this File window, Google Docs Document, 48
SharePoint Server, 47
shareware, 2, 5
shipping packages, 313
ShipTool application, 313
shortcut keys, Gmail, 108
Sicam, Jaime, 13
"Sign me in when Skype starts" box, Skype, 257
Sign Up button, Facebook, 284
Simple Spreadsheet spreadsheet application, 77
Skype Options window, Skype, 262
Skype phone application
    calls, making, 260
    contacts, adding, 258–260
    downloading, 256
    overview, 255–256
    status, setting, 261–262
    text messages, 261
    using, 257–258
    video phone calls, 262–263
Slide button, OpenOffice.org Impress, 90
slide show applications
    books about, 100
    Google Docs Presentation
        application features, 94–98
        downloading, 84
        inserting pictures and video, 96–98
        overview, 83

publishing presentations, 98–99
software, 84
themes, changing, 94–95
Microsoft PowerPoint, 79–81
OpenOffice.org Impress
application features, 86–92
downloading, 84
drawing tools, 89–93
installing, 85
overview, 81–82
OpenOffice.org impress
software, 84
video, adding, 86–89
small business owners, 15, 22–23, 62
SnapFiles web site, 5
social networking applications
Facebook
applications, adding, 295–299
finding people, 292–295
overview, 283
profile, editing, 288–290
setting up, 284–288
Wall, 291–292
LinkedIn, 299
MySpace, 299
Software as a Service (SaaS), *see also* entries
beginning with Google, *see also*
entries beginning with OpenOffice.
org, 3–4
software bugs, 2
sound cards, 21
Source box, Cobian Backup, 200
source code, 3
spam filter, Gmail, 108
Spreadsheet application. *See* Google Docs
Spreadsheet application
spreadsheet applications
Gnumeric, 77
Google Docs Spreadsheet
charts, creating, 73–76
downloading, 63
overview, 59–61
publishing spreadsheets, 76–77
Microsoft Excel, 56–58
OpenOffice.org Calc
colored column headers, 64–66
downloading, 62–63
formulas and functions, 68–73
installing, 63–64
overview, 58–59
publishing as web pages, 66–68

overview, 55
Simple Spreadsheet, 77
Spybot–Search & Destroy, 173
spyware (malware), 189, 192
Starred link, Gmail, 107
Start Blogging button, Blogger, 268
Start Skype button, Skype, 256
storage, 20
students, 33, 62
Subtotal column, OpenOffice.org Calc, 68
Suggested Contacts list, Gmail, 116
Superstars feature, Gmail, 115
SVG (Scalable Vector Graphics), 155
Symantec Norton AntiVirus (NAV),
172–173
Symantec Norton Save & Restore, 85
Symbol shapes tool, OpenOffice.org
Impress, 92

■ T
tables, OpenOffice.org Writer, 46–47
tagging photos, Picasa, 246–248
Task Manager, Gmail, 103
telephone applications. *See* phone
applications
template letterhead, OpenOffice.org Writer,
41
templates, Blogger, 275
Terms of Service, Google Docs Spreadsheet,
76
text, adding to photos with GIMP, 132–140
text editor applications, 219
text messaging
Google Calendar, 119–120
Skype, 261
tracking packages via, 313
Text tool
GIMP, 136
Inkscape, 168
OpenOffice.org Impress, 92
Thomas, Keir, 13
Thunderbird, 205
TimeToMeet group scheduling application,
309
To Whom the Money Goes report, Money
Manager Ex, 224
toolbar
OpenOffice.org Impress, 82
OpenOffice.org Writer, 29
Toolbox window, GIMP, 136
Trash, Gmail, 108

trialware, 2
Tuning tab, Picasa, 245
Turn on Video button, Skype, 263

■U

Ubuntu Linux operating system, 13
Universal CSV Importer Dialog box, Money
 Manager Ex, 220–221
Unpack button, OpenOffice.org, 35
Update job option, AntiVir Personal, 186
upgrading PCs, 10
USB flash drives, 204
user types
 hardware needs by, 19–24
 overview, 14–15

■V

vector math, 154
video, adding to slide shows
 Google Docs Presentation, 96–98
 OpenOffice.org impress, 86–89
Video call button, Skype, 263
video cards, 21–22
video phone calls, Skype, 262–263
"View and edit your profile" link, Facebook,
 288
View Blog link, Blogger, 273
virus protection software
 Avira AntiVir Personal
  complete system scans, 180–182
  downloading, 176
  installing, 176–178
  overview, 173–175
  scheduling routine scans, 183–187
 Lavasoft Ad-Aware, 189
 Norton AntiVirus, 172–173
 overview, 171–172
 Spybot–Search & Destroy, 173
Vostro 420 PC, 23

■W

Wall, Facebook, 291–292
weapons, Runes of Magic, 240
web design applications, 313
web logs (blogs)
 Blogger
  accounts, 266–269
  AdSense, 278–280

  mobile phone usage, 281
  modifying layout, 275–278
  using, 269–275
 overview, 265
 WordPress, 280–281
"what you see is what you get" (WYSIWYG)
 applications, 313
Where the Money Goes report, Money
 Manager Ex, 224
Word application, 25–28
word processing applications
 AbiWord, 53
 Google Docs Document
  collaborating on documents, 47–49
  downloading, 34–35
  downloading files from, 51–52
  folders, creating, 50–51
  overview, 29, 31–33
 KWord, 53
 Microsoft Word, 25–28
 OpenOffice.org Writer
  downloading, 34
  installing, 35–40
  logos, adding, 41–43
  overview, 28–31
  saving as PDF documents, 43–45
  tables, creating, 46–47
WordPerfect word processor application,
 25, 55
WordPress blogging application, 280–281
working groups, 62
World of Warcraft (WoW) game, 227–229
"Write on your own Wall" link, Facebook,
 291
Writer application. *See* OpenOffice.org
 Writer application
WYSIWYG ("what you see is what you get")
 applications, 313

■X

.xls files, 57
.xlsx files, 57
XPs (experience points), Runes of Magic, 233

■Z

zip compression, 201
.zip files, 197, 204–205

You Need the Companion eBook

Your purchase of this book entitles you to buy the companion PDF-version eBook for only $10. Take the weightless companion with you anywhere.

We believe this Apress title will prove so indispensable that you'll want to carry it with you everywhere, which is why we are offering the companion eBook (in PDF format) for $10 to customers who purchase this book now. Convenient and fully searchable, the PDF version of any content-rich, page-heavy Apress book makes a valuable addition to your programming library. You can easily find and copy code—or perform examples by quickly toggling between instructions and the application. Even simultaneously tackling a donut, diet soda, and complex code becomes simplified with hands-free eBooks!

Once you purchase your book, getting the $10 companion eBook is simple:

❶ Visit **www.apress.com/promo/tendollars/**.

❷ Complete a basic registration form to receive a randomly generated question about this title.

❸ Answer the question correctly in 60 seconds, and you will receive a promotional code to redeem for the $10.00 eBook.

2855 TELEGRAPH AVENUE | SUITE 600 | BERKELEY, CA 94705